# Pension Design and Structure

# Pension Design and Structure

## New Lessons from Behavioral Finance

EDITED BY

Olivia S. Mitchell and
Stephen P. Utkus

OXFORD
UNIVERSITY PRESS

# OXFORD

UNIVERSITY PRESS

Great Clarendon Street, Oxford OX2 6DP

Oxford University Press is a department of the University of Oxford.
It furthers the University's objective of excellence in research, scholarship,
and education by publishing worldwide in

Oxford New York

Auckland Bangkok Buenos Aires Cape Town Chennai
Dar es Salaam Delhi Hong Kong Istanbul Karachi Kolkata
Kuala Lumpur Madrid Melbourne Mexico City Mumbai Nairobi
São Paulo Shanghai Taipei Tokyo Toronto

Oxford is a registered trade mark of Oxford University Press
in the UK and in certain other countries

Published in the United States
by Oxford University Press Inc., New York

British Library Cataloguing in Publication Data
Data available

Library of Congress Cataloging in Publication Data
Data available
ISBN 0-19-927339-1

Typeset by Newgen Imaging Systems (P) Ltd., Chennai, India
Printed in Great Britain
on acid-free paper by
Biddles Ltd., King's Lynn, Norfolk

# Preface

In the last two decades, participant-directed DC plans have been an engine of growth for retirement saving around the world. In many countries, the movement to enhance participant choice has also prompted reforms of Social Security systems, by adding personal accounts that permit investment choice.

Reliance on participant direction can, however, spell danger when participants do not save enough, or mismanage their investments during the savings phase, or fail to handle their funds correctly in retirement. Exciting new research blending economics, finance, psychology, and sociology is emerging which will help plan sponsors structure the benefits environment in which these choices take place. This book explores this research and shows in detail how important it is to take into account how "real people" behave—including their lack of self-control, their tendency to procrastinate, their inertia, and their aversion to loss. Drawing on this research, experts then provide key insights regarding pension plan design that can result in more saving and better retirement preparedness.

This book's success bears testimony to the excellent collaboration and fine insights of Steve Utkus, the volume's co-editor. Support for the research described here was generously provided by the Wharton School, along with two other groups at the University of Pennsylvania, the Boettner Center for Pensions and Retirement Research, and the Penn Aging Research Center. In addition, the research effort benefited from support from the Social Security Administration, the Michigan Retirement Research Center, and the Employee Benefits Security Administration of the US Department of Labor. Special funding was provided by Metropolitan Life Insurance Company to help defray publication costs. The Pension Research Council is grateful for the invaluable help of our Senior Partners and Institutional Members, and the careful attention of Victoria Jo and Joseph Hirniak. On behalf of the Pension Research Council at the Wharton School, we thank each of these collaborators, along with the editors and contributors who brought this work to fruition.

Olivia S. Mitchell
Pension Research Council
The Wharton School

## The Pension Research Council

The Pension Research Council of the Wharton School at the University of Pennsylvania is an organization committed to generating debate on key policy issues affecting pensions and other employee benefits. The Council sponsors interdisciplinary research on the entire range of private and social retirement security and related benefit plans in the United States and around the world. It seeks to broaden understanding of these complex arrangements through basic research into their economic, social, legal, actuarial, and financial foundations. Members of the Advisory Board of the Council, appointed by the Dean of the Wharton School, are leaders in the employee benefits field, and they recognize the essential role of social security and other public sector income maintenance programs while sharing a desire to strengthen private sector approaches to economic security.

More information about the Pension Research Council is available at the web site: http://prc.wharton.upenn.edu/prc/prc.html

# Contents

# Figures

# Tables

# Notes on Contributors

**John Ameriks** is Senior Investment Analyst in the Investment Counseling and Research division of the Vanguard Group. Formerly, Dr. Ameriks was a Senior Research Fellow with the TIAA-CREF Institute. His research focuses on individual and household portfolio allocation and savings behavior, and he has written on a variety of topics, including household savings adequacy, income strategies for retirees, life-cycle portfolio allocation, financial planning and wealth accumulation, and the retirement and annuitization decisions of retirement plan participants. Dr Ameriks received a PhD from Columbia University.

**James J. Choi** is a Doctoral Student in Economics at Harvard University. His research explores default choices in 401(k) plans, consumption responses to retirement wealth shocks, the effect of the Internet on trading behavior, and performance evaluation of stock-pickers. He is a National Science Foundation Graduate Research Fellow and a Harvey Fellow of the Mustard Seed Foundation. He received the AB in applied mathematics from Harvard.

**Robert Clark** is a Professor of Business Management and Economics, North Carolina State University. Professor Clark has conducted research examining retirement decisions, the choice between defined benefit and defined contribution plans, the impact of pension conversions to defined contribution and cash balance plans, the role of information and communications on 401(k) contributions, government regulation of pensions, and Social Security. In addition, he has examined the economic responses to population aging, and international pension plans. Professor Clark is a fellow of the Employee Benefit Research Institute and a member of the American Economic Association, the Gerontological Society of America, and the National Academy of Social Insurance. Professor Clark earned the PhD from Duke University.

**Madeleine d'Ambrosio** is Vice President of TIAA-CREF and Executive Director of the TIAA-CREF Institute. There she initiates and supports strategic research and educational programs on issues related to pensions and retirement, insurance, investments, corporate governance, higher education, and financial literacy. Previously, Ms d'Ambrosio worked as an Institutional Consultant at TIAA-CREF where she was responsible for the design and development of TIAA-CREF's Financial Education Seminars and Financial Education for Women programs.

**Matthew Drinkwater** is an Assistant Scientist within the Retirement Research unit of LIMRA International. His responsibilities include studies on Deferred Annuity Owner and Annuitization, Retirement Income Management, an in-depth Annuity Persistency Study, and a Pension Rollover Study. He directs the quarterly U.S. Annuity Persistency Survey and conducts industry sales forecasts and annuitization estimates. Dr Drinkwater received the PhD in psychology from Brown University.

**Esther Duflo** is the Castel Krob Career Development Associate Professor of Development Economics at MIT. In addition to pension topics, she conducts research on development, inequality, and education. Dr Duflo was awarded the Elaine Bennett prize for Economics Research and she was also the recipient of Sloan Foundation research support. She received the PhD in Economics from MIT.

**Gur Huberman** is a Professor at the Graduate School of Business at Columbia University. Dr Huberman's main research interest is behavioral finance. He received the PhD from Yale University.

**Wei Jiang** is Assistant Professor of Finance at Columbia Business School. Previously she was an investment-banking associate. Her current research interests include analysts' forecasting behavior and 401(k) savings and allocation decisions. She received the PhD in Economics from the University of Chicago.

**David Laibson** is Professor of Economics at Harvard University. His research focuses on consumer decisionmaking under uncertainty, including models of hyperbolic preferences and saving behavior. Dr Laibson received the PhD from MIT and the MS from the London School of Economics.

**Annamaria Lusardi** is Associate Professor of Economics at Dartmouth College. Her research focuses on savings and pensions, macroeconomics and the economics of aging. She received the PhD in Economics from Princeton University.

**Donna MacFarland** is Senior Manager of the Institutional Marketing Research Department at Vanguard, where she oversees research, data mining, database marketing, and competitive analyses. Previously Ms MacFarland directed a marketing research consulting firm specializing in business-to-business research; she has also held positions with Merrill Lynch, Citibank, Smith Barney, and the Direct Marketing Association. She received her MBA degree from the University of Connecticut.

**Brigitte Madrian** is an Associate Professor at the Wharton School of the University of Pennsylvania. She is also affiliated with the National Bureau of Economic Research and the Employee Benefit Research Institute. Dr Madrian's research focuses on employee savings behavior in 401(k) plans, and she is best known for her work on automatic enrollment, financial education, company stock, and matching. She was recently awarded the Paul Samuelson Award for Outstanding Scholarly Research on Lifelong Financial Security by TIAA-CREF. Dr Madrian earned the PhD in economics from the Massachusetts Institute of Technology.

**Carolyn Marconi** is a Principal of Vanguard's Marketing Research Group where she oversees company-wide research. Previously she was research director for the Nestle Corporation and Campbell Soup, and she served as an assistant vice president of the Dun & Bradstreet Corporation. She is a Trustee of the Marketing Science Institute (MSI) and a member of the American Marketing Association. Ms Marconi received the MBA from the University of Rhode Island.

**Ann A. McDermed** is retired from the College of Management at North Carolina State University. She has published papers on the economic incentives of pensions and other forms of employee benefits. She received the PhD in Economics from North Carolina State University.

**Andrew Metrick** is an Associate Professor of Finance at the Wharton School. His research focuses on pensions in addition to venture capital, corporate governance, and decisionmaking under uncertainty. Dr Metrick received the PhD and MA from Harvard University.

**Olivia S. Mitchell** is the International Foundation of Employee Benefit Plans Professor of Insurance and Risk Management, the Executive Director of the Pension Research Council, and the Director of the Boettner Center on Pensions and Retirement Research, at the Wharton School of the University of Pennsylvania. She is also a Research Associate at the National Bureau of Economic Research and a CoInvestigator for the AHEAD/ Health and Retirement Studies at the University of Michigan. Professor Mitchell's main areas of research are international private and public insurance, risk management, public finance and labor markets, and compensation and pensions. Mitchell recently served on President Bush's Commission to Strengthen Social Security (www.csss.gov). She received the PhD degree in Economics from the University of Wisconsin—Madison.

**Stan Panis** is Senior Economist at RAND, where his research concentrates on health and financial security among the elderly. Recent projects include analyses of the effects of pensions and health insurance on the retirement timing decisions of married couples; the effects of raising the early and normal Social Security retirement ages on workers' retirement and disability claiming behavior; and the determinants and long-term consequences of premature pension cash-outs. He earned the PhD in Economics from the University of Southern California.

**Emmanuel Saez** is an Assistant Professor of Economics at University of California—Berkeley. His research interests include retirement plan savings decisions, social network effects, taxation and redistribution and evolution of income inequality. Dr Saez received the PhD in economics from MIT.

**Victor Saliterman** is Senior Vice President for CIGNA Retirement & Investment Services, and he is also President of CIGNA Financial Services, Inc., a national discount brokerage unit, and he has management responsibility for CIGNA Bank and Trust Company, FSB. Previously, Mr Saliterman was Senior Vice President of Participant Solutions where he was responsible for communication, education, advice and service. He also has directed investment product development, including the firm's sub-advised manager-of-manager program, marketing for TimesSquare Capital Management, and enterprise strategy and business development. Prior to that he served with Accenture's Strategic Services practice. Saliterman received the MBA from the Wharton School.

**Kshama Sawant** is in the doctoral program in economics at North Carolina State University (NCSU). Her research interests include the economics of aging, the economics of development, macroeconomics, and environmental and resource economics. She received the MS in economics from NCSU.

**Jason Scott** is the Director of Financial Research at Financial Engines, where he models mutual fund and stock returns. His research interests focus on pension economics, and he has written on 401(k) tax benefits, the determinants of defined contribution employee participation, and the impact of pension plan lump sum distribution options on retirement income. Previously Dr Scott worked as a litigation consultant at Cornerstone Research. He earned the PhD in Economics from Stanford University.

**Gary Selnow** is a Professor of Communication at San Francisco State University and Director of the World Internet Resources for Education and Development, a nonprofit corporation that applies information technology to community development, health care, and education in regions affected by war, economic problems, and social unrest. Previously Dr Selnow served in the US Air Force and served as a Fulbright Scholar. He received the PhD degree in communication and psychology from Michigan State University.

**Sheena Sethi-Iyengar** is an Associate Professor of Management at Columbia Business School, where she teaches and conducts research on entrepreneurial creativity and leadership, as well as the cultural factors associated with employee motivation and performance in global organizations. Professor Iyengar recently received the Presidential Early Career Award for her ongoing work in examining cultural, individual, and situational factors that influence people's choice making preferences and behaviors. She earned the PhD in social psychology from Stanford University.

**Barry Sheckley** is the Neag Professor of Adult Learning in the Department of Educational Leadership at the University of Connecticut. His research and practice evaluates how experience enhances adult learning, focusing on how experience contributes to the development of proficiency, the skilled use of knowledge. Previously Dr Sheckley held positions at the New England Center for Community Education and Mohegan Community College. He also served in the US Air Force. Dr Sheckley received the PhD from the University of Connecticut.

**Eric Sondergeld** is Corporate Vice President and Director of Retirement Research at LIMRA; he also founded the Annuity Committee at LIMRA. Previously he worked for The Travelers on individual products, investments, real estate investments, and, most recently, individual annuities. He is a member of the Society of Actuaries, the American Academy of Actuaries, the Association for Investment Management and Research, and the Institute of Chartered Financial Analysts.

**Meir Statman** is the Glenn Klimek Professor of Finance at Santa Clara University. His research explores how investors and managers make financial decisions and how these decisions are reflected in financial markets. Dr Statman has received a Batterymarch Fellowship, a William F. Sharpe Best Paper Award, a Bernstein Fabozzi/Jacobs Levy Outstanding Article Award, and two Graham and Dodd Awards of Excellence. He received the PhD from Columbia University.

**Gregory Stein** manages the Financial Development group at Financial Engines, Inc. His primary role is to oversee the customization of financial technology for Financial Engines' partners and large customers. Greg was awarded the MA degree in economics from Stanford University.

**Stephen P. Utkus** is the Director of the Vanguard Center for Retirement Research, where he conducts and sponsors research on retirement savings and retirement benefits. His current research interests include attitudes and expectations regarding retirement, financial markets and employer-sponsored retirement plans; the psychological and behavioral aspects of participant decisionmaking; trading and investment behavior among retirement plan participants; fiduciary issues arising from retirement programs; and global trends in public and private pension plans. Mr Utkus is a member of the advisory board of the Wharton Pension Research Council, and he is currently a Visiting Scholar at The Wharton School. He received the MBA in finance from The Wharton School.

**Elke Weber** is Jerome A. Chazen Professor of International Business at Columbia University and the Academic Director of the Chazen Institute for International Business at Columbia Business School. She also co-directs the Center for the Decision Sciences, sponsoring cross-disciplinary research and graduate training in the basic and applied decision sciences. Her research focuses on behavioral models of judgment and decisionmaking under risk and uncertainty. Previously she held positions at the University of Chicago, University of Illinois, Ohio State University, the Otto Beisheim Graduate School of Corporate Management, the Center for Advanced Studies in the Behavioral Sciences at Stanford, and the Wissenschaftskolleg (Center for Advanced Study) in Berlin. Dr Weber earned the PhD in Behavior and Decision Analysis from Harvard University.

# Abbreviations

| | |
|---|---|
| AAK | Advice Action Kit |
| APA | American Psychological Association |
| CES-D | Center for Epidemiologic Studies Depression |
| DB | Defined benefit |
| DC | Defined contribution |
| EBRI | Employee Benefit Research Institute |
| ERISA | Employee Retirement and Income Security Act |
| GAO | General Accounting Office |
| HRS | Health and Retirement Study |
| IPRO | Interest Payment Retirement Option |
| IRA | Individual Retirement Account |
| MDO | Minimum Distribution Option |
| MPT | Modern Portfolio Theory |
| PSC | Participant Service Center |
| RTB | Retirement Transition Benefit |
| SMT | Save More Tomorrow |
| SSI | Supplement Security Income |
| SWAT | Systematic Withdrawals and Transfers |
| TDA | Tax Deferred Account |
| TIAA-CREF | Teachers Insurance and Annuity Association-College of Retirement Equities Fund |
| TPA | Transfer Payout Annuity |
| US DOL | US Department of Labor |

# Part I

# Research on Decisionmaking under Uncertainty

# Chapter 1

# Lessons from Behavioral Finance for Retirement Plan Design

*Olivia S. Mitchell and Stephen P. Utkus*

Participant-directed defined contribution (DC) plans have become the cornerstone of the private-sector retirement system around the world. In the United States, participant choice has spread not only to pensions, but also to a great many other aspects of the employee benefit package as well, including healthcare plans, flexible benefit programs, and time-off arrangements. The trend toward giving participants more choice also underlies recent proposals to reform Social Security by adding personal accounts, and Medicare proposals to permit seniors to choose whether they want a public versus a privately managed healthcare plan. Participant-managed DC plans are the main feature of national pension reforms already implemented in many Latin American nations, as well as in Germany, Sweden, and most recently, Russia.

Underlying this global movement spurring participant choice is an implicit assumption about behavior: That the employee–citizen to whom the responsibility of choice has been handed is a well-informed economic agent who acts rationally to maximize his self-interest. To this end, it is assumed that he can interpret and weigh information presented regarding options offered by employers and governments, appropriately evaluate and balance these choices, and then make an informed decision based on a weighing of the alternatives.

Recently, however, a different perspective has emerged regarding how "real" people make economic decisions, one developed by social scientists working at the interface of economics, finance, psychology, and even sociology. This perspective is consistent with the fundamental economic proposition that people can and do try to maximize their self-interest, but it also recognizes that such decisions are often made with less-than perfect outcomes. In the real world, peoples' decisions are subject to "bounded rationality," as Herbert Simon called it (Simon, 1955). Certain types of decisions and problems may be simply too complex for individuals to

The authors are grateful for comments provided by Shlomo Benartzi. Opinions expressed are solely those of the authors. Financial support for this research was provided by the National Bureau of Economic Research and the Pension Research Council.

master on their own. There is also what Mullainathan and Thaler (2000) call "bounded self-control"—individuals have the right intentions or beliefs, but they lack the willpower to carry out the appropriate changes in behavior. And last, there is the problem of "bounded self-interest" or "bounded selfishness" (Mullainathan and Thaler, 2000). This acknowledges that many people do seek to maximize their personal welfare, yet they prove far more cooperative and altruistic than economic theory predicts they will be.

These new notions of how people make decisions have spurred the rapidly growing fields of *behavioral economics and finance*. The central question addressed by this research is how markets work and how consumers make decisions when some (or even many) people labor under such mental or emotional constraints and complications.[1] This research is having a profound impact on the way analysts now view varied aspects of economic and financial life, including the ways in which we understand how people decide to save, invest, and consume.[2] The goal of the present chapter is to evaluate key aspects of this new behavioral research in the light of what it tells us about better ways to design and manage retirement systems. In what follows, therefore, we analyze what insights this literature offers us on how workers decide to save, how they manage their retirement investments, and ultimately how they decide to draw down their assets in retirement. Our aim, in particular, is to understand how workers and retirees might deviate from the rational, all-knowing economic agents that underpin economic theory and often retirement plan design. Finally, we discuss implications of this literature for plan sponsors and policymakers who must design, regulate, and evaluate the institutions that help provide for economic security in old age.

## The Decision to Save

Understanding why people save, and what they invest in, are questions of central importance to economists and policymakers. With the growth of DC saving plans in the United States and around the world, especially plans having a 401(k) or employee contributory feature, it is clear that having a meaningful retirement benefit depends increasingly on participants' decisions to save and invest in their retirement plans.

Neoclassical economic theory casts the saving outcome as the result of people trading off current versus future consumption. Thus, households are thought to compare the benefit gained from consuming their income today, with the benefits of deferring some of that income into the future. This is what is thought to drive contributions to a 401(k) or individual retirement account, with the goal being to save for retirement. The life-cycle model of saving posits that individuals are rational planners of their consumption and saving needs over their lifetimes, taking into account the interests of their heirs (Modigliani and Brumberg, 1954). During their younger years, workers tend to be net dissavers, borrowing from the future by means of debt to boost current consumption; middle-aged individuals become net savers and purchasers of financial assets and enter "accumulation" phase, during which they stockpile assets for the final, retired phase of life. As labor earnings decline or disappear, people then decumulate or draw down their financial assets to finance old-age consumption. According to the tenets of life-cycle theory, people will logically develop assets for retirement that will be sufficient to protect them from unexpected declines in their standard of living in old age.

On balance, the life-cycle theory is thought to do a reasonable job of explaining patterns of household saving behavior. Saving generally rises with income and age, and it is positively associated with education and total wealth. Young households generally have more debt than assets, while prime-aged households do appear to begin saving more and accumulating financial holdings. Finally, in retirement, people do tend to consume portions of their financial assets as they age.[3]

On the other hand, some saving behavior appears to be at odds with the theory. Consider, first, a fundamental question: How good are households at calculating an appropriate saving goal for retirement? Arguably, if the life-cycle analysis is true, households should have some demonstrated skill at estimating their needs for retirement, and analysis of actual savings behavior should demonstrate some reasonably widespread competency at the task. Yet, superficially the retirement savings problem is perhaps an ideal illustration of Simon's "bounded rationality." Being good at retirement savings requires accurate estimates of uncertain future processes, including lifetime earnings, asset returns, tax rates, family and health status, and longevity. In order to solve this problem, the human brain as a calculating machine would need to have the capacity to solve many decades-long time value of money problems, with massive uncertainties as to stochastic cash flows and their timing.

In fact, survey and empirical research suggests that individuals are not particularly good at the retirement savings problem. Relatively few people feel they are able to plan effectively for retirement (Lusardi, Chapter 9, this volume). Indeed, surveys repeatedly find that fewer than 40 percent of US workers have calculated how much they will need to retire on, 30 percent have not saved anything for retirement, and only 20 percent feel very confident about having enough money to live comfortably in retirement (EBRI, 2003).

Furthermore, the empirical evidence suggests that failing to save enough also has serious negative consequences. A recent study of post-retirement consumption patterns indicates that US workers experience an unexpected decline in their standard of living after retirement (Bernheim, Skinner, and Weinberg, 2001). This consumption drop is even more precipitous in the United Kingdom (Banks, Blundell, and Tanner, 1998).[4] Other research suggests that only 30 percent of pre-retirees are fully prepared for retirement at age 65 in the United States (Moore and Mitchell, 2000). Of the remaining group, another 30 percent is likely to close the savings gap by age 65, though this hardly appears to be evidence of a long-term, lifelong rational planner at the heart of the life-cycle model. Finally, fully 40 percent appear unlikely to achieve a reasonable standard of replacement income by age 65. The numbers are much more pessimistic if retirement is planned for age 62, when the median American typically retires.

Behavioral economists would not find it surprising that people struggle with retirement saving in view of the problem's complexity. Indeed, many would take it as *prima facie* evidence that large groups of workers do not "get the saving problem right," contrary to the assumption of rationality and wise planning underlying the life-cycle model.

## The Problem of Self-Control

What might explain this lack of retirement preparation? Behavioralists tend to rely on a straightforward psychological explanation called "lack of willpower." This explanation is often described as "bounded self-control": That is, people try to save for retirement, but they too often prove to be limited in their capacity or desire to execute intentions (Thaler and Shefrin, 1981). In a sense, saving for retirement requires behavior similar to those undertaken in other behavior modification programs such as exercising, dieting, quitting smoking, or following through on New Year's resolutions. It would seem that while people intellectually "understand" the benefits of a specific behavior, and they may even have some idea of how to get started, they have difficulty implementing their intentions. Too often, they struggle to take action, and when they do act, their behaviors are often half-hearted or ineffective.

What evidence is there that problems of self-control may be important deterrents to saving for retirement? One body of researchers offers practical and theoretical insights into how individuals make tradeoffs regarding risk and time. Psychologists have shown that peoples' near-term discount rates are much higher than their long-term discount rates (Laibson, Repetto, and Tobacman, 1998). In Thaler's (1981) formulation, people confronting long-term decisions can exhibit high levels of patience. For instance, they might say "If I can receive an apple in 100 days and two apples in 101 days, I'll be happy to wait the extra day for another apple." But when the decision shifts to the present, their patience wears thin and they think: "I'd rather have an apple today than wait for two tomorrow."[5]

In standard time value of money calculations, discount rates are postulated to remain constant over time, so they do not vary today, tomorrow, or a year from now. Given this assumption, one dollar saved today would be perceived to be worth exponentially more (e.g. $5.74) in 30 years' time

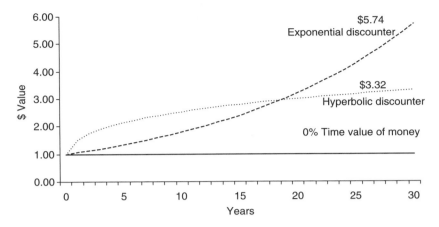

Figure 1-1. Exponential versus hyperbolic discounters—growth of $1 over time.
*Source*: Authors' calculations.

(Figure 1-1). But when individuals are "hyperbolic discounters," they apply high discount rates to the near term and lower discount rates to the future. In this case, one dollar's worth of saving today is perceived as growing more rapidly in the short run, and less in the longer run. Hence the incremental gains from extending one's time horizon are perceived to be relatively modest, compared to those of the conventional "exponential discounter." As illustrated by the increasing slope of the exponential line, exponential savers foresee ever-increasing rewards to deferring consumption by another year. For hyperbolic discounters, rewards are left to accelerate quickly, and then taper off. Put simply, workers who are hyperbolic discounters place a lower value on future benefits and overvalue the present. The application to retirement is clear: They will overconsume today and undersave, as a result of self-control problems when it comes to saving for retirement.

Decision theorists working in this vein seek to understand the self-control problem in a deeper way, delving into the structure and processing mechanisms of the human brain. For instance, Weber (this volume) notes that the brain consists of an older, limbic system shared with lower-order animals, which is the source of emotional or affective decisionmaking; and a more "modern" cerebral layer, which is a late-stage evolutionary trait in humans and the source of conceptual or symbolic processing. Perhaps because of this, processing of emotions typically involves gauging risk in terms of two components: "Dread risk," or the potential for catastrophe, and "uncertainty risk," involving a generalized fear of the unknown or the new. Weber suggests that retirement risks rate low along both dimensions: Few people have a palpable fear of impending disaster or of great uncertainty in their retirement planning, as compared to other risks in their lives.

In Weber's framework, the self-control problem of retirement saving must join both cerebral and emotional decisionmaking simultaneously, if people are to be prompted to take effective action. For example, if one were to experience the risks of retirement in the present so as to stimulate the brain's affective system, people might attempt a real-world experiment such as attempting to live on, say, two-thirds of their income for the next month.

Whether viewed from an economics or a decision theoretic perspective, the self-control problem supports the view of a wide divergence between individuals' desires and their actual behaviors (Saliterman and Sheckley, this volume). A survey of 10,000 employees at a single firm found that 68 percent of participants said their retirement savings rate was "too low" (Choi et al., 2001a). When queried, they reported that they *should* be saving 14 percent of average earnings, whereas in fact, they were only saving about 6 percent. (The remaining one-third of the participants believed their saving patterns were just about right and fewer than 1 percent felt they were saving too much.) Similarly, in Clark et al. (this volume), retirement plan participants reported that they knew they were saving less than they should. In other words, a key obstacle to saving more is not necessarily lack of awareness, but rather the ability to take action on the knowledge. The difficult task is to overcome hyperbolic discounting, to merge conceptual and affective reasoning into a course of effective action.

In recognition of such problems, people often seek to protect themselves through the use of commitment devices, or mechanisms that help foster desirable changes in behavior (cf. Laibson, 1997; and Laibson, Repetto, and Tobacman, 1998). Commitment devices for saving may be an analogue of the fad diet: One way of imposing some degree of discipline on one's wayward behavior is to create some seemingly arbitrary rules about what one can and cannot eat. "Pay yourself first" is a standard commitment device used by financial planners seeking to encourage disciplined saving and budgeting; it is also the principle underlying US payroll-deduction 401(k) plans. These plans are one of the most successful commitment devices in current use, and they are formulated such that contributions are automatically deducted from workers' pay before the money can be spent. Participation rates in 401(k)-type plans, where payroll deduction is the norm, are at least four times as high as for Individual Retirement Accounts (IRA), where structured payroll deductions are uncommon; according to 1997 tax return data, some 27 percent of workers contributed to workplace savings plans, compared with 6 percent contributing to an IRA (CBO, 2003). Other commitment devices include tax refunds and Holiday Clubs, where individuals engage in seemingly irrational economic activity (e.g. loaning money to the government or to their local banks at below-market rates) in exchange for discipline at accumulating savings. Withdrawal restrictions on IRAs and 401(k)s and other retirement plans also appear to be commitment devices: Once the money is allocated to these plans, a psychological and financial hurdle is imposed on accessing the money, helping to counteract lapses in personal willpower.

Other evidence that individuals vary in their capacity for self-control and financial discipline comes from industry surveys of workers' savings and planning behavior. Ameriks, Caplin, and Leahy (2003) as well as Lusardi (Chapter 9, this volume) find that workers' "propensity to plan" has strong positive influence on retirement wealth accumulation. MacFarland et al. (Chapter 6, this volume) indicate that as many as half of pension participants are dis- or uninterested in the financial and retirement planning activities thought necessary to plan successful retirement. In fact, a "planner" paradigm, where the individual consciously pursues retirement saving and investment goals in a disciplined, systematic way, appears to apply to only about half of the retirement plan population. The other half appears singularly unable to impose the self-control needed to solve this problem.

## Framing and Default Choices

Many individuals deviate from standard economic theory in another important way: They can be easily influenced by *decision framing*. Rational economic agents would not be expected to vary their responses to a question based on how it is asked. But in practice, many people do exactly that, both in the savings area and, as we show later, in investment decisionmaking as well. A by-now classic example of decision framing arises with automatic enrollment in retirement saving plans. Under the traditional (non-automatic) approach, the employee would have to make a "positive election" to join the 401(k) plan. By contrast, with automatic enrollment, the employee would be signed up by the employer for the plan at a given percentage contribution rate, and the employee retains the right to opt out of this decision.

This simple rephrasing of the saving question elicits a dramatically different response in plan participation rates. Madrian and Shea (2001) have powerfully shown that when workers are required to opt in, the default decision (or the non-decision) is to save nothing; by dramatic contrast, with automatic enrollment, the default decision proves to be that people save at the rate specified by the employer. For one large US firm, plan participation rates jumped from 37 percent to 86 percent for new hires after automatic enrollment was introduced (Figure 1-2). What this suggests, in the end, is that many workers do not have particularly firm convictions about their desired savings behavior. Merely by rephrasing the question, their preferences can be changed—from not saving to saving.

The impact of automatic enrollment is not just an illustration of framing questions, but also part of a broader behavioral phenomenon, namely the power of the "default option" and its influence on decisionmaking. When confronted with difficult decisions, individuals tend to adopt heuristics (shortcuts)

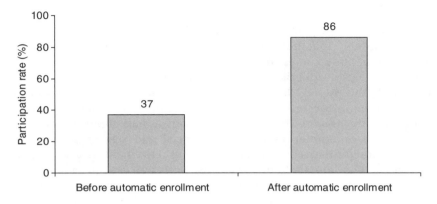

Figure 1-2. Decision framing: The impact of automatic enrollment on new hire plan participation rates.

*Source*: Madrian and Shea (2002).

that simplify the complex problems they face. One simple heuristic is to accept the available default option—that is, rather than making an active choice, accept the choice made by others. And, as noted in 401(k) enrollment, the simplest default is the non-decision: Do nothing.

An emerging literature indicates that individual behavior is easily swayed by default choices.[6] Again, automatic enrollment provides another illustration of the unexpected effects of default behavior. It turns out that while automatic enrollment boosts the number of individuals saving in a retirement plan, it might not actually increase total plan savings (Choi et al., 2001*b*). The reason is that, when automatically enrolled, people who would have voluntarily enrolled in the plan at higher contribution rates or chosen more aggressive investments decide to stick with the low saving rate and conservative investment option set by their employer. Thus, the positive effect is that saving rises for people who formerly did not participate, but an unexpectedly negative result is that saving falls for those who would have enrolled at higher rates and in more aggressive options, but instead elected to adopt the employer's defaults. On net, it appears that these two effects can largely offset one another.

More broadly, Choi et al. (2003) develop a model of a procrastination and default-driven saver and the choice of optimal savings rates. That study argues that optimal defaults for such savers are, in effect, the corner points or defaults of the plan savings problem—a saving rate of 0 percent, a saving rate equal to the employer matching contribution, and a saving rate at the maximum allowed by the plan. Both their theoretical models and the practical evidence on automatic enrollment underscore how profound the impact can be of the selection of a default option.

## Inertia and Procrastination

Evidence on automatic enrollment has also revealed another anomaly about individuals and their saving behavior: The important impact that inertia or procrastination plays on decisionmaking. In Madrian and Shea's (2001) analysis of automatic enrollment, they showed that the benefit of higher plan participation rates appeared to be offset by a profound level of inertia. Most participants remained at the default savings and conservative investment choices set for them by their employer. Once enrolled, participants made few active changes to the contribution rates or investment mixes selected for them by their employer; rather, they simply stayed with what was assigned to them.

Another analysis (Choi et al., 2001a), explored how inertia and default behavior influenced several other defined contribution plan activities: Enrollment, cash distributions at termination, the match level, eligibility, and the impact of education, among others. The authors concluded that, more often than not, many participants followed "the path of least resistance" in their decisionmaking—in effect, making the easiest, rather than the best, decision. Again, the persistence of inertia and what might be called a passive approach to decisionmaking are both indicative of individuals being somewhat imperfect rational economic agents in their retirement and savings decisions.

An illustration of this "desire versus action" compares workers' attitudes expressed after having attended an employee education seminar, with actual behavioral changes recorded on company administrative data systems (Choi et al., 2001a). Immediately following a seminar, for example, all workers not participating in a firm's 401(k) plan indicated in a survey that they would join the plan. In fact, however, over the next 6 months, only 14 percent did so. A similar, though smaller, gap between desire and action was true for other behaviors, including intentions to boost saving, change existing portfolio allocations, or change the mix of future contributions (see Table 1-1).

TABLE 1-1  The Self-Control Problem: Divergence between Desired and Actual Behavior

| Action | Planned Change (%) | Actual Change (%) |
|---|---|---|
| Enroll in 401(k) plan | 100 | 14 |
| Increase contribution rate | 28 | 8 |
| Change fund selection | 47 | 15 |
| Change fund allocation | 36 | 10 |

*Source*: Choi et al. (2001a: table 6).

## Other Influences

These behavioral findings are further supported by new research on the impact of investment choices and peer groups on saving rates. One tenet of contemporary economics is that more choice is better. Yet, as Sethi-Iyengar, Huberman, and Jiang (Chapter 5, this volume) show, offering workers many investment choices can produce "choice overload." In this case, plan participants become overwhelmed with the complexity of the decision, and as a result, pension plan participation is reduced. Faced with complex investment choices, some participants may elect to simplify the decision by following the "default" heuristic (i.e. "Don't decide, don't join the plan.") Similarly, Duflo and Saez (this volume) find that saving decisions can be strongly influenced by peers. For instance, in several striking experiments and case studies, they conclude that people with virtually identical demographic characteristics can have dramatically different saving rates, depending on whether their peers save for retirement. They also demonstrate that communications directed to an individual can influence not only the individual's savings behavior, but also the behavior of others in his or her work group.

## Automatic Saving Plans: Save More Tomorrow

Such behavioral insights into saving behavior have been illustrated in an interesting way in the Save More Tomorrow (or SMT) program developed by Benartzi and Thaler (forthcoming). Under this program, plan participants indicate that they wish to increase their pension saving rates on a regularly scheduled basis, at prespecified future dates (e.g. on their anniversary date with the company). This mechanism is designed to address several behavioral anomalies. First, it recognizes that individuals have self-control problems and benefit from a precommitment device when it comes to retirement saving. Second, it exploits inertia, since people tend to sign up initially and the program is automatically carried out in the future. Third, it recognizes the possibility of hyperbolic discounting: That is, people tend to be averse to saving today but they are willing to push off their commitment to the future—to promise to "save more tomorrow." As hyperbolic discounters, they significantly underestimate the impact of such future commitment. Last, the program exploits money illusion. Thus, participants often think only in terms of nominal take-home pay, so if the savings increase is designed to coincide with pay raises, they tend to believe that the savings increase had little or no cost, even though their real current consumption may have declined by a small amount.

In the initial study, the SMT program was offered to employees at a 300-person firm. Employees were given the option of financial counseling; most signed up for the counseling, and received the advice that they should boost their savings rates by an average of 5 percent. Nearly 80 workers took that

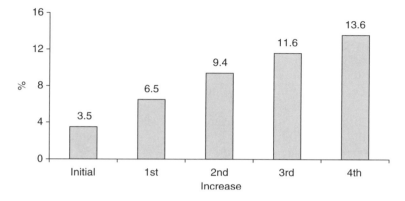

Figure 1-3. The impact of commitment devices and inertia: The impact of SMT on plan saving rates.

*Source*: Benartzi and Thaler (2004).

advice; many more, just over 160, signed up for the SMarT plan instead, which required annual increases of 3 percent. After 3 years, the individuals who signed up for SMT experienced a dramatic increase in their savings rates—from 3.5 percent before the plan began, to 11.6 percent (Figure 1-3).

The popularity of the SMT program provides further evidence of the divergence between real-world employees and the rational agents assumed by many economic theorists working on theoretical saving models. Many people attempt to save for retirement and even appear to know when they are not doing well as they should, but they struggle with exercising the right degree of self-control or willpower. Through inertia and procrastination, default decisions are easiest to maintain, including saving nothing at all, or at one's current rate, particularly if changing behavior requires incurring the costs of saving at a higher level. Reframing the saving decision to include defaults with automatically higher saving rates, and using commitment devices, inertia, and money illusion to address the self-control problems of hyperbolic discounters, all seem useful approaches to address the practical problems associated with the saving decision.

## The Investment Decision

As in the case of the saving problem, the question of how to invest one's money during the accumulation phase has been widely explored in a well-developed model of investment decisionmaking commonly denominated *modern portfolio theory* (MPT). The principles of MPT are at the heart of investment decisionmaking, both in employer-directed defined benefit (DB) plans, and employee-directed DC plans. MPT influences everything from strategic asset allocation decisions in defined benefit DB plans, and investment advice and education programs in defined contribution DC plans, to more technical issues such as performance attribution for investment managers.

In broad-brush terms, MPT seeks to characterize capital market assets, whether stocks or fixed income investments, in terms of their expected mean return and their volatility or variance—hence, the term "mean-variance" investing. Rational investors seek out efficient combinations of securities that optimize risk and return, and a given portfolio is on the "efficient frontier" if it offers the highest return for a given level of risk. Individuals and institutions select from the array of portfolio choices on the efficient frontier based on their expected utility. In their utility preferences, individuals are presumed to be risk-averse, meaning that they penalize, or demand higher compensation for, riskier investments. Also, as risk increases, the compensation they require increases at a faster rate.

One of the important predictions of MPT is that investors will be inadequately compensated for assuming the risks of investing in an individual security. In other words, an efficient capital market will compensate investors only for the aggregate market risk they endure, so there will be no single-stock investments on the efficient frontier. Consequently, rational investors will seek to maximize portfolio diversification and eliminate all stock-specific risk, in the pursuit of optimal portfolio solutions. This principle has been at the foundation of the growth of low-cost index strategies as an investment management style in both DB and DC retirement plans.

Another implication of MPT is the theory of time diversification—the closer one is to an anticipated investment goal where spending from the portfolio begins (such as retirement), the less risky will be the investment portfolio. In practice, financial counselors frequently propose time diversification as a popular investment principle, suggesting, in one popular formulation, that people invest 100 percent minus their age in stocks. The time diversification view is also the basis for most DC education and advisory services, which suggest that older investors should hold more conservative portfolios than younger investors. Yet, this theory has important critics including Paul Samuelson (1989) and Bodie (1995), who suggest that investors ought to hold fixed asset allocation percentages over their entire lifetimes. Finally, richer versions of MPT extend the analysis beyond tradeable securities, to encompass the people's broader wealth portfolio. For example, Campbell and Viceira (2002) and Davis and Willen (2002) suggest that risk and return tradeoffs should encompass illiquid holdings like housing and human capital.

As with saving theory, behavioral economics asks a very fundamental question about investors in general, and plan participants in particular: How good are they at actually understanding and acting on the predictions of mean–variance theory? Arguably, a rational investor should do a reasonable job of constructing mean–variance efficient portfolios, so there should be some evidence of widespread competency at these types of investment decisions. Worrisome for the MPT theorists are some key facts about investor behavior. Of US households who own stocks, the median family owns only two positions, and even the most affluent households hold a median of 15 (Polkovnichenko, 2003). These low levels of diversification fall well short of the number of positions thought to represent a well-diversified portfolio. It appears that for many investors, diversification is more akin to holding a variety of assets rather than the construction of a well-diversified portfolio in an MPT sense.[7] A related diversification puzzle is why, in DC retirement plans, do so many participants overinvest in their employer's stock? A recent study by Mitchell and Utkus (2003) estimated that more than 11 million participants held over 20 percent of their 401(k) account in their employer's stock; of that group, 5 million participants had 60 percent or more in company stock. Finally, broad stock market fluctuations—like the technology bubble of the late 1990s and the subsequent bear market—seem hard to reconcile with a model of the investor as a rational, mean–variance optimizing agent. So do levels of individual and institutional trading in the stock market.

In this section, we first summarize the accumulated evidence on mean–variance behavior among investors—or rather, the case against mean–variance behavior among investors. Much of this research, importantly, has been drawn from participants in DC retirement plans in the United States. We then turn to the attempts to develop alternative theories explaining investor behavior.

## Lack of Firm Preferences

The findings cited earlier on automatic enrollment illustrate that many workers lack firm preferences for saving. Merely by rephrasing the question from a positive to a negative election, workers who were not planning to save suddenly find themselves saving—and workers who would have saved at higher savings rates find themselves saving at the default set by their employer. A similar lack of strong preferences appears to affect investment decisions. Arguably, if investors were rational in a mean–variance sense, one would first expect them to have well-defined preferences over their portfolios. That is, they should have the courage of their convictions. After all, the portfolio they select represents their unique expectations of risk and return, and it is tailored to their own utility preferences.

In fact, retirement plan participants appear to have relatively weak preferences for the portfolio they, in fact, elect (Benartzi and Thaler, 2002). This was found in experiments where workers were given a choice between holding their own portfolio, the portfolio of a median participant in their plan, and the portfolio of the average participant: About eight out of ten participants preferred the median to their own. Only 21 percent continued to prefer the portfolio they initially selected. Furthermore, many found the average portfolio to be quite satisfactory. In other words, pension participants seemed to be quite happy (or perhaps even happier!) with portfolios constructed at the statistical average of their co-workers' behavior, than with the portfolios they themselves constructed.

This finding is supported by psychological literature regarding preference reversals. That is, individuals often do not arrive at a decision with firm preferences in mind; preferences appear not be hard-wired. Rather, individual preferences tend to be situational and emerge at the time a decision is made, based on the conditions and information surrounding that decision. To the extent this is true, preference reversals tend to be more common than might be expected. Individuals who thought not to save find themselves saving; individuals who selected their own portfolio find themselves just as happy, if not happier, with another choice.

## Framing Effects

Just as saving choices can be affected by framing, so too can investment decisions be influenced, sometimes strongly, by framing effects. Much of the research in this area has investigated the impact of investment menu design on participant investment choices in DC retirement plans. The theme underlying this research is that menu design is a more powerful influence on participant decisionmaking than the underlying risk and return characteristics of the investments being offered. In this sense, the investment menu in a retirement plan is an "opaque" frame, which most participants cannot see through, to understand the underlying risk and return characteristics of their investments. Put another way, many participants appear to have weak convictions regarding risk and return, and they can easily be swayed in their decisions by the framing effects of an investment menu.

In one experiment, participants were asked to select an investment mix for their retirement plans given two fund offerings (Benartzi and Thaler, 2001). Some participants were presented with a stock fund and a bond fund; others with a stock fund and a balanced fund; and a third group with a bond fund and a balanced fund. In all three cases, a common strategy was to choose a 50/50 mix of the two funds offered, although many participants did select different weightings. What was striking in the data was the fact that radically different underlying asset allocations ensued, given the different choices offered. For people given the choice of an equity fund and a bond fund, the average allocation to equities was 54 percent. For those offered two equity-oriented portfolios, a balanced fund and an equity fund, the average allocation to equities was 73 percent. And for those offered a balanced and a bond fund, the average allocation to equities was only 35 percent. In a related experiment using investment menus with five funds, the authors found that the asset allocations chosen by participants were again strongly influenced by menu design. If the plan offered several equity funds, participants invested more in equities; when it included more fixed income funds, they chose fixed income options instead.

A different study also asked plan participants to select investments from three different menus, which the authors posed might be similar to the structure of a privatized Social Security account (Benartzi and Thaler, 2001). The investments allowed ranged from A (low risk) to D (high risk). The first menu offered included options A, B, and C; the second menu, just options B and C; and the third menu, options B, C, and D. Comparing options B and C, which were in all three menus, 29 percent of the participants preferred C over B in the first menu; 39 percent in the second menu; and 54 percent in the third menu. In other words, in the first menu, where option C was at the extreme, it was liked least; in the third menu, where option C was the middle choice, it was liked most. As with the asset allocation experiment above, this shows that participants appeared to use a naïve heuristic (i.e. "avoid extremes, pick the middle option") rather than maintain a consistent set of well-ordered risk preferences to select from the investments offered.

Related research indicates that, beyond these menu effects, even simple changes in the way information is presented can influence asset allocation decisions (Benartzi and Thaler, 2001). In one experiment, plan participants were asked to make investment decisions based on reviewing the one-year return profile of US common stocks; in a second experiment, they made decisions based on a 30-year return profile. In the first instance, the average allocation to equities was 63 percent; in the second, 81 percent. The implication is that plan sponsors can alter asset allocations if return data are presented over different holding periods. And as Scott and Stein show (this volume), different types of investment education and information can substantially change retiree investment allocations.

Like the saving research discussed earlier, these findings underscore the powerful influence of framing effects on decisionmaking in retirement plans. Apparently, many plan participants seem to lack well-formed investment preferences, and these preferences appear to be easily altered by the way the choices are presented to them.

## Inertia and Procrastination

As with savings behavior, inertia also plays a large role in investment decisionmaking, in addition to these framing effects. Madrian and Shea (2001) and Choi et al. (2001b) reported high levels of inertia in investment decisionmaking in their studies of participants and automatic enrollment. To further underscore this point, we examined how 2.3 million plan participants at the Vanguard Group allocated their new contributions accounts

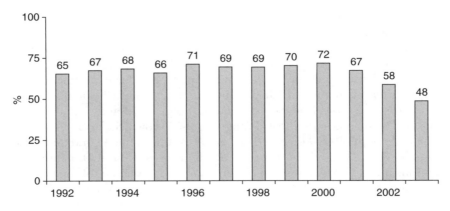

Figure 1-4. Anchoring and adjustment: Current equity contributions by plan entry date % contribution allocated to equity investments.

*Source*: Vanguard Group (2003).

as of June 30, 2003 (Figure 1-4). First, we found that fewer than 10 percent of plan participants change their contribution allocations each year. Further, participants who initially enrolled in their plans near the top of the bull market in 1999, allocated about 70 percent of new contributions to equities in June of 2003, notwithstanding the huge market drop sustained over the preceding 3-year period. Meanwhile, participants who newly enrolled during the first 6 months of 2003, after the 3-year fall in US equity prices, allocated only 48 percent of new monies to equities. While this illustrates how sensitive participant investment decisions at enrollment are to then-current market conditions, it also demonstrates the power of inertia. It seems unlikely that participants enrolled in 1999 would have dramatically different risk preferences than those who enrolled in 2003, yet the recent enrollees were presumably making active choices based on then-current information, whereas earlier enrollees did not react so dramatically to market news.

Figure 1-4 also illustrates "anchoring" effects for pension investors. Anchoring refers to the notion that decisionmaking is strongly influenced by starting values, no matter how arbitrary they may be. Among participants, it appears that the relevant anchor is their initial allocation decision, and subsequent portfolio changes tend to be made with reference to that initial value, rather than on some absolute basis. For instance, participants who enrolled at the peak of the bull market continued to allocate seven out of ten dollars to equities by 2003, over 20 points higher than those enrolling in the first 6 months of 2003.

## The Conundrum of Employer Stock

The use of company stock within US DC plans offers a compelling case study about the relevance of mean–variance models to investor decisionmaking. As noted earlier, Mitchell and Utkus (2003) have calculated that 11 million plan participants have allocations above 20 percent of their account balance in company stock—and 5 million have allocations above 60 percent of their account balance. A conventional economic explanation for this phenomenon is that employers and stockholders seek to promote employee productivity through stock ownership, and so they encourage or mandate large employee holdings of company stock. As rational agents, however, employees who are aware of the risks they are being required to assume, should demand compensation in some other form, such as higher wages or benefits.

There is some support for the "rational agent" view of workers holding company stock. This is because concentrated company stock positions are most common for large firms, and such firms typically pay higher wages and benefits to their employees. Yet, from a behavioral perspective, there is also evidence that concentration stock positions are not solely due to incentive effects; rather, it seems that computational or behavioral errors on the part of participants also help explain the phenomenon. For instance, Mitchell and Utkus (2003) use survey data to uncover evidence of "risk myopia" regarding employer stock, in that many participants rate their employer's stock as *safer* than a diversified equity fund.

Another Vanguard survey (Table 1-2) illustrates that even after the post-Enron publicity surrounding company stock, two-thirds of participants rate their employer stock as safer than, or as safe as, a diversified portfolio of many stocks. Only one-third said it was more risky. What is striking about these results is the comparison between participant risk perceptions and the actual return and volatility of their employer's stock. Looking at the risk ratings first, it is natural to conclude that at least two-thirds of participants are not mean–variance investors when it comes to company stock. They rate stock as safer than or as safe as a diversified portfolio, despite its actual higher volatility than a broad market index: A clear-cut "error" under modern portfolio theory. Arguably one-third of participants did assess the risk correctly, in that they rated their employer's stock as riskier *and* its volatility higher. But it seems implausible to conclude that all participants who understand mean–variance analysis may only be found among the set holding riskier employer stocks; it is more likely that participant do not base their risk perceptions on volatility. Instead, participants' risk ratings are well correlated with the historic relative returns of their employer's stock.

The conclusion that plan participants overlook volatility and focus on returns is supported in Benartzi's (2001) study of pension investments in employer stock. Specifically, he finds that participant allocations were

TABLE 1-2  Perceptions of Company Stock Risk and Return

| Participant Report: Level of Risk in Company Stock[b] | % of Participants | Actual Average Standard Deviation of Company Stock (%)[a] | Actual Average Company Stock Return (%)[a] |
|---|---|---|---|
| **Q. Would you say your employer's stock is more risky, less risky or has about the same level of risk as an investment in a diversified stock fund with many different stocks? (n = 415)** | | | |
| More risky | 33 | 40[b] | −8.8[b] |
| Same level of risk | 42 | 36[b] | −2.0[b] |
| Less risky | 22 | 31[b] | 2.2[b] |
| Don't know | 3 | 35 | −6.0 |
| Total | 100 | | |
| S&P 500 | | 18[b] | −1.1[b] |

[a] Returns and standard deviations of participants' company stock returns for the 5-year period ending September 30, 2003. Standard deviation calculated over 60 months and annualized.

[b] "More risk," "same level of risk" and "less risky" categories are all significantly different from one another at the 95% or 99% level. Standard deviations are all significantly higher than the S&P 500 at the 99% level. Returns for "more risky" ("less risky") are significantly lower (higher) than the S&P 500 at the 99% level.

*Source*: Vanguard Group (2003).

based on extrapolations of the company's historic stock performance. Participants who overweighted their employer's stock based on good past performance then found that those stocks subsequently generated below-average performance. Conversely, those participants who underweighted their employer's stock due to poor past performance subsequently saw the stock becoming an above-average performer.

Participants' allocations were also influenced by whether their employer provided a match in company stock, a phenomenon that Benartzi dubbed the "endorsement effect." The conclusion is that, just as menu design influences participant investment decisions, so too does the employer's plan design decision. Offering a match in company stock encourages participants to hold more in stock than workers whose employers do not match in stock. Other researchers have also argued that past performance, rather than risk, drives participants' portfolio decisions (e.g. Purcell, 2002; Huberman and Sengmueller, 2003; Poterba et al., 2003; Choi et al., Chapter 7, this volume).

## Reliance on Past Performance

Why do investors irrationally rely on past performance and fail to take expected returns as well as risk into account, as modern portfolio theory suggests they should? Two behavioral phenomena may offer some answers. A first issue is the pervasiveness of the "representativeness heuristic" in decisionmaking, explored by Tversky and Kahneman (1974). They found that people tend to see patterns in small series of randomly drawn numbers, and when making decisions, people attempt to impose some order or structure on the information that they see. For example, mutual fund investors might identify a fund manager with 3 years of top performance and conclude that the manager has unusual skill—rather than view it as a random process. Of course, viewed across the universe of thousands of investment managers, a given manager's 3-year track record is just as likely an indication of chance as of skill. The representativeness bias may partly arise due to a framing problem: That is, rather than frame the skill versus luck decision in terms of the universe of all individuals making portfolio decisions, a fund investor may frame it narrowly in terms of the 3-year track record of a single investment manager. As a result, what may actually be a random outcome may instead appear to be logical sequence.

A second issue is that many people appear to be subject to what has been called an "availability heuristic": When faced with difficult decisions, they tend to rely on readily available information. A simple reason that investors may rely on past performance could be because that information is cheaply available. As any plan participant knows, retirement plans and investment companies generate prodigious amounts of past performance data which they make available in statements, on websites, in enrollment materials, and in newsletter updates. Past performance is also pervasive in the media, but very few report systematically on expected returns. Of course, in the United States and elsewhere, reports on past investment performance are often accompanied by the legal disclaimer that "past performance is no guarantee of future results." Yet, one need only compare the size of that disclaimer to the volume of past performance data to understand its limitations in the face of the availability heuristic.

In sum, the representativeness and availability heuristics may help explain why, for example, mutual fund investors invariably chase performance in their fund purchase decisions (Patel, Zeckhauser, and Hendricks, 1991). Patterns suggesting superior performance are constructed from small samples drawn either from skill or luck. And the pervasiveness of past performance data leads to an inevitable reliance on past performance, despite the legal caveats.

## Prospect Theory

If plan participants are not necessarily mean–variance investors, then how do they actually make decisions under uncertainty about their pension investments? This is a complex question, partly because behavioral research in the last 20 years has focused on analyzing how people evaluate

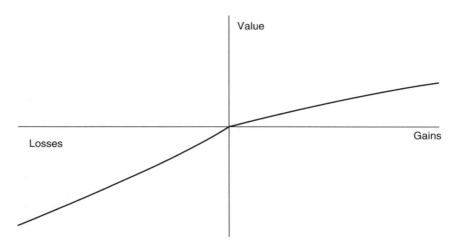

Figure 1-5. Prospect theory value function.

*Source*: Kahneman and Tversky (1979).

risky choices in general; only recently has interest turned to investment decisions.

The seminal theory of risky decisions was offered by Kahneman and Tversky (1979), who modeled individuals as though they made decisions to maximize an S-shaped value function depicted in Figure 1-5. This function differs from conventional utility maximization in two critical ways. First, individuals are thought to consider not how a decision influences total wealth (as in standard utility theory) but rather incremental gains and losses. Second, individuals are modeled as treating gains and losses quite differently. The gain function (to the right of the origin) is concave, while the loss function (to the left of the origin) is convex, with a much steeper slope. What this means is that individuals will experience losses more acutely than gains for a given dollar of gain or loss. Their experimental evidence suggested that the index of loss-aversion is about 2.5: In other words, when evaluating risky gambles, the individual will report that losses are 2.5 times as painful as the equivalent dollar value of gains. For example, if someone were presented with a 50 percent chance of losing $1,000 or a 50 percent chance of gaining an unknown amount, $X, the evidence suggests that many people would not entertain this gamble until the value X is on the order of $2,500 or so.

This approach has come to be known as *prospect theory*, and it has potentially important implications for investment behavior. For instance, investors will seek to lock in certain gains and avoid certain losses. This implies that individuals tend to be risk-averse for a known gain, but they can become risk-seeking in an effort to avoid a certain loss. In addition, actual behavior will depend on the exact sequence of gains and losses and how the individual has incorporated prior gains and losses into current perceptions. For example, suppose an individual wins $100. If offered a reasonable chance to win more money or lose the $100, many people would decline the additional gamble, because of the risk of forfeiting the $100 sure gain. But if offered a choice to win more money while preserving a meaningful part of the $100 gain, many people take the risk. This is known as the "house money" effect: While people are generally risk-averse in the domain of gains, if they feel they are risking someone else's money (e.g. accumulated earnings from prior bets), they become more risk-seeking. On the loss side of the equation, after losing $100, many people will accept a gamble that entails losing significantly more than $100 in an effort to recoup the $100 loss. This represents both the element of risk-seeking in the domain of losses, and the "breakeven" effect. Faced with the realization of a certain loss, many people seek additional risk, in an effort to recoup their investment, contrary to the conventional economic notion that "sunk costs are sunk costs" (i.e. rational agents should ignore realized losses). This approach offers an explanation for why investors have difficulty realizing losses on their investments (a strong desire to avoid loss realization and break even). It also might help explain why they sometimes increase risk-taking in risk equity markets (existing gains appear to be locked in and are "house money" which can be gambled) and in falling markets (existing losses appear temporary and extra risk-taking will help recoup those losses).[8]

Prospect theory and behavioral economics have been deemed relevant to investment decisionmaking in three ways (Kahneman, 2003). First, in the area of gains, investors are often characterized by overconfidence and excessive optimism: People tend to construct forecasts of the future that are typically too rosy. Second, in the area of losses, investor risk-aversion will lead to an unwillingness to realize investment losses, and a premature realization of investment gains (called by Shefrin and Statman the "disposition effect"; 1985). And third, if decisions are less than optimal due to both overconfidence and loss avoidance, the impact of these anomalies will be exacerbated by narrow framing effects. We consider each of these elements in turn.

## Overconfidence

In the domain of gains, one of the important findings of psychology and behavioral economics is that peoples' future forecasts are often characterized by widespread overconfidence and excessive optimism. Overconfidence is a widely documented trait in human decisionmaking: Thus, people systematically overrate their skills on such parameters as driving skills and humor. In business, managers tend to be overconfident about their abilities: For example, managers tend to overpay for mergers and acquisitions because of overoptimistic assessments. Other professionals in a range of diverse fields—in psychology, medicine, investments, engineering, and so on—have demonstrated overconfidence in their decisionmaking. In a study on future life prospects, college students were asked to evaluate the chances of certain positive and negative events occurring in their lives (e.g. having a bright career versus experiencing professional failure; maintaining ongoing good health versus contracting a mortal disease while young; having a happy versus a difficult domestic and emotional life). When asked to judge their own prospects, the students downplayed negative life events and emphasized positive outcomes. What was interesting was that, when asked the same questions of their college roommates, the students were more even-handed in their responses. Similarly, in medical decisionmaking, patients with mortal diseases were shown to be much more optimistic about their future prospects than their professional caregivers. Overall, the accumulated psychological evidence regarding overconfidence in decisionmaking has been described as the "Lake Wobegone" effect, named after a fictional US town described on a popular radio program where "all of the children are above average."[9]

Such overconfidence may partly be the result of an inability to understand accurately the role of random chance in determining the future. As noted above in our discussion on representativeness, people are notoriously poor statisticians, and they find patterns and trends in data that could just as easily be explained by random chance. Individuals appear to significantly underestimate the impact of random chance on their lives, and in hindsight overemphasize the degree of control they have over outcomes. Lack of objectivity might help explain self-evaluations: Individuals generally perceive themselves as better than others—and have better views of themselves than others do. Poor risk calculations certainly play a role in overconfidence: Individuals who are "100 percent sure" of their responses to certain questions are usually wrong 20 percent of the time. Perceived sense of control also plays a role: the stronger one's sense of control, the more powerful one's sense of confidence. Asked about the risks of a disabling car accident, people are much more optimistic when they are driving, than when they are passengers. There is also a gender element at work: Men tend to be more overconfident than women.[10]

Overconfidence probably has some economic, psychological, and even evolutionary positive benefits: For example, it may be the wellspring of risk-taking and entrepreneurial activity, or it may allow fast recovery from life's disappointments. But in the domain of investing, it may also lead to behaviors that are less than optimal and certainly at odds with mean–variance theory. For instance, overconfidence helps explain the high levels of trading activity in equity markets. Barber and Odean (2000) report high rates of turnover, on the order of 75 percent, among households owning brokerage accounts. They calculate that trading is typically hazardous to one's wealth, with active traders earning 11.4 percent over a 5-year period, while the market returned 17.9 percent, and low-turnover accounts 18.5 percent. That study also reports that men trade 45 percent more than women and the difference is even stronger for single men versus single women. Agnew, Balduzzi, and Sundén (2003) suggest that these trading results may be less relevant for retirement plans, since participants could mentally account for brokerage and retirement investments differently.

Other research focuses on affluent male equity investors, and it has confirmed that overconfidence and an emphasis on personal skill are both important attribute of investors, at least in the sample of experienced investors surveyed by De Bondt (1998). Most of these investors exhibited a high level of confidence about the stocks they had selected, while their outlook for the broad market was not as positively biased. They relied on their own skills at selecting companies and tended to downplay the importance of modern portfolio concepts like diversification. From their perspective, it seemed that diversification was less focused on non-correlated stock holdings and more about simple variety. These investors also tended to be surprised about the relationship between the overall market and their own holdings: That is, they downplayed the impact of market forces on their portfolios.[11] These diversification results seem consistent with Goetzmann and Kumar's findings (2001) that individual investors do own multiple stocks, but these are not drawn from uncorrelated industries and sectors so they are not typically diversified in the modern portfolio sense. Statman (Chapter 4, this volume) shows how behavioral theories of risk-taking may be used to formulate alternative theories for portfolio construction.

## Loss-Aversion and the Disposition Effect

If overconfidence helps explain behavior on the "upside" side of the prospect theory ledger, then the "downside" is dominated by aversion to loss realization. This plays out in interesting ways. For instance, as noted above, people are inclined to take a gamble if confronted with the choice of realizing an incurred but not-yet-realized loss, versus taking the gamble in which they might break or lose more. Particularly if there is a reasonable prospect of breaking even and avoiding a loss, many people take the gamble and risk losing even more money. In the investment setting, this manifests itself in what Shefrin and Statman (1985) call the "disposition effect." People who invest in stocks appear to rush to realize gains too quickly: They try to lock in or make certain the gains that they have already realized. On the other hand, they also appear to have trouble "cutting their losses"; that is, they hold onto loss-making stocks too long in the hope of recovering their investment. The impact of this effect on brokerage account investors is not small: Odean (1998a) calculated that investors who sold winning stocks saw those stocks outperform the market by 2 percent in the subsequent year, while investors who kept their losing stocks saw those stocks underperform by market by 1 percent over the same period. In total, the net impact of selling winners too quickly while holding losers cost investors 3 percent per year in terms of portfolio returns. These results also validated the notion of overconfidence in investment decisions: People continued to hold and to sell the wrong stocks, leading to lower returns, despite actual results.

## Narrow Framing

Adding to what has already been discussed, there is evidence that overconfidence and loss-aversion are exacerbated by too narrow a framing of risky decisions (Kahneman, 2003). Few investors would take a gamble involving a 50 percent chance of winning $1,500, versus a 50 percent chance of losing $1,000. (With loss-aversion parameters of around 2.5, most investors would not take the gamble until the gain was closer to $2,500.) Yet, experimental evidence indicates that people are more willing to accept this gamble when they are given the opportunity to play it many times, or when it is framed in terms of changes to their entire net worth. Perhaps, as Kahneman observes, it is more natural for investors to "think small" when facing a one-time gamble, but they may get it right and "think large" if facing sequences of gambles or changes to total wealth.

## The Decumulation Decision

The last phase of financial decisionmaking for retirement happens during the decumulation period. This is likely to occur during later middle age and beyond, and it is the period when most people decide how they will spend down their accumulated assets. Of course, if there were no uncertainty, the rational life-cycler would plan to spend down retirement assets so as to ensure optimal retirement consumption and protect bequest motives (if any). People having saved for retirement via a formal pension scheme would be expected to decumulate their assets just as their non-pensioned counterparts having the same total assets, except insofar as it reduced the retiree's tax obligation (Brown et al., 1999).

In practice, of course, people confront many sources of risk during the retirement period. The most important of these are longevity risk, inflation risk, health risks (leading to unexpected expenses and costs), and capital market risks. All or a combination of these risks can contribute to experiencing consumption shortfalls during retirement—or simply running out of money. So many fundamental uncertainties, further complicated by the psychological considerations discussed above, combine to make it quite difficult for retirees to deftly manage the drawdown process for retirement accounts in old age. In this section, accordingly, we first summarize available evidence on how people deal with longevity risk, then turn to a discussion of inflation risk, and finally conclude with a brief discussion of how to manage capital market risk during the withdrawal period.

## Longevity Risk

People do not know precisely how long they will live, hence they run the risk of exhausting their assets before dying. Such risk exposure can be reduced by consuming less per year during retirement, but of course this simply elevates the chances that a retiree might die with "too much" wealth left over.

One way to offset longevity risk is to buy an annuity with all or part of one's retirement assets (Brown et al., 2001; Mitchell and McCarthy, 2003; Drinkwater and Sondergeld, Chapter 15, this volume). Single premium lifelong annuities are relatively appealing, since they continue to pay benefits as long as the retiree lives, irrespective of whether the retiree outlives the life tables. Indeed, recent survey analysis (Panis, Chapter 14, this volume) finds that retirees holding annuities are more satisfied with their retirement, holding other things constant. Consequently, the implication is that at least partial annuitization may provide peace of mind associated with longevity protection.

Notwithstanding the substantial theoretical appeal of annuities, however, relatively little retirement money is currently devoted to the purchase of annuities in most developed countries. For instance, life annuity purchases in the United States amounted to more than $120 billion in 1999, but the majority of sales were for variable annuities which are used mainly in the accumulation process rather than for decumulation products paying lifetime benefits (Brown et al., 2001). In the group pensions market, there is also growing attention to this issue. Previously, DB plans normally paid either single or joint and survivor life annuities as a matter of course; rarely was any sort of lump sum option available in lieu of the lifetime benefit stream. Of late, however, DB pensions have begun offering lump sum distributions to their retirees, akin to the payouts popularized in the DC world (Moore and Muller, 2002). As a result, workers reaching retirement age with pension coverage are increasingly unlikely to take their benefits as lifetime annuities. Indeed, a recent study found that three quarters of company pension distributions are currently paid as lump sum cashouts rather than as lifetime annuity payments (McGill et al., 2004). In this sense, fewer and fewer retirement plans are providing longevity insurance in the form of lifetime insured annuity benefits.

Several explanations for the declining demand for annuitization in retirement have been offered. One factor is that people may be poorly informed regarding their remaining life expectancies, tending to underestimate the risk of outliving one's income. For instance, a recent industry survey reported that only one-third of the respondents knew that someone who attained the age of 65 had a substantial chance of living beyond his life expectancy (Metlife, 2003). Yet other surveys report that older people's expected survival patterns track actuarial tables relatively closely (Hurd and McGarry, 1995), and retirement asset shortfalls appear uncorrelated with people expecting to die soon in retirement (Mitchell, Moore, and Phillips, 2000). A different factor discouraging annuity purchase is that retirees often have strong bequest motives, and many of them expect to have to pay for long-term care. In such cases, they might elect to hold on to their funds rather than annuitize them on retirement. And of course, to the extent they have Social Security and DB pension plans, they will be less likely to annuitize all their assets since they are partly protected against longevity risk already (Brown et al., 2002).

Three other "rational" explanations may provide insights into why annuity purchases are low despite the fact that baby boomers are moving into retirement age. First is an interest rate factor. The decision to annuitize at a given point in time represents an irreversible decision to "lock in" then-current yields (which underlie the contract pricing). A second is the cost factor: Retirees sometimes see insured products as uncompetitive with pure investments due to the loads levied by the insurance providers. Yet, the loads have decreased substantially over time, and evidence indicates that retirees can expect high "money's worth" for annuity products in many countries (Mitchell, Moore, and Phillips, 2000). Consequently the respectable returns combined with the insurance protection should induce more interest in this payout structure as the baby boomer generation moves into the retirement years. The other main reason lump sums are attractive is that regulations currently permit workers to take a relatively large lump sum computed with a transitorily depressed discount rate, and in many cases this is more economically profitable than leaving the funds in the plan to grow.[12]

Behavioral factors may also explain the low demand for annuities in retirement, including most importantly *loss-aversion*. This arises because some retirees may worry about potential losses to heirs in the event that they die "early," since annuitization typically eliminates the possibility for bequeathing these funds. Adding to the problem is that retirees may heavily discount future benefit coverage in the event that they live a long time in retirement. Such an asymmetric valuation could enhance peoples' probability of taking their pension accruals as a lump sum versus buying a life annuity, and may explain why some argue that "locking up" one's assets in annuities boosts rather than reduces risk. To meet such concerns, some insurers have begun to combine annuity offerings with life insurance, long-term care, and disability benefits, so as to reduce the fear of "losing it all" due to premature death. Employers wishing to help workers with their self-control problem might offer annuities as the default option at retirement, rather than making the lump sum the standard choice.

Nonetheless, it does appear that many people fundamentally undervalue the appeal of a lifetime annuity—sometimes at substantial, if not overwhelming, cost. One fascinating example is a study of annuitization behavior for personnel at the US Department of Defense (DOD) (Warner and Pleeter, 2001). In 1992, about 65,000 officers and enlisted personnel were involved in a program to reduce staffing at the DOD. To this end, they were offered payments from their retirement plan in the form of an annuity or a lump sum. The internal rate of return on the annuity ranged from 17.5 percent to 19.8 percent, at a time when government bond rates were around 7 percent. Economists estimated that all of the officers and half of the enlisted personnel would take the annuity. In the end, contrary to expectations, 52 percent of the officers and 92 percent of the enlisted personnel took the lump sum. In total, the DOD employees forfeited a total of $1.7 billion in economic value, by electing the lump sum over the annuity.

## Inflation and Capital Market Risk

Last, but certainly not least, we turn to the risk of inflation and capital market risk during the retirement period. It is somewhat well known that the common worker is rather poorly informed about volatility in asset returns and inflation rates (Bodie et al., 2002), a problem that also besets him during the retirement period as well. For instance, from the late 1970s to the late 1990s, the United States had a relatively low rate of inflation and rising stock prices that contributed to a widespread belief that equities serve as a good hedge for inflation. Yet, this is not accurate: During the 1970s, inflation moved into double digits, yet stock prices fell by over half in a short 2-year jolt (1974–75). Brown, Mitchell, and Poterba (2000) also confirm that stocks have been a poor inflation hedge in the United States, at least in the short to medium term. For this reason, retirees seeking protection against the destructive impact of inflation over a long retirement period would benefit substantially from holding at least a part of their financial assets in inflation-protected assets such as Treasury Inflation-protected Securities (TIPS).

The fact that workers take lump sums from their pensions, rather than have their funds continue to be managed by the pension fund itself, may also be of concern for several other reasons. One potential explanation is overconfidence: Many people believe they can live well on relatively small asset pools during retirement, yet after leaving work, they then find they run out of money, sometimes within a few months of retirement. This is exacerbated by the fact that the lump sum benefit is often "framed" in a way that induces them to overvalue the lump sum and undervalue the annuity. Offering a retiree a lump sum of $100,000, versus taking a joint and survivor annuity of $600 per month for life, tends to highlight the "massive sum" versus the longevity protection.

Another concern is that, due to lack of self-control, people may be tempted to spend their lump sums once they are out of the pension plan. While recipients do roll over some of their lump sum distributions into Individual Retirement Accounts, they do use a large fraction to pay debts and cover current expenses (Moore and Muller, 2002). A problem with taking a lump sum from the pension, of course, is that the amount withdrawn becomes subject to regular income tax and it may also elicit excise tax if the recipient is younger than age 59½. Finally, many retirees are poorly equipped to manage their investments in old age, perhaps because they never were particularly financially literate, or perhaps they suffer diminished faculties due to poor health and lack of mobility with age. And it is difficult even for experts to undertake the sophisticated calculations required to simultaneously manage the investment portfolio, the drawdown rule, and the target horizon over which these decisions are made (Dus, Maurer, and Mitchell, 2004). Most financial planners are not particularly well versed in these techniques either, nor are their clients. But possibly due to overconfidence, they often expect the money to last longer and earn more than a prudent strategy would dictate.

## Policy and Plan Design Alternatives

Our overview thus far has illustrated how behavioral economics and finance research of the last few years has fundamentally challenged the ways in which plan sponsors, retirement service providers, and policy-makers should think about retirement plan design in the future. At the most inclusive level, behavioral research offers several new insights about the nature of individual decisionmaking in retirement plans, which we enumerate next. After noting these, we turn to several plan design and policy responses to this new body of research.

1. *One lesson is that behavioral research challenges some of the most central assumptions of decisionmaking.* In particular, it challenges the notion that workers are rational, autonomous, microcalculators who exercise independent and unbiased judgment when it comes to their workplace retirement plans. The evidence suggests that people do strive to maximize their self-interest, but for a variety of reasons outlined here, they often fail to act in accordance with the expectations of rational economic and financial theory, in both the accumulation and decumulation phases. Some people have self-control problems when it comes to saving; such individuals could benefit from commitment devices. Others simply overdiscount the future and overvalue the present; such people could benefit from precommitment pension savings programs. Still others might be unduly influenced by defaults and inertia: as a result, their attitudes and action diverge so they very much *want* to save more for retirement, but they do not. Here too, pre-commitment devices can plan an important role. Also, some individuals

do not appear to evaluate their investment portfolios in mean–variance terms; that is, past performance and risk errors cloud their judgment. They are overconfident about the future and have trouble cutting their losses. Some trade too much, think "too small" in terms of gains and losses, and take lump sums when in fact all of these behaviors increase rather than reduce risk.

2. *Another lesson learned is that plan design drives participant decisions, often in unanticipated ways.* Behavioral finance and economics also challenge the notion that pension plan design is a neutral vehicle within which participants make their own choices independently. Because of default, framing, and inertia effects, we have argued that the design of a retirement system or plan has a profound effect on participant investment and saving decisions. Sponsors and policymakers can alter behavior in fundamental ways by choosing different default structures. In particular, the design decisions to set up automatic enrollment, automatic saving, or default investment programs, which makes some saving and investment decisions automatic, are particularly critical.

Using traditional policy and plan design language, DC plans are "employee directed," with employees seen as the active agents while the employer is thought to play a minimal decisionmaking role. In some sense this is a libertarian decisionmaking model, where independent agents can act to maximize their personal welfare within the constraints of the system. But behavioral research sketches a different picture of many workers. These are people with weak or uncertain preferences about basic questions as how much to save, or how much risk to take. Plan design decisions then emit powerful signals about "appropriate" employee behavior, and employer/policymaker design specifications trump independent decisionmaking. Such an environment is consistent with the "paternalistic libertarianism" notion advanced by Thaler and Sunstein (2003), where individuals can be offered choice, but paternalistic elements of retirement plan design play a powerful role in shaping the choices offered.

3. *A third finding is that the standard approach taken in most contemporary DC plans may be counterproductive in encouraging retirement saving.* Generally, participants are told that (i) saving for retirement is optional (since joining the plan is discretionary); (ii) the need to increase saving over time is optional (it requires a voluntary election by the worker); and (iii) investing for retirement should focus on principal stability, rather than taking on risk or balancing the portfolio (since the default fund in most retirement savings plans is a conservative fixed income option). It is interesting that employers and policymakers rely on a model of voluntary choice by the worker in retirement saving plans, although they do not do so in other components of workplace benefits programs. Here, a comparison is instructive between employer retirement saving plans and health insurance. In terms of health plan participation, it has been uncommon for

a US employer offering health insurance to allow employees to drop coverage altogether (particularly without proof of some other health insurance). Employers also regularly make decisions about healthcare plan coverage levels and, for example, types of procedures and catastrophic coverage, rather than leaving such choices to voluntary election by the worker. Perhaps this is because lack of healthcare coverage might be felt immediately in the workplace if a worker became ill, while low levels of retirement saving have no immediate consequence. If this is true, employers may be subject to the same type of "hyperbolic discounting" as many workers, overvaluing present-day risks, and overdiscounting future concerns.

4. *A fourth lesson is that the current education model in 401(k) plans may have reached its effective limits.* Accompanying the growth of participant-directed DC retirement plans has been a large expansion in the provision of workplace education. Much of the educational effort has been motivated by nondiscrimination testing—employers have an incentive to encourage plan use among lower-paid employees, to allow highly paid employees greater ability to contribute to the plan. Other motivations have been employers' desires to promote a popular saving benefit, and to minimize fiduciary liability for participant investment decisions. The current educational model tends to emphasize communication and education activities, both of which are aimed at producing behavioral change (e.g. joining the plan, boosting saving, investing more effectively). Yet, the behavioral literature suggests that for many workers, this model is limited in its applicability. There is the problem of inertia, which we have described as the divergence between desire and effective action. There is also the notion that only part of the workforce is motivated to learn about personal finances or interested in using financial education. Contemporary education practices assume that most workers are rational agents and planners, but the evidence we offer suggests that large numbers of workers simply are not.

As Selnow (Chapter 2, this volume) suggests, an alternative model is that desired behavior must precede education. Mechanisms must be found, whether through plan defaults or delegation to a third party, where workers begin practicing the right behaviors at the outset. Education then can play an ancillary role, explaining the rationale for the defaults and alternative courses of future action. In effect, behavioral economics suggest a reversal in the causality of education: A shift from education driving behavioral change, to initial behavioral change preceding education.

These broad themes—imperfect investors and savers, the critical role of system design, a new model for education—suggest a number of policy and plan design choices. Four issues deserve prominent attention:

1. *Much depends on the DC arrangement in DC plans.* One way to exploit the findings of this rich new behavioral literature would be to alter the

nature of default decisionmaking in US retirement saving plans. Inertia, procrastination, and lack of decisionmaking willpower can be exploited to encourage more retirement saving. An "auto-pilot" 401(k) is one possibility. Also automatic enrollment of all eligible employees; scheduled annual savings increases (as in the Save More Tomorrow plan); and a selection of default investment choices that represent optimal portfolio choices, such as a series of age-based balanced portfolios. In this way, the passive decisionmaker may rely on system design to reach a near-optimal retirement outcome. While workers will still retain the right to "opt out" of this arrangement, allowing for freedom of choice, the system design always directs workers toward desirable saving and investment behaviors.

Auto-pilot 401(k) solutions are not without their drawbacks: Most notably, the automatic enrollment of employees will raise costs above the current model where workers must opt in (e.g. higher employer matching contributions, higher administrative costs for employers and providers). Offsetting these costs, in part, could be the greater asset pool resulting from higher contribution rates over time, as well as higher-fee investments as default options. Just as employees are easily influenced by employer plan design decisions, so employers are influenced by implicit and explicit policymaker directions. Currently, clear-cut regulatory guidance exists only for automatic enrollment components; to generalize this success, some type of regulatory or statutory endorsement for automatic saving and age-based investment choices would be required. A further consideration, of course, is whether the auto-pilot 401(k) model would be an alternative to existing nondiscrimination testing requirements. From a policy perspective, nondiscrimination testing rules were introduced to ensure that low-paid workers take sufficient advantage of tax-deferred retirement savings plans, and that tax benefits of such plans did not accrue solely to the highly paid. An auto-pilot 401(k), perhaps with some standardized eligibility and matching contributions (as in today's "safe harbor" design), might accomplish the same objective in a different way. It would offer other benefits for lower-paid workers as well—including automatic retirement savings increases and better portfolio choices for many.

2. *Simplified menu design in retirement plans could be very useful.* One of the more practical conclusions from behavioral finance is that investment menu design must be closely scrutinized. Iyengar, Huberman, and Jiang (Chapter 5, this volume) describe the "choice overload" hypothesis in detail: Complex investment menus may discourage plan participation. But it is also clear that even simple pension design decisions, such as the composition of equity versus fixed income funds, can also strongly influence participant investment behavior. Certainly, one implication from the research is that many participants lack skills needed to make complex investment choices among highly differentiated options. There is little evidence that participants

are constructing the mean–variance optimal portfolios that employers use to justify the inclusion of different investment classes, styles, and managers. Instead they use informal heuristics, including past performance, to make choices.

As a result, the research suggests that the "laundry list" approach to investment options—where workers are given 50 or 100 choices of funds—will be confusing and demotivating for some. Accordingly, plan sponsors might experiment with tiered investment choices, where communication resources are devoted to educating participants about a limited menu of core options, and additional choices for sophisticated investors could be segregated from the core menu.

More broadly, both employers and policymakers need to rethink the trend toward expanding the myriad and complex active saving decisions presented to workers. Behavioral research suggests that there are natural, inevitable limits to a policy of ever-increasing choices and decisions. For example, tax legislation in 2001 authorized an after-tax version of 401(k) saving plans (dubbed a "Roth" provision, in which contributions are made after-tax and all future earnings and distributions are tax-free). The idea is that employers could offer employees a choice between pre- and post-tax savings in the same plan. The Administration has also recently proposed to create a system of after-tax personal saving accounts which compete with pre-tax workplace saving plans. Whatever the merits of these proposals, it seems likely that adding new choices will further complicate investment and saving decisions. Since the evidence suggests that many workers already struggle with the basic decisions to save, invest, and spend during retirement, it seems likely that new options will further challenge already-burdened decisionmakers.

3. *New approaches are needed to help workers and retirees better manage company stock risk.* Congress and employers have attempted to address the risks of holding excessive company stock through education and educational/disclosure activities, yet the behavioral evidence suggests that this strategy will have limited impact. One problem is inertia; reducing concentrated stock positions requires taking a disciplined approach to selling stock holdings, but few participants tend to follow such a self-motivated, disciplined approach to managing their saving due to inertia and procrastination. Another problem is risk perceptions and the influence of past returns with company stock. Employees significantly underestimate the risks of their own company's stock, and they are also unduly and erroneously influenced by past stock performance. The findings regarding overconfidence and aversion to realizing losses may also come into play with company stock. When workers have too rosy a view of the future but have trouble selling their company stock at a loss, it is unlikely that providing additional information will quickly alter these attitudes and produce changes in investment portfolios.

As in the auto-pilot 401(k) case, one policy option would be to provide employees with an optional statutory mechanism that automatically reduces their exposure to company stock to a given percentage that declined with age (e.g. 20 percent or 10 percent of assets by age 65). For example, a plan might offer a provision that drew down the participant's position steadily each quarter over some prescribed period, say 3 or 5 years. In other words, participants may need a precommitment device that works automatically for them as they near retirement, a concept dubbed as the "sell more tomorrow" idea by the originators of the "Save More Tomorrow" plan.

4. *Sensible plan design includes default choices at retirement.* Current policy has permitted the conversion of pensions from plans that pay life annuities, into programs that give workers a choice to receive their lifelong saving in a lump sum at retirement. Behavioral research suggests that annuity versus lump sum decisions at retirement could be better framed, taking into account participants' understanding of mortality versus investment risks. One question has to do with what should be the default choice. In DB plans, the default has traditionally been an annuity, though more plans are now offering lump sum options. In DC plans, the default is generally a lump sum, with no annuity option. An alternative approach might be to frame the default as some mixture of annuity and lump sum, rather than as an either–or decision. Of course, it would be essential to ensure that the two options are compared on an "apples-to-apples" basis to avoid framing bias. To better preserve the longevity protection that pensions once offered, policymakers may find it sensible to make annuitization the default, and to make loans against the pension accruals more difficult to obtain.

In sum, this research overview on behavioral decisionmaking finds important and valuable new insights into how plan sponsors, benefit plan consultants, and policymakers must rethink pension plan design in this new century. It seems clear that participants can be better served, when they make the hard decisions to accumulate and decumulate retirement assets. It is because retirement saving decisions are, at least an order of magnitude, more complex than other economic decisions, that people need help. The thought process requires a sequence of critical savings and investment decisions over a lifetime, backed by a complex and ongoing forecast of needs and resources. It should not be surprising, then, that for a substantial segment of the workforce, this task proves daunting and discouraging. And for some people, the problem may be so complex that they are forced to rely on decision heuristics that simplify decisionmaking, but may not necessarily produce appropriate outcomes. While much has been learned, a central question remains: How can the various stakeholders strike the best balance between encouragement and compulsion? What system can both preserve participant decisionmaking while offering limits on choice, so as to encourage the outcomes that rational and forward thinking consumers would want for themselves? This volume offers much to inform the debate.

## Notes

[1] For a recent review see Kahneman and Tversky (2000); Mullainathan and Thaler (2000); Shefrin (2003) and Barberis and Thaler (2002). For a review of retirement and portfolio implications, see also Statman (Chapter 4, this volume), Duflo and Saez (Chapter 8, this volume), and Choi et al. (Chapter 7, this volume).

[2] Indeed the 2002 Nobel Prize in economics awarded to Daniel Kahneman and Vernon Smith, recognized the far-reaching importance of this shift in paradigm. The Prize Committee noted "[t]raditionally, much of economic research has relied on the assumption of a 'homo œconomicus' motivated by self-interest and capable of rational decisionmaking. Economics has also been widely considered a non-experimental science, relying on observation of real-world economies rather than controlled laboratory experiments. Nowadays, however, a growing body of research is devoted to modifying and testing basic economic assumptions . . . This research has its roots in two distinct, but currently converging, areas: The analysis of human judgment and decisionmaking by cognitive psychologists, and the empirical testing of predictions from economic theory by experimental economists." (www.mea.uni.mannheim.de/winter/lehre/03-ss/behav.htm)

[3] Aizcorbe, Kennickell, and Moore (2003) summarize results from the 2001 Survey of Consumer Finances, and he finds for example, age-related fluctuations in net worth, financial assets, and debt consistent with the life-cycle hypothesis.

[4] There are methodological or substantive caveats regarding this research, yet on the whole the research does indicate that at least some households are not particularly good at solving the retirement saving problem. Hurd and Rohwedder (2003) find, for example, that households anticipate a 20% drop in consumption, and so the decline in retiree consumption may be rationally anticipated, not unexpected. One concern about Bernheim et al. (2001) is that it uses data on food consumption (both in and out of the home) as a proxy for total consumption.

[5] See also Loewenstein and Prelec (1992), Laibson (1997), and Frederick, Loewenstein, and O'Donoghue (2002). As Thaler recalls, doubts among economists about the consistency of individual time preferences dates back at least to Robert Strotz, who in the mid-1950s wrote that "special attention should be given . . . to a discount function . . . [that] 'overvalues' the more proximate satisfaction relative to the more distant ones . . . ." (cited in Thaler, 1981: 127).

[6] Two examples are drawn from insurance and healthcare (Thaler and Sunstein, 2003). In the United States, in the state of New Jersey, the default option under the state's car insurance regulations offers workers a limited right to sue for damages (with a lower insurance premium). In the neighboring state of Pennsylvania, the default is the regular right to sue; to obtain the limited right to sue and the lower premium, the car driver must make a positive election. In New Jersey, 20% of individuals retain the full right to sue, which requires a positive election, while in Pennsylvania, 75% retain the full right to sue, which is the default. Similarly, the donation of vital organs upon one's death is common in a number of European countries, with over 90% of individuals donating organs; yet, it is comparatively rare in the United States,

with less than 20% making organ donations. In the European countries, organ donation is the default; in the United States, it requires a positive election.

[7] Goetzman and Kumar (2001), De Bondt (1998).

[8] See Thaler and Johnson (1990) for a discussion of break-even thinking and the house money effect.

[9] See Arkes et al. (1995), Odean (1998a), Svenson (1981), Tiger (1979), and Weinstein (1980). Taylor and Brown (1988) point out that overoptimism offers psychological benefits as well.

[10] For an overview of the overconfidence literature, particularly on the ability of individuals to calibrate their forecasts, see Lichtenstein, Fischhoff, and Phillips (1982). Odean (1998a,b) also summarizes findings on overconfidence.

[11] Shefrin (2003) summarizes both these conclusions from De Bondt (1998) and related literature on overconfidence in investing.

[12] It may be worth noting that opting for a lump sum permits retirees to avoid using the unisex mortality tables required by law for employee benefit plans. This could be an appealing result for those who anticipate living less long than the combined male/female life expectancy. Taking the lump sum and spending it also makes the near-poor retiree more likely to be eligible for social welfare benefits payable to the indigent.

## References

Agnew, Julie, Pierluigi Balduzzi, and Annika Sundén. 2003. "Portfolio Choice and Trading in a Large 401(k) Plan." *American Economic Review* 93(1): 193–215.

Aizcorbe, Ana M., Arthur B. Kennickell, and Kevin B. Moore. 2003. "Recent Changes in U.S. Family Finances: Evidence from the 1998 and 2001 Survey of Consumer Finances." *Federal Reserve Bulletin* January: 1–32.

Ameriks, John, Andrew Caplin, and John Leahy. 2003. "Wealth Accumulation and the Propensity to Plan." *Quarterly Journal of Economics* 1007–1048.

Arkes, Hal R., Neal V. Dawson, Theodore Speroff, Frank E. Harrell, Jr., Carlos Alzola, Russell Phillips, Norman Desbiens, Robert K. Oye, and Alfred F. Connors, Jr. 1995. "The Covariance Decomposition of the Probability Score and its Use in Evaluating Prognostic Estimates." *Medical Decision Making* 15(2): 120–131.

Banks, J., Robert Blundell, and S. Tanner. 1998. "Is There a Retirement-Savings Puzzle?" *American Economic Review* 88(4): 769–788.

Barber, Brad M. and Terrance Odean. 2000. "Trading is Hazardous to Your Wealth: The Common Stock Investment Performance of Individual Investors." *Journal of Finance* LV(2): 773–806.

—— 2001. "Boys will be Boys: Overconfidence and Common Stock Investment." *Quarterly Journal of Economics* February: 261–292.

Barberis, Nicholas and Richard Thaler. 2002. "A Survey of Behavioral Finance." NBER Working Paper 9222.

Barberis, Nick and Ming Huang. 2001. "Mental Accounting, Loss Aversion, and Individual Stock Returns." *Journal of Finance* 56(4): 1247–1292.

Benartzi, Shlomo. 2001. "Excessive Extrapolation and the Allocation of 401(k) Accounts to Company Stock." *Journal of Finance* LVI(5): 1747–1764.

—— and Richard Thaler. 2001. "Naive Diversification Strategies in Retirement Saving Plans." *American Economic Review* 91(1): 79–98.

Benartzi, Shlomo and Richard Thaler. 2002. "How Much Is Investor Autonomy Worth?" *Journal of Finance* 57(4): 1593–1616.

—— 2004. "Save More Tomorrow." *Journal of Political Economy,* 112(1) February: 164–187.

Bernheim, B. Douglas, Jonathan Skinner, and Steven Weinberg. 2001. "What Accounts for the Variation in Retirement Wealth among U.S. Households?" *American Economic Review* 91(4): 832–857.

Bodie, Zvi. 1995. "On the Risk of Stocks in the Long Run." *Financial Analysts Journal* 51(3): 18–22.

Bodie, Zvi, Brett Hammond, and Olivia S. Mitchell. 2002. "A Framework for Analyzing and Managing Retirement Risks." In *Innovations in Financing Retirement,* eds. Zvi Bodie, Brett Hammond, Olivia S. Mitchell, and Stephen Zeldes. Philadelphia, PA: University of Pennsylvania Press: 3–19.

Brown, Jeffrey, Olivia S. Mitchell, and James Poterba. 2000. "The Role of Real Annuities and Indexed Bonds in an Individual Accounts Retirement Program." In *Risk Aspects of Investment-Based Social Security Reform,* eds. John Y. Campbell and Martin Feldstein. Chicago: NBER, University of Chicago Press, pp. 321–360.

—— 2002. "Mortality Risk, Inflation Risk, and Annuity Products." In *Innovations in Financing Retirement,* eds. Zvi Bodie, Brett Hammond, Olivia S. Mitchell, and Stephen Zeldes. Philadelphia, PA: University of Pennsylvania Press, pp. 175–197.

Brown, Jeffrey, Olivia S. Mitchell, James Poterba, and Mark Warshawsky. 1999. "Taxing Retirement Income: Nonqualified Annuities and Distributions from Qualified Accounts." *National Tax Journal* LII(3) September: 563–592.

—— 2001. *The Role of Annuity Markets in Financing Retirement.* Cambridge, MA: MIT Press.

Campbell, John Y. and Luis M. Viceira. 2002. *Strategic Asset Allocation: Portfolio Choice for Long-Term Investors.* Oxford: Oxford University Press.

Choi, James, David Laibson, Brigitte Madrian, and Andrew Metrick. 2001*a*. "Defined Contribution Pensions: Plan Rules, Participant Decisions, and the Path of Least Resistance." NBER Working Paper 8655.

—— 2001*b*. "For Better or For Worse: Default Effects and 401(k) Savings Behavior." NBER Working Paper 8651.

—— 2003. "Passive Decisions and Potent Defaults." NBER Working Paper 9917.

Congressional Budget Office (CBO). 2003. "Utilization of Tax Incentives for Retirement Saving." August. www.cbo.gov.

Davis, Steven J. and Paul Willen. 2002. "Income Shocks, Asset Returns, and Portfolio Choice." In *Innovations in Retirement Financing,* eds. Zvi Bodie, Brett Hammond, Olivia Mitchell, and Stephen Zeldes. Philadelphia, PA: University of Pennsylvania Press: 20–49.

De Bondt, Werner. 1998. "A Portrait of the Individual Investor." *European Economic Review* 42: 831–844.

Dus, Ivica, Raimond Maurer, and Olivia S. Mitchell. 2004. "Betting on Death and Capital Markets in Retirement: A Shortfall Risk Analysis of Life Annuities versus Phased Withdrawal Plans." Pension Research Council Working Paper 2004.

Employee Benefit Research Institute (EBRI). 2003. *Retirement Confidence Survey: A Summary of Results.* www.ebri.org/rcs/2003/03rcssof.pdf.

Frederick, Shane, George Loewenstein, and Ted O'Donoghue. 2002. "Time Discounting and Time Preference: A Critical Review." *Journal of Economic Literature* 40(2): 351–401.

Goetzmann, William N. and Alok Kumar. 2001. "Equity Portfolio Diversification." NBER Working Papers 8686.

Huberman, Gur and Paul Sengmueller. 2003. "Company Stock in 401k Plans." Columbia University Working Paper.

Hurd, Michael D. and Kathleen McGarry. 1995. "Evaluation of Subjective Probability Distributions in the HRS." *Journal of Human Resources* 30(5): S268–S292.

Hurd, Michael and Susann Rohwedder. 2003. "The Retirement-Consumption Puzzle: Anticipated and Actual Deadlines in Spending at Retirement." NBER Working Paper No. w9586.

Kahneman, Daniel. 2003. "The Psychology of Risky Choices." Address before the Investment Company Institute, May 2003, Washington DC.

Kahneman, Daniel and Amos Tversky. 1979. "Prospect Theory: An Analysis of Decision Under Risk." *Econometrica* 47(2) March: 263–291.

—— 2000. *Choices, Values and Frames*. Cambridge, MA: Russell Sage Foundation and Cambridge University Press.

Laibson, David I. 1997. "Golden Eggs and Hyperbolic Discounting." *Quarterly Journal of Economics* 112(2) May: 443–478.

Laibson, David I., Andrea Repetto, and Jeremy Tobacman. 1998. "Self Control and Saving for Retirement." *Brookings Papers on Economic Activity* I: 91–196.

Lichtenstein, Sarah, Baruch Fischhoff, and Lawrence Phillips. 1982. "Calibration of Probabilities: The State of the Art to 1980." In *Judgment Under Uncertainty: Heuristics and Biases*, eds. Daniel Kahnemann, Paul Slovic, and Amos Tversky. Cambridge: Cambridge University Press: 306–334.

Loewenstein, George and Drazen Prelec. 1992. "Anomalies in Intertemporal Choice: Evidence and an Interpretation." *Quarterly Journal of Economics* 57: 573–598.

Madrian, Brigitte C. and Dennis F. Shea. 2001. "The Power of Suggestion: Inertia in 401(k) Participation and Savings Behavior." *Quarterly Journal of Economics* 116(4): 1149–1187.

McGill, Daniel, Kyle Brown, John Haley and Sylvester Schieber. 2004. *Fundamentals of Private Pensions*, 8th edn. Oxford: Oxford University Press, 2004.

MetLife. 2003. *The MetLife Retirement Income IQ Test: Findings from the 2003 National Survey of American Pre-Retirees*. New York: Metlife Mature Market Institute, June.

Mitchell, Olivia S. and David McCarthy. 2003. "Annuities for an Ageing World." In *Developing an Annuities Market in Europe*, eds. E. Fornero and E. Luciano. London: Elgar.

Mitchell, Olivia S. and Stephen P. Utkus. 2003. "Company Stock and Retirement Plan Diversification." In *The Pension Challenge: Risk Transfers and Retirement Income Security*, eds. Olivia S. Mitchell and Kent Smetters. Oxford: Oxford University Press: 33–70.

——, James Poterba, Mark Warshawsky, and Jeffrey Brown. 1999. "New Evidence on the Money's Worth of Individual Annuities." *American Economic Review* December: 1299–1318.

——, James Moore, and John Phillips. 2000. "Explaining Retirement Saving Shortfalls." In *Forecasting Retirement Needs and Retirement Wealth*, eds. Olivia S. Mitchell, Brett Hammond, and Anna Rappaport. Philadelphia, PA: Univ. of Pennsylvania Press: 139–166.

Modigliani, Franco and R. Brumberg. 1954. "Utility Analysis and the Consumption Function: An Interpretation of Cross-section Data." In *Post-Keynesian Economics*, ed. K. K. Kurihara. New Brunswick, NJ: Rutgers University Press.

Moore, James and Olivia S. Mitchell. 2000. "Projected Retirement Wealth and Saving Adequacy." In *Forecasting Retirement Needs and Retirement Wealth*, eds. Olivia S. Mitchell, Brett Hammond, and Anna Rappaport. Philadelphia, PA: Univ. of Pennsylvania Press: 68–94.

Moore, James H., Jr. and Leslie A. Muller. 2002. "An Analysis of Lump-sum Pension Distribution Recipients." *Monthly Labor Review* 125(5) May: 29–46.

Mullainathan, Sendhil and Richard H. Thaler. 2000. "Behavioral Economics." NBER Working Paper 7948.

Odean, Terrance. 1998*a*. "Are Investors Reluctant to Realize Their Losses?" *Journal of Finance* 53(5): 1775–1798.

——1998*b*. "Volume, Volatility, Price and Profit: When All Traders are Above Average." *Journal of Finance* 53(5): 1887–1933.

Patel, Jayendu, Richard Zeckhauser, and Darryll Hendricks. 1991. "The Rationality Struggle: Illustrations from Financial Markets." *American Economic Review* 81: 232–236.

Polkovnichenko, Valery. 2003. "Household Portfolio Diversification." Working paper presented at the Rodney White Center for Financial Research conference, Household Portfolio Choice and Financial Decision-Making, March.

Poterba, James, Joshua Rauh, Steven Venti, and David Wise. 2003. "Utility Evaluation of Risk in Retirement Saving Accounts." NBER Working Paper 9892.

Purcell, Patrick J. 2002. "The Enron Bankruptcy and Employer Stock in Retirement Plans." *CRS Report for Congress*. US GOP. Code RS21115.

Samuelson, Paul A. 1989. "The Judgment of Economic Science on Rational Portfolio Management: Timing and Long-Horizon Effects." *Journal of Portfolio Management* 16: 4–12.

Shefrin, Hersh. 2003. *Beyond Greed and Fear: Understanding Behavioral Finance and the Psychology of Investing*. Oxford: Oxford University Press.

—— and Meir Statman. 1985. "The Disposition to Sell Winners Too Early and Ride Losers Too Long: Theory and Evidence." *Journal of Finance* 40(3) July: 777–790.

Simon, Herbert A. 1955. "A Behavioral Model of Rational Choice." *Quarterly Journal of Economics* 69 February: 99–118.

Svenson, Ernest O. 1981. "Are We All Less Risky and More Skillful Than Our Fellow Drivers?" *Acta Psychologica* 47: 143–148.

Taylor, Shelley E. and Brown, Jonathan D. 1988. "Illusion of Well-Being: A Social Psychological Perspective on Mental Health." *Psychological Bulletin* 103: 193–210.

Thaler, Richard and Cass R. Sunstein. 2003. "Libertarian Paternalism." *American Economic Review* 93(2): 175–179.

—— and Eric Johnson. 1990. "Gambling with the House Money and Trying to Break Even: The Effects of Prior Outcomes on Risky Choices." *Management Science* 36(6): 643–660. Reprinted in Richard Thaler, *Quasi-Rational Economics*. New York: Russell Sage Foundation, 1994.

—— and H. M. Shefrin. 1981. "An Economic Theory of Self-Control." *Journal of Political Economy* 89(2): 392–406.

—— 1981. "Some Empirical Evidence on Dynamic Inconsistency." *Economic Letters* 8: 201–207. Reprinted in Richard Thaler, *Quasi-Rational Economics.* New York: Russell Sage Foundation, 1994.

—— and Shlomo Benartzi. 1999. "Risk Aversion or Myopia? Choices in Repeated Gambles and Retirement Investments." *Management Science* 45(3): 364–381.

Tiger, Lionel. 1979. *Optimism: The Biology of Hope.* New York.

Tversky, Amos and Daniel Kahneman. 1974. "Judgment Under Uncertainty: Heuristics and Biases." *Science* 185: 1124–1131.

Warner, John T. and Saul Pleeter. 2001. "The Personal Discount Rate: Evidence from Military Downsizing Programs." *American Economic Review* 91(1): 33–53.

Weinstein, N. 1980. "Unrealistic Optimism About Future Life Events." *Journal of Personality and Social Psychology* 39: 806–820.

# Chapter 2

# Motivating Retirement Planning: Problems and Solutions

*Gary W. Selnow*

Retirement saving advocates face one of the most daunting communication tasks imaginable. They seek to promote within the labor force a willingness to set aside scarce resources for some distant age that the worker may or may not reach, for rewards that the worker may or not achieve, at a price today that the worker may not wish to pay. This is a tough sell, however, recent research and an old theory lend some guidance and encouragement. This chapter looks at the nature of the challenge and the rationale for some interesting solutions.

To motivate our discussion, though, I offer a story from the Balkans which helps illuminate how some people view their financial circumstances to be driven by fate. It takes place on a river that forms the border between Slovenia, part of the former Yugoslavia, and Austria, part of the West. People tell of a Slovenian fisherman who had been laboring for hours but had not caught a fish; the poor fellow had felt not even the tug of a fish on his line. Meanwhile, on the other side of the river in Austria, a young boy was reeling in fish by the bucketful. He would toss out his line, and before it struck the water's surface, a fish would leap up and grab the hook in mid-air. Eventually, the fisherman could bear it no longer and looked about for a way to cross the river. Since he could find no boats or bridges, the Slovenian man shouted at the boy, "Hey, how did you cross the river?" The boy stared back for a moment, and then yelled back, "I was born here!"

In short, fate—in our case, financial fate—is often determined from birth. Depending on which side of the river you are born on, you can live a charmed life or a life of toil and frustration. The hard truth is, some people need not bother with plans for retirement: This problem is settled for them at birth. Most people, however, find themselves on the wrong shore and accept this as their fate. That being so, one job for retirement savings planners is to show people how they can get to the other side of the river, where the retirement fishing is good.

Investing for retirement is different from just about anything else people are asked to do. Along nearly every dimension, tucking away money today for a more secure tomorrow violates basic human inclinations. The savings ethic is resistant to nearly all of the motivators we commonly use to encourage desired behaviors, which robs retirement planning advocates of the most useful and effective tools to stimulate wise investment decisions.

In thinking about these problems, I reflect on the challenges I have faced over the years in recent years, persuading people to alter their behaviors. Most recently, we set out to tackle the HIV/AIDS tragedy in Africa, and our communication work has had some real success. Nevertheless, tackling the AIDS problem, as overwhelming as that is, is quite different from the challenges communicators face getting people to save for retirement. In the regions where I work, people see the evidence of AIDS all around them. Each morning they arise to the palpable devastation wrought by the plague, each night they fall asleep haunted by their private fears that it will infect them as well. Stories from communities being slaughtered by AIDS chill the soul. Our message of caution and hope is well received because the audience is ready. Moreover, opinion leaders figure prominently in our design as we work closely with traditional healers and birth attendants who are revered within the communities. Our job is to establish credibility, connect the behaviors with the outcomes, and teach about alternatives.

By contrast, retirement issues have less conspicuous consequences, and they lack the stunning horrors that reign in AIDS-infected communities. Moreover, in the AIDS work, the lapse time between behavior and consequence is much shorter, and the outcomes are more certain. These conditions enable us to use persuasive methods not available to advocates of retirement savings, because as important as retirement preparations may be, their structure deprives advocates of many tools.

Another of our recent assignment involves the development of attitudes favorable toward reconciliation, in places where reconciliation is a four-letter word. We work throughout the Balkans—in Croatia, Bosnia, Montenegro, Kosovo, and now Serbia—to encourage people of different ethnicities to live together in peace. We have seen some evidence of steps in the right direction where isolated communities that once quite literally battled over backyard fences, have begun to patch up old wounds. This is taking place with the efforts of many indigenous and international organizations, but I would like to think that we have made a contribution. In places that exaggerate the differences between people, we emphasize the features that people share. We join parents through their children at multiethnic schools, and more recently we have connected people through medical programs. Illness does not discriminate: Heart disease, asthma, cancer, and HIV/AIDS, cut a cruel swath across the human race. Our programs remind people that everyone shares these assaults, and there are bigger enemies that stand over us all. Attitudes and behaviors here, too, are structurally different from the attitudes and behaviors retirement planners seek to change. Where I work, people have lived through the consequences of corrosive thinking and destructive actions. They know that a bad decision or a good one can manifest itself immediately to their benefit or to their ruin. And again, retirement issues are unlike these issues and they do not allow supporters to tap the human motivators that we can access in our work. Problems faced by retirement savings advocates are quite different and quite frustrating.

It is also worth noting that techniques which increase voting, garner political support, improve diet and exercise, get people to brush their teeth, paint their houses, and vaccinate their children, are fundamentally different from getting people to save for retirement. No matter how I size it up, the conclusion is the same retirement savings issues are unique in several ways:

*First, the payoff for behavioral change is quite uncertain.* Saving for retirement is a gamble, and the truth is, no one can promise that money set aside will ever come back to us. We may die, financial markets may crash, and events on this troubled and treacherous planet can change our fates.

*Second, workers do not easily buy the idea of payoffs in the distant future.* For a here-and-now, instant-gratification society, this is troubling. Ben Franklin advised us that if we wanted to be wealthy, we should "think of saving as well as getting." For many people today, Ben's advice falls on deaf ears.

*Third, the promise of pleasure tomorrow means pain today.* This is a hard sell. Setting aside even a few dollars each month is most painful when the need for cash is greatest—when one is raising children, buying a home, paying for education. A pleasant and secure retirement is a daydream, when the mortgage comes due and the kids need braces.

*Fourth, the wrong decision yields instant gain.* This is the flip side: When the worker chooses *not* to save that $100, he is immediately rewarded with $100 that he can enjoy in the here-and-now. Instant gratification is very familiar.

*Fifth, there is no immediate tangible reward.* One's sacrifices, good judgments, loyalties to one's future-self, yield little today of the self than a vague satisfaction. Citizens of the material world are motivated by fast automobiles, handsome clothes, good food, and drink: These are the rewards and symbols of success. Money planted deep for retirement bears none of those harvests, and it returns only a promise bound to a probability. The contingent–reward link is broken, which undermines a powerful behavioral motivator.

*Sixth, the saving decision can be postponed without immediate penalty.* Workers suffer little today if they fail to save for tomorrow; they deprive themselves of nothing, now, and they walk away from this unfulfilled duty unaltered and unharmed.

*And finally, there are no functional deadlines.* People believe they do not have to save today and do not have to save tomorrow. The immediate rewards for deciding to save grow no greater and the punishments for declining to save become no more severe. It is not like failing to pay the mortgage, or the water bill, since letting those deadlines go, makes quick trouble. With retirement savings, there is always tomorrow and the day after tomorrow.

As a result, the pressures of immediate gratification, delayed benefit, the unknown, the uncertain, the uncomfortable, the deferrable, all ally against the wiser choices. And they also strip retirement planning advocates of powerful human motivators and inducements. Furthermore, the details of retirement savings are complicated for average people. The laws and rules are esoteric and ever-changing. Too many options confuse people: SEP plans, 401ks, 402ks, IRAs, 403bs and the rest, form in the public mind, a confusing stew of options that for many people are easier left for another time, another place.

On top of all this, most young people are firmly convinced they will always be young; belief in one's immortality is a mighty force. And, peer pressure is scarce: Discussions about financial preparations for retirement do not arise spontaneously around the water cooler, and friends do not pressure one another about retirement set-asides.

Finally, Social Security is an easy palliative. Although ill-fated, under-funded, and precariously unprotected, Social Security is, in many people's minds, that secret place for comfort when thoughts tread near retirement savings. Consequently, judgments become clouded by complexities, legal-ities, choices, norms, and expectations. Sometimes it seems a wonder anyone bothers to save for retirement at all. Yet, many people do save and the question is what motivates them to do so? The literature suggests a vari-ety of reasons, programs, and conditions that lead to or are associated with retirement savings decisions. For one, older people save more than younger people (Hogarth, 1991; Zhong, 1994); more educated people save more than less educated people; employees with higher incomes put aside more than employees with lower incomes (Zhong, 1994). We would be sur-prised to learn otherwise. These facts are good to know, but not prescript-ive. Retirement advocates cannot do much here, other than urge people to attend college then wait for them to age and earn more money.

The literature says, further, that people with a future orientation save more than people who live for the here and now (Munnell, Sundén, and Taylor, 2000). A popular analyst proposes that people who are content with what they have—and thus seek fewer possessions—are those more likely to save for the years beyond (Richey, 2002). But how this can be of use to motivate peo-ple who live for today, or those who are not content with what they have? Maybe advisers could promote favorable attitude formation by dislodging cultural preoccupations with the present, but this would acquire house-to-house combat in a society where a focus on the present is woven into the fabric of every popular message, of every public and private institution. Consider that Congress looks no further than the next election, companies plan quarter-by-quarter, and public policy fixes on immediate impact.

What about other motivators? For example, education can build knowl-edge that can inspire a rational person to action. To be sure, education about saving is a consistent theme in the literature: People aware of the need to save and familiar with investment options are more likely to set aside money for later. The cause and effect relationships are not entirely clear in many studies: Does education bring about investment decisions, or do investment decisions stimulate an interest in learning about saving? Either way, many analysts believe that education is the key.[1] Joo and Grable (2000) argue that workplace financial education boosts the likelihood of having a retirement investment or savings program. They argue, further, that family and consumer economists can help individuals plan for retirement with additional financial education. Hershey and Mowen (2000) find that training programs designed to boost financial knowledge trigger advanced planning activities, and they also demonstrate the value of audience segmentation based on attitudinal characteristics.

Whether education relates favorably to retirement planning behaviors because it cultivates skills, nurtures attitudes, or simply responds to predispositions, is less important than the finding of education's relevance. This is a comfort, because the last thing I want to suggest is that we have been barking up the wrong tree. But I do suggest that, so far, our educational approach has been vulnerable to the natural resistance people display toward investing in their distant futures. Yes, education impacts many employees, but the alarming fact remains that 70 percent of American workers have not even calculated their financial needs for retirement, half have made negligible contributions to their retirement funds, and fully 15 percent have saved nothing for their later years (EBRI, 2002). So large numbers of employees remain untouched by the best efforts of educators who would teach them about the virtues of salting away funds for later.

Is there a way around the natural defenses against retirement savings? Is there a way to defeat the resistance, the reluctance, the refusal of employees who balk at the advice to save? Is there a better way to cross the river? Maybe the answer is yes. Several researchers have been looking at the value of automatically enrolling employees in retirement investment programs. I believe this automatic enrollment approach may be the way to end-run the natural blocks evident in the persuasion-resistant activity. They also tap into a theory that I believe has great relevance to this discussion.

To elaborate on this point, I make reference to the work of Choi et al. (2001*a*), who reported that "automatic enrollment has a dramatic impact on retirement savings behavior: 401(k) participation rates at all three firms (they studied) exceed 85 percent." The researchers found that participants usually anchored at the lowest saving default rates, and in the most conservative vehicles, but this does not detract from the fact that enrollment led to dramatic participation. Why does automatic enrollment have the impact they reported? Choi and his co-authors also find that employees follow the "path of least resistance" (Choi et al., 2001*b*). In other words, it is easier to keep on doing what you are doing, than it is to change. So for sailing ships and employees alike, steering straight ahead is easier than changing course. Once the employee is enrolled, they stay enrolled; if they are not enrolled, they remain not enrolled. The lesson is clear: Enroll employees automatically and plan sponsors will have set them on the proper course for the other side of the river.

This interesting research brought to mind a book by psychologist Daryl Bem, who in his book, *Beliefs, Attitudes, and Human Affairs* (1970), discusses a theory whose arrangement of variables violates convention. Most of us subscribe to the notion that people first acquire knowledge, from knowledge we form attitudes, and from the attitudes flow our consequent behaviors. Knowledge shapes attitudes, and then behavior. But Bem argues that sometimes behavior comes first. Sometimes we find ourselves behaving in a certain way, and we infer from that behavior our attitudes. In Bem's words, "(it is a) common assumption that one cannot change the behavior of (people) until one has changed 'hearts and minds' first . . . in fact, one of the most effective ways of changing the 'hearts and minds' of (people) is to change their behavior first" (Bem, 1970: 3). His examples include racial integration during the early 1950s and 1960s, citing instances where people with the strongest positive attitudes toward integration were those who were positioned to experience integration first-hand. Further, other research on integration demonstrated that "the cause-effect sequence most often appears to be 'behavior first, then attitudes'" (Bem, 1970: 68).

A good example of this point occurred when President Truman banned segregation in the armed forces with a stroke of the pen in 1948. The very fact of suspicious whites having to live and work and serve with blacks paid off in the striking improvement of attitudes. Of course, attitudes about race changed for blacks as well as for whites. Military people, by virtue of the government's power to impose behavior on the troops, had for years been well ahead of civilians on attitudes toward racial matters.

Another example of knowledge first, then attitudes, occurred in California during the 1990s. Over a period of time, California tightened regulations on cigarette smoking, first restricting smoking in public buildings and, then in workplaces and in restaurants; then curtailing smoking outside near the doors of public buildings, workplaces, and restaurants; and most recently, in 1998, the State banned smoking in bars, the last citadels for smokers (California Department of Health Services, 2001). Currently, Californians are allowed to smoke only in caves with fewer than two occupants and in aluminum kayaks anchored beyond the 3-mile limit!

What has been the result? The California Department of Health Services reports the following: "During the 1990s in California, smoking *behaviors* and *attitudes* about smoking have changed, as measured by the California Tobacco Surveys and other data sources (emphasis added). The net effect has been not only a drop in smoking rates at twice the national average, but a corresponding change in public attitudes toward smoking as well. Were attitudes changing anyway? Perhaps, but the behavioral changes imposed by the regulations are likely responsible for the accelerated shifts in the way people have come to view smoking."

Even if behavior changes first and then attitudes, how does this work? Bem emphasizes two dynamics. First, cognitive dissonance is key. This is the uncomfortable sense that develops when we act in a way that is incongruous with our beliefs. Second, self-perception theory suggests inasmuch as we infer the attitudes of others by observing their behaviors, we often infer our own attitudes by observing our own behaviors. We behave according to situational demands and then infer from that what our beliefs must be. We do this because we dislike the discomfort of incongruity between behaviors and beliefs, and because we believe we are rational and logical and hence interpret our self-conceptions by way of what we see in our own behavior.

One condition must be in place: We must see ourselves as having an escape, and having at least some choice in the behavior. Why? Because if we believe we are coerced, the force of coercion becomes the obvious explanation for our behaviors rather than our supporting beliefs. So, people seem logical and consistent—or at least they like to believe this about themselves—and accordingly, their behaviors cue our attitudes as long as they have at least some choice in the matter.

What does behavior-first have to do with automatic enrollment? What does it have to do with getting people to the other side of the river? The studies show that automatic enrollment with an easy escape offers the initial behavior. People may stay the course of least resistance, but effort alone may not explain the fact that nine of ten employees stay with an automatic retirement savings program after 6 months, and after 36 months the enrollment numbers remain about a third higher than for employees not under automatic enrollment plans. In other words, people who examine their savings behavior may infer that their own values and beliefs actually support the merits of retirement savings. Automatic enrollment imposed the initial behavior. The path of least resistance may help employees stay the course, and the fact that they were enrolled and could unenroll at any time of their choosing—but did *not* unenroll—may actually lead to altered beliefs about savings.

One further point bears mention. If attitudes do, in fact, change in light of behavior, then we might anticipate reasonable success with automatic upgrading of enrollment programs as well. Research finds that "employees do succeed in raising their contribution rates if they are given a low-effort opportunity to sign up for an automatic schedule of increases in their contribution rate" (Choi et al., 2001*b*). Why is this so? It must be more than "stay the course," because even the low-effort opportunity requires some action that we would not reasonably expect, unless supporting attitudes were in place. Employees who have come to look favorably at the concept of retirement saving and accept the practice at the entry level are more likely to accept incremental increases. The hard work has been done; the basic belief has been forged. Automatic enrollment, coupled with automatic upgrades proposed the "Save More Tomorrow" plan advocated by Benartzi and Thaler (2004), fit reasonably well into the "behavior-first" model of attitude formation.[2]

An automatic enrollment approach has a real chance of success because it skirts the natural impediments to employee-initiated investment plans noted earlier. The delay and uncertainty of payoffs, the deferral of rewards, the imposition of sacrifices and other pains and suffering of initiating a retirement savings plan become less relevant. The behavior-first model begins with automatic enrollment, but it must not end there. Employee education will continue to play a significant role. The huge advantage of behavior-first is that it puts in place the mechanisms of attitude change that could not only make employees more supportive of savings behaviors, but can also heighten their interests in educational messages. Automatic enrollment programs should, therefore, include employee educational elements that prepare people for their active involvement in the ongoing maintenance and fine-tuning of their retirement savings plans. Approaches to employee education laid out by many advocacy groups are not only valid, but they are essential to the long-term success of the plan. With education, we complete the cycle: Behavior, attitudes, and knowledge, knowledge, attitudes, and behavior—each element supporting the other in maintaining the employees' involvement in retirement savings.

Fortified by ongoing employee education, automatic enrollment has genuine appeal because it begins where other approaches hope to end, and it appears promising because it sets in motion dynamics often overlooked. The nice thing about the behavior-first approaches is that they come at little cost, they preserve employee discretion, and they do not replace the need for ongoing education and similar interventions that arm employees with tools for greater control of their own financial futures. This is a promising and fruitful means of helping people to the other side of the river.

## Notes

[1] See, for instance, Richardson (1993), Taylor-Carter, Cook, and Weinberg (1997), Bernheim, Garrett, and Maki (1997) and many others.

[2] Benartzi and Thaler (2004), discuss a "Save More Tomorrow" plan where employees agree in advance to earmark a portion of their future pay increases for retirement savings. Promise today to pay more tomorrow, but this time, put it in writing. They report considerable success noting that 78% who were offered the plan chose to use it; almost everyone who joined remained in it through two pay raises, and four out of five stayed with it into the third pay raise; and the average saving rates increased from 3.5% to 11.6% in 28 months.

## References

Bem, Daryl J. 1970. *Beliefs, Attitudes and Human Affairs*. Belmont, CA: Wadsworth.

Benartzi, Shlomo, and Richard H. Thaler. 2004. "Save More Tomorrow: Using Behavioral Economics to Increase Employee Saving." *Journal of Political Economy* 112(1): February 164–187.

Bernheim, Douglas B., Daniel M. Garrett, and Dean M. Maki. 1997. "Education and Saving: The Long-term Effects of High School Financial Curriculum Mandates." National Bureau of Economic Research Working Paper No 6085.

California Department of Health Services. 2001. "California Tobacco Control Program: A Decade of Progress: Results from the California Tobacco Survey, 1990–1999." Prepared by the Cancer Prevention and Control Program, University of California, San Diego, December 26.

Choi, James J., David Laibson, Brigitte Madrian, and Andrew Metrick. 2001*a*. "For Better or For Worse: Default Effects and 401(k) Savings Behavior." Pension Research Council Working Paper 2002–2.

——— 2001*b*. "Defined Contribution Pensions: Plan Rules, Participant Decisions, and the Path of Least Resistance." Pension Research Council Working Paper 2002–3.

The Employee Benefit Research Institute (EBRI). 2002. The American Savings Education Council (ASEC), and Mathew Greenwald and Associates (MGA). Retirement Confidence Survey www.asec.org/media/pr143.htm.

Hershey, Douglas A. and John C. Mowen. 2000. "Psychological Determinants of Financial Preparedness for Retirement." *The Gerontologist* 40(6): 687–697.

Hogarth, J. M. 1991. "Asset Management and Retired Households: Savers, Dissavers and Alternators." *Financial Counseling and Planning* 2: 97–122.

Joo, So-hyun and John Grable. 2000. "A Retirement Investment and Savings Decision Model: Influencing Factors and Outcomes." *Consumer Interests Annual* 46: 1–7.

Munnell, Alicia H., Annika Sundén and Catherine Taylor. 2000. "What Determines 401(k) Participation and Contributions?" Center for Retirement Research at Boston College CRR WP 2000–12, December.

Richardson, Virginia E. 1993. *Retirement Counseling: A Handbook for Gerontology Practitioners.* New York: Springer.

Ritchey, Matt. 2002. "Your Most Important Financial Decision". From the "Motley Fool Website" www.fool.com/news/foth/2002/foth020322.htm.

Taylor-Carter, Mary Anne, K. Cook, and C. Weinberg. 1997. "Factors Influencing Attitude Toward Retirement and Retirement Planning Among Mid-life University Employees." *Journal of Applied Gerontology* 13: 143–156.

Zhong, Lucy X. 1994. "Factors Associated with Bond and Stock Holdings." *Consumer Interests Annual* 40: 359–360.

## Chapter 3

# Who's Afraid of a Poor Old Age? Risk Perception in Risk Management Decisions

*Elke U. Weber*

The initial decision to save anything at all, the consideration of plan providers and investment vehicles, the periodic examination and readjustment of one's investment portfolio, all constitute a risk management process with important individual and societal consequences. There is little question that the financial and social implications of low saving rates and of inappropriate investment strategies are significant and far-reaching. And yet the risk of being financially ill-prepared for one's sunset years keeps few of us awake at night, and it engenders little legislative enthusiasm among our politicians. This chapter argues that it is the lack of any visceral perception of risk or danger that is responsible for the inadequate allocation of personal and collective resources to deal with this issue. By inadequate allocation of resources, I refer to both financial resources and, perhaps even more importantly, attentional resources.

Behavioral decision research is well positioned to predict the neglect we observe. In what follows, I review theory and empirical evidence to document two claims:

1. Affect is the wellspring of action: When we encounter or anticipate consequences that engender positive affect, we act in ways that will maintain those consequences. Negative affect, on the other hand, serves as a trigger to take action that will avoid aversive consequences in the future. Fear, for example, motivates us to remove ourselves from the fear-provoking situation or to change the environment in ways that reduce the fear. Visceral reactions such as a fear or anxiety serve as an early warning system that some risk management action is in order.

2. Perceived risk, and in particular, people's visceral reactions to risky situations, often has little correspondence to other measures of risk that consider either the information-theoretical uncertainty of outcomes or the magnitude and dispersion of material consequences. Instead, visceral judgments of risk (which fuel self-protective action) are determined by a small number of situational characteristics that elicit affective reactions as part of our evolutionary heritage.

In what follows, I show that the risk of providing inadequately for one's retirement years and the risk of being vested in underperforming assets are ill-suited on every dimension to elicit subjective *feelings* of risk. As a result, it is not surprising that people fail to allocate the attentional resources to retirement planning and retirement saving maintenance that they deserve, based on their financial importance to our lives. I conclude by considering the implications of psychological models of decisionmaking for the design of procedures or institutions that improve on the current state of affairs.

## Behavioral Decision Research and Theory

### Associative/Affective versus Analytic Processing

People process information in two fundamentally different ways, mediated by different neural substrates when they make judgments or arrive at decisions (Epstein, 1994; Sloman, 1996; Chaiken and Trope, 1999; Slovic et al., 2002). The first system, which is evolutionarily older, and thus shared with lower animals, works by way of similarity and associations. It requires real world knowledge (i.e. experienced decisionmakers make better decisions than novices), but its basic mechanisms seem to be hard-wired. Experience-based thinking is intuitive, automatic, and fast. It relies on images and associations, linked by experience to emotions and affect (feelings that something is good or bad). This system transforms uncertain and threatening aspects of the environment into affective responses (e.g. fear, dread, anxiety) and thus represents *risk* as a *feeling* (Loewenstein et al., 2001), which tells us whether it is safe to walk down a dark street or drink a strange-smelling liquid. The second processing system works by analytic algorithms and rules, including those specified by normative models of judgment and decisionmaking (e.g. the probability calculus, Bayesian updating, formal logic, and utility maximization). It is slower and requires awareness and conscious control.

These two processing systems typically operate in parallel and interact with each other. Neuroscientists have demonstrated that logical argument and analytic reasoning cannot be effective unless it is guided by emotion and affect (Damasio, 1994). We become aware of the simultaneous presence and operation of the two systems mainly in those situations where they produce different outputs. Thus, the question of whether a whale is a fish produces an affirmative answer from the similarity-based processing system ("a whale sure looks like a big fish"), but a negative response from the analytic, rule-based system ("it can't be a fish because it is warm blooded").

### Affect and Risk Perception

Much evidence from cognitive, social, and clinical psychology demonstrates that risk perceptions are influenced by association and affect-driven processes as much or more than by analytic processes (Loewenstein et al., 2001). In cases where the outputs from the two processing systems disagree, the affective, association-based system usually prevails. Even in seemingly "objective" contexts, such as financial investment decisions, subjective and largely affective factors have been shown to influence perceptions of risk. For example, Holtgrave and Weber (1993), showed that both affective variables (e.g. dread) and cognitive–consequentialist variables (e.g. outcomes and probabilities) are necessary to predict people's perception of risk in the financial and health/safety domain.

Differences in risk perception lie at the heart of many interpersonal and societal disputes about the best course of action. They appear to be the result of differences in affective reactions to risky situations as the result of prior experiences or general orienting disposition or worldview (Dake, 1991). Familiarity with a risk (e.g. acquired by daily exposure) lowers perceptions of its riskiness, with the result that technical experts perceive the risk of such technologies as nuclear power generation to be much lower than members of the general public (Fischhoff et al., 1978). Hertwig et al. (Forthcoming) describe the affective processing and updating mechanisms by which personal experience with rare events (e.g. negative consequences that have a low probability of occurrence) leads to a greater risk taking (and lower risk perception) than the statistic description of the same events. Numerous studies show differences in risk perception between men and women, with women judging health, safety, and recreational risks (Slovic, 1987; Flynn et al., 1994; Finucane et al., 2000) and also financial and ethical risks (Weber et al., 2002) to be larger and more problematic than men. This gender difference in perceived riskiness reverses only in the social domain, in which women have greater familiarity with risks and risk taking (Weber et al., 2002). This tendency of women to worry more about financial risks is consistent with the result observed by Sethi-Iyengar, Huberman, and Jiang (this volume) to enroll in voluntary pension plans in greater numbers and make larger contributions. Weber and Hsee (1998, 1999) find differences in the perception of financial risks between American and Chinese investors—with Chinese investors perceiving the risks of investment options to be lower and showing greater willingness to invest in risky options—and then explain these differences in risk ratings and expressions of worry by cultural differences in social collectivism. Chinese investors tend to have larger social networks (family members and associates) to which they can turn for material support than American investors; these networks provide implicit insurance against catastrophic risks, and thus lower both the objective and experienced level of risk.

These studies and many others show that differences in risk perception but not (so much) differences in risk attitude are responsible for group or individual differences in risk-taking behavior, that is, differences in preference for risky decision alternatives (Weber and Milliman, 1997). Risk taking and risk attitude have been conceptualized in several ways (Weber, 1999, 2001*a*). The most promising and consistent approach seems to be provided by models that allow for the fact that individuals or groups may differ in their subjective *perception of risk* and in their *risk attitude*, (i.e. reaction to risk), which some people find exciting and pleasurable (and thus seek out) and most people evaluate negatively (and thus avoid). While there are individual differences in risk attitude (i.e. positive or negative reaction towards risk, as it is perceived), probably mediated by biological differences in optimal arousal levels, differences in risk perception (mediated by culturally determined differences in worry and concern about possible adverse consequences) are a far better predictor of risk taking.

## Measuring Risk Perception

At least three different paradigms have studied subjective risk perception, with the goal of explaining individual and group differences in perceived risk (Weber, 2001*b*). Studies within the first measurement paradigm, known as axiomatic studies, have focused on the way in which people subjectively transform objective risk information (i.e. possible consequences of risky choice options such as mortality rates or financial returns and their likelihood of occurrence) in ways that reflect the impact that these events have on their lives (cf. Weber, 2001*b*; Palmer, 1996). The conjoint-expected risk model, for example, allows for the possibility that upside variability in financial returns has a different and usually smaller effect on perceived riskiness than downside variability (Luce and Weber, 1986). Studies within the second paradigm, called the sociocultural group, have examined the effect of group and culture-level variables on risk perception (e.g. Douglas and Wildavsky, 1982). Research within the third or psychometric paradigm is of greatest interest to our discussion, since it explicitly addresses people's emotional reactions to risky situations. It shows that these psychological/affective risk dimensions strongly influence judgments of the riskiness of physical, environmental, and material risks in ways that go beyond their objective consequences (Fischhoff et al., 1978; Slovic, Fischhoff, and Lichtenstein, 1984).

## Dread and Predictability as Determinants of Perceived Risk

The psychometric paradigm uses psychophysical scaling and multivariate analysis techniques to identify the characteristics of hazards that affect people's quantitative judgments about their perceived riskiness. Figure 3-1 shows a two-dimensional factor space that has been replicated across numerous studies covering both lay people and technical experts judging large and diverse sets of hazards in multiple countries (Slovic, 1987). Factor 1, labeled "dread risk," captures aspects of the described hazards that speed up our heart rate and make us anxious as we contemplate them: Perceived lack of control over exposure to the risk, with consequences that are

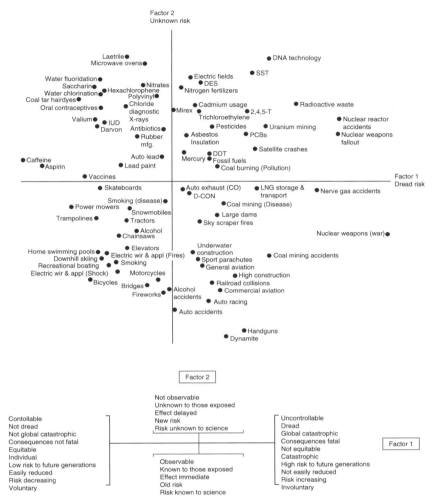

Figure 3-1. Location of 81 hazards in a two-dimensional space derived by factor analysis from the intercorrelations of 15 risk characteristics.

*Note*: Each factor is made up of a combination of characteristics, as indicated by the lower diagram.

*Source*: Slovic (1987).

catastrophic, and may have global ramifications or affect future generations. At its high (right-hand) end, we find such hazards as nuclear weapons
fallout, nuclear reactor accidents, or nerve gas accidents or attacks. Factor 2,
labeled "unknown risk," refers to the degree to which exposure to a hazard
and its consequences are predictable and observable: how much is known

about the hazard and is exposure easily detected? At the high (top) end, we find chemical hazards and radiation, which might kill exposed parties without their awareness, and DNA technology which has unforeseeable consequences not yet tested by time.

## Perceived Risk of Inadequate Pension Saving

It is an interesting and instructive exercise to place the hazard of not having adequate financial means in one's old age into the two-dimensional space of Figure 3-1. Most people would probably characterize it as a risk that is controllable, non-fatal, observable, and predictable, which would place it into the "harmless–harmless" lower-left quadrant, comparable to such hazards as riding a bicycle or owning and operating a home swimming pool.

Yet, in addition to its psychological risk-dimension profile, other factors also contribute to the fact that the prospect of financial destitution in old age carries low emotional intensity and perceived threat. Trope and Liberman (2003) argue convincingly that people construe future events differently, depending on their temporal distance to them. In particular, events in the distant future (an invitation to give a conference paper 2 years from now, or retirement 20 or 30 years from now) tends to be construed in terms of abstract features, whereas events close to us in time (the upcoming trip on Monday to attend the long-scheduled conference, or the possibility to escape winter chills for a week with an advertised last-minute travel special to Bermuda) are construed in very concrete terms. A number of interesting behavioral phenomena derive from this construal difference. One difference between the abstract versus concrete representation of the consequences of possible actions important for our discussion lies in their discrepancy in affective strength, or visceral salience and impact. Abstract representations of consequences in the distant future (e.g. "living on 60 percent of your current income") lack concrete associations connected to emotional reactions, essentially by definition. In contrast, concrete representations of choice alternatives in the present or in the near future (e.g. "buying the 5-bedroom, 4 bath, ocean-front bungalow you saw last week, that will provide space and recreation for your growing family") tend to be saturated with affective associations.

The difference in the richness and concreteness of the representation of anticipated consequences of close versus distant consequences (and thus in their affective strength) may well lie at the root of observed problems of self-control, arising from impatience and impulsivity in obtaining desirable outcomes (Mischel, Grusec, and Masters, 1969; Laibson, 1997) or procrastination with undesirable tasks (O'Donoghue and Rabin, 1999). Duflo and Saez (Chapter 8, this volume) drew the analogy between obstacles to adequate pension saving and obstacles to successful dieting, and they address the self-control issues therein. Both pension saving and dieting require the sacrifice of concrete, immediate, benefits, for the sake of abstract, distant goals. While these phenomena can and have been modeled by hyperbolic time discounting functions (Ainslie, 1975; Loewenstein and Elster, 1992), at a behavioral process level it most likely is the strong positive affect associated with immediate consequences that drives impulsive consumption decisions. The affective impoverishment of both the positive and the negative distant future consequences of current actions related to retirement saving puts any decision options that would increase positive consequences and decrease negative consequences in the distant future at a distinct disadvantage.

## Affect, Risk Perception, and Action

Visceral factors, including emotions and affect, have a potent impact on behavior (Loewenstein, 1996). In general terms, visceral states such as hunger or fear have the effect of focusing attention and motivation on activities and forms of consumption associated with the visceral factor. In the context of risk management, the specific hypothesis we propose is the following: A visceral perception of some risk is a necessary condition for any action taken to manage the risk. Putting it negatively, a purely analytic judgment of risk will have little or no impact on behavior. In situations where choice options with affective reactions to possible consequences compete with choice options that have no affective associations, people's attentional focus hypothesis will predict decisions that favor consideration of the former and neglect of the latter.

Is there any evidence for the view that the affect generated by a potentially dangerous situation drives action to reduce the affect-flagged risk, and that the absence (or removal) of the affective risk perception component reduces the likelihood of risk management actions? Evidence comes from a variety of sources. Damasio (1994) argues that decisionmakers encode the consequences of alternative courses of action affectively, and that such "somatic markers" are an essential input into future decisions. The prefrontal cortex of the brain seems to play a critical role in translating cognitive inputs from the cortex into terms that the emotional mind can understand. A study was conducted in which patients suffering damage to the prefrontal cortex and normal subjects played a game in which the objective was to win as much money as possible (Bechara et al., 1997). Players earned hypothetical money by turning over cards on which were written either monetary gains or losses. On any given turn, subjects could draw from any of four decks, two of which included high payments ($100) and two of which contained lower payments ($50). The high-paying deck, however, also included occasional very large losses, to the point where these decks had a net negative expected value. The investigators found that both normal subjects and prefrontal subjects began by sampling from all four decks, and both groups avoided high-paying decks immediately after penalty cards were encountered. But compared to normal respondents, prefrontal patients returned to the high-paying decks more quickly after suffering a loss. As a result of this tendency, the prefrontal subjects often went "bankrupt" in spite of a (reportedly) strong desire to win and a thorough understanding of the game. One possible interpretation of the prefrontal patients' behavior is that even though they "knew" the high-paying deck was risky, their inability to experience fear when contemplating a draw from one of those decks made risky draws more palatable. Consistent with this interpretation, subsequent research has examined the behavior of normal subjects in this task, and it found that those people who showed higher affective reactions to negative events (as measured by two standard scales) were more likely to sample from the lower-paying, but safer decks of cards (Peters and Slovic, 2000).

Additional support for the idea that affect plays an important role in behavioral intentions and actual behavior comes from a series of studies by Slovic and collaborators. In a typical study, participants free-associate about a concept of interest to the experimenters. For health-related behaviors such as smoking or exercising (Benthin et al., 1995), respondents might be asked to list everything that comes to mind when they hear the word "cigarette" or "jogging." In the financial domain, they might be asked to list everything that comes to mind when they hear the name of a new company on the stock market (Slovic et al., 2000). Trained raters subsequently evaluate the positive and negative affective connotations of the responses elicited in these free associations. Both for health-related behaviors and for investment decisions, these ratings of the (positive or negative) affective tone of respondents' free associations show strong correlations with their propensity to act. Thus, people with more positive imagery about exercising tend to exercise more, those with more negative imagery toward smoking tend to smoke less, and those who have more positive associations with a given company are more likely to buy its stock.

## Single Action Bias

There is another class of suboptimal risk management response that is at least consistent with the role of affect as a flag for action. Weber (1997) coined the phrase *single action bias* for the following phenomenon observed in a wide range of contexts (e.g. medical diagnosis, farmers' reactions to climate change). Decisionmakers are very likely to take one action to reduce a risk that they encounter, but they are much less likely to take additional steps that would provide incremental protection or risk reduction. The single action taken is not necessarily the most effective one, nor is it the same for different decisionmakers. However, regardless of which single action is taken first, decisionmakers have a tendency to stop from taking further action, presumably because the first action suffices in reducing the feeling of fear or threat. Thus, Berbaum et al. (1991) found that radiologists looking for abnormalities in X-rays often halt their search after finding one lesion, leaving additional lesions undetected. Weber (1997) found that farmers who became concerned about climate change in the early 1990s were likely to change either something in their production practice (e.g. irrigate), their pricing practice (e.g. ensure crop prices through the futures market), or lobby for government interventions (e.g. ethanol taxes). But they hardly ever engaged in more than one of those actions, even though a portfolio of protective actions might have been advisable. The fear of climate change seemed to set a "flag" that some action was required, but it remained in place only until one such action was taken. Thus, any single protective action had the effect of taking down the "impending danger flag."

While such behavior might have served humans well in evolutionary history, where single actions generally sufficed to contain important risks, purely affect-driven, single-action biased responses may not be sufficient in more complex environments where a portfolio of risk management actions is advised. The single-action bias illustrates the connection between visceral reaction to some risk and risk management actions. In the absence of a fear or dread response to the prospect of economic destitution in old age, purely affect-driven risk management decisions will likely result in insufficient responsiveness to the risk.

## Implications for Pension Decisionmaking

Our review of the behavioral decision literature tells us a great deal about how retirement saving decisions ought to be guided and structured. We structure our consideration of implications around the different component decisions that people encounter as part of the retirement risk management process. There are at least three classes of decisions: (i) The initial decision to save towards retirement at all, above and beyond any legally mandated contributions, and how much to put away; (ii) choice between plan providers and investment vehicles; and (iii) the decision to periodically examine and rebalance one's investment portfolio. Since others (Sethi-Iyengar, Huberman, and Jiang, Chapter 5, this volume; Statman, Chapter 4, this volume) have plenty to say about behavioral decision research results that speak to decisions in Class 2, I restrict myself to implications regarding decisions in Classes 1 and 3. In the course of considering lessons and implications, I also think of other decision situations offering useful parallels for retirement investment decisions.

### Whether to Save for One's Retirement and How Much

These decisions clearly suffer from the lack of attention to distant conse-quences of one's actions (i.e. the disproportionate temporal discounting) that people experience when considering tradeoffs between choices that result either in sacrifices in consumption now, or in sacrifices in consumption in the distant future. I have argued that the reason for this attentional neglect lies in the abstract representation of distant-future consequences and in the psychological risk dimension profile of the hazard. Contemplating the consequences of inadequate pension saving does not result in an affective reaction of fear or worry. As a result, no "flag" gets set that indicates the presence of some "clear and present danger" which mandates some protective action. In addition to retirement saving decisions, individual or societal decisions to manage such risks as climate change and species depletion fall into the same category of threats that fail to elicit fear or anxiety. In the absence of such anxiety, the impetus to take action is greatly reduced. A clear implication of this analysis is the prescription to engage decisionmakers in exercises that will concretize the consequences of their current choices. If it is the abstract and often statistical nature of information about consequences in the distant future that is responsible for the lack of visceral reaction to potentially serious circumstances, we ought to find ways to turn those statistics into experiential consequences that *do* carry affective associations, perhaps in the form of simulation games that dramatize and illustrate life at 60 percent of one's current budget levels.

Another factor distinguishing the retirement problem from the relationship between fear and action described above, is the fact that any contemplation of one's eventual demise and death is existentially disquieting and unpleasant. In this respect, retirement-related decisionmaking is analogous to decisionmaking about organ donation or estate planning. Such decisions involve topics that decisionmakers find inherently unpleasant, and thus any consideration of these questions tends to be avoided, not because of lack of attention or because of lack of an affective signal, but because the topic generates negative affect in the present. Setting the right kind of defaults for decisions where such avoidance behavior might be expected may be the best way to help people make decisions more in line with their own preferences and long-term self-interest, and certainly more in line with societal interests. European countries, for example, differ in the default preference assumed when citizens fail to make a decision on whether or not to donate some or any of their organs after death. In those countries that assume, as a default, that people want to donate their organs (i.e. action is required to opt *out*), compared to those countries that assume that people do not want to donate their organs (i.e. action is required to opt *in*), the rates of declared and actual organ donations are dramatically larger, and they are typically closer to those proportion of people who express a positive attitude towards organ donations in opinion surveys (Johnson and Goldstein, 2003). In those cases where the deliberation necessary to make a deliberate decision has aversive elements (e.g. the contemplation of one's own death), it may well be a mark of enlightened paternalism to set non-action or non-decision defaults in ways that maximize the well-being of the reluctant decisionmakers over time (Statman, this volume). The experiments reported by Benartzi and Thaler (2004) show that the lessons from organ donation transfer to the design of voluntary pension investment plans. Making contributions the default outcome that happens when employees fail to make a deliberate decision seems to align participation and saving rates more closely to participants' long-term interests.

## Whether and When to Examine and Rebalance One's Retirement Investment Portfolio

In addition to low savings rates, retirement savings account maintenance presents another problem. Several studies show that the median number of changes that people make to their pension investment portfolio over their lifetime may be zero (Samuelson and Zeckhauser, 1988; Ameriks and Zeldes, 2000; Benartzi and Thaler, 2004). Part of the reluctance to spend time or energy on retirement saving maintenance decisions is undoubtedly related to the two mechanisms discussed in the last section. First, failure to take any maintenance action does not have consequences that frighten the decisionmaker in any way, and the taking of some action does not result in immediate delight. Second, every revisit of a retirement saving decision is an unwelcome reminder of pending decline and eventual death.

Recent behavioral decision research on decision modes, that examine the qualitatively different ways in which people make decisions, may provide some additional insights for the design of procedures or institutions to promote more optimal retirement saving behavior (Weber, 1998). This research suggests that people use a much broader range of decision modes than traditionally studied in psychology, economics, and management science. For example, Yates and Lee (1996) coined the term *decision modes* in their description of particular methods or strategies for arriving at decisions and distinguished between analytic, rule-based, and automatic decision modes. Weber (1998) proposes a similar, though somewhat more differentiated taxonomy of modes. While the *analytic* decision mode of arriving at a decision by explicit or implicit weighing the costs and benefits of different alternatives has received most of decision-theoretical and empirical attention, a recent content analysis of the twentieth-century American and Chinese novels, thought to be representative of contemporary decisions and decision processes, shows that only about one-third of even the major decisions in these novels were described as having been made in an analytic mode (Weber et al., 2004). Two other decision modes were just as common, or even more common: *Affect-based* decisions, in which people base their decision on their immediate, holistic, affective reaction to different choice alternatives, with affect-guided approach and avoidance reactions as the primary decision process (Epstein, 1994; Loewenstein et al., 2001); and *recognition-and-rule-based* decisions, where people recognize the decision situation as a member of a category for which a best action is known (Simon, 1990). As soon as the decision situation has been classified, an "if–then" rule is activated, which implements the known best action. Examples include the rule of a recovering alcoholic never to accept any alcoholic beverage, or a dieter's rule never to eat after 5 PM. Many other explicitly and consciously rule-based decision situations involve self-control issues (Prelec and Herrnstein, 1991).

In sum, the evidence reviewed here suggests that cost–benefit decisions about whether to engage in some retirement portfolio review may not result in a decision that is in a person's long-term financial best interest. This is because the costs of taking action are immediate and concrete, and the benefits distant and abstract. Similarly, an affect-driven decision will not result in a retirement portfolio review. Failure to take action does not frighten people and anticipation of taking this action does not delight. Nevertheless, procedures that encourage the establishment of rules ("once a year, when I get my annual account report, I review my investment portfolio"), analogous to the rules we set and follow about visiting dentists and doctors for checkups at regular intervals, and the use of a rule-based decision mode for this purpose, hold much stronger promise. Social influence techniques of the type discussed by Duflo and Saez (this volume) can be used to establish the required behavioral norms.

# References

Ainslie, George. 1975. "Specious Reward: A Behavioral Theory of Impulsiveness and Impulse Control." *Psychological Bulletin* 82: 463–496.

Ameriks, John and Stephen Zeldes. 2000. "How Do Household Portfolio Shares Vary with Age?" Columbia University Working Paper.

Bechara, Antoine, Hanna Damasio, David Tranel, and Antonio R. Damasio. 1997. "Deciding Advantageously Before Knowing the Advantageous Strategy." *Science* 275: 1293–1295.

Benarzi, Shlomo and Richard H. Thaler. 2004. "Save More Tomorrow: Using Behavioral Economics to Increase Employee Saving." *Journal of Political Economy.* 112(1): 164–187.

Benthin, Alida, Paul Slovic, Paul Moran, Henry Severson, Chris K. Mertz, and Meg Gerrard. 1995. "Adolescent Health-threatening and Health-enhancing Behaviors: A Study of Word Association and Imagery." *Journal of Adolescent Health* 17: 143–152.

Berbaum, Karl S. et al. 1991. "Time Course of Satisfaction of Search." *Investigative Radiology* 26: 640–648.

Chaiken, Shelly and Yaacov Trope. 1999. *Dual-Process Theories in Social Psychology.* New York: Guilford.

Dake, Karl. 1991. "Orienting Dispositions in the Perception of Risk: An Analysis of Contemporary Worldviews and Cultural Biases." *Journal of Cross-Cultural Psychology* 22: 61–82.

Damasio, Antonio R. 1994. *Descartes' Error: Emotion, Reason, and the Human Brain.* New York: Avon.

Douglas, Mary and Aaron B. Wildavsky. 1982. *Risk and Culture: An Essay on the Selection of Technological and Environmental Dangers.* Berkeley, CA: University of California Press.

Epstein, Seymour. 1994. "Integration of the Cognitive and the Psychodynamic Unconscious." *American Psychologist* 49: 709–724.

Finucane, Melissa L., Paul Slovic, Chris K. Mertz, James Flynn, and Theresa A. Satterfield. 2000. "Gender, Race, Perceived Risk: The 'White Male' Effect." *Health, Risk, & Society* 2: 159–172.

Fischhoff, Baruch, Paul Slovic, Sarah Lichtenstein, Stephen Read, and Barbara Combs. 1978. "How Safe is Safe Enough? A Psychometric Study of Attitudes Towards Technological Risks and Benefits." *Policy Sciences* 9: 127–152.

Flynn, James, Paul Slovic, and Chris K. Mertz. 1994. "Gender, Race, and Perception of Environmental Health Risks." *Risk Analysis* 14(6): 1101–1108.

Hertwig, Ralph, Greg Barron, Elke U. Weber, and Ido Erev. Forthcoming. "Decisions from Experience and the Effect of Rare Events." *Psychological Science.*

Holtgrave, David and Elke U. Weber. 1993. "Dimensions of Risk Perception for Financial and Health Risks." *Risk Analysis* 13: 553–558.

Johnson, Eric J. and Dan G. Goldstein. 2003. "Do Defaults Save Lives?" *Science* 302(5649): 1338–1339. November 21.

Kraus, Neil, Torbjorn Malmfors, and Paul Slovic. 1992. "Intuitive Toxicology: Expert and Lay Judgments of Chemical Risks." *Risk Analysis* 12: 215–232.

Krimsky, Sheldon and Dominic Golding. 1992. *Social Theories of Risk.* Westport, CT: Praeger-Greenwood.

Laibson, David. 1997. "Golden Eggs and Hyperbolic Discounting." *Quarterly Journal of Economics* 112: 443–477.

Loewenstein, George. 1996. "Out of Control: Visceral Influences on Behavior." *Organizational Behavior and Human Decision Processes* 65: 272–292.

—— and Jon Elster (eds.) 1992. *Choice Over Time.* New York: Russell Sage.

Loewenstein, George F., Elke U. Weber, Chris K. Hsee, and Edward Welch. 2001. "Risk as Feelings." *Psychological Bulletin* 127: 267–286.

Luce, R. Duncan and Elke U. Weber. 1986. "An Axiomatic Theory of Conjoint, Expected Risk." *Journal of Mathematical Psychology* 30: 188–205.

Madrian, Brigitte C. and Dennis Shea. 2001. "The Power of Suggestion: Inertia in 401(k) Participation and Savings Behavior." *Quarterly Journal of Economics* 116(4): 1149–1187.

Mischel, Walter, Joan Grusec, and John C. Masters. 1969. "Effects of Expected Delay Time on the Subjective Value of Rewards and Punishments." *Journal of Personality and Social Psychology* 11: 363–373.

O'Donoghue, Ted and Matthew Rabin. 1999. "Doing It Now or Later." *American Economic Review* 89: 103–124.

Palmer, Christina G.S. 1996. "Risk Perception: An Empirical Study of the Relationship Between World View and the Risk Construct." *Risk Analysis* 16: 717–723.

Peters, Ellen and Paul Slovic. 2000. "The Springs of Action: Affective and Analytical Information Processing in Choice." *Personality and Social Psychology Bulletin* 26: 1465–1475.

Prelec, Drazan and Richard Herrnstein. 1991. "Preferences or Principles: Alternative Guidelines for Choice." In *Strategy and Choice,* ed. R. J. Zeckhauser. Cambridge, MA: MIT Press.

Rottenstreich, Yuval and Chris K. Hsee. 2001. "Money, Kisses and Electric Shocks: On the Affective Psychology of Probability Weighting." *Psychological Science.*

Samuelson, William and Richard J. Zeckhauser. 1988. "Status Quo Bias in Decision Making." *Journal of Risk and Uncertainty* 1: 7–59.

Simon, Herbert A. 1990. "Invariants of Human Behavior." *Annual Review of Psychology* 41: 1–19.

Sloman, Steven A. 1996. "The Empirical Case for Two Systems of Reasoning." *Psychological Bulletin* 119(1): 3–22.

Slovic, Paul. 1987. "Perception of Risk." *Science* 236: 280–285.

—— 1999. "Trust, Emotion, Sex, Politics, and Science: Surveying the Risk-assessment Battlefield." *Risk Analysis* 19(4): 689–701.

——, Melissa Finucane, Ellen Peters, and Donald G. MacGregor. 2002. "Rational Actors or Rational Fools: Implications of the Affect Heuristic for Behavioral Economics." *Journal of Socio-Economics* 31(4): 329–342.

——, Baruch Fischhoff, and Sarah Lichtenstein. 1984. "Behavioral Decision Theory Perspectives on Risk and Safety." *Acta Psychologica* 56: 183–203.

Trope, Yaacov and Nera Liberman. 2003. "Temporal Construal." *Psychological Review* 110: 403–421.

Weber, Elke U. 1997. "Perception and Expectation of Climate Change: Precondition for Economic and Technological Adaptation." In *Psychological Perspectives to Environmental and Ethical Issues in Management*, eds. M. Bazerman, D. Messick, A. Tenbrunsel, and K. Wade-Benzoni. San Francisco, CA: Jossey-Bass: 314–341.

—— 1998. "From Shakespeare to Spielberg: Predicting Modes of Decision Making." Presidential Address, Annual Meeting, Society of Judgment and Decision Making, Dallas, TX.

—— 1999. "Who's Afraid of a Little Risk? New Evidence for General Risk Aversion." In *Decision Science and Technology: Reflections on the Contributions of Ward Edwards*, eds. J. Shanteau, B. A. Mellers, and D. Schum. Norwell, MA: Kluwer Academic Press: 53–64.

—— 2001a. "Personality and Risk Taking." In *International Encyclopedia of the Social and Behavioral Sciences*, eds. N. J. Smelser and P. B. Baltes. Oxford, UK: Elsevier Science Limited: 11274–11276.

—— 2001b. "Decision and Choice: Risk, Empirical Studies." In *International Encyclopedia of the Social and Behavioral Science*, eds. N. J. Smelser and P. B. Baltes. Oxford, UK: Elsevier Science Limited: 13347–13351.

—— and Chris Hsee. 1998. "Cross-cultural Differences in Risk Perception but Cross-cultural Similarities in Attitudes Towards Risk." *Management Science* 44: 1205–1217.

—— 1999. "Models and Mosaics: Investigating Cross-cultural Differences in Risk Perception and Risk Preference." *Psychonomic Bulletin & Review* 6: 611–617.

—— and Richard Milliman. 1997. "Perceived Risk Attitudes: Relating Risk Perception to Risky Choice." *Management Science* 43: 122–143.

——, Daniel Ames, and Ann-Renee Blais. 2004. "How do I Choose Thee? Let Me Count the Ways:" A Textual Analysis of Similarities and Differences in Modes of Decision Making in the USA and China. *Management and Organization Review* 1: 1–32.

——, Ann-Renee Blais, and Nancy E. Betz. 2002. "Domain–Specific Risk Attitude Scale: Measuring Risk Perceptions and Risk Behaviors." *Journal of Behavioral Decision Making* 15: 263–290.

Yates, J. Frank and John W. Lee. 1996. "Chinese Decision Making." In *Handbook of Chinese Psychology*, ed. M. H. Bond. Hong Kong: Oxford University Press: 338–351.

# Chapter 4

# Behavioral Portfolios: Hope for Riches and Protection from Poverty

*Meir Statman*

As the boom of the late 1990s gave way to the bust of the early 2000s, and defined benefit (DB) plans gave way to defined contribution (DC) plans, individual investors struggled to understand their responsibilities and look for help from employers, financial services companies, government entities, investment professionals, and academics. We argue in this chapter that behavioral portfolio theory offers a good description of investor behavior and a basis for good policy prescriptions.

Behavioral portfolio theory is an alternative to mean–variance portfolio theory, a theory that is founded on expected utility theory (Shefrin and Statman, 2000). Van Neumann and Morgenstern (1944) developed expected utility theory from Bernoulli utility theory, the principles of which are illustrated in the observation that most people prefer a sure $1 over a gamble with the same expected value, such as one that offers a 50 percent chance to win $2 and a 50 percent chance to win nothing. Expected utility theory says that the utility of money increases at a lower rate than its amount, as depicted in the concave Bernoulli utility function graphed in Figure 4-1. So, while the expected value of the 50–50 gamble for $2 or nothing is equal to a sure $1, its expected utility is less than the utility of a sure $1. The observation that people generally prefer a sure $1 over a gamble with the same expected value has been offered as evidence that people are risk-averse.

Expected utility theory and mean–variance portfolio theory banished risk-seeking and gambling from theory, but gambling is easier to banish from theory than from real life. The Commission on the Review of National Policy toward gambling (1976) in *Gambling in America* describes the attempts of the Christian church to banish gambling in the early days of Christianity:

Gambling was forbidden to early Christians, but an evasion of the code continued for centuries, extending often to the clergy itself. Constantinople, the seat of the Church, was also the 12th Century gambling capital of the world. (p. 5)

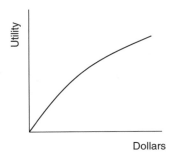

Figure 4-1. Bernoulli's utility function.
*Source*: Lopes (1987).

Figure 4-2. Friedman–Savage's utility function.
*Source*: Lopes (1987).

Centuries later, the Dickenson Report, part of the deliberations leading to the 1934 Securities Act, said (Ellenberger and Mahar, 1973):

It must always be recognized that the average man has an inherent instinct for gambling in some form or other. It has been recognized as a social evil, always inveighed against since early times. No method of combating it has ever been completely successful.

The road to behavioral portfolio theory started more than a half century ago, when Friedman and Savage (1948) noted that hope for riches and protection from poverty share roles in our human behavior; people who buy lottery tickets often buy insurance policies as well. Consequently people are risk-seeking enough to buy lottery tickets in the concave middle portion of their utility function (see Figure 4-2), while they are risk-averse enough to buy insurance in the convex outer portions. Four years later, Markowitz wrote two papers that reflect two very different views of behavior. In one (1952*b*), he created mean–variance theory, based on expected utility theory; in the other (1952a), he extended Friedman and Savage's insurance–lottery framework. People in mean–variance theory, unlike people in the insurance–lottery framework, would never buy lottery tickets; they are always risk averse, never risk-seeking.

Friedman and Savage observed that people buy lottery tickets because they aspire to reach higher social classes, whereas they buy insurance as protection against falling into lower social classes. Markowitz (1952b) fine-tuned the Friedman/Savage observation by noting that people aspire to move up from their *current* social class or "customary wealth." So people with $10,000 might accept lottery-like odds in the hope of winning $1 million, and people with $1 million might accept lottery-like odds in the hope of winning $100 million (see Figure 4-3). Kahneman and Tversky (1979) extended this line of research into prospect theory, which describes the behavior of people who accept lottery-like odds when they are below their levels of aspiration, but reject such odds when they are above their levels of aspiration (Figure 4-4).

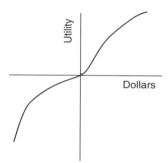

Figure 4-3. Markowitz's customary wealth utility theory.
*Source*: Lopes (1987).

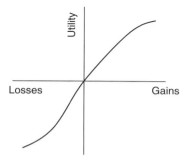

Figure 4-4. Kahneman and Tversky's prospect theory utility function.
*Source*: Lopes (1987).

Prospect theory is different from expected utility theory and mean–variance theory in a number of ways. First, while mean–variance consumers choose among alternatives based on effect of outcomes on the *levels* of their final wealth, people in prospect theory choose based on the effect of outcomes on *changes* in their wealth, relative to their reference point. Markowitz's "customary wealth" is a common reference point. Second, while mean–variance consumers are always risk-averse, people in prospect theory are risk-averse when changes in wealth are perceived as gains, but they are risk-seeking when all changes in wealth are perceived as losses. Third, mean–variance consumers treat risk objectively, by its probabilities, but prospect theorists overweight small probabilities. Overweighting may cause people to be risk-seeking in the domain of gains, such as when they purchase lottery tickets, or it may cause them to be risk-averse in the domain of losses, such as when they purchase insurance against losses that have small probabilities, such as when they buy insurance against plane crash at the airport, just before they board their flight. Finally, mean–variance theory assumes that frames do not affect choice, prospect theory emphasizes that frames greatly affect choices.

Consider an experiment that illuminates the features of prospect theory. Imagine that you face a choice of a pair such that one is A or B and the other is C or D, where

- A = a sure gain of $24,000
- B = a 25 percent chance to gain $100,000 and a 75 percent chance to gain nothing
- C = a sure loss of $75,000
- D = a 75 percent chance to lose $100,000 and a 25 percent chance to lose nothing.

The evidence shows that more people chose A than B, and more people chose D than C. This common pattern poses a puzzle for mean–variance theory, since people are predicted to be risk-averse in mean–variance theory, never risk-seeking. While the choice of A over B is consistent with risk-aversion, the choice of D over C is not. Note that the $25,000 expected gain of B (25 percent of a $100,000 gain) is greater than the sure $24,000 gain of A, so the common choice of A over B is consistent with risk-aversion. However, the election of D over C indicates that such people behave as if they are risk-seeking. Note that the expected $75,000 loss of D (75 percent of a $100,000 loss) is equal to the sure $75,000 loss of C, but D is riskier than C since it can impose a $100,000 loss.

One reason for this analysis is that choices depend on frames. For example, the common choice of the A and D combination is stochastically dominated by the less frequently chosen B and C. Note that A and D offers a 25 percent chance to win $24,000 and a 75 percent chance to lose $76,000, while B and C offers a 25 percent chance to win more, $25,000, and a 75 percent chance to lose less, $75,000. Even though the instructions indicate that the choice among A, B, C, and D is concurrent, people tend to frame the choice into one from A and B and one from C or D, overlooking the link between the two choices and its relationship to the final levels of their wealth. Indeed, researchers found that when people are asked directly whether they would prefer winning $25,000 instead of winning $24,000, and losing $75,000 instead of losing $76,000, all chose the more favorable amounts, the amounts associated with the stochastically dominating B and C.

In general then, in the context of portfolio construction, these findings imply that people do not choose well-diversified portfolios. In particular, people ignore covariance among security returns, and therefore choose stochastically dominated portfolios that lie below the mean–variance efficient frontier.

## Behavioral Portfolio Theory

A central feature in behavioral portfolio theory is the observation that investors view their portfolios not as a whole, as prescribed by mean–variance portfolio theory, but as distinct layers in a pyramid of assets, where layers are associated with particular goals and where attitudes towards risk vary across layers.[1] One layer might be a "downside protection" layer, designed to protect investors from being poor. Another might be an "upside potential" layer, designed to give investors a chance at being rich. Investors might behave as if they hate risk in the downside protection layer while they behave as if they love risk in the upside potential layer. These are normal, familiar investors, investors who buy insurance policies while they also buy lottery tickets.

In the simple version of behavioral portfolio theory, investors divide their money into two layers, a downside protection layer designed to protect them from poverty, and an upside potential layer designed to make them rich. Investors in the complete version of the theory divide their money into many layers corresponding to many different goals and levels of aspiration.

Seeing behavioral portfolios as pyramids of assets is consistent with investment advice. Consider, for example, the investment pyramid that the Putnam mutual fund company (Putnam Investments, 2003) prescribes to its investors, presented in Figure 4-5. Income funds in the Putnam Pyramid are "[d]esigned to provide a regular stream of income," and their place is at the bottom of the pyramid, while growth funds are "[d]esigned to help build the value of your investment over time," and their place is at the top of the pyramid. This structure is also reflected in the upside potential and downside protection layers of "core and satellite" and "risk budget" portfolios. Pietranico and Riepe (2002) describe "Core and Explore," Schwab's version of core and satellite, as comprised of a well-diversified "core," serving as the

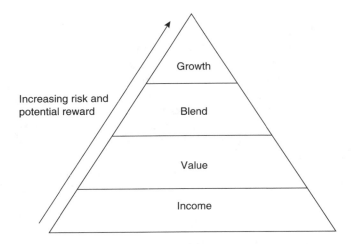

Figure 4-5. Portfolios as layered pyramids.
*Source*: Putnam Investments (2003).

"foundation" layer of the portfolio and a less diversified layer of "explore," seeking "returns that are higher than the overall market, which entails greater risk." Similarly, Waring et al. (2000) describe portfolios where the risk budget is allocated to active funds while the safe budget is allocated to index funds.

One might argue that while portfolios are described as layered pyramids consistent with behavioral portfolio theory, investors consider them as a whole, consistent with mean–variance portfolio theory. But such argument is not supported by the evidence. Consider, for example, Question 13 in Fidelity Investments (2003) Asset Allocation Planner:

If you could increase your chances of improving your returns by taking more risk, would you:

1. Be willing to take *a lot* more risk with *all* your money.
2. Be willing to take *a lot* more risk with *some* of your money.
3. Be willing to take *a little* more risk with *all* your money.
4. Be willing to take *a little* more risk with *some* of your money.
5. Be unlikely to take much more risk.

Answers 1 and 3 make sense within the mean–variance framework. In that framework, only the risk of the overall portfolio (i.e. *all* your money) matters. But answers 2 and 4 make no sense within the mean–variance framework. This is because answers 2 and 4 segment the portfolio into layers where investors are willing to take *a lot more risk* or *a little more risk* with *some* of their money. Mean–variance investors have single attitude toward risk, not a set of attitudes, layer by layer. In contrast, behavioral investors have many attitudes toward risk, layer by layer. So they might be willing to take *a lot more* risk with *some* of their money.

Mean–variance investors construct the mean–variance efficient frontier by identifying portfolios with highest level of expected wealth for each level of standard deviation. The counterpart in behavioral portfolio theory to standard deviation in mean–variance portfolio theory is the probability that wealth might fall below the aspiration level. Behavioral investors construct the behavioral efficient frontier by identifying the portfolios with the highest level of expected wealth for each probability that wealth would fall below the aspiration level (see Figures 4-6a and b).

Mean–variance portfolio theory posts that security returns follow a normal distribution, but that behavioral investors prefer securities with non-normal, asymmetric distributions that combine downside protection, in the form of a floor, with upside potential (Shefrin and Statman, 2000). Call options combine a floor with upside potential and so do bonds, stocks,

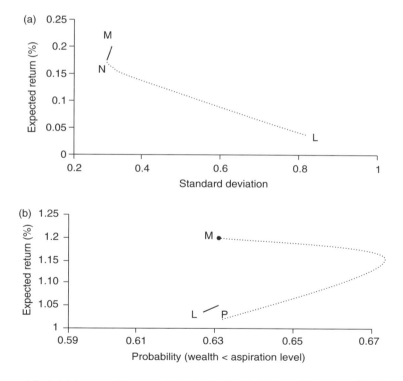

Figure 4-6. (a) Mean–variance and (b) behavioral efficient frontiers with $1.00 in assets and a $1.30 aspiration level.

*Source*: Shefrin and Statman (2000).

and lottery tickets. Indeed, "limited liability" is an important feature that endears stocks to the hearts of behavioral investors. Behavioral investors choose "deep in the money" securities, such as Treasury bills, bonds and equity participation notes for the downside protection layers of their portfolios, "in the money" securities, such as stock mutual funds and individual stocks, for the middle layers of their portfolios and "out of the money" securities, such as call options and lottery tickets for the upside potential layers of the portfolios.

While securities with normal distributions are not optimal for behavioral investors, they do provide a comparison between behavioral efficient frontiers and mean–variance efficient frontiers when investors can choose only from securities with normal distributors (Shefrin and Statman, 2000). Behavioral investors, like mean–variance investors, tend to consider their portfolio as a single account, so behavioral investors with low aspirations are likely to choose diversified portfolios, while those with high aspirations are likely to choose undiversified portfolios. Moreover, behavioral investors with high aspirations are likely to choose lottery-like securities, shunned by mean–variance investors.

Consider an investor with $1 and a (high) aspiration level of $1.30 who can choose security L, security M, or combinations of both. Security L is lottery-like, with an expected return of 2 percent and a standard deviation of 90 percent, while security M has an expected return of 20 percent and a standard deviation of 30 percent.[2] The mean–variance efficient frontier extends from M to N in Figure 4-6(a), where N is the portfolio with the lowest standard deviation. Mean–variance investors with no aversion to risk place their entire $1 in security M, while risk-averse mean–variance investors divide their $1 between securities M and L along the M–N efficient frontier. Yet, a portfolio composed entirely of lottery-like L is not on the mean–variance efficient frontier, because it is dominated by other portfolios, including the one composed entirely of M. In contrast, a portfolio composed entirely of L is on the efficient frontier of a high-aspiration behavioral investor, since it provides the highest probability of reaching the aspiration level. The behavioral efficient frontier extends from L to P and includes M. The probability of reaching the aspiration level in P is higher than the probability in M, but M offers higher expected returns than P (see Figure 4-6b).[3]

Behavioral investors who choose lottery-like L do so because they have high aspirations, not because they like risk. In that, they are similar to the Dubins and Savage (1976) investor who is in a casino with $1,000 and desperately aspires to have $10,000 by morning. The optimal portfolio for this investor is concentrated in a single bet, one that offers a chance, however small, of winning $10,000. An investor who diversifies his bets does worse than one who concentrates them in a single bet since he has virtually no chance of winning the aspired $10,000.

While the single account version of behavioral portfolio theory is useful for comparisons with mean–variance portfolio theory, investors in practice think of their portfolio not as a single account but as a pyramid of many accounts or many layers. In the two-layer version of behavioral portfolio theory, investors divide their portfolio money into a downside protection layer with a low aspiration level, designed to protect them from poverty, and an upside potential layer with a high aspiration level, designed for a shot at riches. A diversified portfolio of cash, bonds, and stock mutual funds comes close to an optimal sub-portfolio for the downside protection layer while an undiversified portfolio consisting of one or a few stocks comes close to an optimal sub-portfolio for the upside potential layer. The overall portfolio where the two layers are added together is likely to contain large proportions of one or few stocks.

Consider an investor who is pulled equally strongly by the desire for downside protection and the desire for upside potential so he divides his $2 into two equal parts, $1 for the downside protection layer and $1 for the upside potential layer. Imagine that the aspiration level of that investor for the downside protection layer is $1, a level that is low relative to the $1.20 aspiration level for the upside potential layer. Imagine that there were two securities, X and Y, both of which have normally distributed returns. X has an expected return of 16 percent with a standard deviation of 20 percent, while Y has an expected return of 10 percent with a standard deviation of 15 percent. The correlation between the returns of X and Y is zero.

Now we contemplate behavioral efficient frontier for the downside protection layer. A portfolio consisting entirely of Y offers an expected wealth of $1.10 along with a 25.2 percent probability that the aspiration level will be missed. Portfolio Y is not on the efficient frontier since it is dominated by portfolio Z. Portfolio Z, combining $0.50 of X with $0.50 of Y, has the lowest probability of missing the aspiration level, 14.9 percent, along with higher expected wealth, $1.13. Figure 4-7 shows the efficient frontier for the downside protection layer, extending from Z to X. Next, consider the efficient frontier for the upside potential layer. Figure 4-8 shows that the frontier consists of a concentrated bet on security X. Any other portfolio is inferior since it provides a lower expected wealth with a higher probability of missing the aspiration level.

In sum, behavioral investors allocate their assets to upside potential and downside layers of a portfolio pyramid. While they place great importance on the upside potential layers of their portfolios, they do not necessarily neglect the downside protection ones. Indeed, behavioral investors form their portfolios as if they fill the downside protection layers of their portfolios first, before they move on to fill the upside potential ones. Many gamblers do the same. *Gambling in America* (1976) reported that gamblers have more substantial downside protection layers than non-gamblers and the proportions of both stock owners and bond owners among gamblers is

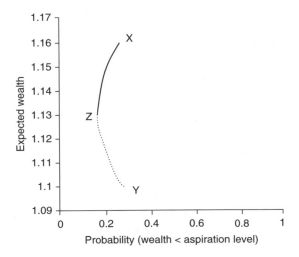

Figure 4-7. Behavioral efficient frontier for an investor with $1.00 in the downside protection layer and a $1.00 aspiration level.

*Source*: Shefrin and Statman (2000).

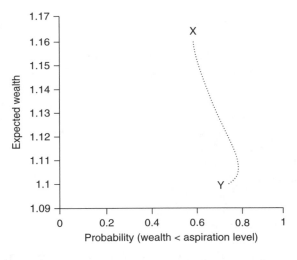

Figure 4-8. Behavioral efficient frontier for an investor with $1.00 in the upside potential layer and a $1.20 aspiration level.

*Source*: Shefrin and Statman (2000).

higher than their proportions among non-gamblers. Moreover, "gamblers were more likely to have their future secured by social security and pension plans than non-gamblers and hold 60 percent more assets . . . " (1976: 66).

## Public Policy

Mean–variance theory offers portfolio descriptions that investors do not follow. By contrast, behavioral portfolio theory offers descriptions of pyramid portfolios that are much closer to reality. Investors want downside protection layers in their portfolios but they want upside potential layers as well. But what should we prescribe as the right balance between upside potential and downside protection? And what should we prescribe as the right balance between freedom and paternalism?

One problem is that people have begun suing advisers and employers who let them concentrate their portfolios in stocks. Mitchell and Utkus (2003) illustrate the tradeoff between upside potential and downside protection in their discussion of the consequences of holding company stocks in DC plans. They simulated three hypothetical portfolios, one invested entirely in company stock, one invested entirely in a stock market index, and one divided equally between company stock and stock market index. They found that portfolios concentrated in company stock offer great upside potential, with a 5 percent chance of accumulating more than $4.1 million after 30 years. In contrast, the corresponding accumulation figure for the stock market portfolio is only $2.7 million. Yet, while the stock market index offered lesser upside potential, it offered greater downside protection. The lowest accumulation with the stock market index was $281,000 while the lowest accumulation with company stock was $66,000.

Should financial advisers, employers, and government entities let investors concentrate their portfolios in company stock? Should they let investors concentrate their portfolios in stocks? Public policy has always fluctuated between the desire for upside potential and the desire for downside protection, just it has fluctuated between the desire for freedom and the desire for paternalism. People opt for freedom when times are good and upside potential seems near, but evidence suggests they clamor for paternalism after it turns out that they have sacrificed downside protection for dashed hopes of upside potential.

This pattern has long historical roots in the United States. In the early 1900s, as investors pressed for "blue sky" laws when their reach for upside potential brought loss of downside protection. The value of Kansas farmland more than doubled during the 1900–10 period and this new prosperity attracted investment promoters. A commentator at the time noted (Bateman, 1973: 766): "the state of Kansas, most wonderfully prolific and rich in farming products, had a large proportion of agriculturists not versed in ordinary business methods. The State was the happy hunting ground of promoters of fraudulent enterprises; in fact, their frauds became so barefaced that it was stated that they would sell building lots in the blue sky in fee simple. Metonymically they became known as the blue-sky merchants and the legislation intended to prevent their frauds was called Blue Sky Law."

The 1911 Kansas Blue Sky law empowered state officials to deny registration to any security judged unfair, unjust, or inequitable to any class of investors. By 1933, every state except Nevada had adopted blue sky laws. Carosso (1970: 164) noted the paternalistic nature of these laws, "Never before had a state sought to prevent its citizens from making unwise decisions." The paternalistic blue sky framework competed with the freedom-based disclosure framework as the basis for the 1933 and 1934 acts that established the SEC and underlie the regulation of investors and investments to this day. Congressman Huston Thompson took the leadership role in crafting a new securities law in 1933, shortly after President Roosevelt's inauguration and his draft combined blue sky features with disclosure ones.

Several argued against the blue sky features in Thompson's bill. Rayburn told Roosevelt that the Thompson bill was too stringent and Roosevelt quickly agreed, for two reasons: First, he wished to enact a securities bill rapidly and was concerned that a debate would delay enactment; and second, he felt most strongly about the disclosure principle. Disclosure is the principle that underlies the acts of 1933 and 1934, but paternalism has not been vanquished, reflected in Social Security.

Social Security was created to satisfy a need for downside protection. Moss (2002) wrote that the "Social Security Act represented a sweeping response to the problem of worker insecurity" and quoted President Roosevelt's words:

We can never insure one hundred percent of the population against one hundred percent of the hazards and vicissitudes of life, but we have tried to frame a law which will give some measure of protection to the average citizen and to his family against the loss of a job and against poverty-ridden old age. (2002: 180)

Clearly, the pendulum has begun to swing from freedom to paternalism, as the boom of the late 1990s has given way to the bust of the early 2000s. Further, it appears that the pendulum is swinging from concern over upside potential to downside protection.

## Conclusion

Over a half century ago, Friedman and Savage (1948) described people as they are, people who hope that a lottery ticket will lift them into a higher social class, while they trust that an insurance policy will protect them from falling into a lower social class. While Friedman and Savage assigned equal roles to lottery tickets and insurance policies in their insurance–lottery framework, research by Markowitz took us to a fork in the road (1952a,b). On one hand, Markowitz extended Friedman and Savage's framework, assigning to lotteries a role as big as the role of insurance. On the other, the mean–variance framework, Markowitz (1952b) assigned to lotteries no role at all. While the mean–variance road is the better-traveled road the insurance–lottery road is the better road. Here, we have shown how Kahneman and Tversky (1979) developed the thinking into prospect theory, while Shefrin and Statman (2000) pressed further to develop behavioral portfolio theory.

While some researchers and policymakers may lament the fact that people are attracted to lotteries, others might accept it and help people strike a balance between hope for riches and protection from poverty. Finding the balance is the challenge as governments offer to both Social Security and lotteries, corporations offer their employees both mutual funds and company stocks, and the financial services industry offers its investors both bond funds and Internet stocks.

## Notes

[1] Friedman and Savage (1948), Markowitz (1952b), and Kahneman and Tversky (1979) form the basis of Shefrin and Statman's (2000) behavioral portfolio theory.
[2] The argument would be similar if the expected return of L were negative, as is the case of a lottery.
[3] Behavioral investors do not borrow to leverage their investments. Mean–variance investors without the ability to borrow might concentrate their portfolios in one security, but it would not be lottery-like stock L.

## References

Bateman, Hal. 1973. "State Securities Registration: An Unresolved Dilemma and a Suggestion for the Federal Securities Code." *Southwestern Law Journal* 27: 759–789.

Carosso, Vincent. 1970. *Investment Banking in America.* Cambridge, MA: Harvard University Press.

Commission on the Review of National Policy Toward Gambling. 1976. *Gambling in America.* Washington, October.

Dubins, Lester E. and Leonard J. Savage. 1975. *How to Gamble If You Must: Inequalities for Stochastic Processes,* 2nd Ed. New York, Dover: McGraw Hill.

Ellenberger, J. S. and Ellen Mahar. 1973. Legislative History of the Securities Act of 1973 and Securities Exchange Act of 1934, Vols 1–10. South Hackensack, NJ: Law Librarians' Society of Washington, DC, Fred B. Rothman and Co.

Fidelity Investments. 2003. "Asset Allocation Planner Questionnaire." www.fidelity.com.

Friedman, Milton and Leonard J. Savage. 1948. "The Utility Analysis of Choices Involving Risk." *Journal of Political Economy* 56(4): 279–304.

Kahneman, Daniel and Amos Tversky. 1979. "Prospect Theory: An Analysis of Decision Making Under Risk." *Econometrica* 47(2): 263–291.

Kritzman, Mark, 1992. "Asset Allocation for Individual Investors." *Financial Analyst Journal* January–February: 12–13.

Lopes, Lola, 1987. "Between Hope and Fear: The Psychology of Risk." *Advances in Experimental Social Psychology* 20: 255–295.

Loss, Louis and James Seligman. 1989. *Securities Regulation.* Boston, MA: Little, Brown.

Markowitz, Harry. 1952a. "Portfolio Selection." *Journal of Finance* 7(1): 77–91.

——— 1952b. "The Utility of Wealth." *Journal of Political Economy* 60(2): 151–158.

Mitchell, Olivia and Stephen Utkus. 2003. "The Role of Company Stock in Defined Contribution Plans." In *The Pension Challenge: Risk Transfers and Retirement Income Security*, eds. Olivia Mitchell and Kent Smetters. Oxford: Oxford University Press: 33–70.

Moss, David A. 2002. *When All Else Fails: Government as the Ultimate Risk Manager.* Cambridge: Havard University Press.

Pietranico, Paul and Mark Riepe. 2002. "Core & Explore—Details." Charles Schwab and Company. www.schwab.com.

Putnam Investments. 2003. www.putnam.com/individual.

Shefrin, Hersh and Meir Statman. 2000. "Behavioral Portfolio Theory." *Journal of Financial and Quantitative Analysis* 35(2): 127–151.

Von Neumann, John and Oscar Morgenstern. 1944. *Theory of Games and Economic Behavior.* Princeton, NJ: Princeton University Press.

Waring, Barton, Duane Whitney, John Pirone, and Charles Castille. 2000. "Optimizing Manager Structure and Budgeting Manager Risk." *The Journal of Portfolio Management* 26(3): 90–104.

# Part II
# Implications for Retirement Plan Design

# Chapter 5

# How Much Choice is Too Much? Contributions to 401(k) Retirement Plans

*Sheena Sethi-Iyengar, Gur Huberman, and Wei Jiang*

It is commonly supposed that the more choices we have, the better off we are—that the human ability to manage and the desire for choice are infinite. From classic economic theories of free enterprise, to mundane marketing practices that offer aisles of potato chips and soft drinks, the desire for infinite choice pervades our institutions, norms, and customs. Ice cream parlors compete to offer the most flavors while major fast-food chains urge customers to "Have it your way." Furthermore, the challenges of choice are not merely confined to snack foods. With today's plethora of retirement savings plans, important life decisions have also become a matter of choice, where employees become consumers, contemplating alternative career options and multiple investment opportunities.

These days, most workers cannot expect to retire on Social Security alone; therefore people are increasingly turning to company pension plans to help them save for retirement. Firms offer 401(k) plans in order to attract new employees, encourage superior performances from current employees, and increase employee retention. The 401(k) plan, named for section 401(k) of the Internal Revenue Code, permits employees of qualifying companies to set aside tax-deferred funds with each paycheck. While the employer is responsible for establishing a 401(k) plan, employees must decide what percentage of their paycheck will be deducted for their plans. Employees can legally contribute up to 25 percent of their annual earnings as long as the amount does not exceed the legal cap (which was $12,000 in 2003). Over the past decade the number of employer-provided retirement plans has skyrocketed from under 100,000 in 1990, to over 400,000 by 2002.

While the promise of a greater variety of plans seems beneficial, is there such a thing as too much choice? Indeed, if we look beyond the number of plans available, and we examine the options within the plans themselves,

The authors acknowledge the contributions of Steve Utkus, who made available the data essential for conducting this analysis and provided the authors constructive feedback throughout the process. The authors would also like to thank Gary Mottola for his considerable time and effort.

we find even more decisions waiting to be made. Most 401(k) plans offer employees a myriad of investment opportunities from mutual funds, insurance companies, and/or banks. Indeed, some providers even allow employees to invest in individual stocks, and on global capital exchanges allowing for maximum portfolio diversification. But, does bigger necessarily mean better? When large companies woo potential employees with a smorgasbord of options, do these options actually enhance employee welfare?

Inherent to consumerism is the assumption that choice is both desirable and powerful. Psychological theory and research have similarly presumed that choice is invariably beneficial. Repeatedly, across many domains of inquiry, psychologists have contended that the provision of choice can increase the individual's sense of personal control (e.g. Rotter, 1966; Taylor and Brown, 1988; Taylor, 1989) and feelings of intrinsic motivation (e.g. deCharms, 1968; Deci, 1981; Deci and Ryan, 1985). In turn, personal control and intrinsic motivation have been correlated with numerous physical and psychological benefits, including greater task enjoyment, enhanced task performance, and increased life satisfaction. Indeed, even seemingly trivial or wholly illusory choices have been shown to have powerful motivating consequences (e.g. Langer, 1975; Langer and Rodin, 1976; Dember et al., 1992).

More recently, however, a few researchers have demonstrated potential limitations to this assumption. Rather than presuming the benefits of choice to be ubiquitous, Iyengar and Lepper (2000) examined the consequences of offering choosers an extensive range of alternatives, in which the differences among options were relatively small. They hypothesized that choosers will be intrinsically motivated by the actual provision of extensive choices, because such contexts allow for maximal opportunity in the achievement of personal preference matching. Nonetheless, the very act of making a choice from an excessive number of options might result in "choice overload," in turn lessening both the motivation to choose and the subsequent motivation to commit to a choice.

Field and laboratory experiments were conducted in which the intrinsic motivations of participants encountering limited as opposed to extensive choices were compared (Iyengar and Lepper, 2000). In one compelling field demonstration, a tasting booth for exotic jams was arranged at Draeger's, a California gourmet grocery store. This grocery store is of particular interest because its salient distinguishing feature is the extraordinary selection it offers, especially when compared with large grocery chains. For instance, Draeger's offers roughly 250 different varieties of mustard, 75 different varieties of olive oil, and over 300 varieties of jam. Shoppers are frequently offered sample tastes of this enormous array of available products; consequently, Draeger's provided a particularly conducive environment for a naturalistic experiment, using tasting booths.

As customers passed the tasting booth, they encountered a display with either 6 or 24 different flavored jams. The number of passers-by who approached the tasting booth and the number of purchases made in these

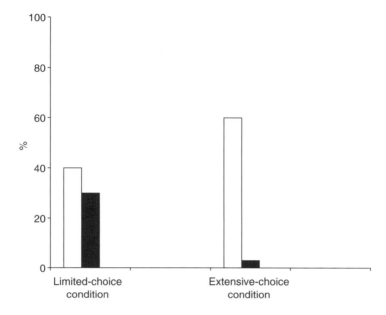

Figure 5-1. Comparison of jam sampling versus purchasing in limited and extensive-choice conditions.

*Note*: White bars: Percentage of passers-by who approached the tasting booth; Solid bars: Percentage of "approachers" who subsequently purchased jam.

*Source*: Iyengar and Lepper (2000).

two conditions served as dependent variables. The results indicated that although extensive choice proved initially more enticing than limited choice, limited choice was ultimately more motivating. Thus, 60 percent of the passers-by approached the table in the extensive-choice condition as compared to only 40 percent in the limited-choice condition. However, as depicted in Figure 5-1, 30 percent of the customers who encountered the limited selection actually purchased a jam, while only 3 percent of those offered the extensive selection made a purchase.

This study's results challenge a fundamental assumption underlying classic psychological theories of human motivation and economic theories of rational choice; that is, that having more choice is necessarily more desirable and intrinsically motivating. These findings from this study show that an extensive array of options can at first seem highly appealing to consumers, yet it also can reduce subsequent motivation to purchase the product. Even though consumers presumably shop at this particular store in part because of the large number of selections available, having "too much" choice seems, nonetheless, to have hampered their later motivation to buy.

Subsequent laboratory experiments not only support the "choice overload" hypothesis, but they also provide insight into the potential mediators of this hypothesis (Iyengar and Lepper, 2000). In one experiment, this time involving displays of Godiva chocolate, participants once again encountered either a limited or an extensive array of option, and were asked to make a choice. Unlike the jam study, however, before being given the opportunity to sample the selection they had made, choosers' expectations about their choices were assessed. Participants provided predictions about how satisfied they would be with their stated preference—whether they expected the choice they made to be merely "satisfactory," or "among the best." After making their choices, participants were asked to provide ratings of their enjoyment, difficulty, and frustration during the choice-making process. Later, after sampling their choices, they again provided ratings of satisfaction and regret.

Study participants either sampled a chosen Godiva chocolate from a limited selection of six, or an extensive selection of 30. At the time they made their choices, participants reported enjoying the process more when choosing from the display of 30 chocolates as opposed to the display of six. Subsequently, however, participants choosing from the selection of six proved more satisfied and more likely to purchase chocolates again, as compared to participants choosing from a selection of 30. Collectively, these results suggest that choosers may experience frustration with complex choice-making processes, and that dissatisfaction with their choices—stemming from greater feelings of responsibility for the choices they make—may lead to a lower willingness to commit to one choice.

It is not that people are saddened by the decisions they make in the face of abundant options, but rather that they are rendered unsure, burdened by the responsibility of choosing optimally. In theory, the burden of choosing experienced by choosers in these studies should have been insignificant, since the task of choosing among chocolates or jams is less about distinguishing between "right" and "wrong" choices and more about the identification of personal preferences. Nevertheless, the findings demonstrate that the offer of overly extensive choices in relatively less consequential choice-making contexts can have significant demotivating effects. Participants in both the jam and chocolates studies proved less likely to buy these products when confronted with an overwhelming array of choices.

Perhaps the phenomenon of *choice overload* may be further exacerbated by contexts in which (i) the costs associated with making the "wrong" choice, or even beliefs that there are truly "wrong" choices, are much more prominent; and/or (ii) substantial time and effort would be required for choosers to make truly informed comparisons among alternatives. The more choosers perceive their choice-making task to necessitate expert information, the more they may be inclined not to choose. In such cases, in fact, they may even surrender the choice to someone else—whom they presumably see as more expert (de Charms, 1968; Langer and Rodin, 1976; Schulz, 1976; Zuckerman et al., 1978; Lepper, 1983; Deci and Ryan, 1985; Malone and Lepper, 1987; Taylor, 1989). In Schwartz's (1994) terms, one important paradox confronting the modern world is that as the freedom of individuals expands, so too does people's dependence on institutions and on other people.

## The Effect of Choice Overload on 401(k) Plan Contributions

Given that the choice overload phenomenon was observed in less consequential choice-making contexts (i.e. when choosing jams and chocolates), to what extent might it also hold for major life decisionmaking situations? To test its presence in more consequential decisionmaking, we examined employees' decisions about whether—and how much—to participate in the 401(k) retirement benefit plan offered to them by their employers. The ramifications of employee investment decisions are potentially life-changing. Contributions to the 401(k) protect employees' income from being taxed, thus allowing employees to save more for their retirement. Moreover, employers often match employee contributions to the 401(k). One might have predicted participation rates to be at an all-time high, given the plethora of options available to employees and the ease with which many employees can transfer funds using the Internet. In fact, from 1998 to 2001, the average 401(k) plan has boosted its available investment options by 21 percent (Mottola and Utkus, 2003).

A Hewitt Associates survey as cited in *The Washington Post* shows that participation in 401(k) plans dropped to 68.2 percent of workers at the end of 2002, from 71 percent a year earlier (*Washington Post*, 2003). Additionally, the average 401(k) participant contributes less than 7 percent of pre-tax salary, even though financial advisors encourage a contribution of 10 percent or more of pre-tax salary (Financial Planning Association, 2002). Why are participation rates so low, despite an ever-increasing array of plan offerings? Could it be that the provision of more 401(k) plan options does *not* have a positive effect on employee willingness to participate in a plan? Instead, does the consequentiality of the investment decision, combined with employee intimidation by the complex details of the various plan offerings, contribute to a pronounced choice overload effect, resulting in a greater likelihood of investors choosing not to choose?

We test this hypothesis by examining 401(k) participation rates among clients of the Vanguard Group, an investment management company. The firm provided records of contributions to 401(k) plans at both the plan and individual levels for the year 2001. We identified employees as participants in the 401(k) plans if they contributed any part of their salary to the plan. We made no distinctions among participants based on the amount they contributed as long as it was above $0. Those employees who chose not to contribute any part of their salary to a 401(k) were designated non-participants. The sample included 926,104 records for 899,631 employees of 647 plans in 69 industries. We excluded any employee hired after January 1,

2001 (10 percent), who was less than 18 years old (0.02 percent), or whose annual salary was less than $10,000 or above $1,000,000 (7.51 percent), leaving an analysis group of 793,794 people. The records identified 442,544 of these people as male and 264,471 as female, and the mean age was 43. The mean and median salaries were $61,150 and $47,430, respectively. Over 71 percent of the employees contributed positive amounts to tax-deferred accounts in 2001, and 75 percent of the accounts had positive balances in tax-deferred accounts. The savings rate was 5.2 percent, and 12.2 percent of 401(k) participants contributed the maximum amount in 2001 (which was an annual limit of $10,500).

We analyzed how individual and plan characteristics affect individual participation, and in particular, whether more funds offered correlated negatively with participation rates. The empirical regression examined the effect of the number of offered funds (which ranged from 2 to 59) on the employee likelihood of participating in the 401(k) plan.[1] Our regressions controlled for both employee and plan-level characteristics.[2] Employee-level data is particularly important because it is generally inappropriate to estimate a relation on an aggregate level and then infer that an analogous relation holds at the individual level. For example, our data shows that at plan level, a $10,000 increase in average compensation, everything else equal, would increase average contribution by $480, while at the individual level, the same coefficient is $907. In some cases, even the sign of certain factors could be reversed (C.F., 2001).

The regressions, controlled for several employee attributes: Annual compensation in $10,000 (COMP); gender (FEMALE); age in years (AGE); the wealth rank (1–24) of the nine-digit zip code neighborhood where the individual lives, WEALTH);[3] and the length (in years) of the individual's tenure with the current employer. Plan-level attributes for which we controlled were average compensation in $10,000 (COMP_MEAN), average age (AGE_MEAN), average tenure (TENURE_MEAN), average wealth rank (WEALTH_MEAN), number of employees in natural logo (NEMPLOY), the rate of web registration among participants in the plan in percentage points (WEB), a variable indicating whether the plan allowed individuals to take loans out of their tax-deferred savings. Some 541 plans covering 88 percent of the employees offered loans, and about 17 percent of those employees had a positive loan balance at the end of 2001, with a median loan balance of $4,373. Also controlled was the rate (in percentage points) at which employers matched employee contributions (MATCH); and a variable indicating whether the company's own stock was offered. There were 125 plans covering 59 percent of the employees in this population who were offered company-owned stock (COMPSTK). Most importantly, the number of funds offered (NFUNDS) was a key regressor.

As shown in Table 5-1, if a plan offered more funds, this depressed probability of employee 401(k) participation. Other things equal, every ten funds

TABLE 5-1 Determinants of Individual Participation in DC Plans (2001) (DepVar: Plan Participation rate, %)

| | Linear Probability | | | | Probit | | | | | |
| | Pooled Regressions | | Within–Between | | Log-Linear | | | Linear | | |
| | (1) | | (2) | | (3) | | (4) | | (5) | | | (6) | | |
| | COEF | t | COEF | t | COEF | t | COEF | t | COEF | t | Marginal Pr | COEF | t | Marginal Pr |
|---|---|---|---|---|---|---|---|---|---|---|---|---|---|---|
| CNST | 197.44 | 6.13 | 216.88 | 6.26 | 206.39 | 5.73 | 278.13 | 6.22 | 845.14 | 114.88 | — | 172.37 | 41.23 | — |
| **I. Individual characteristics** | | | | | | | | | | | | | | |
| COMP | 15.12 | 0.162 | 22.19 | 0.190 | 15.00 | 0.175 | 15.19 | 0.101 | 57.00 | 0.406 | 15.31 | 7.84 | 0.068 | 2.54 |
| FEMALE | 5.73 | 0.406 | 7.74 | 0.809 | 4.35 | 0.879 | 6.12 | 0.108 | 19.57 | 0.401 | 5.26 | 17.60 | 0.375 | 5.71 |
| AGE | 0.47 | 0.078 | 0.38 | 0.091 | 0.39 | 0.123 | 0.47 | 0.048 | 1.10 | 0.132 | 0.29 | 2.09 | 0.124 | 0.68 |
| AGE² | -0.01 | 0.002 | 0.00 | 0.000 | 0.00 | 0.000 | -0.01 | 0.001 | -0.01 | 0.001 | 0.00 | -0.02 | 0.001 | -0.01 |
| WEALTH | 5.96 | 0.049 | — | — | 5.91 | 0.064 | 5.91 | 0.034 | 23.29 | 0.142 | 6.25 | 2.9 | 0.056 | 0.94 |
| TENURE | 1.28 | 0.080 | 1.32 | 0.101 | 1.17 | 0.132 | 1.22 | 0.045 | 4.63 | 0.067 | 1.24 | 5.10 | 0.063 | 1.65 |
| TENURE² | -0.03 | 0.002 | -0.03 | 0.003 | -0.03 | 0.005 | -0.03 | 0.001 | -0.11 | 0.002 | -0.03 | -0.12 | 0.002 | -0.04 |
| **II. Plan policy variables** | | | | | | | | | | | | | | |
| LOANS | -3.69 | 3.765 | -2.67 | 44.500 | — | — | -1.02 | 3.778 | -12.9 | 0.639 | -3.46 | -4.58 | 0.607 | -1.49 |
| MATCH | 0.18 | 0.015 | 0.18 | 0.015 | — | — | 0.18 | 0.017 | 0.68 | 0.007 | 0.18 | 0.59 | 0.006 | 0.19 |
| COMPSTK | 2.89 | 1.338 | 2.94 | 1.598 | — | — | 3.11 | 1.139 | 6.46 | 0.423 | 1.74 | 7.45 | 0.406 | 2.42 |
| NFUNDS | -0.2 | 0.083 | -0.17 | 0.058 | — | — | -0.21 | 0.077 | -0.61 | 0.037 | -0.16 | -0.57 | 0.034 | -0.19 |

TABLE 5.1 Continued.

| | Linear Probability | | | | | | Probit | | | | | |
| | Pooled Regressions | | | | Within–Between | | | | Log-Linear | | | Linear | | |
| | (1) | | (2) | | (3) | | (4) | | (5) | | | (6) | | |
| | COEF | t | COEF | t | COEF | t | COEF | t | COEF | t | Marginal Pr | COEF | t | Marginal Pr |
| III. Plan-level controls | | | | | | | | | | | | | | |
| COMP_MEAN | -1.09 | 3.759 | -0.72 | 1.014 | 3.75 | 4.808 | 3.20 | 5.000 | -10.63 | 0.756 | -2.86 | 2.35 | 0.123 | 0.76 |
| WEALTH_MEAN | 0.69 | 2.300 | — | — | -0.90 | 2.903 | -0.69 | 2.654 | 4.88 | 0.424 | 1.31 | -3.98 | 0.219 | -1.29 |
| AGE_MEAN | 1.47 | 0.274 | 1.55 | 0.463 | 1.04 | 0.486 | 1.31 | 0.376 | 4.41 | 0.096 | 1.18 | 4.36 | 0.088 | 1.41 |
| TENURE_MEAN | -1.06 | 0.275 | -1.20 | 0.423 | -0.82 | 0.371 | -1.08 | 0.282 | -3.52 | 0.074 | -0.95 | -3.64 | 0.069 | -1.18 |
| WEB | 0.07 | 0.063 | 0.14 | 0.059 | 0.17 | 0.063 | 0.14 | 0.059 | 0.29 | 0.022 | 0.08 | 0.71 | 0.019 | 0.23 |
| NEMPLOYEES | -2.88 | 0.331 | -3.29 | 0.593 | -3.37 | 0.832 | -3.73 | 0.789 | -9.23 | 0.119 | -2.48 | -10.82 | 0.110 | -3.51 |
| $R^2$ | 0.19 | | 0.16 | | 0.18 | | 0.16 | | 0.18 | | 0.33 | 0.12 | | 0.23 |

Note: The all-sample participation rate is 70.8%. All coefficients are multiplied by 100. Columns (1)–(4) are results from a linear probability model. COMP and WEALTH are expressed in dollars. The standard errors are obtained by bootstraps (50 replications) that adjust for both heteroskedasticity (both within and across groups, and group-specific disturbances) and within group correlation (due to the group-specific disturbance). Columns (5) and (6) report results from probit estimation. Pseudo $R^2$ and incremental probability of correct prediction are reported for goodness-of-fit. Marginal probabilities are calculated by setting all non-dummy variables at their mean values, and all dummy variables at zero. In column (6), COMP is expressed in $10,000, and WEALTH is expressed in IXI ranks from 1 to 24. The number of observations is 793,794.

Source: Authors' computations.

added was associated with 1.5 percent to 2 percent drop in participation rate. Figure 5-2 illustrates the decline of participation rates as a function of number of funds offered, controlling for all other variables listed in Table 5-1 (by setting them at their mean values). If there were only two funds offered, participation rates peaked at 75 percent, but when there were 59 funds offered, participation rates dipped to a low of approximately 60 percent. The majority of the plans included in this data set offered between 10 and 30 options, yet Figure 5-2 shows that plans offering (fewer than 10 plans) had significantly higher employee participation rates. Although the number of plans that offered between 30 and 60 options was few, there is a distinctive trend, which suggests that the decline in participation rates is exacerbated as offerings increased further.

While other researchers have considered some of the issues covered here, our results are particularly compelling because of the size and nature of the data used, namely actual employee records (including non-participants' records) from hundreds of 401(k) plans. Our findings have important implications for sponsors designing investment menus for 401(k) plans, as well as for policymakers considering private accounts within Social Security.

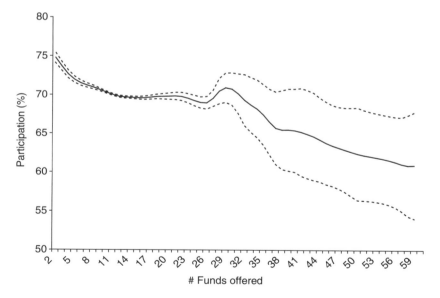

Figure 5-2. The relation between participation and number of funds offered.

*Notes*: The graph plots the relation between the plan participation rate. Explanatory variables except the number of funds offered are set at their respective mean values and the number of funds offered using a two-stage parametric estimation method. The dotted lines represent the 95% confidence intervals.

*Source*: Authors' analyses.

Both sponsors and policymakers may intuitively feel that limiting the number of options to a manageable few is desirable based on considerations such as the demographics of participants/employees, their investment knowledge or experience, and the complexity of investment decisionmaking generally or from the options themselves. Our research provides a quantitative basis for this intuition.

Recently, there has also been a trend to offer "fund windows" or "brokerage accounts," in which employees are offered hundreds or thousands of securities. A fund window is an investment structure that significantly expands 401(k) plan investment choices by allowing participants to choose from funds beyond their main investment options. Although record-keeping for assets in the fund window is usually performed on the same system as the main 401(k) investments, the funds in the window are considered distinct from the main options (Hewitt Associates, 2001). With brokerage accounts, employees are permitted to trade virtually any US stock, bond, or mutual fund; the problem, of course, is if they are not informed, they run the risk of investing rashly.

Plan providers who continue to present participants with a plethora of options including brokerage accounts and fund windows might perhaps consider "tiering" the options. This could include focusing communication activities on a core set of investment options, with more limited information about the larger number of choices (or perhaps just a reference to where the information can be found—for example, a website). As an example, a plan could offer two tiers of investments including ten main funds in Tier I, and 60 in the fund window in Tier II. Another possibility, rather than offering a menu of 100 or 1,000 options, is to present participants with a menu of 10 options plus one—with the last being "many more choices."

Pension fiduciary law requires the plan sponsor to investigate fund options, provide manageable choices to employees, and offer educational programs through which employees can verse themselves in their options. Yet, often employees fail to avail themselves of the necessary information. Industry evidence indicates that half of all these participants never contact their money managers in any given year, and those who do tend to be affluent, higher-balance participants. Perhaps in attempting to provide employees with a generous number of 401(k) options, employers may actually intimidate rather than induce employees to invest in personal retirement plans. One way to combat the dangers of choice overload in which employees "choose not to choose," is to implement for "libertarian paternalism," a phrase recently coined to describe institutional efforts to affect individuals' behavior while respecting their freedom of choice. Sunstein and Thaler (2003) who develop this notion, propose that people's preferences often are ill-informed, which leads to decisions, that are unduly influenced by default rules, framing effects, and starting points (Sunstein and Thaler, 2003). An employer aware of such issues could react by steering employee choices in a welfare-promoting direction, yet without eliminating their freedom of choice. In the present case, the libertarian paternalist employer would design the plan carefully so as not to offer too much choice to employees. In order to ensure that employees engage in some form of retirement savings, the employer might declare a "standard" or default 401(k) plan into which workers are automatically enrolled, if they do not elect to opt out. While this is currently permitted by US pension regulation, but it may actually be dictated by the tenets of libertarian paternalism.

## Notes

[1] Strictly speaking, we lack data on the total number of funds offered by each plan, so we approximate it by counting the number of funds used by at least one participant in each plan. As a result, the number of funds offered could be under estimated for plans with few employees and/or with low participation ratios. Given that the average plan in our sample had 1,486 employees, the measurement error should be minimal. If a bias arises from this approximation, it will bias against finding a demotivating effect of more choices.

[2] Specifically the following empirical equation was estimated:

$$y_{ij}^* = \beta_0 + \bar{\beta}_1 X_{ij} + \bar{\beta}_2 \bar{X}_j + \bar{\beta}_3 Z_j + \delta_j + \varepsilon_{ij},$$

$$y_{ij} = \begin{cases} \underline{v}, & if\ y_{ij}^* < \underline{v} \\ \bar{v}, & if\ y_{ij}^* > \underline{v} \\ y_{ij}^*, & otherwise \end{cases}.$$

Here, $y_{ij}^*$ is the *desired* contribution made by individual $i$ in plan $j$. $y_{ij}$ is the *observed* contribution which is doubly censored at $\underline{v} = 0$ and $\bar{v} = 10,500$. There are three sets of regressors. $X_{ij}$ is a set of individual characteristics variables; $\bar{X}_j$ represents the plan-level averages of individual characteristics; and $Z_j$ is a set of plan policy variables. The disturbance can be decomposed into a plan-specific error, $\delta_j$, assumed uncorrelated across difference plans, and an individual disturbance, $\epsilon_{ij}$, which is independently distributed across individuals. Both $\delta_j$ and $\epsilon_{ij}$ could be heteroskedastic across different plans and/or individuals, but are assumed to be independent of the regressors. From an economic analysis perspective, the meaningful contribution is the "desired contribution," and not necessarily the observed one. For example, if next year the 401(k) contribution cap is raised from $12,000 to $15,000, those who are currently contributing $12,000 would likely contribute more because their desired contribution is greater than the observed level. Personal and plan attributes both determine desired contribution, but the latter is only partially observed.

[3] A company called IXI collects retail and IRA asset data from most of the large financial services companies, Vanguard being one of them. IXI then aggregates the data from all the companies at the Zip+4 level. IXI divides the total of retail and IRA assets in each Zip+4 by the number of households (based on US Census data) to determine the average assets for each Zip+4. This enables IXI to assign a code (from 1 to 24) at the Zip+4 level which indicates about how much money in investable assets people living in each particular Zip+4 have. A Zip+4 has, on

average, about 10–12 houses in it. So, the IXI system works under the premise that peoples' financial situation is similar to that of their immediate neighbors, which is a reasonable premise. Further, using the wealth level of the neighborhood, instead using that of the individual under consideration, eliminates spurious correlation between current contribution and accumulated wealth. The term "wealth" used here includes bank, brokerage, and mutual fund investment assets.

# References

de Charms, Richard. 1968. *Personal Causation.* New York: Academic Press.

Deci, Edward L. 1981. *The Psychology of Self-determination.* Lexington, MA: Heaths.

—— and R. M. Ryan. 1985. *Intrinsic Motivation and Self-determination in Human Behavior.* New York: Plenum Press.

Dember, William N., Tracy L. Galinsky, and Joel S. Warm. 1992. "The Role of Choice in Vigilance Performance." *Bulletin of the Psychonomic Society* 30: 201–204.

Financial Planning Association. 2002.

Hewitt Associates. 2001.

Iyengar, Sheena S. and Mark Lepper. 2000. "When Choice is Demotivating: Can One Desire Too Much of a Good Thing?" *Journal of Personality and Social Psychology* 76: 995–1006.

Langer, Ellen J. 1975. "The Illusion of Control." *Journal of Personality and Social Psychology* 32: 311–328.

—— and Judy Rodin. 1976. "The Effects of Choice and Enhanced Personal Responsibility for the Aged: A Field Experiment in an Institutional Setting." *Journal of Personality and Social Psychology* 34: 191–198.

Lepper, Mark R. 1983. "Social Control Processes and the Internalization of Social Values: An Attributional Perspective." In *Social Cognition and Social Development,* eds. E. T. Higgins, D. N. Ruble, and W. W. Hartup. New York: Cambridge University Press: 294–330.

Malone, Tom W. and Mark R. Lepper. 1987. "Making Learning Fun: A Taxonomy of Intrinsic Motivations for Learning." In *Aptitude, Learning and Instruction: Vol. 3. Cognitive and Affective Process Analysis,* eds. R. E. Snow and M. J. Farr. Hillsdale, NJ: Erlbaum: 223–253.

Mottola, Gary R. and Stephen P. Utkus. 2003. "Can There Be Too Much Choice In a Retirement Savings Plan?" The Vanguard Group Inc. Malvern, PA: Vanguard Center for Retirement Research.

Rotter, Julian B. 1966. "Generalized Expectancies for Internal Versus External Locus of Control of Reinforcement." *Psychological Monographs* 80: 1–28.

Schulz, Richard. 1976. "Effects of Control and Predictability on the Physical and Psychological Well-being of the Institutionalized Aged." *Journal of Personality and Social Psychology* 33: 563–573.

Schwartz, Barry. 1994. *The Costs of Living: How Market Freedom Erodes the Best Things in Life.* New York: W. W. Norton & Company.

Sunstein, Cass R. and Richard H. Thaler. 2003. "Libertarian Paternalism Is Not An Oxymoron." *University of Chicago Law Review.*

Taylor, Shelley E. 1989. *Positive Illusions: Creative Self-deception and the Healthy Mind.* New York: Basic Books.

Taylor, Shelley E. and Jonathon D. Brown. 1988. "Illusion and Well-being: A Social-psychological Perspective on Mental Health." *Psychological Bulletin* 103: 193–210.

*Washington Post.* 2003. "401(k)s: Remember Them?" June 22, F4.

Zuckerman, Miron, Joseph Porac, David Lathin, R. Smith, and Edward L. Deci. 1978. "On the Importance of Self-Determination for Intrinsically Motivated Behavior." *Personality and Social Psychology Bulletin* 4: 443–446.

# Chapter 6

# "Money Attitudes" and Retirement Plan Design: One Size Does Not Fit All

*Donna M. MacFarland, Carolyn D. Marconi,
and Stephen P. Utkus*

Worker-directed defined contribution (DC) savings plans have become the dominant form of retirement plan in many countries. More than 40 percent of US private sector workers are DC participants, about twice the percentage covered by defined benefit (DB) plans. Most of these employees are in participant-directed 401(k) plans, in which workers make voluntary saving and investment choices, encouraged by federal tax benefits and employer matching contributions (Vanguard 2002*a*).

As these plans have grown, so, too, have employer and policymaker expectations for worker behavior. In an ideal world, workers would be expected to join these plans and take full advantage of the tax and savings advantages they offer. In pursuit of retirement security, rational participants would be expected to calculate an adequate savings rate and construct an optimal investment portfolio. When they change jobs, participants would be expected to avoid tax penalties and not spend their assets. At retirement, with lump sum distributions being the common form of benefit payment, workers would be expected to generate a suitable income stream from their savings for their life, managing mortality risk and avoiding the premature depletion of assets.

This set of expectations regarding participant behavior we refer to here as the "planner model." Workers in participant-directed retirement plans are supposed to exhibit many of the characteristics of a good financial planner. Perhaps symbolic of the "planner model" was the recent announcement of a new national coalition designed to promote "comprehensive financial planning" in the United States (Business Wire, 2002). This new organization encourages Americans to undertake 10 tasks to "retire on your terms," including calculating savings goals, learning about Social Security and employer plans, and creating a retirement plan. Many analysts measure success of DC plans in precisely this way, by comparing actual participant behavior with what a good financial planner might recommend or do. For example, determining the adequacy of one's current savings rate is a critical financial planning task.

Accordingly, in its annual survey of retirement readiness, the Employee Benefits Research Institute (EBRI) asks Americans whether they have calculated their retirement savings goal (EBRI, 2002). In the 2002 survey only, 32 percent had, and this was down from 39 percent in 2001.

Being well informed about retirement plan design and investments is also an important characteristic of a financial planner. Education is, therefore, a cornerstone of the defined contribution plan services offered to employers; it is also a focus of public policy at the Department of Labor, the Securities and Exchange Commission, and now the new Office of Financial Education within the US Treasury.[1] To gauge progress along these lines, several well-publicized industry and academic studies surveys have documented the gap between what participants actually know and what a well-trained financial planner might know. For example, in terms of retirement benefit information, Gustman and Steinmeier (2001) report that "misinformation or lack of information about retirement benefits is the norm" among individuals near retirement. Meanwhile, Merrill Lynch (2002) reports that 54 percent of Americans over 30 think that a 401(k) plan is guaranteed, and this was also true of those expecting to rely on a 401(k) plan for retirement income. In terms of investment knowledge, Vanguard (2002*a*) and Merrill (2002) report that sizeable groups have no clear expectation of future stock market returns, or expect annual returns in excess of 20 percent. Also Vanguard (2002*a*) and John Hancock Financial Services (2001) report that the typical participant rates his or her own company stock as safer than a diversified stock fund. These reports attract headlines because they underscore the difference between the "planner model" and real-world participants.

It should be no surprise that all workers do not all conform to the planner model. Even a casual survey would suggest that individuals appear to differ markedly in their interest in money and retirement planning. Some individuals are saving and planning enthusiasts, motivated and excited about learning about whatever they need to know needed to make them successful in retirement. Others are indifferent or averse to saving, money matters, and discussion of retirement finances. The idea of heterogeneous saving preferences is, of course, not new. In classical literature, the idea surfaces in Aesop's Fables, where an ant works ceaselessly to gather corn for the winter, while a grasshopper pursues a life of leisure. In 1834, the economist John Rae attempted to explain a country's wealth in terms of its "effective desire for accumulation."[2] In his *Principles of Economics*, Alfred Marshall (1920) spoke of heterogeneous savings preferences not among countries, but among individuals:

One will reckon a distant benefit at nearly the same value which it would have for him if it were present; while another who has less power of realizing the future, less patience and self-control, will care comparatively little for any benefit that is not near at hand.

Arthur Pigou wrote about the tendency of human beings to discount the future, but he could have just as well been describing the grasshopper's dilemma: "our telescopic faculty is defective, and we, therefore, see future pleasures, as it were, on a diminished scale."[3] More recently, Laibson (1997, Laibson et al., 1998) and others have utilized hyperbolic discounting models to explain people's tendency to overvalue the present and undervalue the future.

This chapter attempts to apply this broad observation—that individuals have heterogeneous savings preferences—to the world of designing participant-directed retirement savings plans. Specifically, we examine how individual workers' attitudes vary towards the topics or interests thought to be necessary for optimal behavior in DC plans, including issues as saving for the future, taking equity market risk, and creating a retirement plan. We segment workers participating in or eligible for an employer-sponsored DC plan into five "money attitude" clusters: Groupings of similar attitudes and expectations regarding various aspects of financial and retirement management. What we find, not surprisingly, is that people differ substantially in their enthusiasm for the types of planning activities needed to be successful in conventional DC plans. In other words, not all workers are planners; rather, they come in many attitudinal "sizes."

## Prior Research

Much of the existing economics literature explaining saving behavior in DC retirement plans focuses on how saving rates vary according to employer-provided incentives and participant demographics.[4] Researchers have found a positive statistical relationship between 401(k) plan participation and employer matching contributions, though there is some debate as to whether it is the mere presence or the actual magnitude of the match that matters more.[5] Plan saving rates have also been analyzed in terms of the demographic variables—income and age—at the heart of the neoclassical model of saving (i.e. that higher-income and/or older workers save more). Various researchers have also linked saving behavior to sex, race, education, job tenure, home ownership, and the presence of another retirement plan in the workplace.

Employer plan design is also thought to influence employee savings behavior—most notably the presence of 401(k) loans[6] and workplace education. In terms of education, Bernheim and Garrett (1996), Bayer, Bernheim, and Scholz (1996) and Lusardi (Chapter 9, this volume) report that education raises both participation and savings rates. Active use of financial training programs appears to boost participation rates and saving rates more than merely making information available. Education has its greatest impact among low and middle-income households, probably because upper-income households are constrained by Internal Revenue Service contribution limits in their ability to boost saving. Of course, while education may successfully boost plan saving rates, this is distinct from saying that participants are well-educated about retirement plan decisions, given the results of the surveys cited in our introduction.

More recent research has sought to examine the non-economic or psychological factors that influence savings decisions. One notion is the importance of plan design "framing" effects, in which design choices by the sponsor influence participant decisions. Madrian and Shea (2001) report that automatic enrollment (in which newly eligible employees are enrolled at a default savings rate and in a default investment option) raises participation rates dramatically. It also eliminates differences in participation rates due to income, age, job tenure, sex, and race. Yet, this research raises a provocative question—why does a saving decision framed in negative terms yield such dramatically different results than one framed in positive terms? The worker-as-planner would not be expected to vary saving behavior depending on how the question is asked by the employer.

Choi et al. (2002a, b) document the role that inertia plays in automatic enrollment and in plan decisions generally. Not only do many participants exhibit inertia when automatically enrolled by staying at low default savings rates and in conservative default investment options, but also some participants who would have saved more or would have chosen different options decide to accept the default choices made for them. Perhaps if participants were fully rational agents with well-formed preferences, their choices would not be as easily swayed by the default options established by their employer.

In the same vein, inertia can be used to induce participants to save more, especially when they would otherwise be reluctant to do so. Under the "Save More Tomorrow" (or SMT) plan, by Benartzi and Thaler (2004), workers agree to have their plan contributions increased regularly in the future (e.g. by 1 percent a year on their anniversary). They found that workers in one firm were more willing to use the SMT feature than to agree to a one-time increase in saving rate recommended by a financial planner. Over time, these workers ended up saving more than the planner had originally recommended. In this way, higher saving was produced by a combination of a technique in which painful savings decisions were postponed into the future, and inertia thereafter.

Another vein of academic research has addressed the impact of social and peer group dynamics within an organization. Duflo and Saez (Chapter 8, this volume) report that peer groups play an important role in helping individuals gather information and make informed decisions.

Finally, in a related vein, research by industry groups has sought to analyze participant savings behavior in terms of common outlooks or beliefs. The EBRI has classified Americans into several "personality types" based on their common beliefs or attitudes in the annual Retirement Confidence Survey. These groups are created based on statistical segmentation or clustering techniques that aggregate people according to their common responses to a battery of questions. In its 2002 survey, EBRI classified workers into Planners, who enjoy financial and retirement planning; Savers, who are disciplined about saving but risk-averse about investing in the capital markets; Strugglers, who while interested in saving are often beset by financial problems; Impulsives, who are not disciplined in savings habits; and Deniers, who do not think about financial matters and deny that retirement security is possible.

## Data and Methodology

The goal of present is to understand how attitudinal perceptions toward "money" and, more specifically, "retirement planning," are linked to behavior around plan participation or non-participation, as well as participant equity holdings and account activity. Our current research, like the EBRI study before it, develops an attitudinal segmentation of retirement plan participants and eligible non-participants. Importantly, however, we augment our survey results with administrative records on saving behavior (including plan eligibility and plan participation), and account behavior (including equity investment holdings, the level of account interaction, and the use of loans). In this way, our findings are linked not only to psychological attitudes expressed in the survey portion of the study, but also to actual participant behavior. The analysis had two phases: A qualitative phase, in which structured interviews were used to elicit possible attitudes regarding "money" and "retirement planning" from a small group of workers; and a quantitative phase, in which a much larger sample population was asked to respond to a battery of attitudinal statements regarding money and retirement planning.

### Qualitative/Interview Phase

Working with an independent research organization researchers at The Vanguard Group conducted 40 1-h, in-depth, one-on-one interviews with 16 participants in defined contribution plans for which Vanguard provides record-keeping services; 14 participants in retirement plans administered by other organizations; five non-participants; and five retired participants.[7] These interviews included participants employed full-time and participating in a 401(k) or 403(b) retirement saving program; non-participants were required to be full-time employees in an organization offering a 401(k) or 403(b) savings plan. Interview candidates were selected to provide a mix of blue-collar and white-collar positions; within the limited sample, we attempted to include participants who varied by age, sex, and race.

The interviews, held in 1999, were organized around an unstructured interviewing technique, in which interviewees were asked a series of open-ended questions in a number of categories. These included general questions about the role of money and finances in their lives; the individuals or events in their lives that influenced their approach to money (which elicited many comments about savings role models); and a number of retirement topics, including the role of a workplace savings plan and reasons for use (or lack of use), savings goals, and expectations for retirement. Interviewees were also asked about the sources of information, advice, and education they used to make decisions. The interviews closed with some creative imagery around planning for retirement, the future, retirement, and savings.[8] A panel of observers was trained to take verbatim notes, which were used as input to the subsequent design of a questionnaire in the quantitative phase.

Following the interviews, a team of researchers synthesized the interview notes, from which three patterns emerged. One group of interviewees clearly had a strong interest and orientation toward money management and retirement planning: This group was tentatively named "planners" by the research team. A second set of interviewees seemed uninterested in money issues or retirement planning: These were given the name "avoiders." And a third set of interviewees seemed somewhere in between: Diligent and motivated about saving for the future, often out of a sense of responsibility for others, but at the same time, not particularly interested in retirement planning or financial matters per se. This third group the team referred to as the "doers": Individuals who "did what they're supposed to" in terms of saving for the future (or for others). An important output from the qualitative phase was a battery of 48 potential attitude statements that could be used to describe the feelings, emotions, and attitudes expressed by the interviewees regarding money and retirement planning.

## Quantitative/Survey Phase

During the quantitative phase, we sought to verify the existence of distinct attitudinal segments in the population, quantify what portion of the retirement plan population they represented, and investigate differences that might emerge in terms of attitudes, behavioral variables (e.g. participation rate, equity allocation, account usage), and demographic variables. A questionnaire was designed to incorporate a series of attitudinal statements drawn from the interviews, and this survey was administered via telephone in 2000. A total of 1,141 respondents participated in the telephone survey, which averaged 20 min in length. Respondents were a random sample drawn from a universe of participants and eligible non-participants among Vanguard recordkeeping plans. Participation and eligibility status was drawn from our administrative systems, not from the survey respondents. A summary of respondent's demographics can be founded in Table 6-1.

The survey included a variety of demographic, behavioral, and usage questions to reveal the types of information that respondents relied on when making financial decisions. After the survey, we added additional administrative data, including asset allocation to equities, transaction activity,

TABLE 6-1  Study Sample: Quantitative Phase

| | Participants | Non-Participants | Total |
|---|---|---|---|
| **I.  Sample size** | | | |
| 401(k) | 599 | 300 | 899 |
| 403(b) | 216 | 26 | 242 |
| Total | 815 | 326 | 1,141 |
| **II.  Sample demographics** | | | |
| *Median age Gender* | ↑45 | 40 | 44 |
| Male (%) | 67 | 66 | 67 |
| Female (%) | 33 | 34 | 33 |
| *Household income* | | | |
| Under $25,000 | 4% | 12% | 5% |
| $25,000–<$45,000 | 18 | 29 | 21 |
| $45,000–<$75,000 | 34 | 37 | 36 |
| $75,000 or more | 32 | 36 | 17 |
| *Race* | | | |
| White (%) | ↑83 | 77 | 82 |
| African-American | 6 | ↑10 | 7 |
| Other | 8 | ↑11 | 9 |
| *Marital status* | | | |
| Married (%) | ↑77 | 60 | 73 |
| Not married, living with partner | 2 | 4 | 2 |
| Single | 11 | ↑19 | 13 |
| Divorce | 8 | ↑16 | 10 |
| Widowed | 1 | 2 | 2 |
| *Workstage*[a] | | | |
| Beginning (%) | 12 | ↑32 | 17 |
| Middle | ↑55 | 37 | 50 |
| End | 32 | 29 | 32 |
| *Education* | | | |
| Some high school (%) | 2 | 5 | 2 |
| High school graduate | 22 | 29 | 23 |
| Some College or Associates degree | 36 | 45 | 38 |
| 4 year College or higher | ↑41 | 22 | 37 |
| *Occupation* | | | |
| Clerical (%) | 7 | 8 | 7 |
| Blue collar | 22 | ↑33 | 25 |
| White collar/professional | ↑58 | 37 | 52 |
| *Children under age 18* (%) | 45 | 52 | 47 |

[a] Workstage is defined as respondents' perception of the point they are in their working career.

*Note*: ↑/↓ indicates significantly higher or lower (participants versus non-participants) at the 95% confidence level. Plan participants had an account balance of at least $100 in their Vanguard record-keeping account. Non-participants were eligible for plan enrollment but non-participating.

*Source*: Authors' computations.

"channel utilization" (the frequency of retirement plan transactions, whether via a telephone associate, an automated voice response unit, or the Internet), and loan activity.

Survey attitudinal responses were then analyzed using a statistical procedure known as "cluster analysis." Cluster analysis is a multivariate statistical technique designed to group objects (in this case, retirement plan participants and eligible non-participants) based on similar characteristics (their responses to the 26 attitudinal questions). The statistical technique defines a cluster or segment in such a way as to minimize differences among individual members within a cluster, while maximizing the differences across the clusters. In effect, it is a way of determining natural groupings within a data set, although researchers can influence these groupings by the statistical methods employed.

Cluster solutions were generated using an iterative, non-hierarchical *k*-means clustering procedure.[9] For further analysis, we selected a five-segment clustering solution, chosen because it was easy to understand and communicate. Each cluster also represented a reasonably large subsegment of the retirement plan population, with the smallest segment accounting for 14 percent of the population and the largest for 26 percent. Finally, each cluster was given a name designed to evoke its attitudinal preferences.

## Results: The Five "Money Attitudes" Segments

Table 6-2 provides a list of the 26 attitudinal statements used in the survey, as well as the corresponding mean scores for respondents in each cluster of

TABLE 6-2  Attitude Segments—Survey Responses

|  | *Successful Planners* | *Up & Coming Planners* | *Secure Doers* | *Stressed Avoiders* | *Live-for-Today Avoiders* |
|---|---|---|---|---|---|
| *Vision of retirement* | | | | | |
| I am generally optimistic about my financial future | 8.4 | 7.0 | 7.4 | 5.9 | 6.2 |
| It's pointless to plan for retirement, it's too far away | 1.3 | 1.7 | 2.0 | 2.1 | 6.0 |
| *Interest in retirement and financial planning* | | | | | |
| I make time to plan and review my finances | 8.5 | 6.5 | 6.1 | 4.7 | 5.2 |
| I enjoy managing my money | 8.6 | 7.5 | 6.2 | 5.0 | 5.6 |
| I don't like dealing with money and finances | 1.8 | 3.4 | 4.5 | 6.2 | 5.1 |

TABLE 6-2 *Continued.*

|  | Successful Planners | Up & Coming Planners | Secure Doers | Stressed Avoiders | Live-for-Today Avoiders |
|---|---|---|---|---|---|
| I feel stressed out when I think about planning my future retirement | 2.0 | 4.2 | 3.2 | 6.4 | 5.0 |
| My leisure time is more important to me than taking out time to plan for retirement | 3.4 | 4.1 | 4.9 | 4.8 | 5.5 |
| I am more focused on day-to-day responsibilities than on planning my future retirement | 4.4 | 5.3 | 6.0 | 7.5 | 6.6 |
| Preparing for retirement takes too much time and effort | 1.9 | 3.0 | 3.4 | 4.2 | 5.1 |
| *Preparation for retirement* | | | | | |
| I'm in a position to meet all of my financial goals for retirement | 8.4 | 5.5 | 6.6 | 3.9 | 4.6 |
| I know the amount of money I will need to have saved up in order to retire well | 7.8 | 6.0 | 5.9 | 3.5 | 4.8 |
| I worry about having enough money for retirement | 4.3 | 7.3 | 4.4 | 8.3 | 5.7 |
| *Savings behavior/deferral of gratification* | | | | | |
| I'm disciplined at saving | 8.4 | 6.2 | 6.8 | 4.6 | 4.6 |
| I usually pay off credit cards at the end of every month | 8.2 | 6.7 | 7.4 | 5.1 | 5.5 |
| I'm not willing to make sacrifices to save more for retirement | 3.1 | 3.6 | 4.1 | 4.3 | 4.9 |
| I'd rather spend today than save for the future | 2.2 | 3.1 | 3.1 | 3.9 | 5.2 |
| I get a lot of satisfaction from saving for the future | 8.6 | 7.8 | 7.1 | 6.3 | 5.3 |
| *Equity risk-taking* | | | | | |
| I have made a lot of money in the last few years in the stock market | 6.9 | 4.4 | 3.1 | 2.4 | 3.0 |

TABLE 6-2 *Continued.*

| | Successful Planners | Up & Coming Planners | Secure Doers | Stressed Avoiders | Live-for-Today Avoiders |
|---|---|---|---|---|---|
| I am willing to take substantial financial risks if it could mean a higher return | 6.7 | 7.3 | 4.3 | 5.5 | 5.8 |
| To retire well you have to be willing to take substantial investment risks | 5.7 | 6.5 | 4.0 | 5.7 | 5.5 |
| I am not a risk taker when it comes to investing my money | 4.2 | 4.4 | 7.3 | 6.6 | 5.3 |
| *Financial knowledge/ information/advice* | | | | | |
| A lot of financial information is confusing to me | 3.0 | 5.2 | 5.3 | 7.7 | 5.6 |
| I'm willing to tell a financial advisor all my financial details | 6.5 | 6.6 | 5.5 | 7.1 | 4.9 |
| I like to get financial advice from professional advisors but then make my own decision | 7.7 | 7.5 | 6.4 | 7.1 | 6.5 |
| I feel confident in my investment skills | 7.7 | 5.7 | 5.0 | 3.4 | 5.1 |
| *Other* | | | | | |
| Social Security will provide most of my retirement needs | 1.7 | 2.0 | 2.5 | 2.2 | 3.8 |
| *Plan participants only* | | | | | |
| Joining the 401(k)/403(b) plan was an easy decision | 9.8 | 9.4 | 9.1 | 9.1 | 7.9 |
| I find it easy to save with my 401(k)/403(b) plan | 9.3 | 9.0 | 8.6 | 8.7 | 7.5 |
| I follow the progress of my 401(k)/403(b) plan closely | 8.6 | 7.7 | 6.5 | 5.8 | 6.0 |
| I am willing to tap my 401(k)/403(b) plan for needs other than retirement | 3.0 | 3.5 | 3.1 | 4.1 | 4.5 |
| I think 401(k)/403(b) plans are too complicated to understand | 1.9 | 3.0 | 3.7 | 4.4 | 4.7 |

TABLE 6-2 *Continued.*

|  | *Successful Planners* | *Up & Coming Planners* | *Secure Doers* | *Stressed Avoiders* | *Live-for-Today Avoiders* |
|---|---|---|---|---|---|
| *Non-participants only* | | | | | |
| Deciding not to join the 401(k)/403(b) plan was an easy decision | 5.6 | 4.5 | 5.7 | 4.8 | 5.3 |
| I would find it easy to save if I had a 401(k)/403(b) plan | 6.4 | 7.2 | 6.0 | 7.0 | 5.7 |
| I wish I had enrolled in a 401(k)/403(b) plan | 4.9 | 7.1 | 5.1 | 8.0 | 5.6 |
| I think 401(k)/403(b) plans are too complicated to understand | 1.9 | 3.6 | 3.6 | 3.9 | 4.7 |
| N | 237 | 298 | 229 | 212 | 165 |

*Notes*: Eligible non-participants and participants were asked to rank each of the following statements on a scale of "1" to "10" where "10" means "strongly agree" and "1" means "strongly disagree." Statements were randomized; headings were for reference only and not read to the respondents. Shading illustrates highest response in each category.

*Source*: Authors' computations.

the five "money attitude" clusters. Table 6-3 summarizes key features of each cluster, while Figure 6-1 provides a snapshot of the size of each attitudinal segment. About one-fifth (21 percent) of the retirement plan population (participants and eligible non-participants) may be characterized as *Successful Planners*. These individuals have a strong, goal-oriented vision of a successful retirement. They enjoy planning for the future and are optimistic that they are well prepared for retirement. They are disciplined savers, and they derive a high level of personal satisfaction from the act of saving for the future. They are comfortable with equity risk-taking, and they rely on an extensive array of information sources to make decisions.

*Up & Coming Planners* accounted for another quarter (26 percent) of the retirement plan population. They possess many of the attitudes and preferences of Successful Planners—a strong, goal-oriented vision of retirement; an abiding interest in retirement planning; a disciplined approach to savings; and an equity orientation in their investment strategy. Where they differ from Successful Planners is in the degree of confidence about their plans. They lack the degree of optimism, the feeling of assured success, that the Successful Planners have achieved—hence the "Up & Coming" designation.

The *Secure Doer* segment accounted for one-fifth (20 percent) of the retirement plan population. The term "Doer" originated from the original

TABLE 6-3 Attitude Segments: Highlights of Attitudinal Characteristics

| | Successful Planners | Up & Coming Planners | Secure Doers | Stressed Avoiders | Live-for-Today Avoiders |
|---|---|---|---|---|---|
| N | 237 | 298 | 229 | 212 | 165 |
| (%) | (21) | (26) | (20) | (19) | (14) |
| **Vision of Retirement** | Possess a strong vision with clear goals and aspirations | Similar to Successful Planners but with some uncertainty | Less goal-focused; willing to adjust lifestyle to resources | Worried about the future and money; not goal- or vision-oriented | Not focused on the future at all |
| **Interest in retirement and financial planning** | Enjoy planning and dealing with finances; derive satisfaction from managing money | Enjoy dealing with finances, planning, money management | Strong interest in saving for the future, not as concerned with planning or managing their money | Stressed out and confused by financial planning, money- but interested in learning more | Little interest in planning; not stressed; would rather "live for today" than "plan for tomorrow" |
| **Preparation for retirement** | Optimistic they will meet retirement goals; least concerned about having enough money | Not yet in a position to meet retirement goals but optimistic about the future | Optimistic about retirement; likely to save sufficiently for future | Pessimistic about having enough money for retirement | Have not considered retirement needs; have highest degree of confidence in Social Security |

| | | | | | |
|---|---|---|---|---|---|
| **Savings behavior/ deferral of gratification** | Disciplined savers; derive satisfaction from saving | Disciplined savers; enjoy savings process | Willing to save for future | Savings impeded by confusion, worry | Little satisfaction from saving; leisure time more valuable; retirement "too far away" |
| **Equity risk-taking** | Willing to take risks for higher return | Have made money in stocks, but are less confident than Successful Planners | Less willing to take equity market risk | Least confident of their investment skills | Middle-of-the-road attitudes toward risk-taking |
| **Sources of financial information** | Many-plan provider, media, Internet, adviser, employer | Many, like Successful Planners | Employer, plan provider, or adviser | Employer, plan provider | Employer, plan provider |
| **Other** | Older and more affluent; more active with the Internet | Younger than Successful Planners | Older and more affluent | Nonparticipants regret not having joined plan; participants wish they had started sooner | Somewhat younger than all other groups |

*Source*: Authors' computations.

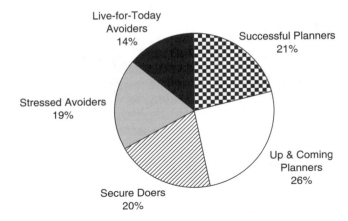

Figure 6-1. Five "money attitude" segments.
*Source*: The Vanguard Group (2002).

interviews, during which the research team observed a pattern of individuals having strong interest in savings, particularly out of a sense of responsibility or duty toward themselves or others. The term "Secure" originates from this segment's relative aversion to stock market risk. Secure Doers appear to have a high level of interest in saving, but they are more security-conscious in their investment strategy and less willing to take on equity market risk. Their orientation to saving behavior, rather than retirement planning, is also reflected in a number of other attitudinal characteristics. Individuals in this segment are not particularly interested in money management, and retirement and financial planning; there would be few personal finance hobbyists in this segment. Unlike the two Planner categories, who have strong goal-oriented visions of retirement, Secure Doers do not appear to have a strong view of their retirement goals. In fact, they appear to be more willing to adjust their lifestyle to available resources rather than pursue a given set of goals with discipline.

The fourth segment is the *Stressed Avoiders*, which accounted one-fifth (19 percent) of the retirement plan population. Stressed Avoiders find financial matters to be a source of stress, anxiety, and confusion—all of which combine to create obstacles to planning a successful financial future. They do not appear to be particularly goal-oriented in thinking about the future. Worry, concern, stress, and pessimism are the emotions which most often surface when they confront financial issues. Of all of the segments, this group is least confident in its investing skills.

The final segment is the *Live-for-Today Avoiders*, which represented 14 percent of the retirement plan population. This group is not necessarily overwhelmed by the emotional aspects of money and retirement planning, but instead is uninterested in the future at all. Since they live for the present, they derive little or no satisfaction from saving for the future; leisure time is more valuable than any time spent on planning efforts.

## Demographic and Behavioral Characteristics

Besides differing in attitudes, the segments also differ in terms of certain demographic and behavioral characteristics (see Table 6-4). Plan participation

TABLE 6-4 Attitude Segments—Behavioral and Demographic Characteristics

|  | Successful Planners | Up & Coming Planners | Secure Doers | Stressed Avoiders | Live-for-Today Avoiders |
|---|---|---|---|---|---|
| N | 237 | 298 | 229 | 212 | 165 |
| (%) | (21) | (26) | (20) | (19) | (14) |
| *Behavioral characteristics* |  |  |  |  |  |
| Plan participation rate[a] (%) | 90 | 81 | 71 | 62 | 64 |
| Full participants[b] (%) | 51 | 29 | 26 | 19 | 26 |
| % invested in equities[c] | 76 | 72 | 56 | 55 | 62 |
| Mean number of investment exchanges in 12 month period[d] | 2.4 | 2.6 | 1.4 | 1.6 | 2.0 |
| Mean number of contacts to Vanguard[e] | 18.8 | 9.6 | 2.7 | 6.6 | 5.9 |
| % who have taken a loan[f] | 11 | 20 | 9 | 17 | 20 |
| *Demographic characteristics* |  |  |  |  |  |
| Age[g] | Older (45) | (42) | Older (45) | Younger (43) | Younger (43) |
| Income[h] (in$) | Higher income (93K) | (61K) | (67K) | Lower income (55K) | Lower income (47K) |
| Occupation[i] | More professional/ managerial | — | — | More general labor | More general labor, skilled trades |
| Education[j] | More grad school | — | More grad school | — | More high school or less |

TABLE 6-4 *Continued.*

| | Successful Planners | Up & Coming Planners | Secure Doers | Stressed Avoiders | Live-for-Today Avoiders |
|---|---|---|---|---|---|
| Gender[k] | — | — | — | More female | — |
| Race[l] | Smaller minority | — | — | Higher minority | Higher minority |
| Married (%)[m] | 85 | 73 | 76 | ↓63 | ↓64 |
| Job/plan tenure[n] | — | — | — | — | — |

[a] Participation rates among all segments are statistically significantly different, except for Stressed and Live-for-Today Avoiders.

[b] Participating at maximum allowed by plan (prior to 2001 pension reform). Successful Planner rate is statistically significant compared with all others; Up & Coming rate, compared with Stressed Avoiders; differences between Up & Coming Planners and two Avoider groups are not statistically significant.

[c] Exposure to equities is significantly higher among Successful Planners and Up & Coming Planners compared with others than among other segments.

[d] Both Planner segments are more likely to make exchanges within their accounts.

[e] Successful Planners have the highest frequency of contact with Vanguard compared with all other segments; Secure Doers, the lowest.

[f] Loan activity is significantly higher among Up & Coming Planners and Live-for-Today Avoiders.

[g] Successful Planners and Secure Doers were more likely to be older, while Live-for-Today Avoiders were more likely to be younger.

[h] Incomes of Successful Planners were statistically significantly higher than other segments, while incomes of Stressed Avoiders and Live-for-Today Avoiders were lower than the three other segments.

[i] While Successful Planners had a statistically significant higher proportion of professional or managerial employees, Stressed Avoiders and Live-for-Today Avoiders had higher proportions of general labor employees compared with most other segments.

[j] Successful Planners and Secure Doers had a somewhat higher proportion of graduate school training, while Live-for-Today Avoiders had a statistically significant higher high school or less population.

[k] While all segments were majority male, Stressed Avoiders was the only category with a statistically significant higher percentage of female gender.

[l] Minorities have a statistically higher representation in the two Avoider segments, albeit small, than in any other segment.

[m] Marriage rates among Successful Planners were statistically significantly higher; while both Avoiders had significantly lower rates of marriage.

[n] There were no statistically significant differences in job or plan tenure, with the average person at their current company between 11 and 13 years, and the average participant in their employer's plan for 8–9 years.

*Note*: This table summarizes key behavioral and demographic characteristics of each segment. Major statistically significant differences in variables among the segments at a 95% confidence level are described in the footnotes. Behavioral characteristics were drawn from administrative systems; demographic characteristics, from survey responses. No entry under the demographic variables means that there were no statistically significant differences compared with all other groups.

*Source*: Authors' computations.

rates, our primary metric of saving behavior, varied significantly across four of the five groups—from a high of 90 percent for Successful Planners to a low of 62 percent for Stressed Avoiders. (Participation rates for the two groups of Avoiders, at 62 percent for Stressed Avoiders and 64 percent for Live-for-Today Avoiders, were not statistically significantly different.) At the extremes, Successful Planners are more likely to be older, better paid, have better jobs or education, and have larger retirement savings than other segments. They are also the most likely to be active in managing and interacting with their accounts. These seem to include many of the characteristics of the "over-confident males" that Barber and O'Dean (2001) have analyzed (though in our survey, two-thirds of the respondents were male and so it was not possible to differentiate the impact of gender on a statistically significant basis).

At the other extreme, Live-for-Today Avoiders were more likely to be younger, lower paid, with manual or labor jobs and lower levels of education. Both Avoider categories were somewhat more likely to be minority rather than white; women were somewhat more prominent in the Stressed Avoider category.

In reviewing these results, several caveats should be kept in mind. First, each segment is a statistical construct, and the boundaries are not precisely defined. Thus, individuals and typical demographic groups will not fit perfectly into a given category. Second, the results represent a snapshot in time, raising several interesting questions of whether attitudes change over time and what factors could influence those changes. These remain for future research.

An important question raised by these segments is causality: Do psychological states determine financial outcomes, or is it the other way around? For example, in the data there is a rough correlation between assets, income, age, and "planner" status. Is this because people who are older or who accumulate more assets become more motivated around appropriate financial attitudes and behavior, and so become more planner-like? Or is it that planners are more likely to be richer, given their vision of retirement, disciplined savings approach, and equity market orientation? Another way to restate this question is that, perhaps with sufficient time and resources, both financial and educational, most people actually become planners. However, for some groups of people, there is never sufficient time and resources. They come to realize the importance of planner attributes too late in their lives (if at all).

One critique of attitudinal segmentation studies is that, in the end, it is behavior that is relevant, not personal beliefs and attitudes. As long as individuals end up saving something, whether they express an interest in saving or other financial activities per se may be immaterial. Research on the adequacy of saving rates casts some doubt on the belief that workers are saving adequately in the first place. Moore and Mitchell (2000) note that about

40 percent of pre-retirees appearing to be ill-prepared to achieve some reasonable measure of retirement security. Moreover, it is clear from the data we analyze that attitudes do matter and are linked to specific behavioral differences. Overall, participants with certain "desirable" sets of retirement saving attitudes do behave differently from other participants, in terms of plan participation, investment decisions, and engagement with their retirement plan account.

## Implications of Money Attitudes

Our findings indicate that at least half of the plan population does not conform to a "planner" set of attitudes and expectations. Such a result has important implications for the ways in which retirement plans are designed. Here, we highlight three: The degree of participant direction in retirement saving plans (and of employee choice in benefit packages broadly); the role of negative versus positive elections in plan design and public policy; and the design of financial education programs, both in the workplace and as part of a national campaign to promote financial literacy.

### Degree of Participant Direction

Participant-directed pension plans are based on an implicit model of the "worker as planner," with each employee seen as a proactive, engaged agent making fully informed decisions about their financial futures. But the "money attitudes" research suggests that the "planner" model does not fit all.

If a large subset of the working population fails to take an active interest in retirement planning, retirement plans that rely on participants' voluntary decisions will be limited in their ability to assure retirement security. And unfortunately, a sizeable fraction of plan participants appears to have little or no interest in retirement planning or in plan participation. For instance, the average participation rate for participant-directed DC plans was approximately 75 percent in 2001. Using plan-weighted data, if participation is calculated across the entire DC system, participation rates are closer to 66 percent (Vanguard, 2002c). Defined contribution plans rely upon a well-intended incentives-based approach to promoting savings including federal 401(k) tax deductions, employer matching contributions, and workplace education programs. Nevertheless, such incentives fall on some deaf ears, with one out of three eligible participants failing to join their workplace saving plan. One way employers can address the problem of inadequate plan participation is to offer employer contributions that are not contingent on voluntary savings decisions by participants. Many large and medium-sized employers already do this, either through DB programs or other DC plans with employer contributions (e.g. money purchase and profit-sharing plans). For policymakers, the "money attitudes" research raises two questions: What incentives can be implemented to increase employer contributions which are not contingent on participant saving behavior? And to what extent should some baseline employer contributions be mandatory? Mandating employer contributions creates disincentives for employers to adopt plans, a concern that must be weighed against the sizeable population not voluntarily taking advantage of existing workplace plans.

Yet, this research does not suggest a retreat from plans relying on voluntary participant contributions and a shift to solely employer-funded plans. This is because in our sample, at least half the population appears to have the attributes needed to optimize decisions in a participant-centric plan. Many others who are not classified as planners still do make voluntary contributions to a 401(k) plan. The question, it seems, is not whether public policy or employer plan design should take an "either–or" approach to participant versus employer direction in plan design. Rather, it is to what degree both types of plan designs should be encouraged in order to optimize the retirement system for workers with a variety of attitudinal types.

Our research also suggests that a limit on the number of choices offered to workers might make sense. Iyengar and Lepper (2000) raise questions about the demotivating effects of too much choice in the choice among consumer products, and Iyengar, Huberman, and Jiang (Chapter 5, this volume) extend the choice research to retirement plans. This work underscores the fact that too much choice within a 401(k) plan can modestly reduce plan participation rates. While some choice is better than none, it is not at all clear that an ever-expanding set of choices is superior to a reasonable but small menu of choices. In the employee benefits world, choice is proliferating—in consumer-directed health care plans, in choice among types of retirement plan, and in proposed models for the reform of employee benefits law.[10] These models all rely on the success of a participant-directed DC plan as their reference point. Our research suggests that not all individuals with have the appropriate attitudes thought necessary to make successful decisions in such programs.

## Negative Elections and Default Choices—The "auto-pilot 401(k)"

The behavioral economics literature cited earlier suggests a possible course of action, both in terms of policy and plan design, for addressing workers' varying "money attitudes." To address the fact that large groups of workers do not conform to the planner model of behavior, both policy and plan design could seek to encourage negative, rather than positive, choices—default outcomes, rather than proactive decisionmaking.

Consider a possible reformulation of the traditional 401(k) plan along negative-decision lines. First, all eligible participants would be automatically enrolled in the workplace plan. Because automatically enrolled participants remain at low savings rates, as Madrian and Shea (2001) have noted, participants' deferral rates would need to be increased automatically over time, using the Benartzi and Thaler (2004) Save More Tomorrow concept. For workers who "opted out" of a savings program, there could be a provision for re-enrollment after a certain time in order to promote savings behavior on an ongoing basis. In terms of investment choices, fiduciary law might be amended to encourage sponsors to select diversified balanced portfolios, perhaps defined by current age, as default investment options. Alternatively, the law itself might include statutory definitions of default options, eliminating much of the employer decisionmaking and liability in the selection of investment defaults. We call this the "auto-pilot 401(k)" in which optimal savings and investment decisions occur by default, without the active engagement of the employee. Auto-pilot 401(k)s, in effect, attempt to reduce the degree of active decisionmaking in participant-directed plans for many workers, while preserving choice and flexibility for others.

Auto-pilot plan designs would come at some cost. Provider and employer administrative costs would rise, as many small accounts would be created through automatic enrollment. Absent any change in plan design, employers would face additional costs for matching contributions for the newly enrolled participants who were previously non-participating. One way to offset some of those costs might be to make these automatic features an alternative to nondiscrimination testing. Nondiscrimination testing is designed to ensure that plans are not created exclusively to benefit high-paid workers, and that low-paid workers participate in sufficient numbers. Since automatic enroll-ment, automatic savings increases and age-based default balanced funds would likely achieve these same public policy goals, such a set of features could be a "safe harbor" alternative to traditional nondiscrimination testing.

The idea is that when a sizeable group of workers is disinterested in retirement and financial planning, plan design can be rethought so that doing nothing—being non-proactive, demotivated or uninterested when it comes to money and finances—can result in a near-optimal (if not optimal) retirement outcome as well.

## Financial Literacy and Education

Current financial education programs in the workplace seem designed to meet the needs of Planners. Implicit in the delivery of extensive financial education materials is the idea of a motivated, interested audience. But our attitudinal segments reveal that at least half of the audience has a low level of interest in the topics addressed by such programs. Paradoxically, while education seems targeted at the Planner attitudinal segments, workplace education is only one source of financial information for them. They also turn to the general media, the Internet, financial publications, advisers, and others to make financial decisions.

Our results suggest that financial literacy programs, whether in the work-place or some other venue be refocused away from Planners, who are more naturally inclined to seek out many sources of financial information, and toward other attitudinal segments, where reliance on employer education is greater. This seems particularly true of enrollment materials. Emphasizing the importance of retirement and providing extensive investment education in enrollment materials seem ideally suited to the interests of Successful or Up & Coming Planners (and possibly to sponsors and policymakers who are themselves Planners). Yet, it runs exactly contrary to the present-day focus on Live-for-Today Avoiders, and it can even increase the level of financial complexity thought to be a hurdle to Stressed Avoiders.

Financial education could be redirected in three specific ways. First, education materials might increasingly focus on present-day benefits. Tangible benefits, such as matching contributions, or intangible benefits such as "making the most of your money today" or "avoiding financial confusion," are techniques to appeal attitudinally to non-Planners (Selnow, Chapter 2, this volume). Second, educational materials need to be vastly shortened simplified. Non-Planner audiences simply were not interested in an extensive tutorial on money management or retirement planning. And finally, education must be explicit and directive. Avoiders and even Secure Doers do not seem particularly interested in conceptual training in personal finance, while Planners relish it (Vanguard, 2002c). Indeed, for some participant segments, the "educational" model—in which educational activities result in specific attitudinal and behavioral changes—may no longer be suitable. For the non-Planner segments, a more suitable solution may be explicit savings and investment advice. Attitudinal segments may help improve the delivery of such advisory programs within DC programs. Advice programs that require little effort or complex data gathering are likely to appeal to Secure Doers and Avoiders. Perhaps the ideal approach for this audience would be a default fund or managed 401(k) account, in which investment decisions are fully delegated to a third party or service provider. Sophisticated advice capabilities on the Internet, especially those that require active involvement, are probably better suited to Planners. Attitudinal issues may be one reason that complex Internet tools have not been widely adopted by participants within retirement plans.

## Conclusions

With the growth of voluntary, participant-directed DC saving plans, expectations for the types of decisions made by workers have also risen. Like experienced financial planners, workers are now expected to optimize a series of saving, investment, tax, and spending decisions throughout their working and retirement years. Yet, participants' interests and attitudes towards important planning activities, like saving for the future, taking equity market risk, or developing a retirement plan, are quite heterogeneous. Only half of the retirement saver population can be thought of as possessing the "planner" characteristics needed to optimize retirement results in defined contribution plans, so the planner model does not fit all. The other half of the retirement plan population diverges from this "planner model" in important ways. We have identified five "money attitude" groups of workers—Successful Planners, Up & Coming Planners, Secure Doers, Stressed Avoiders, and Live-for-Today Avoiders—with distinct behavioral, demographic, and attitudinal preferences toward money and retirement planning.

The existence of these attitudinal segments has important implications for public policy, retirement plan design, and education and communications practices. First, it suggests a natural limit to the current model of participant direction, in which knowledgeable and motivated agents make well-informed choices about their future. A significant proportion of the population, it appears, is disinclined to be interested in the key activities or attitudes needed to make informed choices. While there may be educational or other techniques that will overcome this resistance, our research results suggest a tougher-than-anticipated road ahead for such efforts. Second, our research suggests that because not all participants are interested in making active and well-informed financial choices, there may be a greater role for negative elections, default choices, investment advice, and managed 401(k) accounts—that is, techniques designed to increase the level of "non-participant-direction" (or "other-person-direction") in participant-directed plans. Third, the results of this chapter suggest new approaches to financial education, with greater emphasis on simpler decisions, less information, reduced complexity, and fewer choices. This new approach is applicable whether education is provided in the workplace or as part of a public campaign for financial literacy.

## Notes

[1] Plan Sponsor (2002) notes that both communication materials and participant education are key attributes in the evaluation of retirement plan service vendors. In the public arena, the Department of Labor has sponsored a Retirement Education Savings Campaign and has published a 20-page guide to financial fitness; see www.dol.gov/ebsa/savingsmatters.html. The SEC's investor education programs have a prominent location on their website—see www.sec.gov. Information on the US Treasury's new Office of Financial Education can be found at www.treas.gov/offices/domestic-finance/financial-institution/fin_ed.html.

[2] As cited in Frederick, Loewenstein, and O'Donoghue (2002: 4).

[3] As cited in Frederick, Loewenstein, and O'Donoghue (2002: 6).

[4] See for instance Papke (1995), Papke and Poterba (1995), Clark and Schieber (1998), Even and MacPherson (1999) and Munnell, Sundén, and Taylor (2000).

[5] Papke (1995) and Bassett, Fleming, and Rodrigues (1998) suggest that it may be only the existence of an employer match, rather than its size, that influences savings behavior.

[6] See Munnell, Sundén, and Taylor (2000).

[7] In addition, we interviewed 15 plan sponsors about participant attitudes regarding money and financial planning.

[8] The interviewees were asked to select a Tarot card image representing their approach to money. Visualization techniques were also used earlier during the interviews: For example, interviewees were asked to close their eyes and visualize certain aspects of planning for retirement, such as the time when they first enrolled.

[9] Before the surveys were analyzed using cluster analysis, mean substitution was applied, meaning that respondents who failed to respond to a particular attitudinal statement were assigned the mean response. Attitude statements were also centered within a respondent, by subtracting the mean score for an attitude from each respondent's score. Centering the data removes the "yea-sayers" and "nay-sayers" from the sample—individuals who always respond at the extremes of a scale.

[10] See Macey and Young (2002). In their reform proposals, workers might have far-reaching discretion to direct employer and employee benefits contributions among a wide array of retirement, health, and wealth and other benefits choices.

# References

Barber, Brad M. and Terrance O'Dean. 2001. "Boys Will be Boys: Gender, Overconfidence, and Common Stock Investment." *Quarterly Journal of Economics* 116(1): 261–292.

Bassett, William F., Michael J. Fleming, and Anthony P. Rodrigues. 1998. "How Workers Use 401(k) Plans: The Participation, Contribution and Withdrawal Decisions," *National Tax Journal* 51(2): 263–289.

Bayer, Patrick J., B. Douglas Bernheim, and J. Karl Scholz. 1996. "The Effects of Financial Education in the Workplace: Evidence from a Survey of Employers." NBER Working Paper 5655.

Benartzi, Shlomo. 2001. "Excessive Extrapolation and the Allocation of 401(k) Accounts to Company Stock." *Journal of Finance* LVI(5): 1747–1764.

Benartzi, Shlomo and Richard Thaler. 2004. "Save More Tomorrow: Using Behavioral Economics to Increase Employee Saving." *Journal of Political Economy* 112(1) February: 164–187.

Bernheim, B. Douglas and Daniel M. Garrett. 1996. "The Determinants and Consequences of Financial Education in the Workplace: Evidence from a Survey of Households." Stanford University Department of Economics Working Paper 96-007.

Business Wire. 2002. "Senator Bob Dole to Inaugurate National Retirement Planning Week." November 18. www.retireonyourterms.org.

Choi, James, David Laibson, Brigitte Madrian, and Andrew Metrick. 2002a. "For Better or For Worse: Default Effects and 401(k) Savings Behavior." NBER Working Paper 8651.

——— 2002b. "Defined Contribution Pensions: Plan Rules, Participant Decisions, and the Path of Least Resistance." NBER Working Paper 8655.

Clark, Robert L. and Sylvester J. Schieber. 1998. "Factors Affecting Participation Rates and Contribution Levels in 401(k) Plans." In *Living with Defined Contribution Pensions*, eds. Olivia S. Mitchell and Sylvester J. Schieber. Philadelphia, PA: University of Pennsylvania Press, pp. 69–97.

Duflo, Esther and Emmanuel Saez. 2000. "Participation and Investment Decisions in a Retirement Plan: The Influence of Colleagues' Choices." NBER Working Paper 7735.

——— 2002. "The Role of Information and Social Interaction in Retirement Plan Decisions: Evidence from a Randomized Experiment." NBER Working Paper 8885.

Employee Benefit Research Institute (EBRI). 2002. *Retirement Confidence Survey.* www.ebri.org/rcs/2002/02rcssof.pdf.

Even, William E. and David A. Macpherson. 1999. "Employee Participation in 401(k) Plans." Pepper Institute Working Paper 99-54.

Frederick, Shane, George Loewenstein, and Ted O'Donoghue. 2002. "Time Discounting and Time Preference." *Journal of Economic Literature* 40(2): 351–401.

Gustman, Alan L. and Thomas L. Steinmeier. 2001. "Imperfect Knowledge, Retirement and Saving." NBER Working Paper 8406.

Hinz, Richard P. and John A. Turner. 1998. "Pension Coverage Initiatives: Why Don't Workers Participate?" In *Living with Defined Contribution Pensions*, eds. Olivia S. Mitchell and Sylvester J. Schieber. Philadelphia, PA: University of Pennsylvania Press: 17–37.

Iyengar, Sheena and Mark Lepper. 2000. "When Choice is Demotivating: Can One Desire too Much of a Good Thing?" *Journal of Personality and Social Psychology* 76: 995–1006.

John Hancock Financial Services. 2001. *Insight into Participant Investment Knowledge and Behavior.* Seventh Defined Contribution Plan Survey. Boston.

Laibson, David I. 1997. "Golden Eggs and Hyperbolic Discounting." *Quarterly Journal of Economics* 112(2) May: 443–478.

——, Andrea Repetto, and Jeremy Tobacman. 1998. "Self Control and Saving for Retirement." Brookings Papers on Economic Activity I: 91–196.

Macey, Scott and Gretchen Young. 2002. "The Future of Employee Benefits: A Call for Reform." *Benefits Law Journal* 15(2): 5–25.

Madrian, Brigitte C. and Dennis F. Shea. 2001. "The Power of Suggestion: Inertia in 401(k) Participation and Savings Behavior." *Quarterly Journal of Economics* 116(4): 1149–1187.

Marshall, Alfred. 1920. *Principles of Economics.* Macmillan and Co., Ltd. Library of Economics and Liberty.

Merrill Lynch. 2002. *The Merrill Lynch 2002 Retirement Survey: Examining America's Changing Attitudes, Expectations and Behavior.*

Moore, James F. and Olivia S. Mitchell. 2000. "Projected Retirement Wealth and Saving Adequacy." In *Forecasting Retirement Needs and Retirement Wealth*, eds. Olivia S. Mitchell, P. Brett Hammond, and Anna M. Rappaport. Philadelphia: University of Pennsylvania Press: 68–94.

Munnell, Alicia H., Annika Sundén, and Catherine Taylor. 2000. "What Determines 401(k) Participation and Contributions?" Center for Retirement Research (CRR) Working Paper 2000-12.

Papke, Leslie E. 1995. "Participation in and Contributions to 401(k) Pension Plans." *Journal of Human Resources* 30(2): 311–325.

—— and James M. Poterba. 1995. "Survey Evidence on Employer Match Rates and Employee Savings Behavior in 401(k) Plans." *Economic Letters* 49(3): 313–317.

Plan Sponsor. 2002. "2002 Plan Sponsor DC Survey." *Plan Sponsor* November: 38–78.

Vanguard. 2002*a. Vanguard Participant Monitor: Expecting Lower Market Returns in the Near Term.* Malvern, PA: Vanguard Center for Retirement Research.

——2002*b. How America Saves: A Report on Vanguard Defined Contribution Plans.* Malvern, PA: Vanguard Center for Retirement Research.

——2002*c. Using "Money Attitudes" to Enhance Retirement Communications.* Malvern, PA: Vanguard Center for Retirement Research.

# Chapter 7

# Employee Investment Decisions about Company Stock

*James J. Choi, David Laibson, Brigitte Madrian, and Andrew Metrick*

Recent high-profile cases have illustrated the dangers of employee investment in company stock. These debacles are unlikely to be the last ones, or even the most severe. Companies with more than 50 percent of retirement assets in company stock are common, and fractions over 80 percent continue to prevail at such large companies as Procter & Gamble, Anheuser-Busch, and Pfizer.[1]

The concentration of retirement wealth in company stock is a clear violation of diversification principles. Recently, several studies have quantified the economic costs of this concentration. Muelbroek (2002) uses a Sharpe-ratio approach and finds that the average diversification cost of company stock is about 42 percent of its value. Ramaswamy (2003) uses option-pricing techniques to compute the cost of insuring the extra risk of company stock. For a range of plausible parameter values, he finds that this insurance would be prohibitively expensive.[2]

Despite these high costs, companies continue to offer employee stock in their retirement plans. There are many potential explanations for this behavior, but none are entirely satisfying. For example, employers may believe that stock compensation is inexpensive relative to cash, that there are strong incentive or morale effects, or that friendly employees will aid management in a takeover or other proxy battle. Mitchell and Utkus (2003) review these arguments and find little evidence to support them. The only explanation with any significant empirical support is tax-driven: Dividends paid to certain employee ownership plans are tax-deductible at the corporate level. Liang and Weisbenner (2002) find a significant relationship between company stock fractions of total contributions and dividend payout. Nevertheless, this finding can explain only part of the puzzle, as many firms without any

The authors thank Hewitt Associates for their help in providing the data. They are particularly grateful to Lori Lucas and Jim McGhee at Hewitt. Choi acknowledges financial support from a National Science Foundation Graduate Research Fellowship. Laibson and Madrian acknowledge financial support from the National Institute on Aging (R01-AG-16605 and R29-AG-013020 respectively). Laibson also acknowledges financial support from the MacArthur Foundation.

dividends still have significant employee ownership of company stock in their plans.

Even when employers offer their stock, of course, it does not mean that employees must buy it. While many plans make matched contributions in company stock, and some of these plans restrict employees' rights to sell this stock for some period of time, there is still a significant amount of discretionary contributions to company stock. Benartzi (2001) was the first to investigate this behavior and provided an interesting explanation for it. Using a sample of about half of the S&P 500 companies, he found that discretionary contributions to company stock are positively correlated with the past returns on that stock. He posited that this correlation was due to employees' extrapolation of past returns when forming expectations about future returns. Liang and Weisbenner (2002) confirmed his result for a larger number of companies over a longer time period.

Both of these prior studies rely on firm-level data drawn from SEC filings, which report a firm's average contribution fraction to company stock. Thus, these studies use data for a large number of firms to analyze cross-sectional relationships between firm characteristics and employee discretionary contributions to company stock. Our analysis looks at some similar questions, but our approach is distinct and complementary: We use time-series variation in returns at three large firms' 401(k) plans, from 1992 to 2000, to identify the effect of returns on the company stock choices of 94,191 plan participants. Our objective is to use this time-series variation to better understand the mechanisms by which past returns influence employee investment. Specifically, we attempt to measure the extent of "feedback" investing in company stock, to analyze whether participants are momentum or contrarian investors. Momentum investors trade with a trend, adding to their holdings after high returns; contrarian investors do the opposite. An active finance literature has developed in the past few years to look at the empirical evidence on feedback trading.[3] By focusing on a salient asset class—company stock—we hope to make a contribution to this literature while at the same time providing useful insights for the policy debate on company stock investment.

## Description of Our Data

The data used to examine these patterns were provided by Hewitt Associates, a large benefits administration and consulting firm. From Hewitt's roster of clients, we identified three large companies, which we denote here as Alpha, Delta, and Gamma, which offered company stock as an investment option. We obtained detailed data on individual participant in each plan, with two components. The first is panel data on every transaction that occurred in the plans since Hewitt took over the plan administration. These data go from January 4, 1993 to October 20, 1999 for

Alpha; January 31, 1994 to January 26, 2000 for Delta; and April 3, 1996 to March 3, 2000 for Gamma. The second component of the data is cross-sectional, taken at year-end 1998 and 1999, which reports participant data on demographics, hire, and enrollment dates, and balance for all participants with a positive balance or plan activity in 1998 or 1999. We will refer to December 31, 1999 as the "final date." None of these companies are financial services or technology companies.[4]

Table 7-1 summarizes information on participants' demographic statistics who were active in the plans at the final date (a subset of the 94,191 total employees). The average plan balance for these participants was $89,172. The most comparable cross-sectional data to ours is the EBRI/ICI sample of 401(k) plans, which covers about 35 percent of the assets in the 401(k) universe. Holden and VanDerhei (2001) report that average plan balances at the end of 1999 are broken down by plan size, and they find that average plan balances are positively correlated with the number of participants in the plan (this is mainly because larger companies tend to have started plans earlier, thus giving more time for balances to be accumulated). For plans with over 10,000 participants—like all three of our plans—they report an average balance of $73,672, which is quite comparable.

Table 7-2 breaks down the contribution fraction and asset holdings into three non-disjoint asset classes. Company stock contribution fractions were approximately 17 percent at Alpha, 5 percent at Delta, 12 percent at Gamma, and 10 percent as a participant-weighted average across the three companies. The holdings in company stock were similar to the contribution fractions at Gamma, but they were significantly higher at Alpha (32 percent versus 17 percent) and Delta (8 percent versus 5 percent). The disparity at Alpha is partly due to the fact that Alpha made matching contributions in company stock and placed some tenure restrictions on selling these contributions. Like most clients of Hewitt Associates, Delta and Gamma did not match in company stock and placed no restrictions on the holdings of company stock.

TABLE 7-1 Demographic Summary Statistics

| | |
|---|---|
| Average age | 45.0 |
| Average salary ($) | 55,830 |
| Average tenure at company (years) | 15.8 |
| Average elected contribution rate (%) | 8.73 |
| Average plan balance ($) | 89,172 |
| Percent who traded in 1999 (%) | 39.3 |
| Total companies | 3 |
| Total participants (all years) | 94,191 |

*Note*: Unless otherwise noted, all figures are as of year-end 1999.

*Source*: Authors' calculations.

TABLE 7-2  Summary Statistics on Equity Holdings

|  |  | Company Stock (%) | Other Equities (%) | All Equities (%) |
|---|---|---|---|---|
| Company Alpha | Contributions | 16.6 | 51.8 | 68.4 |
|  | Holdings | 31.5 | 39.7 | 71.2 |
| Company Delta | Contributions | 4.5 | 49.6 | 54.1 |
|  | Holdings | 8.1 | 48.6 | 56.7 |
| Company Gamma | Contributions | 12.0 | 52.1 | 64.1 |
|  | Holdings | 11.4 | 53.5 | 64.8 |
| Participant-weighted total | Contributions | 9.9 | 50.8 | 60.7 |
|  | Holdings | 17.7 | 46.0 | 63.6 |

*Note*: Discretionary contributions and year-end balances held that in equities in 1999.

*Source*: Authors' calculations.

These holdings fractions are somewhat lower than the averages reported by Holden and VanDerwei (2001) using the EBRI/ICI database. They found that, among larger plans (>5,000 participants) with similar investment offerings to our sample companies, the average holding of company stock was 24 percent of the portfolio. Note, however, that many of the plans in this class of the EBRI/ICI sample were similar to company Alpha, in that they matched contributions in company stock and imposed some trading restrictions on these matched contributions. Nevertheless, even Alpha had lower company stock holdings than the average company that matched in company stock.

While the main focus of the chapter is on company stock, it is also useful to know the relationship between past returns and employee allocations to other asset classes. These relationships are not only interesting in themselves, but they are also important for knowing whether changes in company stock investments crowded out other equities. We consider two other asset classes in the chapter: "Total equity" includes all equity holdings, domestic and international, including company stock,[5] and "other equity," which is total equity minus company stock.

Our focus on the initial contribution fractions to these asset classes, subsequent changes in these contribution fractions, and trades across the classes. Before turning to these analyses, it is useful to examine the empirical frequency of changes and trades. Figure 7-1 plots the likelihood of ever having made a change to contribution fractions, or a trade as a function of tenure in the plan. By 3 years after initial enrollment, almost half percent of participants had made at least one change to their initial contribution fraction, and 47 percent had made a trade.[6] These two groups overlap significantly, so that their union comprises only 58 percent of the full sample. By 6 years after enrollment, these percentages were over 70 percent for either of the two activities separately, and 80 percent for either.

Figure 7-2 plots the frequency of trades per year for all individuals that had at least 3 years' participation as of the final date. Within this whole

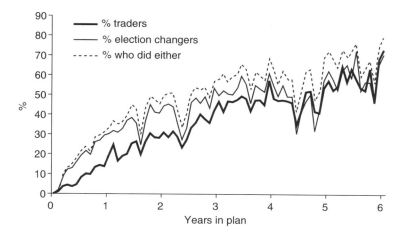

Figure 7-1. Likelihood of trading, changing elections, or doing either at least once, by tenure in plan, 12/31/1992 to 3/6/2000.

*Notes*: We examine all people for whom we have data since their initial enrollment in the plans. The graph depicts the percent of participants who have made at least one trade, changed their discretionary contribution allocations at least once, or done either, plotted against the number of years we observe them in the plan.

*Source*: Authors' calculations.

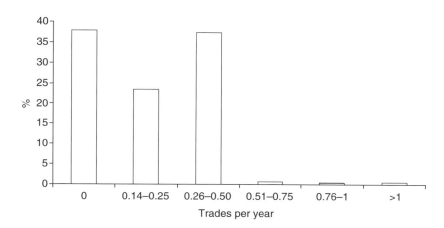

Figure 7-2. Histogram of participant trades per year, 1999 participants.

*Notes*: We examine all people who are active in the plans as of year-end 1999 and who have been participating for at least three years. We divide the total number of times a participant has traded in our data by the number of years we observe the participant. The graph is a histogram of this ratio.

*Source*: Authors' calculations.

group, 38 percent never made a trade. The next highest grouping was between 0.26 and 0.50 trades per year, with 37 percent of participants falling into this range. Very few participants made more than half a trade per year. Overall, these trading frequencies are somewhat higher than for the typical firm in the Hewitt universe, most likely because these firms were "early adopters" of the Internet channel for trading and other participant activities (Choi et al., 2002*a*).

## Analysis of Initial Contribution Fractions

To investigate the initial contribution fraction, we use a Tobit regression equation of the following form,

$$Y_i = \alpha + \beta X_i + \varepsilon_i, \tag{1}$$

where $Y_i$ is the fraction of company stock (censored below at 0 and above at 1) other equity, or total equity out of the total contribution: $X_i$ is a vector of firm-level and participant-level characteristics that may explain the cross-sectional pattern of flow decisions; and $\varepsilon_i$ is a participant-level error term. While we employ panel-data notation to distinguish among participants and initial dates, these regressions used only one observation per participant. The sample included every participant with positive balances or plan activity in 1998 or 1999. For each member of the sample, we included a single observation made on the date he first enrolled in their plan, and all explanatory variables for that participant $(X_i)$ are measured on that same date.

We include several firm-level variables in the $X_i$ vector. The main variables of interest are the past returns on company stock and on the overall stock market. Since we seek to separate common shocks (stock market returns) and firm-specific shocks (company stock returns), we include two past return variables. *SP500* is the past return for the S&P 500 in the one year (253 trading days) preceding the enrollment of participant $i$. That is, if participant $i$ enrolled on date $t$, then *SP500$_i$* is the return from trading date $t - 253$ to trading date $t - 1$. *CSTOCK$_i$* is the excess return over the S&P 500 for the company stock of participant $i$. Like *SP500*, it is measured over the preceding 253 trading days. Thus, all participants who enrolled on the same date $t$ will have identical *SP500* values; all participants who enrolled on the same date $t$ at the same company will have identical *CSTOCK* values. For notational convenience, we drop the $i$ subscripts for the remainder of this discussion. Previous research suggests that investment behavior is also influenced by the variance of past returns. Thus, we include two variance measures in $X$. *Std(SP500)* and *Std(CSTOCK)* are the standard deviations of the daily returns on the S&P 500 and company stock over the 253 trading days preceding the enrollment of participant $i$. Finally, we include a separate fixed effect and trend for each company, and omit a regression constant term.

We also include several participant-level variables as elements of $X$. Consistent with past work, we posit that total equity fractions are related to age, probably in a hump-shaped relationship with equity fractions first increasing and then decreasing later in life. (Consistent relationships across studies have been elusive in the literature, however.[7]) We include *Age* and *Age²* as elements of $X$. In addition, several studies show that overall equity holdings are positively related to salary; including Holden and VanDerhei (2001). For company stock, however, they find little relationship between salary and company stock fractions, with just a hint of slight negative tilt at the highest salary levels. Since we lack data on wealth, we rely on salary as a proxy and include the log of annualized salary for the year of enrollment as an element of $X$.

Company stock contributions may also be related to job tenure. Workers with longer tenure at enrollment could differ from other participants along several dimensions. Since they have been at the company longer, they may have more human capital dedicated to the company, which should induce lower contributions to company stock, other things equal. On the other hand, they may have a greater loyalty to the company and feel more of a duty to invest in company stock. Finally, workers who first participate later in their careers may have waited to do so because they are less financially sophisticated. This lower sophistication may be correlated with poorer diversification and higher contributions to company stock. The relative importance of these different factors is an empirical question, though Holden, VanDerhei, and Quick (2000) report a positive relationship in their study. Accordingly we include a variable, *TENURE*, which is the log of 1 + job tenure (in years), as an element of $X$.

Estimated coefficients are reported in Table 7-3. The dependent variable is the percent of the participant's pay invested in company stock in column 1, other equity in column 2, and total equity in column 3. The results show a strong impact of past returns on the initial contribution fractions to company stock. The coefficients on both *SP500* and *CSTOCK* are positive and significant when the dependent variable is company stock (column 1); conversely, the coefficients on these two variables are negative and significant when the dependent variable is other equity (column 2). These respective coefficients are positive but insignificant for total equity (column 3).

This pattern of results suggests that when company stock returns are high, newly enrolled participants contribute a higher fraction of their flows to company stock and a lower fraction of their flows to other equity; on net, the fraction of flows allocated to all equity (total equity) tends to cancel. Thus, these past returns—both the marketwide (*SP500*) and company-specific (*CSTOCK*)—have mostly a compositional effect on overall equity holdings.

TABLE 7-3  Initial Contribution Allocation, 11/30/1992 to 2/17/2000, as a Function of Asset Returns Prior to Plan Enrollment

| | Company Stock | Other Equities | All Equities |
|---|---|---|---|
| SP500 | 0.80** | −0.46** | 0.04 |
| | (0.07) | (0.06) | (0.07) |
| CSTOCK | 0.45** | −0.14** | 0.07 |
| | (0.04) | (0.03) | (0.04) |
| Std(SP500) | −12.76* | −3.36 | −2.21 |
| | (5.16) | (4.10) | (4.79) |
| Std(CSTOCK) | −12.13** | −2.47 | 0.39 |
| | (3.55) | (2.91) | (3.41) |
| Salary | −0.08** | 0.16** | 0.11** |
| | (0.01) | (0.01) | (0.01) |
| Age/100 | 0.02 | 0.26 | 0.24 |
| | (0.50) | (0.41) | (0.48) |
| $Age^2$/1000 | 0.04 | −0.09 | −0.05 |
| | (0.06) | (0.05) | (0.06) |
| Tenure | 0.02* | −0.06** | −0.04** |
| | (0.01) | (0.01) | (0.01) |
| Company Trend α | 0.02** | 0.02** | 0.02** |
| | (0.01) | (0.00) | (0.00) |
| Company Trend δ | −0.08** | 0.17** | 0.14** |
| | (0.01) | (0.01) | (0.01) |
| Company Trend γ | 0.07** | 0.06** | 0.08** |
| | (0.02) | (0.02) | (0.02) |
| σ(ε) | 0.76** | 0.69** | 0.80** |
| | (0.01) | (0.01) | (0.01) |

*Significant at the 5% level.
**Significant at the 1% level.

Notes: The dependent variable in column 1 is the percent of the participant's first payroll contribution that went to company stock, the dependent variable in column 2 is the percent of the participant's first payroll contribution that went to other equities, and the dependent variable in column 3 is the percent of the participant's first payroll contribution that went to all equities. Coefficients shown are for tobit regressions censored at 0 and 1. SP500 is the cumulative return on the S&P 500 for the 253 trading days prior to the participant's enrollment in the plan. CSTOCK is the cumulative return in excess of the S&P 500 on company stock for the 253 trading days prior to participant enrollment. Std(SP500) and Std(CSTOCK) are the standard deviations of the S&P 500 and company stock returns, respectively, over the 253 trading days prior to the participant's enrollment. Salary is the log of annual salary in the year of enrollment (in 1999 CPI-deflated dollars), Age is the participant's age at the time of enrollment, $Age^2$ is the square of Age, and Tenure is the log of one plus the years between the participant's original hire date and plan enrollment date. Company Trend x is the years between December 31, 1980 and the participant's enrollment if the participant is in Company x, and zero otherwise. σ(ε) is the standard deviation of the latent variable's residual. Coefficients on fixed-effect company dummies and a constant are not shown. Standard errors are reported in parentheses below the point estimates.

Source: Authors' calculations.

For the other independent variables, we find results consistent with previous studies. The coefficients on *age* and *age*$^2$ (column 3), while not significant, are consistent with a hump-shaped relationship between the total equity fraction and age. The relationship between salary and total equity is positive and significant, while the relationship between salary and company stock fraction is negative and significant.

One possible criticism of these results is that the standard errors may be understated. If firm-specific shocks induce correlated behavior across participants enrolling around the same time, then the assumption of cross-sectionally independent residuals would be violated, and the standard errors would be biased downward. For example, if firms changed their communication strategies to new participants, then these new strategies could induce correlated behavior. In this case, it would appear that we have more independent observations than we really do.

A comment is in order regarding this possibility. First, the regression specification controls for firm-specific differences in average behavior (with fixed effects) and for firm-specific changes in this average behavior over time (with trend variables for each firm). To also control for firm-specific shocks would require a specification of the correlation structure induced by such shocks, and this requires imposing more structure on the model which may not be appropriate. Instead, we perform a simple robustness check by assuming an extreme case: perfect correlation for all participants who enroll on the same day. To do this, we compute the average percentage allocated to each asset class by all participants who enrolled on each day. We then perform a separate time-series regression of these averages for each firm on the firm-specific independent variables used in equation (1). Furthermore, we allow for error correlation across days by computing Newey–West (1987) robust standard errors. Even in this extreme case, the evidence confirms that past returns affect contribution allocations.

The strongest evidence is for the company stock fraction, where two of the three firms show a positive and significant impact of past company stock returns on the company stock fraction, and one of the companies shows a positive and significant impact of past S&P 500 returns.[8] For other equity, the results are consistent with participant-level evidence in Table 7-3: Coefficients on company stock are negative and significant for two firms, and the coefficients on S&P 500 are negative (but insignificant) for all three firms. For total equity, these results again appear to cancel, with no strong pattern to the coefficient signs. Thus, it appears that past returns have mainly a compositional effect within total equity as for the individual-level results in Table 7-3, with high past returns leading to higher fractions allocated to company stock and lower fractions allocated to other equity.

## Analysis of Changes in Contribution Fractions

After examining snapshots of flows and the impact of past returns on these snapshots, we now turn to an examination of the determinants of the changes in these flows. To explore how past returns affect changes to flow fractions, we shift attention away from returns preceding enrollment to focus on returns preceding specific changes.

Table 7-4 summarizes the results of Logit regressions for the probability that a participant boosts his company stock fraction (column 1), other equity fraction (column 2), and total equity fraction (column 3). The dependent variable is an indicator variable equal to one if the fraction is increased and zero otherwise. Explanatory variables are as before except that *SP500* and *CSTOCK* represent for the year immediately preceding the contribution fraction change. The sample includes every change made by any participant who was active in the plans at year-ends 1998 or 1999.[9]

The results demonstrate more evidence of the powerful impact of past returns on participant behavior. As in the previous section, that the coefficient on *CSTOCK* is again positive and significant for the company stock regressions (column 1). In this case, however, the coefficient is also positive (and nearly significant) for other equities, so it appears that company stock does not crowd out other equities when contributions are changed. The net effect of *CSTOCK* on total equity is positive and significant (column 3). Another contrast with Table 7-3 is that the coefficient on *SP500* is negative and significant for company stock (column 1) and is positive and significant for the total equity fraction. In this case, high returns on the marketwide component of company stock returns induce a shift away from company stock and towards other equity, with a new effect of shifts towards equity and away from other assets (column 3). Overall, participants act like momentum investors for total equity.

As in the previous section, there may be concern that the standard errors in Table 7-4 could be understated, due to firm-specific shocks. To check robustness, we again collapse all participant observations on each trading day down to a single observation for each firm. To do this, we construct a new dependent variable, $Y_{mnt}$, for each asset class $m$ (company stock, other equity, or total equity) at each firm $n$ on every trading date $t$. $Y_{mnt}$ is a fraction, where the numerator is the number of participants in firm $n$ who increased their flow fraction to asset $m$ on date $t$, minus the number of participants in firm $n$ who made an allocation change to any fund on date $t$ but did not increase their flow fraction to asset $m$. The denominator is all participants at firm $n$ who made any allocation change on date $t$. We then estimate separate time series regressions for each firm, to determine whether the qualitative results from Table 7-4 also hold here. The answer is yes: several coefficients are significant and have the same sign as their analogues in Table 7-4.[10] These significant coefficients are negative for one firm on *SP500* and positive for two firms for *CSTOCK* in the company stock

TABLE 7-4  Probability of Increasing Contribution Fraction, 12/31/1992 to 3/3/2000, as a Function of Asset Returns Prior to the Election Change

|  | Company Stock | Other Equities | All Equities |
|---|---|---|---|
| SP500 | −2.09** | 2.85** | 1.02** |
|  | (0.10) | (0.08) | (0.08) |
| CSTOCK | 0.59** | 0.06 | 0.23** |
|  | (0.04) | (0.03) | (0.03) |
| Std(SP500) | −148.70** | 39.67** | −47.97** |
|  | (5.45) | (4.58) | (4.60) |
| Std(CSTOCK) | 1.62 | −5.40 | 16.49** |
|  | (3.97) | (3.42) | (3.40) |
| Salary | −0.14* | 0.02 | −0.09** |
|  | (0.02) | (0.02) | (0.02) |
| Total Balances | −0.14** | −0.08** | −0.13** |
|  | (0.01) | (0.01) | (0.01) |
| Age /100 | 2.66** | 3.73** | 4.18** |
|  | (0.69) | (0.58) | (0.58) |
| $Age^2/1000$ | −0.23** | −0.47** | −0.40** |
|  | (0.08) | (0.07) | (0.07) |
| Tenure | −0.01 | 0.04** | 0.18** |
|  | (0.01) | (0.01) | (0.01) |
| Company Trend $\alpha$ | 0.40** | −0.36** | −0.20** |
|  | (0.01) | (0.01) | (0.01) |
| Company Trend $\delta$ | 0.02 | −0.10** | −0.02** |
|  | (0.01) | (0.01) | (0.01) |
| Company Trend $\gamma$ | 0.22** | −0.00 | −0.23** |
|  | (0.01) | (0.01) | (0.01) |

\* Significant at the 5% level.
\*\* Significant at the 1% level.

*Notes*: This table presents the results of a binary logit regression of the probability a particip-ant increases the fraction of his or her contribution to company stock (column 1), other equities (column 2), and all equities (column 3), conditional on making a change to his or her contribution allocations. *SP500* is the cumulative return on the S&P 500 for the 253 trading days prior to the participant's first contribution after an election change. *CSTOCK* is the cumulative return in excess of the S&P 500 on company stock for the 253 trading days prior to the post-change contribution. *Std(SP500)* and *Std(CSTOCK)* are the standard devia-tions of the S&P 500 and company stock returns, respectively, over the 253 trading days prior to the post-change contribution. *Salary* is the log of annual salary in the year of the post-change contribution, and *Total Balances* is the log of total balances in the plan in the calendar month prior to the change, both in 1999 CPI-deflated dollars. *Age* is the particip-ant's age at the time of the post-change contribution, $Age^2$ is the square of *Age*, and *Tenure* is the log of one plus the years between the participant's original hire date and the post-change contribution. *Company Trend x* is the years between December 31, 1980 and the par-ticipant's post-change contribution if the participant is in company *x*, and zero otherwise. Coefficients on fixed-effect company dummies and a constant are not shown. Standard errors are reported in parentheses below the point estimates.

*Source*: Authors' calculations.

regressions; positive for two firms on *SP500* and negative for one firm on *CSTOCK* in the other equity regressions; and positive for one firm on *SP500* in the total equity regressions. Meanwhile, no coefficients are significant with the opposite sign from their analogues in Table 7-4.

## Analysis of Trading Behavior

The previous sections analyzed the determinants of contribution fractions–investment flows—to company stock and other equity. Many researchers focus on flows because these data allow for the cleanest test of the impact of past returns on investment decisions. By contrast, studies of asset holdings and past returns suffer from an obvious problem: High returns through price appreciation on any given asset will tend to increase the fraction of that asset in overall holdings, even if investors take no action. Nevertheless, it is asset *holdings*, not *flows*, that drive the long-run distribution of wealth. In an extreme scenario, one could imagine that all participants rebalance their holdings on a regular basis, so that differences in flows cause only minor long-run differences in their portfolio allocations.

For example, consider a participant who wanted to have 5 percent of his overall holdings in company stock. Suppose further that this participant allocated 20 percent to company stock at initial enrollment, because the participant had not yet decided to limit company stock to 5 percent of his or her overall portfolio. In later years, he or she could change the contribution fraction in company stock to 5 percent, but would still need to rebalance the participants' holdings periodically, to ensure that the 5 percent fraction was maintained. It may be the case that it is found to be simpler to rebalance his or her holdings periodically to 5 percent and ignore the flow component in the short run. If so, even though contribution fractions might appear to be influenced by returns prior to enrollment, we would not notice any long-run impact of these fractions on portfolio diversification.

To examine this possibility, we look at the rebalancing decision ("trades") with the same methods used to study changes in the flow fraction. We take every trade initiated by employees who have positive balances or plan activity in 1998 or 1999, and then we estimate a separate Logit regression for each asset class, where the dependent variable takes on a value of one if the trade increased holdings in that asset class and zero otherwise.[11]

Results appear in Table 7-5, and the key evidence appears in column 1. Here we see that returns one year prior to the trade on both components of company stock returns (*CSTOCK* and *SP500*) induce participants to trade *out* of company stock, but only for SP500 is there a significant effect. For both components, high returns induce participants to substitute away from company stock and towards other equities, with positive and significant coefficients on both components in column 2. These results are consistent with "profit-taking" behavior found in other studies where investors tended

TABLE 7-5  Probability of Trading into Asset Class, 1/4/1993 to 3/6/2000, as a Function of Asset Returns Prior to Trade

|  | Company Stock | Other Equities | All Equities |
|---|---|---|---|
| SP500 | −2.18** | 2.31** | 0.09 |
|  | (0.06) | (0.05) | (0.05) |
| CSTOCK | −0.01 | 0.31** | 0.07** |
|  | (0.02) | (0.02) | (0.02) |
| Std(SP500) | −159.70** | 71.28** | −62.22** |
|  | (4.24) | (3.86) | (3.71) |
| Std(CSTOCK) | −36.62** | −20.47** | −26.88** |
|  | (2.33) | (2.26) | (2.14) |
| Salary | 0.04** | 0.08** | 0.02 |
|  | (0.01) | (0.01) | (0.01) |
| Total Balances | −0.07** | −0.02** | −0.03** |
|  | (0.01) | (0.00) | (0.00) |
| Age/100 | 4.47** | −2.83** | 1.24** |
|  | (0.56) | (0.50) | (0.48) |
| $Age^2/1000$ | −0.52** | 0.26** | −0.09 |
|  | (0.06) | (0.05) | (0.05) |
| Tenure | 0.07** | −0.05** | 0.03** |
|  | (0.01) | (0.01) | (0.01) |
| Company Trend $\alpha$ | 0.50** | −0.26** | 0.15** |
|  | (0.01) | (0.01) | (0.01) |
| Company Trend $\delta$ | 0.10** | −0.12** | 0.05** |
|  | (0.01) | (0.01) | (0.01) |
| Company Trend $\gamma$ | 0.56** | −0.26** | 0.05** |
|  | (0.02) | (0.01) | (0.01) |

*  Significant at the 5% level.
** Significant at the 1% level.

Notes:  This table presents the results of a binary logit regression of the probability a participant makes a trade increasing his or her holdings in company stock (column 1), other equities (column 2), or all equities (column 3), conditional on the participant trading. SP500 is the cumulative return on the S&P 500 for the 253 trading days prior to the trade. CSTOCK is the cumulative returns in excess of the S&P 500 on company stock for the 253 trading days prior to the trade. Std(SP500) and Std(CSTOCK) are the standard deviations of the S&P 500 and company stock returns, respectively, over the 253 trading days prior to the trade. Salary is the log of annual salary in the year of the trade, and Total Balances is the log of total balances in the plan on the day of the trade, both in 1999 CPI-deflated dollars. Age is the participant's age at the time of the post-change contribution, $Age^2$ is the square of Age, and Tenure is the log of one plus the years between the participant's original hire date and the trade date. Company Trend x is the years between December 31, 1980 and the participant's trade if the participant is in company x, and zero otherwise. Coefficients on fixed-effect company dummies and a constant are not shown. Standard errors are reported in parentheses below the point estimates.

Source:  Authors' calculations.

to sell "winner" stocks and hold "loser" stocks (Odean, 1998; Grinblatt and Keloharju, 2001). Somewhat paradoxically, the net effect on total equity is positive and significant for the *CSTOCK* component, perhaps because rising prices on company stock induce participants to feel wealthier and less risk-averse.

We next perform an analogous analysis at the firm level, using the same approach described in previous sections. The dependent variable here is the number of participants who increased their holdings of the respective asset class on day *t*, minus the number of participants who made any trade but did not increase their holdings of the respective asset class on day *t*, all divided by the number of participants who made any trade on day *t*. We estimate separate regressions for each asset class for each firm. Even in this extreme case, this evidence indicates that past returns affect contribution allocations. Consistent with the results of Table 7-5, we find that the coefficient on *SP500* is negative and significant for one firm, and it is negative but insignificant for the other two. For other equity, the coefficients on *SP500* are positive and significant for all three firms. Overall, then, it appears that participants act as contrarians in their trades for company stock.

## Conclusions

Our analysis has studied the decisions of almost 100,000 individual 401(k) participants, seeking a better understanding of the determinants of employee discretionary investment in company stock. We study three companies, which include many participants, though the sample is still small relative to the universe of 401(k) participants, and it includes a relatively low level of company stock holdings. The great detail in the data, however, allows for an analysis at several different stages in the 401(k) process, and our main conclusion is that past returns matter at every stage. Thus, high returns on company stock for the year prior to enrollment induce participants to make higher initial contributions to company stock. Furthermore, high returns over any one-year period induce participants to increase these contribution fractions. High returns on company stock have the opposite effect on trading decisions: High past returns induce participants to reallocate their portfolios away from company stock and toward other equities. Thus, participants are momentum investors when making decisions about investment flows, but they appear to be contrarian investors when making trading decisions.

Our results allow us to build on the important work of Benartzi (2001), who found a positive relationship between past returns on company stock and current contributions to company stock, with the strongest results for past 10-year return, and weaker results for shorter horizons. We can explain that result as the combination of several forces. First, when participants join, they are influenced by the past returns, including the past one-year return. Some participants never alter their initial contribution fractions, and so while specific past years may seem influential at any point in time, the influence of the most recent year will be limited. Second, some participants do make change, but these changes are infrequent, and fewer than 40 percent make changes in any given year. These changes are influenced by prior returns, but the influence of the most recent year tends to be limited. Taken together, initial contributions and contribution changes are both influenced by one-year returns, but these years are spread out over a long period. Consequently, if we seek to understand the relationship between current contributions and past returns, the longer period appears better at the company level.

The most interesting and policy-relevant findings pertain to the relationship between asset holdings and past returns. Absent frequent rebalancing, high returns on assets will tend to increase the portfolio allocation to these assets. This makes it difficult to directly test for a relationship between asset holdings and past returns on these assets. The best we can do is to try to infer these relationships by looking at different decisions made by investors. Since most previous studies have used cross-sectional snapshots of holdings and contribution fractions, they have logically focused on the latter as the cleanest source of data. These studies find—as do we—that high past returns on company stock tend to increase contribution fractions to company stock. Nevertheless, the time-series data used here show that trading decisions may work to mitigate some of this effect. Since high past returns induce participants to substitute out of company stock, the strong relationship between past returns and contributions is less dangerous for asset allocation than it might appear.

## Notes

[1] The original source for these percentages is Schultz and Francis (2002), reported by Mitchell and Utkus (2003).

[2] For example, he notes that "a 25-year-old employee who wanted to buy an insurance policy on company stock that he cannot reallocate until he is 50 years old" would have to pay $739 per $1000 of value.

[3] For a discussion of this literature, see Goetzmann and Massa (2002).

[4] Several other recent papers have used participant-level panel data to explore different aspects of 401(k) investment behavior, but none of these papers have focused on company stock. See Agnew, Balduzzi, and Sunden (2003), Ameriks and Zeldes (2001), Choi et al. (2002a, b).

[5] Omitting international funds from the definitions of other equity and total equity does not qualitatively alter the results of the paper. For balanced funds, we include the fraction of that fund targeted to equities.

[6] These figures omit trades and allocation changes that were initiated by the plan administrators.

[7] Ameriks and Zeldes (2001) survey this literature and discuss new evidence from a survey of TIAA-CREF participants.

[8] Complete results are not presented here but are available from the authors on request.

[9] We omit changes made at Gamma in November 1996 and April 1998 because numerous funds were shut down in those months, so allocation changes then may have been due to the plan administration automatically shifting contributions away from the closed funds.

[10] Complete results are not presented here but are available from the authors on request.

[11] We omit trades that were initiated by plan administrators.

# References

Agnew, Julie, Pietro Balduzzi, and Annika Sunden. 2003. "Portfolio Choice, Trading, and Returns in a Large 401(k) Plan." *American Economic Review* L (93): 193–205.

Ameriks, John and Steve Zeldes. 2001. "How do Household Portfolios Vary with Age." Columbia University Working Paper. New York.

Benartzi, Shlomo. 2001. "Excessive Extrapolation and the Allocation of Company Stock to Retirement Accounts." *Journal of Finance* 56(5): 1747–1764.

Choi, James J, David Laibson, and Andrew Metrick. 2002*a*. "How Does the Internet Affect Trading? Evidence from Investor Behavior in 401(k) Plans," *Journal of Financial Economics* 64(3): 397–421.

Choi, James J., David Laibson, Brigitte Madrian, and Andrew Metrick. 2002*b*. "Defined Contribution Pensions: Plan Rules, Participant Choices, and the Path of Least Resistance." In *Tax Policy and the Economy*, ed. James Poterba. Cambridge: MIT Press: 67–113.

Goetzmann, William N. and Massimo Massa. 2002. "Daily Momentum and Contrarian Behavior of Index Fund Investors." *Journal of Financial and Quantitative Analysis* 37(3): 375–389.

Grinblatt, Mark, and Matti Keloharju. 2001. "What Makes Investors Trade?" *Journal of Finance* 56(2): 589–616.

Holden, Sarah and Jack VanDerhei. 2001. "401(k) Plan Asset Allocation, Account Balances, and Loan Activity in 1999." *Investment Company Institute Perspective* 7(1).

Holden, Sarah, Jack VanDerhei, and Carol Quick. 2000. "401(k) Plan Asset Allocation, Account Balances, and Loan Activity in 1998." *Investment Company Institute Perspective* 6(1): 1–24.

Liang, Nellie and Scott Weisbenner. 2002. "Investor Behavior and the Purchase of Company Stock in 401(k) Plans—The Importance of Plan Design." University of Illinois Working Paper. Champaign.

Mitchell, Olivia S. and Stephen P. Utkus. 2003. "The Role of Company Stock in Defined Contribution Plans." In *The Pension Challenge: Risk Transfers and Retirement Income Security*, eds. Olivia S. Mitchell and Kent Smetters. Oxford: Oxford University Press: 33–70.

Muelbroek, Lisa. 2002. "Company Stock in Pension Plans: How Costly Is It?" Harvard Business School Working Paper 02-058.

Odean, Terrance. 1998. "Are Investors Reluctant to Realize Their Losses?" *Journal of Finance* 53(5): 1775–1798.

Ramaswamy, Krishna. 2003. "Company Stock and Pension Plan Diversification." In *The Pension Challenge: Risk Transfers and Retirement Income Security*, eds. Olivia S. Mitchell and Kent Smetters. Oxford: Oxford University Press: 71–88.

Schultz, Ellen E. and Theo Francis. 2002. "Companies' Hot Tax Break: 401(k)s." *Wall Street Journal.* January 31: C1.

# Chapter 8

# Implications of Pension Plan Features, Information, and Social Interactions for Retirement Saving Decisions

*Esther Duflo and Emmanuel Saez*

There is growing concern in many nations about low levels of retirement saving. For most US families, employer pensions are the main source of cash income during retirement, over and above Social Security benefits (Poterba, Venti, and Wise, 1996). Yet, in the last 25 years, traditional defined benefit (DB) and employer plans with mandatory employee participation have steadily been replaced with Tax Deferred Account (TDA) retirement plans such as 401(k)s and 403(b)s, where employees choose whether to participate and how much to save for their retirement (Poterba, Venti, and Wise, 2001). As a result, many US workers now must make decisions about how much to save for their retirement, instead of being passive participants in their employer's DB pension plan. This makes it very important to understand how retirement savings decisions are made.

Deciding how much to save is a complicated decision, which requires processing a substantial amount of information and making intertemporal tradeoffs. It is clear that many households lack the financial education required to think about the saving problem as a standard intertemporal optimization problem, let alone to find the optimal solution. It is, therefore, plausible to think that participation and investment decisions in 401(k)s will be affected by factors other than standard economic maximization. Indeed, the recent empirical literature on 401(k)s has identified several of these channels: Default rules (Madrian and Shea, 2001; Choi et al., 2003, 2004), the possibility to commit now for the future (Benartzi and Thaler, 2004), information and peer effects (Bernheim and Garrett, 2000; Duflo and Saez, 2002, 2003; Madrian and Shea, 2002; and Choi and Garrett, 2000, Chapter 7, this volume).

Some recent research is based on actual experiments, either natural such as when a firm changes its retirement benefit policy, or prospective, in

The authors thank Abhijit Banerjee, David Card, David Laibson, Brigitte Madrian, and Olivia Mitchell for very helpful comments and discussions. They gratefully acknowledge financial support from the National Science Foundation (SES-0078535).

a randomized trial design where researchers can evaluate the impact of a specific channel on enrollment. The experimental approach has important advantages over previous analysis. First, it does not posit *a priori* models of savings behavior, and therefore the results are not dependent on behavioral assumptions. Second, experiments allow the researcher to raise new questions and provide new evidence on questions deemed irrelevant in standard approaches. As a result, the scope of investigation of saving problems has been considerably expanded so as to provide better understanding of the determinants of saving. Finally, experiments can allow researchers to develop research designs in order to answer very specific questions. We will see that, in many instances, the answers to those questions are very sensitive to the exact set-up, and therefore many experiments are called for in order to yield a solid sense of the key elements affecting the decision to save for retirement through employer sponsored benefit plans.

The goals of this chapter are twofold. First, we summarize the key features of the findings from studies that have used experimental or quasi-experimental methods. In our view, four main facts emerge from the literature. First, default rules in employer retirement benefits plans have a very important impact on retirement savings decisions. As Madrian and Shea (2001) have strikingly shown, shifting from the default rule in 401(k) plans from no-enrollment to automatic enrollment has a dramatic impact on the enrollment rates of new employees, and thus effect persists for several years. Second, the ability to commit now for the future also influences the willingness to participate. The "Saving More Tomorrow" plan proposed by Benartzi and Thaler (2004), whereby employees can decide to allocate automatically a fraction of their future pay raises to 401(k) contributions, produced a dramatic increase in the level of 401(k) savings. Third, network effects seem to be important. Duflo and Saez (2002) show that employees' enrollment and contribution choices are influenced by the choices of colleagues within departments, within a large university. Fourth, information has some impact on participation decisions, but this effect is fairly small. Duflo and Saez (2003) conduct an experiment showing that attendance to information sessions on retirement benefits within a single large university, has a significant effect on the subsequent 401(k) enrollment rates.

Finally, we will identify the gaps in the existing knowledge and propose new randomized experiments. Most of these could be conducted in the workplace, and they would fill important gaps in our understanding of the determinants of retirement savings.

## What Experiments Have Shown Thus Far

### Default Rules and Commitment

Several studies have analyzed how changes in the default rule for 401(k) enrollment and contributions within a single large firm influences the enrollment rates of new employees (Madrian and Shea, 2001). Enrollment rates for new employees increased from about 50 to over 80 percent. After the change, over three quarters of new employees remained in the default money market fund allocation, even though very few employees hired before automatic enrollment picked this particular outcome, and a money market fund is unlikely to be the optimal investment for long-term retirement savings.

How should we interpret the evidence on the impact of default rule? One possibility is that people do not take the time to make decisions about their 401(k) decision, or they assume that the firm has made the right choice for them. A different possibility is that the small cost involved in calling the benefits office to drop out of the 401(k) plan is actually large enough to prevent people from "acting on impulse," to disenroll. This second explanation recognizes that people can make short-run decisions that will hurt them in the long run: The value of today's consumption is very high, relative to the value of consumption in any future period. This means that, the individual will actually regret having consumed too much today, in the future. By enrolling employees by default, the firm provides employees with a commitment device. Even though the commitment is not particularly constraining, it appears sufficient to protect individuals from themselves.

If this is in fact the right explanation, then individuals should actually value the opportunity to commit themselves for the future by enrolling in the 401(k). The problem, however, is that in order to enroll today, they must give up consumption today. They would rather start giving up consumption *starting tomorrow*. The "Save More Tomorrow" (SMT) experiment developed by Shlomo Benartzi and Richard Thaler (2004) was meant to test exactly the possibility that workers would be willing to commit today to save *future* salary increases. Their analysis gave employees in a mid-sized company the option to commit in advance to allocate a portion of their future salary increases toward retirement savings. The vast majority of people (78 percent) who were offered the SMT plan elected to use it, and the vast majority of those who joined remained in it through at least three pay raises. Average contribution rates in the 401(k) plan for SMT plan participants increased from 3.5 to 11.6 percent of pay, over the course of 28 months.

## Information and Peer Effects

Several studies have investigated whether peer effects play an important role in retirement savings decisions. Using individual data on employees of a large university, Duflo and Saez (2002) study decisions to enroll in the 401(k) plan along with the choice of the mutual fund vendor for people who choose to enroll. The research question was whether people are influenced by the decisions of other employees in the same department. Results consistently suggest that peer effects are important: There is little difference in participation *within* departments, but larger variance in participation rates *across* departments, and individual participation rates are correlated with predicted participation in their peer groups.[1]

An interesting related experiment also sheds light on the role of information and social interactions in decisions to enroll in 401(k) retirement plans (Duflo and Saez, 2003). Here, a random sample of employees in a subset of departments was encouraged to attend a benefits information fair organized by the employer, who offered them a $20 monetary reward for attendance. We set a variable $D = 1$ were the treated departments where some letters were sent and by $D = 0$ were the control departments where no letters were sent. Within the treated departments, each employee not previously enrolled in the 401(k) plan had a probability $1/2$ of receiving the letter promising the $20 monetary reward for attendance. We denote by $L = 1$ the treated employees who did receive the letter, and by $L = 0$ the employees who did not. Our experiment included only employees not yet enrolled in the 401(k) shortly before the fair.

Attendance rates at the benefits fair are reported for each group in Panel A of Table 8-1. For employees in control departments ($D = 0$), the fair attendance rate was only 5 percent, whereas in treated departments ($D = 1$), the fair attendance rate was above 20 percent. Within treated departments, the attendance rate was 28 percent for employees who received the letter, more than five times larger than in control departments. Interestingly, the attendance rate of employees in treated departments who did not receive the letter was 15 percent, three times higher than in control departments, even though those employees did not receive a monetary reward for attending. Therefore, this shows that there were important spillover effects within departments in the decision to attend the benefits fair: Employees who received the letter did induce some of their colleagues to attend the fair with them.

Panel B of Table 8-1 displays 401(k) enrollment rates 5 and 11 months after the fair, for each of the groups. The enrollment rates in treated departments remained significantly higher (by about 20 percent) than in control departments after 5 and 11 months, although the difference was small is absolute terms (1 and 1.4 points, respectively). Interestingly, within treated departments, the enrollment rate of those who did receive the letter is no higher than for those who did not.

Three interpretations, not mutually exclusive, can account for these results (Duflo and Saez, 2003). First, they could be explained by social effects at the department level. Fair attendees might be able to spread information gleaned from the fair in their departments, and therefore increase the enrollment rates of their colleagues, even if the latter did not attend the fair themselves. Second, the results might be explained by differential treatment effects. Employees who went to the fair only because of the financial reward are likely to be different from those who participate because of their colleagues, and it is plausible to think that the treatment effect would be larger for the latter group than for the former. Finally, the results could be explained by motivational reward effects. Paying people to attend the fair

TABLE 8-1 Descriptive Statistics of Fair Attendance and 401(k) Participation, by Groups

| | Untreated Departments (Group $D = 0$) | Treated Departments | | |
| --- | --- | --- | --- | --- |
| | | All (Group $D = 1$) | Treated (Group $D = 1$, $L = 1$) | Untreated (Group $D = 1$, $L = 0$) |
| *Panel A: Benefits fair attendance*[a] | | | | |
| Fair attendance rate[b] among non-401(k) enrollees | 0.049 (0.005) | 0.214 (0.006) | 0.280 (0.01) | 0.151 (0.008) |
| Observations | 2,018 | 4,126 | 2,020 | 2,106 |
| *Panel B: 401(k) participation*[c] | | | | |
| 401(k) participation rate after 4.5 months | 0.040 (0.005) | 0.049 (0.004) | 0.045 (0.005) | 0.053 (0.005) |
| Observations | 1,861 | 3,726 | 1,832 | 1,894 |
| 401(k) participation rate after 11 months | 0.075 (0.0065) | 0.088 (0.005) | 0.089 (0.0071) | 0.088 (0.007) |
| Observations | 1,633 | 3,246 | 1,608 | 1,638 |
| *Panel C: Response rate to additional questionnaire* | | | | |
| Response rate | 0.352 (0.0402) | 0.452 (0.018) | 0.440 (0.0201) | 0.464 (0.0405) |
| Observations | 142 | 765 | 612 | 153 |

[a] Panel A includes all individuals not enrolled in the 401(k) plan by September 2000.

[b] Average fair participation in the non-treated department was obtained from the registration information collected at the fair. Since only 75% of the participants registered, participation was adjusted by a proportionality factor.

[c] 401(k) participation rates are obtained from administrative data.

*Notes*: Standard errors in parentheses.

*Source*: Authors' analyses.

could have affected their subjective motivation and therefore the perceived value or quality of the information they obtained at the fair.

Next we turn to new evidence from a follow-up questionnaire mailed after the fair. We believe this information helps to show that the important decision about how much to save for retirement is affected by small shocks, such as a very small financial reward and/or the influence of peers, and thus it does not seem to be the consequence of an elaborate decision process.

Five months after the benefits fair, a follow-up questionnaire was sent to 917 employees. This included two questions designed to measure employee knowledge of university retirement benefits system, as well as questions to elicit information on alternative retirement savings options available and to measure the extent of procrastination. The questionnaire, reproduced in the Appendix, provides additional perspectives regarding how the information obtained at the fair boosted 401(k) enrollment, despite the fact that the response rate was under 50 percent (Panel C of Table 8-1).[2] Clearly, people who responded are a select group. For example, those who responded to the questionnaire were eight percentage points more likely to enroll in the 401(k) after 6 months, compared to those who received it but did not return the survey (the standard error is 1.7 percentage points). The questionnaire itself had no causal effect on participation, because the enrollment rate in departments where we sent questionnaires did not increase relative to others.[3] Thus, this difference is entirely due to selection.[4] Moreover, those who received the questionnaire and did not respond were less likely to enroll in the 401(k) after 6 months, than those who did not get the questionnaire.[5]

Results from the follow-up survey appear in Table 8-2. People who answered the questionnaire were more likely to have attended the fair than people who did not: In the treated group, 43 percent of the questionnaire respondents attended (while 28 percent of the entire treated population attended), and in the control group, 29 percent of the respondents attended (compared to 15 percent). The attendance difference (14 percent) is similar to the difference in fair attendance between the two groups as a whole (13 percent) recorded at the fair. Respondents overall reported very high satisfaction rates with the fair. Yet, satisfaction was significantly higher for the control group than for the treatment group (95 versus 85 percent), and the difference was almost as large as the difference in fair attendance. Panel A thus suggests either that the marginal fair participant induced by the reward was less likely to find the fair useful (thus supporting the hypothesis of differential treatment effects), or that having received the letter reduced fair satisfaction (supporting the motivational reward effect hypothesis).

Panel B of Table 8-2 reports responses to the question "Why are you not enrolled in the 401(k) plan?" for those who reported that they were not enrolled (none of them were actually enrolled). They could check as many answers as were applicable. Individuals in the treatment group were less likely to report that they lacked information (20 versus 30 percent), the difference was significant at the 10 percent level. They were more likely to say that they wanted to enroll soon but had not yet found the time (45 versus 36 percent), although the $t$-statistic was just 1.3.[6] All other reasons for not contributing were mentioned equally often by both groups, with "plan to enroll soon" being the single most often cited reason for not contributing. In Panel C, we match this answer with their subsequent behavior. Actual behavior was correlated with intention (virtually no one who did not declare that he intended to enroll did so) but it fell well short of intention. Among untreated individuals, 17 percent of those who indicated they planned to enroll did so, but among treated individuals, 10 percent did so.[7]

TABLE 8-2  Analysis of Answers to Follow-Up Questionnaire[a] and Standard Errors of the Difference Corrected for Clustering at the Department Level[b]

| | Treated Departments | | |
| --- | --- | --- | --- |
| | Treatment (Received Invitation) | Control | Difference |
| **A. Fair participation and impressions** | | | |
| Benefits fair participation | 0.43 | 0.29 | 0.14 |
| | (0.03) | (0.05) | (0.06) |
| Benefits fair satisfaction (for those who attended the fair) | 0.85 | 0.95 | −0.10 |
| | (0.03) | (0.05) | (0.05) |
| Observations | 301 | 70 | |
| **B. Response to question "Why are you currently not enrolled in the 401(k)?"** | | | |
| Not enough information | 0.20 | 0.31 | −0.11 |
| | (0.03) | (0.06) | (0.06) |
| Cannot afford to save for retirement | 0.33 | 0.37 | −0.04 |
| | (0.03) | (0.06) | (0.08) |
| Plan to enroll soon but no time to do it yet | 0.45 | 0.35 | 0.09 |
| | (0.03) | (0.06) | (0.07) |
| Other ways to save for retirement | 0.22 | 0.24 | −0.02 |
| | (0.03) | (0.05) | (0.06) |
| Observations | 255 | 62 | |
| **C. Enrollment 6 months after the questionnaires** | | | |
| Plan to enroll soon | 0.10 | 0.17 | −0.07 |
| | (0.03) | (0.09) | (0.1) |
| Do not plan to enroll soon | 0.02 | 0.00 | 0.02 |
| | (0.01) | | (0.01) |
| **D. Response to question "Where do you obtain information about benefits?"** | | | |
| Benefits fair | 0.37 | 0.25 | 0.12 |
| | (0.03) | (0.05) | (0.05) |
| Benefits information packet | 0.77 | 0.93 | −0.16 |
| | (0.02) | (0.03) | (0.04) |
| Personal visit to the Benefits Office | 0.12 | 0.08 | 0.04 |
| | (0.02) | (0.03) | (0.05) |
| Other information seminar | 0.20 | 0.21 | −0.01 |
| | (0.02) | (0.05) | (0.05) |
| Colleagues | 0.25 | 0.31 | −0.06 |
| | (0.03) | (0.06) | (0.05) |
| Family or friends | 0.26 | 0.24 | 0.03 |
| | (0.03) | (0.05) | (0.05) |
| Administrative officer | 0.05 | 0.01 | 0.03 |
| | (0.01) | (0.01) | (0.02) |
| Observations | 300 | 71 | |

TABLE 8-2 *Continued.*

|  | Treated Departments | | |
|---|---|---|---|
|  | Treament (Received Invitation) | Control | Difference |
| *E. Knowledge about benefits* | | | |
| Reported knew own 401(k) status | 0.94 | 0.99 | −0.05 |
|  | (0.01) | (0.01) | (0.02) |
| Reported knew the number of vendors | 0.74 | 0.71 | 0.02 |
|  | (0.03) | (0.06) | (0.06) |
| Gave correct answer about 401(k) status | 0.89 | 0.94 | −0.06 |
|  | (0.02) | (0.03) | (0.03) |
| Gave correct answer about pension plan | 0.60 | 0.61 | 0.00 |
|  | (0.03) | (0.07) | (0.07) |
| Observations | 235 | 56 | |

[a]  All statistics are weighted by population weight.
[b]  Sample is restricted to treated departments.

*Source*: Authors' analyses.

Thus, treated individuals were more likely to have good intentions, but they were also more likely to procrastinate.

Panel D shows the answer to the question "Where do you obtain information about the 401(k) plan?" Not surprisingly, those in the treatment group were more likely to say that they obtained it from the fair (and the difference, 11 percent, is close to the 14 percent difference in fair attendance). However, they were *less* likely to obtain information from the benefits information *packet* (77 versus 93 percent). Those two sources of information thus appear to be substitutes. Other sources of information seem to be used equally by both groups.

Panel E reports answers to the knowledge questions. The first question asked whether the employee was not enrolled in the 401(k) plan (when we sent the letter, none of them were). Second, we asked them whether they knew the number of vendors with whom their Defined Contribution (DC) benefits could be invested. Employees were automatically enrolled in the DC plan at that firm, and they could choose to invest their contributions with four different vendors. Many employees had more than one vendor. If they did not make a choice, the benefits office randomly allocated them to one vendor. The results show that treatment and control groups were about as likely to know the number of vendors: 74 and 71 percent, respectively, ventured to answer the question, and in total 60 percent of each group gave the right answer.[8] However, those who received the letter were significantly less likely to report knowing their 401(k) plan status (94 versus 99 percent), and they were also less likely to give the correct answer (89 versus 94 percent).[9]

This could reflect some over-confidence on their part, since the letter was sent only to those who were not contributing. The finding lends some support to the motivational reward hypothesis: In the group where fair attendance was high, the treated group had less knowledge than the group that was not directly treated.

In summary, then, our results show that participation in the fair did not have a large impact on the information set of those who received the letter. In fact, they seem to have substituted fair attendance for individual research. The result was that they were more unsure about their actual 401(k) status, and to wrongly report themselves as contributing even though they were not. However, they were less likely to think that they suffered from a lack of information, and they were more likely to plan to enroll soon. Of course, this does not imply that the fair had no impact on the information set of those who went to the fair without the letter (used here as the control group).

## Discussion

This experiment had two striking findings bearing further comment. First, there was a large spillover effect at the fair attendance stage. Second, despite the large remaining difference in fair attendance, there was no difference in 401(k) plan participation between treated and untreated individuals within treated departments, while there was a significant difference in 401(k) plan participation between treated and untreated departments. As noted above, the fair attendance results are a clear indication of social effects in the decision to attend the fair, but interpreting the 401(k) plan participation results is more delicate. These could be due to social effects, differential treatment effects, motivational reward effects, or a combination of all three. Yet, the three different explanations have a common feature: They all suggest that the decision to participate in the 401(k) plan is affected by small changes in the environment, and not only by the information content of the fair.

If our results were entirely explained by the social effects hypothesis, this would imply that peer effects are very strong, as compared to the direct effect of the fair. This could arise in two cases. One case would posit that the fair conveys useful information to the fair participant which is then completely diffused to his entire department. This could explain why individuals who received the letter did not participate in the 401(k) plan any more than their colleagues who did not, and both, in turn participated more than individuals in control departments. A second case would propose that when people see more colleagues attending the fair (or they see others receive a letter inviting them to attend the fair), they are directly induced to enroll in the 401(k) plan, irrespective of what those who went to the fair learned at the fair or decided to do. Such peer effects do not seem to stem from rational "herd behavior" in an environment where information is scarce or difficult to obtain (Banerjee, 1992; Bikhchandani, Hirshleifer, and Welch, 1992). At the same time, however, there is clearly no strong social pressure to conform to the decisions of the majority regarding the 401(k) plan (as was true, for example, in Munshi, 2000).

Yet another explanation for our results is that the treatment effects may have been different for the various groups: It was positive for those who attended the fair because of their colleagues, but zero for those who attended because of the monetary reward. Yet, even if the results were entirely due to such differential treatment effects, so that social interactions play no role in explaining the 401(k) enrollment rate results, social network effects are still responsible for the increase in fair attendance among the untreated individuals in treated departments. Hence, social network effects still prompted some people to take steps which ultimately led them to change their 401(k) plan participation decisions.

As noted, the results could also be partly explained by the motivational reward effect. If true, this would also indicate that individuals' decisions can be influenced by small non-economic factors. When attending the fair on their own, they were influenced by it, but they were not induced to go by a $20 reward. A small perturbation in their motivation to attend the fair thus influenced their final decision, which again indicates that decision-making processes can be influenced by small changes in the environment.

In summary, a common theme across all these explanations is that the participation decision is influenced by things other than new information about costs and benefits of the 401(k) plan. Consequently, the decision to participate in the 401(k) plan is not purely the outcome of a sophisticated process of information-gathering and careful considerations of the alternatives. This conclusion is consistent with a growing body of evidence on retirement saving behavior showing that people believe that their saving rate is too low (Choi et al., 2002), but that their plans to increase it are rarely followed by action (Choi et al., 2002; Madrian and Shea, 2002), and that retirement decisions are characterized by very strong inertia and adherence to default rules (Madrian and Shea, 2001; Choi et al., 2003). It is important to emphasize, however, that the studies discussed analyze only the decision to enroll and contribute to a 401(k) plan. Starting to contribute to a 401(k) plan does not necessarily imply increased real saving, since individuals may offset 401(k) savings by reducing other saving or increasing their debt. Measuring the effects on total saving would require more data on overall assets and liabilities.

## Future Research

Next, we sketch several further experiments to shed light on questions regarding the 401(k) enrollment decisions that remain unanswered.

These experiments could be conducted within one large employer (in which case, employees within the firm would be randomly allocated to different groups), or at several companies (in which case, employers would be randomly allocated to different groups, and all employees would be treated similarly within a firm). Answering these questions would improve our understanding of the determinants of savings for retirement better, and can help design plans that will better serve both employees and employers.

## Seminars versus Fairs

More focused information, in smaller groups, could have a larger impact than a large-scale benefits fair: some groups are particularly in need of information, and do not receive it through the regular channels such as a general benefits fair. For example, the Bush administration proposed a retirement plan that would match up to 50 percent of the first $1,000 of IRA or 401(k) contributions for low-income earners. Since eligibility conditions depend in a complicated way on income and marital status, it could be difficult to access precisely for the low-income families whom this reform targeted. Employers might use payroll information to determine who is likely to be eligible, and target information to these individuals through specialized seminars.[10]

Many firms offer benefits information sessions to their employees.[11] The impact of such sessions could be enhanced if they were combined with some of the interventions proposed below. New employees typically must make a number of decisions (e.g. regarding health and flex benefits), so it could be a good time to reach them. Compulsory information sessions for new employees might be a method of informing new hires without requiring financial incentives. Such sessions, however, might have no impact if the "motivational reward" effect is too large, since employees might feel that they are forced to attend and stop paying attention altogether. Measuring the impact of compulsory information sessions on new hires' decisions could be very useful.

## Signing Up on the Spot

At the information session studied by Duflo and Saez (2003), the university did not offer enrollment on the spot; instead, employees interested in the 401(k) plan had to pick up an enrollment packet to take home. Quite plausibly, the additional effort required and the time lapse could be enough to undermine their resolve to enroll in the plan, especially if the reason that default rules matter is because people are simply reluctant to spend any time thinking about saving. In contrast, the "Save More Tomorrow" experiment offered people the option to enroll *right away* in the plan, which had greater success.

Three different hypotheses on the impact of default rules are as follows: there is information in the proposed default, individuals do not think at all about retirement; and the default is a commitment device that protects individuals from themselves. To distinguish between these, we propose three different experiments. First, one could compare the impact of regular information sessions with sessions where the employees could enroll on the spot, assisted by someone from the benefits office. To detect a clean effect, employees would be randomly allocated to sessions with or without on the spot enrollment. Second, information sessions with on the spot enrollment could be combined with default rules. The information session could deliver exactly the same message as before, but now enrollment would be the default option in one case, and non-enrollment would be the default option in a second case. Combining these two interventions would provide six groups that can be compared with each other:

(1) no enrollment by default; no information session;
(2) no enrollment by default; information session with no option to change choices on the spot;
(3) no enrollment by default, information session with option to change choices on the spot;
(4) enrollment by default, no information session;
(5) enrollment by default, information session with no option to change choices on the spot; and
(6) enrollment by default, information session with option to change choices on the spot.

If the enrollment rates were higher in group 3 than in group 2, we could conclude that the lack of salience of the 401(k) decision plays a big role in the enrollment decision. In other words, focusing people's attention on the question, and getting them to make a decision at the moment when they are focused, could have an important impact on the enrollment decision. It would also confirm that people spend very little time thinking about very important financial questions, a conclusion which seems to emerge from existing evidence, as argued above. If there were a difference in enrollment rates of groups 2 and 3, but not between groups 5 and 6, we could additionally conclude that when individuals think about the problem, they actually decide to remain in the 401(k).

A comparison between groups 2 and 4 (versus groups 1 and 3) would also shed light on whether people interpret the default as information. When the information session has taken place, people receive direct information on what an employer thinks is appropriate, and in both cases, they receive exactly the same information. Of course, the fact that the firm decides to enroll the individual by default could be additional information. But if the only reason why the default matters was that people see it as a signal, we should see a much smaller difference between groups 2 and 4 than between groups 1 and 3. To make it even clearer, the information session could provide precise recommendations, which differed across types of individuals. In this case, the default enrollment (common across individuals) should provide no additional information, and if it still mattered, it would be for non-learning reasons.

To summarize, an experimental design combining variations on default options, the ability to enroll right after an information session, and the ability to commit for the future, would allow plan designers and researchers to understand more clearly what determines saving decisions.

## Effect on Saving

The central question of interest remains whether access and contributions to a 401(k) plan increase net saving, or whether people offset additional 401(k) saving with less other saving. The answer to this question is of course critical: If 401(k) contributions crowd out other forms of saving, there is little reason to offer tax subsidies to these programs. Many researchers have tried to evaluate whether, in fact, 401(k) plans boost total saving, but the analysis remains controversial.[12]

The key reason why the question is very difficult to answer is that one cannot simply compare saving by workers enrolled in 401(k) with that of workers who are not enrolled. People who do enroll may be otherwise financially more savvy, and therefore likely to invest more, even in the absence of a 401(k) plan. Even comparing employees in firms that offer a plan to those in firms which do not offer a plan may not solve the problem, if firms that offer 401(k) plans employ different types of people (Poterba et al., 1996). The ideal experiment would be to randomly offer 401(k) plans, or to boost 401(k) contributions of some workers but not others, and then to measure the impact on net saving. Of course, this particular experiment cannot be conducted. On the other hand, contribution rates in 401(k) plans can be significantly increased, by default rules and commitment devices, and some of the experiments we propose above could have the same impact. For example, one could track the saving rate of individuals hired just before and just after the introduction of default 401(k) enrollment, and compare their saving and asset accumulation patterns over several years. Another possibility would be to offer the "Save More Tomorrow" program to a random group of individuals within a firm, and compare the subsequent saving of those offered the program, versus the rest. Of course in so doing, it would be important to compare all the assets of those subjected (or not subjected) to the new policy. The difference between the saving rates across the two groups could then be normalized by the difference in 401(k) participation in the two groups, to obtain an estimate of the effect of 401(k) enrollment on net saving. Ideally, both groups of individuals would be followed over several years, making such a study expensive and yet these data would also provide the most useful insights on the most important questions.

## Appendix: Questionnaire Sent 5 Months After the Benefits Fair

Please answer the following 6 simple questions. You can check the "don't know" answer if you are not sure of an answer. Your answers will remain strictly confidential and will be used for no purpose other than this study.

(1) In addition to your Basic Retirement Account, the university makes a monthly contribution of 3.5 percent of your monthly salary to an Individual Investment Account(s). You decide how this contribution should be invested from a list of four investment companies.

Through how many investment companies are you currently investing this contribution?

–One . . .
–Two . . .
–Three . . .
–Four . . .
–Don't know . . .

(2) The university offers a supplemental retirement plan called the Tax-Deferred Account (TDA) program. Through the TDA program, you can add to your retirement savings by contributing a portion of your salary on a pre-tax basis. You pay no taxes on these savings or the investment income until you withdraw your funds. You decide how much to contribute and the university deducts your contributions from your paycheck. You choose how to invest your savings from a wide range of funds offered by four different vendors.

Are you currently enrolled in the Tax-Deferred Account (TDA)?

–Yes . . .(go to question 4)
–No . . .
–Don't know . . .

(3) [To be filled out only if you are not currently enrolled in the TDA]
Why are you currently not enrolled in the TDA (check all answers that apply)?

–You do not have enough information on the TDA: . . .
–Right now, you cannot afford to save for your retirement: . . .
–You plan to enroll soon, but did not have the occasion to do it yet: . . .
–You save for your retirement through other means: . . .

(3b) If you check the last answer, which other means are you using to save for retirement:

–TDA through spouse's employer: ...
–Individual Retirement Account (IRA): ...
–Employer provided pension plan (own): ...
–Employer provided pension plan (spouse): ...
–Other mutual funds: ...
–Other ...

(4) [To be filled out by everybody]
From which of the following sources do you get information about the retirement plans (check all that apply)?

–The benefits information fair: ...
–Benefits information packet: ...
–You came in person to the Benefits office: ...
–You attended an information seminar: ...
–Colleagues: ...
–Family or friends: ...
–The Administrative Officer of your department: ...
–None ...

(5) Did you attend the university benefits information fair in the fall?

–Yes: ...
–No: ...

(6) If you did, did you find it useful?

–Yes: ...
–No: ...

## Notes

[1] While this evidence is suggestive, it might be contaminated by omitted variables, correlated within the group, and correlated with the observed variables used to predict aggregate participation rates.

[2] This is a common problem. The survey on savings intention by Choi et al. (2002a) had a response rate of 33%.

[3] This result is well in line with previous results by Bayer, Bernheim, and Scholz (1995) showing that distributing pamphlets or advertisement about benefits is not enough to change employees' behavior.

[4] Since we have shown above that the questionnaire had no causal effect on enrollment, this is also a sign of selection.

[5] In addition, the selection seemed to work differently in treated versus control departments: The response rate for treated departments was 45% (Panel C), while it was only 35% in control departments. It may thus not be very informative to compare the responses across samples. On the other hand, network effects within departments

seem to have played an important role here too. The response rates among treated and untreated individuals within treated departments were essentially identical. A plausible explanation is that those who had received the fair invitation letter were able to tell their colleagues that the researchers delivered on the promise of sending the reward. Since the response rates are the same, the assumption that the selection process is the same is reasonable. Thus, we can compare the response among treated and untreated individuals within treated departments. These responses are not representative of the population in general, but representative of the segment of the population that tends to respond to this type of questionnaire.

[6] The difference is 9%, almost as large as the difference in fair participation: A simple IV on the probability to report that one wants to enroll on whether an individual went to the fair, using the letter as instrument, would thus give a coefficient very close to 1, which is also what Madrian and Shea (2002) obtain: Virtually all seminar attendees who were not yet enrolled in the plan were intending to enroll soon after the seminar.

[7] This is in the ballpark of other studies. Following the survey conducted by Choi et al. (2001a), 14% of those who intended to enroll in the TDA did. Following the financial education session in Madrian and Shea (2002), 14% of the attendees (who all intended to enroll) did.

[8] Those who did not answer are counted as having given the wrong answer.

[9] Incidentally, this level of misclassification underscores the importance of working with administrative data when studying 401(k) savings behavior.

[10] In the university we studied, many potentially eligible employees would need to be reached with information sessions in Spanish, for example.

[11] A phone survey we conducted with Fortune 500 companies revealed that 71% of them conduct these sessions. See also other studies in this volume.

[12] Poterba, Venti, and Wise (1996) argue that 401(k)s have increased saving while Engen, Gale, and Scholz (1996) argue they did not. Poterba, Venti, and Wise (2001) summarize the most recent research on those issues.

# References

Banerjee, Abhijit. 1992. "A Simple Model of Herd Behavior." *Quarterly Journal of Economics* 107: 797–817.

Bayer, Patrick, Douglas Bernheim, and Karl Scholz. 1996. "The Effects of Financial Education in the Workplace: Evidence from a Survey of Employers." NBER Working Paper 5655.

Benartzi, Shlomo and Richard Thaler. 2004. "Save More Tomorrow: Using Behavioral Economics to Increase Employee Saving." *Journal of Political Economy* 112(1) February: 164–187.

Bikhchandani, Sushil, David Hirshleifer, and Ivo Welch. 1992. "A Theory of Fads, Fashion, Custom, and Cultural Change as Informational Cascades." *Journal of Political Economy* 100: 992–1026.

Choi, James, David Laibson, Brigitte Madrian, and Andrew Metrick. 2002. "Defined Contributions Pensions: Plan Rules, Participants Choices, and the Path of Least Resistance." In *Tax Policy and the Economy, Vol. 16*, ed. James Poterba. Cambridge, MA: MIT Press: 67–113.

—— 2003. "Benign Paternalism and Active Decisions: A Natural Experiment in Savings." Harvard University Working Paper.

——2004. "For Better or for Worse: Default Effect and 401(k) Savings Behavior." In *Perspectives on the Economics of Aging,* ed. David A. Wise. Chicago, IL: University of Chicago Press.

Duflo, Esther and Emmanuel Saez. 2002. "Participation and Investment Decisions in a Retirement Plan: The Influence of Colleagues' Choices." *Journal of Public Economics* 85: 121–148.

——2003. "The Role of Information and Social Interactions in Retirement Plan Decisions: Evidence From a Randomized Experiment." *Quarterly Journal of Economics* 118(3): 815–842.

Engen, Eric M., William G. Gale, and John Karl Scholz. 1996. "The Illusory Effect of Saving Incentives on Saving." *Journal of Economic Perspective* 10: 113–138.

Madrian, Brigitte and Dennis F. Shea. 2001. "The Power of Suggestion: Inertia in 401(k) Participation and Savings Behavior." *Quarterly Journal of Economics* 116: 1149–1187.

——2002. "Preaching to the Converted and Converting those Taught: Financial Education in the Workplace." University of Chicago Graduate School of Business Working Paper.

Munshi, Kaivan. 2000. "Social Norms and Individual Decisions During a Period of Change: An Application to the Demographic Transition," University of Pennsylvania Working Paper.

Poterba, James, Steven Venti, and David Wise. 1996. "How Retirement Saving Programs Increase Saving." *Journal of Economic Perspectives* 10: 91–112.

——2001. "The Transition to Personal Accounts and Increasing Retirement Wealth: Macro and Micro Evidence." NBER Working Paper 8610.

# Part III

# Consequences for Retirement Education

# Chapter 9

## Saving and the Effectiveness of Financial Education

*Annamaria Lusardi*

This chapter uses information from the Health and Retirement Study (HRS) to examine the financial situation of older households. We show that many families arrive at retirement with little or no wealth, and with rather simple portfolios: The major asset that families own is their house, and around 30 percent of households hold stocks. Yet, many families, in particular those with low education, hold neither high return assets (stocks, IRAs, business equity), nor basic assets such as checking accounts. Next I evaluate the reasons for such low wealth accumulation and simple portfolios. I contend that planning costs play a role in explaining many families' financial situation. To assess the importance of such costs, I examine whether the provision of financial education via retirement seminars fosters savings and investment in stocks. My evidence indicates that seminars can foster saving, particularly for those with low education and those who save little. We also found that, by offering financial education, wealth can be increased sharply, close to 20 percent in the total sample, and much more for families at the bottom of the distribution and those with low education. Retirement seminars also increase total wealth inclusive of pension and Social Security for both high and low education families. Our estimates are comparable with findings of Clark et al. (Chapter 10, this volume), who also confirm that financial education can boost saving, particularly for those with low financial literacy.

## Previous Studies

Previous studies have shown that many households make poor provision for retirement. Women appear particularly vulnerable to the death of their spouses and a husband's death can precipitate the widow's entry into

The author thanks Rob Alessie, Patty Anderson, Steve Donahue, Al Gustman, Amy Harris, David McCarthy, Joe Piacentini, Doug Staiger, and especially Olivia Mitchell for suggestions and comments. Nicholas Duquette and Crandall Peeler provided excellent research assistance. The research was supported by the US Department of Labor, Employee Benefits Security Administration, the Michigan Retirement Research Center, and TIAA-CREF. Expressed opinions are solely those of the author.

poverty (Weir and Willis, 2000). Using a nationally representative sample of older Americans, Warshawsky and Ameriks (2000) import their current wealth into one of the most popular financial planners. They find that about half of working middle-class American households will not have fully funded retirements, and many will actually run out of resources very shortly into retirement. One of the problems these authors, and others (Lusardi, 2002) emphasize is that many households have limited resources until late in their life cycles, or they start saving so late that it is impossible to accumulate much. These results are consistent with Hurd and Zissimopoulos (2000), who examine subjective information about past saving behavior. When asked to evaluate their saving, a stunningly high proportion of respondents, 73 percent, indicated they saved too little over the past 20 and 30 years. Similar findings are reported by Moore and Mitchell (2000), who determine how much wealth (including Social Security and pensions) older households have, and how much they would need to save if they wished to preserve consumption levels after retirement. They conclude that most older households will not be able to maintain current levels of consumption into retirement without additional saving. In particular, the median HRS household would still have to save an additional 16 percent of income to smooth consumption after retirement.

Other studies corroborate the lack of preparedness for retirement: For instance, the national Retirement Confidence Survey indicates that a large proportion of workers has done little or no planning for retirement (EBRI, 2001). Only 39 percent of workers tried to determine with some accuracy how much they needed to save to fund their retirement, whereas a decade previously, around one-third of workers indicated that they had tried to calculate how much money they needed to save for retirement. When asked why the calculation was not attempted, many respondents replied that it was too difficult and they did not know where to find help to do it.

Lack of planning is also pervasive among older workers, 5–10 years from retirement, according to Lusardi (2000, 2002). These findings are consistent with several other studies that show many workers lack the information necessary for making saving decisions. For instance, Gustman and Steinmeier (1999b) report that many workers are poorly informed about their Social Security and pension benefits, and they often err about the type of pension plan they have and the benefits associated with it. EBRI (2001) suggests that more than half of current workers expect to reach full eligibility for Social Security benefits sooner than they actually will. An earlier EBRI survey (1996) shows that only 55 percent of workers knew that government bonds provided a lower rate of return (over the past 20 years) than the US stock market. Other researchers, including Bernheim (1998) and MacFarland et al. (this volume), also show that workers are often ill-equipped to make saving plans.

An important finding by Lusardi (1999, 2002) is that planning has effects on both saving behavior and portfolio choice. Households whose head does not plan for retirement accumulate much less wealth than households whose head does do some planning. This result holds true even after accounting for many determinants of wealth and including levels of pension and Social Security wealth. In addition, households that do not plan are less likely to invest in high return assets such as stocks.

Furthermore, planning for retirement is considered an important but difficult task, so many employers have started offering financial education to their employees. Financial education is particularly prevalent among firms offering DC pensions, where workers have to make their own decisions on how to allocate pension funds. An important question, then, is whether these initiatives have any effects on worker behavior.

A few studies have looked at the effects of financial education in the work place on private savings or contributions to pension funds.[1] Empirical findings are mixed: There is evidence of some positive effect of financial education on saving and pensions, but the form of education seems to matter. For example, Bernheim and Garrett (2003) and Bayer, Bernheim, and Scholz (1996) find that programs that rely on print media (newsletters, plan description, etc.) have generally no effect on pension participation and contributions, even though the quality of financial information seems to matter (Clark and Schieber, 1998). By contrast, retirement seminars are found to be effective, but they seem to affect only certain aspects of behavior—for example, pension participation and the amount of contributions—but not total saving levels (McCarthy and Turner, 1996; Bernheim and Garrett, 2003). These and other similar studies suffer from severe data shortcomings, since they lack information about workers' characteristics, the characteristics of their pension plans and total wealth levels. There remain questions regarding the appropriate measures of wealth when looking at accumulation for retirement, and how to treat housing when calculating retirement wealth. Some studies claim that few elderly sell their houses after retirement and even fewer use contracts such as reverse mortgages to access their housing wealth.[2] Most importantly, most previous studies do not consider pension and Social Security wealth, two major components of total household retirement savings. Leaving out these components of wealth and/or concentrating on narrow definitions of accumulation can have important effects on the empirical findings. In what follows, I evaluate data from the HRS, which provides rich information about household characteristics and wealth measures.

## Empirical Approach

The HRS offers unique information that overcomes many of the shortcomings of previous research on saving and financial education. This survey, covering a nationally representative sample of US households born 1931–41, provides detailed information on wealth and the retirement process with a focus on health, labor markets, and economic and psycho-social factors.

Questions about wealth are asked to the most financially knowledgeable person in the household.[3]

Five types of HRS information are critically important to understand saving and its interaction with planning, past economic circumstances, expectations about the future, individual preferences, and pension and Social Security wealth. The HRS provides several indicators about planning: How much respondents have thought about retirement, whether they attended a retirement seminar, and whether they asked Social Security to calculate their retirement benefits. Hence, I concentrate mostly on the effects of retirement seminars. Moreover, the HRS provides information on several past negative and positive shocks, including past unemployment, episodes of distress, inheritances, insurance settlements, and money received from relatives and friends. Most importantly, the survey reports information about anticipated future resources and future events. This is critically important since decisions to save are intrinsically related to the future. In the HRS, respondents are asked to report how likely it is that future home prices will increase more than the general price level, and how likely it is that Social Security will become less generous in the future. Respondents are also asked to report their expectation of living to ages 75 and 85, to work full-time after ages 62 and 65, and to lose their job in the next year.[4] In addition, respondents are asked to report the chance they will have to give major financial help to family members in the next 10 years.

Another not yet well-explored dimension along which households can differ is preferences, (e.g. risk aversion or impatience), both of which play a pivotal role in saving decisions. One can infer preference information from the HRS using the model developed by Barsky et al. (1997), who explore people's willingness to take gambles, to construct proxies for risk aversion. Demographic variables that could be related to the impatience— such as education, race, and country of origin—are also present in the survey. Additionally, questions on smoking, drinking, health practices, and regular exercise may be used to proxy for individual heterogeneity.

In the HRS, it is possible to link to the Social Security records of respondents and use that information to calculate Social Security wealth.[5] For any household who did not provide consent to link to Social Security records, we have used imputed Social Security wealth.[6] It is also possible to construct pension wealth from the self-reported pension information.[7] Thus, the data set offers a very complete measure of household resources to examine saving behavior.

## Household Saving Close to Retirement

Before looking at how financial education influences retirement wealth, it is useful to first describe two measures of household (non-pension) accumulation. The first measure, which I call liquid net worth, is defined as the sum of checking and saving accounts, certificates of deposit and Treasury bills, bonds, stocks, and other financial assets minus short-term debt. The second measure, which I call total net worth or simply net worth, is obtained by adding IRAs and Keoghs, housing equity, other real estate, business equity, and vehicles to liquid net worth. Table 9-1 displays the major components of wealth including retirement assets (IRAs and Keoghs) and housing equity. All values are given in 1,992 dollars and the sample includes all financial respondents between the age of 50 and 61 who are not partially or fully retired.

The first important result is that there are tremendous differences in wealth holdings for households on the verge of retirement in the HRS. While some households have amassed large amounts of wealth, others have accumulated very little. Considerable differences in wealth are to be expected, because permanent income (or average income over the lifetime) varies widely. But the actual variation, from $850 in net worth for households at the 10th percentile to $475,000 in the 90th percentile, is far larger than variation in permanent income. It is also apparent that housing is an important asset in many household portfolios, and furthermore many people have no assets other than home equity. As mentioned before, whether housing equity serves to sustain consumption at retirement is in dispute. Retirement assets such as IRAs have been one of the fastest growing components of household wealth in the last two decades, but the evidence shows that ownership and the amounts invested in such tax-favored assets

TABLE 9-1  Pre-retirement Household Wealth in the 1992 HRS Components of Household Wealth (Excluding Social Security and Pensions)

| Percentile | Liquid Net Worth $ | IRAs and Keoghs $ | Housing Equity $ | Total Net Worth $ |
|---|---|---|---|---|
| 5 | −6,000 | 0 | 0 | 0 |
| 25 | 0 | 0 | 0 | 27,980 |
| 50 | 6,000 | 0 | 42,000 | 96,000 |
| 75 | 36,000 | 15,000 | 85,000 | 222,200 |
| 90 | 110,000 | 45,000 | 150,000 | 475,000 |
| 95 | 199,500 | 75,000 | 200,000 | 785,000 |
| Mean | 46,171 | 16,492 | 61,613 | 227,483 |
| (Std. Dev.) | (178,654) | (49,754) | (100,646) | (521,467) |

*Notes*: This table includes HRS households whose head is 50–61 years old and not fully or partially retired. The total number of observations is 5,292. All figures are weighted using survey weights. Liquid net worth is defined as the sum of checking and savings accounts, certificate of deposits and Treasury bills, bonds, stocks, and other financial assets minus short-term debt. Total net worth is defined as the sum of liquid net worth, IRAs and Keoghs, housing equity, business equity, other real estate, and vehicles. All values are expressed in 1,992 dollars.

*Source*: Authors' computations.

are heterogeneous across the sample. Even though not shown in the table, a substantial portion of total net worth is accounted for by business equity:[8] households owning one or more businesses are fairly rare (only 15 percent of the sample), but their wealth holdings are large, median holdings are worth $75,000.[9] A second important point to note in Table 9-1 is the prevalence of households that arrive close to retirement with little or no wealth; one quarter of HRS households have less than $30,000 in total net worth. Of course, total net worth is only a partial measure of accumulation since it omits Social Security and pension wealth; nevertheless, it is difficult to borrow against retirement assets.

Wealth holdings across education, which can proxy for permanent income, appear in Table 9-2. What is clear is that wealth differences both within and across groups remain large. Wealth holdings are very low for households whose financial respondent has less than a high-school education, while households whose head is college-educated have more than twice the wealth (considering medians) of households with high-school education. If one considers a restricted measure of wealth such as liquid net worth, the scenario worsens considerably. Many of the households with low education have little or zero holdings of financial assets and little net worth.

To account for the fact that normal or permanent income varies across households and is one of the most important determinants of wealth, in the empirical work I always consider wealth as a ratio of permanent income. Permanent income has been constructed by regressing total household income on a set of household demographics (age, sex, race, marital status, region), workers characteristics (working in small firms, working part time, belonging to unions), occupation and education dummies and these occupation interacted with age, and the subjective expectations of income changes in the future (whether future income will increase or decrease, subjective probability of losing work next year and that health will limit work activity in next 10 years).

TABLE 9-2 Pre-retirement Household Wealth by Education in the 1992 HRS

| Education Level | Number of Observations | Liquid Net Worth $ | | Total Net Worth $ | |
|---|---|---|---|---|---|
| | | Median | Mean | Median | Mean |
| Elementary | 329 | 0 | −707 | 9,000 | 82,215 |
| Less than high school | 1,042 | 100 | 16,429 | 39,000 | 110,324 |
| High school | 1,876 | 5,500 | 29,668 | 90,000 | 183,678 |
| Some college | 1,041 | 10,000 | 47,312 | 122,700 | 243,571 |
| College | 800 | 28,000 | 90,910 | 186,000 | 358,848 |
| More than college | 204 | 41,000 | 175,160 | 234,000 | 636,366 |

*Notes*: This table reports the distribution of liquid and total net worth across education groups. All figures are weighted using survey weights.

*Source*: See Table 9-1.

TABLE 9-3  Asset Ownership by Education in the 1992 HRS (%)

| Assets and Liabilities | Elementary School | Some High School | High School | Some College | College | More than College | Total |
|---|---|---|---|---|---|---|---|
| Check and saving | 0.30 | 0.63 | 0.85 | 0.90 | 0.95 | 0.95 | 0.82 |
| CDs | 0.03 | 0.14 | 0.28 | 0.29 | 0.34 | 0.30 | 0.26 |
| Bonds | 0.00 | 0.01 | 0.04 | 0.07 | 0.14 | 0.27 | 0.07 |
| Stocks | 0.01 | 0.10 | 0.24 | 0.34 | 0.51 | 0.55 | 0.28 |
| IRAs and Keoghs | 0.05 | 0.16 | 0.41 | 0.48 | 0.62 | 0.71 | 0.41 |
| Other assets | 0.02 | 0.07 | 0.13 | 0.20 | 0.25 | 0.36 | 0.16 |
| Businesses | 0.05 | 0.09 | 0.13 | 0.20 | 0.18 | 0.29 | 0.15 |
| Housing | 0.48 | 0.64 | 0.80 | 0.80 | 0.82 | 0.83 | 0.74 |
| Real estate | 0.15 | 0.18 | 0.27 | 0.37 | 0.41 | 0.49 | 0.30 |
| Vehicles | 0.59 | 0.79 | 0.92 | 0.94 | 0.95 | 0.97 | 0.89 |
| Debt | 0.24 | 0.36 | 0.40 | 0.44 | 0.38 | 0.37 | 0.39 |

*Notes*: This table reports the ownership of assets across education groups. The number of observations is 5,292. Figures are weighted using survey weights.
*Source*: See Table 9-1.

More information on the composition of wealth in household portfolios by education groups is given in Table 9-3. Results show that wealth is concentrated among households whose financial respondent has at least a high-school education; this group is also more likely to holds stocks and bonds. Focusing on households with low education shows that over one-third of Hispanics have only an elementary school education, and almost 60 percent have less than a high-school education. Among Blacks, 40 percent have less than a high-school education. Another important and striking feature among Blacks and Hispanics is that they lack many of the assets common to the portfolios of wealthier households, such as stocks, bonds, and IRAs and few have even a checking account. In this sample, 57 percent of Black households and 47 percent of Hispanic households have a checking account, a finding consistent with results for younger households (Lusardi, Cossa, and Krupka, 2001).

## The Role of Financial Education

Many factors can explain the heterogeneity of wealth holdings close to retirement. Households with low permanent incomes, those who are hit by many shocks, and people who are impatient or expect large capital gains on their assets, may save differently from others. In addition, planning costs can explain some of the differences in wealth. To help confront the problem of planning costs, some employers have started to offer some form of financial education in the workplace. By providing information and improving financial literacy, the hope is that seminars will reduce planning costs and foster savings. Nevertheless, there is still much uncertainty regarding the effects of seminars on savings. Several studies discern a positive correlation between attending a retirement seminar and private wealth or contributions to pension funds, yet it is not completely clear what this correlation means. Attending retirement seminars is largely voluntary, so it is possible that those who attend seminars are more likely to have an interest in them, for example, because they have large wealth holdings. Thus, it may be wealth levels that drive participation in retirement seminars, but not the other way around. Similarly, attending retirement seminars could simply reflect individual characteristics, such as patience and diligence, both of which are also likely to affect wealth accumulation. Attending a retirement seminar could then simply be a proxy for individual characteristics and attitudes towards saving, rather than a measure of the effects of providing information, improving financial literacy, and/or reducing planning costs. Furthermore, as reported by Bernheim and Garrett (2003), retirement education is often remedial, and thus offered in firms where workers do very little savings. Since few data sets have enough information to allow researchers to sort these effects out, findings regarding the effects of retirement seminars are often difficult to interpret.

I seek to remedy these shortcomings by using the HRS to examine the effectiveness of retirement seminars. One advantage is that the HRS provides rich information on individual characteristics that might affect saving. Another is that the detailed HRS information is more complete than those used in previous studies; for example, Bernheim and Garrett (2003) use limited and noisy data about private savings and other studies have only information about pension contributions and pension wealth but no information about private wealth.

To illustrate the strength of the HRS financial education variables, Table 9-4 reports two indicators of planning activities: (i) whether the respondent has attended a meeting on retirement and retirement planning organized by his/her spouse's employer and (ii) whether he or she has asked Social Security to calculate retirement benefits (of husband or spouse). The results show that respondents who are male, white, and married are more likely to have attended a seminar. Households whose head has low education or comes from a family of low education are less likely to have attended a seminar. Of course, this might occur if such families work in firms that tend not to offer such seminars. Nevertheless, similar findings are obtained when considering those who have asked Social Security to calculate their retirement benefits. Again, the better-educated, higher-income, white, and married respondents are more likely to ask for information about Social Security benefits. Households who plan are also more likely to have a pension and to invest in retirement assets such as IRAs and Keoghs.

Several other household characteristics are also considered, including whether the financially knowledgeable person in the household smokes or stopped smoking, drinks heavily, thinks he or she should cut down on drinking, does not exercise, and has talked to a doctor about health. All of

TABLE 9-4 Planning Activities Undertaken by HRS Pre-Retirees

| Characteristics | Attended Retirement Seminar | Asked SS to Calculate Benefits | Total Sample |
|---|---|---|---|
| *Demographics* | | | |
| Age 50–53 | 0.32 | 0.28 | 0.36 |
| Age 54–57 | 0.38 | 0.34 | 0.36 |
| Age 58–61 | 0.29 | 0.38 | 0.27 |
| White | 0.85 | 0.90 | 0.79 |
| Male | 0.58 | 0.54 | 0.51 |
| Married | 0.72 | 0.73 | 0.61 |
| Less than high school | 0.06 | 0.09 | 0.22 |
| High school | 0.30 | 0.38 | 0.36 |
| More than high school | 0.63 | 0.53 | 0.42 |
| Family of origin has high education | 0.58 | 0.55 | 0.47 |
| *Income and wealth* | | | |
| Income < $25,000 | 0.11 | 0.14 | 0.29 |
| Have pension | 0.84 | 0.60 | 0.49 |
| Have IRAs or Keoghs | 0.63 | 0.63 | 0.41 |
| *General attitudes* | | | |
| Heavy smoker | 0.10 | 0.15 | 0.18 |
| Stopped smoking | 0.45 | 0.42 | 0.37 |
| Drink heavily | 0.04 | 0.05 | 0.05 |
| Feel should cut down on drinking | 0.21 | 0.20 | 0.20 |
| Do not exercise | 0.27 | 0.37 | 0.46 |
| Talk to a doctor about own health | 0.83 | 0.81 | 0.77 |
| *Subjective expectations* | | | |
| Expectation that health will limit work activity in the next 10 years+ | 0.36 | 0.38 | 0.39 |
| Expectations to live to age 75 or more | 0.68 | 0.67 | 0.65 |
| Expectations to work full-time after age 62+ | 0.43 | 0.49 | 0.52 |
| Expectations that SS will become less generous | 0.59 | 0.62 | 0.59 |
| Expectation that house prices will increase faster than prices in the next 10 years | 0.46 | 0.48 | 0.49 |
| # of observations | 506 | 1,191 | 5,292 |

*Notes*: This table reports the proportion of respondents who have attended a retirement seminar or asked Social Security to calculate retirement benefits. All figures are weighted using survey weights. + indicates that the means are calculated on the sample of workers only.

*Source*: See Table 9-1.

these correlate strongly with planning activities and underscore the finding that individual heterogeneity should be taken into account in the empirical work (see also MacFarland, Marconi, and Utkus, Chapter 6, this volume).

When looking at the probabilities of future events, another important and unique source of information in the HRS, one finds that those who attend a retirement seminar or asked Social Security to calculate retirement benefits are less likely to work full-time after age 62. Those who plan are also somewhat less likely to report that they expect house prices to increase more than the general price level in the next 10 years.

To assess the importance of seminars on retirement wealth accumulation, I regressed wealth measures on an indicator variable for whether respondents have attended a retirement seminar and an extensive set of controls.[10] The dependent variable is the ratio of non-pension wealth to permanent income, in some cases also controlling on pension and Social Security wealth. First, I consider financial net worth, which adds IRAs and Keoghs to liquid net worth, and next I consider total net worth; both are divided by permanent income. Even after this normalization, variation in the ratio of wealth to permanent income remains wide. Households in the first quartile of the distribution have financial wealth that is only 1 percent of income, while in the third quartile, financial wealth is approximately equal to permanent income. Considering net worth, households in the first quartile hold wealth equal to approximately 75 percent of their permanent income, while at the third quartile, they hold three times the amount of permanent income. Among the explanatory variables, I use age and age squared (the latter to capture the hump-shaped profile of wealth holdings), and also I evaluate demographic factors, such as the total number of children, the number of children still living at home, sex, race, country of birth, marital status, region of residence, and education. Permanent income is included among the regressors to account for the fact that accumulation can vary across levels of permanent income and to test whether rich households are simply a scaled-up version of poor households. The model also accounts for health status, past shocks, measures of risk aversion and impatience, and future expectations as described above. Additionally, the model accounts for whether households have pensions since these workers are more likely to work at firms that offer retirement seminars.

I also account for other motives to save, apart from providing for retirement. For instance, some may save to leave a bequest to future generations, which I account for by using information on people's reported intention of leaving bequests to heirs[11] and expectations of giving financial help to family member in the future, and I allowed for a precautionary saving by including the subjective variance of earnings risk calculated from the expectation of losing their job in the coming year.[12] I also account for the fact that households accumulate little because they can rely on help from relatives and friends in case they run into severe financial difficulties in the future. Conversely, the possibility of receiving bequests is controlled by a variable indicating whether at least one parent is alive. The model also incorporates the respondent's subjective expectation of future events that can affect wealth accumulation, for example his/her expectation that Social Security will be less generous or that house prices will increase more than the general price level.

To explore the impact of retirement education, I turn next to the empirical results. If education is likely to be offered to workers who most need it, one might expect the effect to be stronger at the lower quartiles of the wealth distribution and among those with low education. Thus, I perform quartile regressions and I also perform regressions across different education groups since, as reported above, least educated families save very little and invest in simple assets.

The main empirical results are summarized in Table 9-5 (detailed results appear in the Appendix. Retirement seminars affect the lowest two quartiles of the wealth distribution and they also affect the lowest two quartiles

TABLE 9-5  The Effect of Retirement Seminars on Retirement Accumulation

|  | Total Sample (%) | 1st Quartile (%) | Median (%) | 3rd Quartile (%) |
|---|---|---|---|---|
| *A. Financial net worth* | | | | |
| Total sample | 17.6** | 78.7** | 32.8** | 10.0 |
| Low education | 19.5 | 95.2** | 30.0** | 8.8 |
| High education | 13.1 | 70.0** | 19.4** | 10.2 |
| *B. Total net worth* | | | | |
| Total sample | 5.7 | 29.2** | 8.7 | 0.5 |
| Low education | 3.4 | 27.0** | 7.1 | 4.0 |
| High education | 7.3 | 26.5** | 6.5 | 3.6 |
| *C. Total net worth +* *Pensions* | | | | |
| Total sample | 20.5** | 32.7** | 26.8** | 19.5** |
| Low education | 20.7** | 31.4** | 14.6* | 18.2** |
| High education | 19.4** | 39.3** | 31.2** | 17.6** |
| *D. Total net worth +* *Pensions and Social* *Security* | | | | |
| Total sample | 16.0** | 18.6** | 20.4** | 17.2** |
| Low education | 12.7** | 14.7** | 12.7** | 9.5** |
| High education | 17.7** | 25.4** | 25.8** | 17.0** |

*Notes*: This table reports the percentage changes in different measures of retirement accumulation resulting from attending retirement seminars. See Data Appendix for full estimates.
\* Indicates that the estimates from which percentages are based are statistically significant at the 10% level.
\*\* Indicates that the estimates from which percentages are based are statistically significant at the 5% level.
*Source*: See Table 9-1.

of the distribution across education groups. Estimated effects are sizable, particularly for the least wealthy. Overall, attending seminars appears to increase financial wealth by approximately 18 percent (Table 9-5, Panel A). This effect derives mainly from the bottom of the distribution, where wealth increased by more than 70 percent. The effect is also large for those with least education with increases in financial wealth close to 100 percent. The reason for such large percentage changes is that households at the bottom of the wealth distribution and those with low education have little financial net worth and increases of $2,000—the average change in wealth for those with low education that attend a retirement seminar—represent very large percentage increases.

Results for net worth show a similar pattern. Attending a retirement seminar increases net worth in the sample by approximately 6 percent. Again, the effect is mostly coming from those at the bottom of the net worth distribution. For the lowest quartile, attending a retirement seminar increases wealth by close to 30 percent. Seminars affect mostly those with less than a high-school education, increasing wealth by 27 percent for those with low education and at the bottom of the wealth distribution. The effect of seminars decreases steadily as one moves to higher quartiles of wealth (Table 9-5, Panel B).

Note that these estimates may be a lower bound of the effectiveness of retirement seminars, because the HRS provides no information about when the seminars were attended. If workers attended them recently, changes in saving behavior might not have affected wealth yet. Given that wealth is a stock, it takes time for seminars to affect it. The data set also contains no information on the content, length, and features of the seminars and, as mentioned in MacFarland, Marconi, and Utkus (Chapter 6, this volume), these could be important in evaluating and designing seminars. These estimates may also be small because of the large set of controls included in the regressions. Controlling for a smaller set of variables tends to boost estimates for retirement seminars (Lusardi, 2003). Nevertheless, regressions showed that it is important to control for the individual heterogeneity present in savings data.

## More Comprehensive Retirement Resources Measures

To extend my analysis, I take into account two additional sources of retirement resources: Social Security and pension. For the median 10 percent of wealth-holding households in the HRS, as much as 60 percent of total wealth is accounted for by Social Security and pensions (Gustman and Steinmeier, 1999a). Overall, pensions and Social Security account for half or more of total accumulation for households in all but the top decile of the wealth distribution.

Pension wealth is not evenly distributed, accounting for 7 percent for those in the bottom quarter of wealth holders, but 31 percent for those in the 75th to the 95th percentile of households (Gustman et al., 1999), while the effect of Social Security on the distribution of wealth is equalizing. As one moves up the wealth distribution, the share of total accumulation due to pensions increases while the share of Social Security falls (Gustman et al., 1999).

Incorporating a more comprehensive measure of total wealth accumulation into the analysis is not without pitfalls. One reason is that pensions and Social Security are not liquid: It is hard (if not impossible) to borrow against such wealth and it is not clear that households with large pension wealth can use it to smooth consumption prior to retirement. Second, complex calculations are required to determine pension and Social Security wealth (Gustman and Steinmeier, 1999b), and many workers lack information on their pension.[13] Nevertheless, these two components are so sizable that it is important to analyze the effects of financial education on broader measures of net worth.

In what follows, I first consider a measure of pension wealth, as reported by HRS workers, which I sum to total net worth. I next add Social Security wealth (measured as of the time of the interview) to the previous measure. Hence, these models assess whether attending a retirement seminar influences not just total net worth but also accumulations in pension and Social Security wealth. Panels C and D of Table 9-5 (and Appendix Tables A9-4 and A9-5) report the effects of seminars on these more comprehensive measures of wealth.

Retirement seminars affect not only financial and net worth but also total accumulation patterns. The economic significance of the estimated effects is also in line with previous estimates. Overall, attending seminars increases net worth inclusive of pensions by about 20 percent and total net worth inclusive of pensions and Social Security by 16 percent. When using these comprehensive measures of wealth, I find that all education groups are affected by retirement education and estimates are significant as well for every quartile of total accumulation.

## Extensions

One possible concern in the evaluation of the effectiveness of retirement seminars is that seminars may not be offered exogenously. That is, firms may be more likely to offer seminars if they think workers are unprepared for retirement. Moreover, workers who attend such seminars may do so because they have a great deal of wealth and of course, as argued by Selnow (Chapter 2, this volume), the cause and effect relationship between saving and financial education are not entirely clear. If one could identify variation in attending retirement seminars that did not result from differences in saving, then it might be possible to distinguish between the hypothesis that knowledge causes the accumulation of wealth, and the hypothesis that wealth causes the acquisition of knowledge. This can be analyzed via randomized experiments, as in Duflo and Saez (Chapter 8, this volume) or by using instrumental variables. This latter approach confirms the finding reported previously: Retirement seminars are found to foster wealth accumulation even when using instrumental variables estimation (Lusardi, 2003).

Additionally, seminars affect accumulation not only by changing how much people save, but also how they invest their portfolios. Several authors have emphasized that there can be large transaction and learning costs associated with investing in stocks, which may explain why so many households, particularly those with low education, do not invest in stocks (Haliassos and Bertaut, 1995; Vissing-Jorgensen, 2002). As reported by Lusardi (2003), retirement seminars influence the ownership of stocks: Those who have attended seminars are more likely to hold stocks. Furthermore, employees with low wealth holdings are most affected by seminars, reinforcing the conclusion that education is remedial and mainly influences those households who otherwise might not hold stocks. Analysis by education groups confirms that those with low education and lower wealth (less than $60,000) respond to retirement seminars by purchasing more stocks, but there is no effect of seminars for those with high education. This may explain why the effects of seminars are present and significant even for restricted measures of accumulation, such as financial net worth, which includes stocks.

Our estimates compare well with other works: For example, they are consistent with the findings of Bernheim and Garrett (2003) that also show that virtually all measures of retirement accumulation are higher when the respondent's employer offers financial education. Most importantly, as in this work, the effect is concentrated on the 25th and 50th percentile of accumulation and decreases or disappears at higher percentiles, a finding difficult to rationalize simply by appealing to tastes for saving. It is also consistent with the findings of Clark and Schieber (1998) that employer-provided education programs that increase the quality and type of financial information increase participation rates as well as contributions in pension plans. This may explain why the effects of retirement seminars get stronger when I consider measures of wealth inclusive of pension. Our findings are overall consistent with the work of Clark et al. (Chapter 10, this volume), who show that those individuals with less financial knowledge such as women are more likely to change their saving behavior after attending a financial education seminar, again suggesting that seminars may help those who display more difficulties in saving.

To put estimates in perspective, I have examined the effects of retirement seminars across other relevant determinants of wealth. For those in the first quartile of the net worth to permanent income ratio distribution, attending a seminar has as large an effect as not smoking or having received inheritances or money from relative and friends. The effect is also comparable to have high education: College or more than college education.

When looking at those with low education, seminars have a similar effect on net worth as having pensions. Given the difficulties or costs of changing these other variables, retirement seminars may represent a viable alternative to stimulate savings.

Other studies, such as Garman (1998) and the references therein, have argued that financial education increases workers productivity and reduces absenteeism to deal with personal financial matters and overall absences from work. The value to employers of these benefits of financial education is estimated at around $400, a figure easily above the costs of providing financial education. While these studies are often qualitative and based on small samples, they represent initial evidence from which to build more research. If saving stimulus improves household well-being, retirement seminars may be a worthy initiative. Examining data for workers who have already retired, Lusardi (2002) shows that those who did not plan are more likely to report a less satisfying retirement. Since lack of planning is usually associated with low wealth, this may explain the link to retirement satisfaction. A similar finding is reported by Panis (Chapter 14, this volume), who finds that retired respondents with low wealth are much less likely to report a satisfying retirement. Similarly, respondents with lower net worth report more frequent signs of depression.

## Conclusions

This chapter examines how retirement seminars help explain the wide differences in retirement accumulation that we observe across older households. The results show that seminars are remedial and appear to affect those at the bottom of the wealth distribution the most. The effects become even stronger for every education group and every quartile of the wealth distribution if pension and Social Security wealth are included in the household wealth measures.

These estimates imply that retirement seminars can influence the accumulation of both net worth and broader measures of wealth. Both financial and net worth can increase by 20 percent and a lot more across subgroups of low education when workers attend retirement seminars. A broader wealth measure, inclusive of pension and Social Security relative to permanent income, rises by 15–20 percent for both high and low-education families.

While the provision of information and the reduction of planning costs could play an important role in improving the financial security of many US households, it should be recalled that only a small number of workers currently attends retirement seminars. Consequently, many remain untouched by employers' efforts to provide financial education. This fact represents an important topic for future research and a challenge for policymakers. Moreover, many of the households with low education or at the bottom of the wealth distribution are minorities, particularly Blacks and Hispanics. They not only save little but often do not hold any high-return and tax-favored assets or even simple assets such as checking accounts. To understand the saving behavior and the effectiveness of financial education for these groups, it may be important to study them in isolation.

## Data Appendix

The data used in this chapter are taken from the 1992 wave of HRS. The HRS is a representative sample of individuals born in the year 1931–41 (approximately 51–61 at the time of the interview), through Blacks, Hispanics, and Floridians were oversampled. The individual deemed most knowledgeable about the family's assets, debts, and retirement planning was asked questions on housing, wealth, and income. As described in more detail in the text, one distinctive feature of the HRS is the attention paid to expectations about future events. A second innovation of the HRS is the use of bracketing or unfolding techniques to reduce the missing data problems in the measurement of financial variables. In the HRS, respondents who reported they did not know or refused to provide an estimate of the size of a net worth component were asked to report the value in a set of brackets. Smith (1995) and Juster and Smith (1997) evaluate these techniques and a detailed description of their advantages in improving the accuracy of information about household wealth.

The sample for the initial analysis I deleted respondents who were partially or fully retired at the time of the interview, and only financial respondents were considered between the ages of 50 and 61. The final sample for empirical analysis (Tables 9A-2–A-5) additionally deletes respondents who lack information on the variables used in the empirical estimation. The self-employed are not asked many of the questions about subjective future probabilities so they are deleted from the sample. Similarly, expectations about changes in income are not asked to respondents who are not working, so they are also excluded from the sample. Since the distribution of the ratio of total and financial net worth to permanent income is so wide, I trim the distribution and exclude the top and bottom 1 percent, resulting in a total number of observations of 3,265. Appendix Table 9A-1 reports descriptive statistics of variables used in the empirical estimation. The original sample which only excluded respondents who are retired or younger than 50 and older than 61 had 5,292 observations; the decrease to 3,265 is mainly due to the fact that some questions were only asked to respondents who were working. There is little reason to believe that the final sample suffers from self-selection. With respect to the original sample, the final sample covers respondents who are a little younger, more likely to be white (the fraction white is 0.79 initially versus 0.818 in my sample), more likely to be born in the United States (0.89 initially versus 0.924 in my sample), a bit more educated (0.11 have a college degree versus 0.129 in my sample). Overall, differences between these two samples are small.

# Appendix

TABLE 9A-1  Descriptive Statistics

| Variables | Mean | (Std.Dev.) |
|---|---|---|
| Financial net worth/permanent income | 0.758 | (1.261) |
| Total net worth/ permanent income | 2.590 | (2.628) |
| (Total net worth + pension)/permanent income | 4.214 | (3.512) |
| (Total net worth + pension + SS worth)/ permanent income | 6.727 | (3.741) |
| Stock ownership | 0.290 | (0.454) |
| Have not thought about retirement | 0.224 | (0.417) |
| Attended a retirement seminar | 0.126 | (0.332) |
| Age | 54.40 | (3.857) |
| # of children at home | 0.806 | (1.009) |
| Male | 0.507 | (0.500) |
| White | 0.818 | (0.385) |
| US born | 0.924 | (0.264) |
| Married | 0.624 | (0.484) |
| Divorced | 0.185 | (0.389) |
| Widowed | 0.086 | (0.282) |
| Separated | 0.035 | (0.177) |
| Northeast region | 0.224 | (0.417) |
| Midwest region | 0.249 | (0.433) |
| West region | 0.185 | (0.389) |
| High school | 0.388 | (0.487) |
| Some college | 0.214 | (0.410) |
| College | 0.129 | (0.336 |
| More than college | 0.106 | (0.308) |
| Excellent health | 0.276 | (0.447) |
| Very good health | 0.331 | (0.470) |
| Good health | 0.275 | (0.447) |
| Past unemployment | 0.361 | (0.481) |
| Past shocks | 0.328 | (0.469) |
| Received inheritances | 0.197 | (0.397) |
| Received money from relatives | 0.080 | (0.271) |
| Received money from insurance settlements | 0.057 | (0.233) |
| High risk aversion | 0.647 | (0.478) |
| Moderate risk aversion | 0.130 | (0.336) |
| Medium risk aversion | 0.108 | (0.311) |
| Permanent income /1000 | 51.846 | (20.990) |
| Expectation to live to 75 | 0.660 | (0.276) |
| Expectation that SS will be less generous | 0.605 | (0.289) |
| Expectation that house prices will go up | 0.480 | (0.286) |
| Expectation to give major financial help to family | 0.406 | (0.307) |
| Heavy smoker | 0.168 | 0.374 |
| Heavy drinker | 0.048 | (0.214) |
| No regular exercise | 0.416 | (0.493) |
| Talks to doctors about health | 0.783 | (0.412) |
| Bequest | 0.420 | (0.493) |
| Parents still alive | 0.686 | (0.464) |
| Variance of income | 2.010 | (7.687) |
| Can rely on help from relatives and friends | 0.431 | (0.495) |
| # of observations | 3,265 | |

Source: See Table 9-1.

TABLE 9A-2 Determinants of Financial Net Worth Accumulation in the 1992 HRS

| | Total Sample | | 1st Quartile | | Median | | 3rd Quartile | |
|---|---|---|---|---|---|---|---|---|
| | Coeff. | Std. Err. | Coeff. | Std. Err. | Coeff. | Std. Err. | Coeff. | Std. Err. |
| Constant | −0.274 | 3.000 | −0.036 | 0.494 | −0.958 | 1.753 | 2.216 | 3.575 |
| Seminar | 0.137** | 0.065 | 0.088** | 0.011 | 0.134** | 0.040 | 0.103 | 0.086 |
| *Health* | | | | | | | | |
| Excellent health | 0.144* | 0.080 | 0.058** | 0.013 | 0.071 | 0.048 | 0.146 | 0.102 |
| Very good health | 0.091 | 0.075 | 0.076** | 0.012 | 0.073 | 0.045 | 0.108 | 0.095 |
| Good health | 0.069 | 0.074 | 0.048** | 0.012 | 0.025 | 0.044 | 0.088 | 0.093 |
| *Pos./Neg. shocks* | | | | | | | | |
| Past unemployment | −0.004 | 0.047 | −0.023** | 0.008 | −0.027 | 0.028 | −0.055 | 0.061 |
| Past shocks | −0.287** | 0.045 | −0.067** | 0.008 | −0.13** | 0.028 | −0.279** | 0.059 |
| Received inheritances | 0.248** | 0.055 | 0.043** | 0.009 | 0.254** | 0.034 | 0.350** | 0.072 |
| Money from relatives | 0.229** | 0.077 | 0.022 | 0.013 | 0.118** | 0.049 | 0.301** | 0.103 |
| Money from insurance | 0.490** | 0.101 | 0.089** | 0.017 | 0.359** | 0.063 | 0.570** | 0.133 |
| *Risk aversion* | | | | | | | | |
| High risk aversion | −0.113* | 0.068 | 0.007 | 0.011 | 0.004 | 0.041 | 0.021 | 0.087 |
| Medium risk aversion | −0.127 | 0.084 | 0.036** | 0.014 | 0.020 | 0.052 | 0.042 | 0.109 |
| Moderate risk aversion | −0.186** | 0.088 | 0.014 | 0.015 | −0.019 | 0.054 | −0.126 | 0.113 |
| *Subjective expectations* | | | | | | | | |
| Expectation to live to 75 | 0.022 | 0.081 | −0.020 | 0.014 | −0.029 | 0.049 | 0.042 | 0.103 |
| Expecting SS more gener. | 0.067 | 0.073 | 0.007 | 0.012 | 0.015 | 0.044 | 0.105 | 0.095 |
| Expecting house price up | −0.261** | 0.075 | −0.029** | 0.013 | −0.064 | 0.045 | −0.280** | 0.096 |
| Expectation to give help to family | 0.167** | 0.070 | 0.031** | 0.012 | 0.025 | 0.042 | 0.126 | 0.092 |

| | | | | | | | | |
|---|---|---|---|---|---|---|---|---|
| *Bequests and help* | | | | | | | | |
| Bequests | 0.312** | 0.043 | 0.099** | 0.007 | 0.203** | 0.027 | 0.428** | 0.057 |
| Parent alive | −0.068 | 0.050 | 0.011 | 0.008 | −0.011 | 0.030 | −0.004 | 0.064 |
| Can rely on help | 0.031 | 0.043 | 0.027** | 0.007 | 0.045* | 0.026 | 0.053 | 0.056 |
| *General attitudes* | | | | | | | | |
| Heavy smoker | −0.179** | 0.058 | −0.038** | 0.010 | −0.09** | 0.036 | −0.190** | 0.077 |
| Heavy drinker | −0.028 | 0.099 | −0.002 | 0.017 | −0.015 | 0.060 | −0.015 | 0.127 |
| No regular exercise | −0.091** | 0.045 | −0.022** | 0.008 | −0.06** | 0.028 | −0.099* | 0.059 |
| Talk to doctor about health | 0.161** | 0.052 | 0.016* | 0.009 | 0.035 | 0.032 | 0.172*** | 0.067 |
| *Income and pension* | | | | | | | | |
| Permanent inc./1000 | −0.004 | 0.003 | 0.0008 | 0.0005 | −0.0005 | 0.002 | −0.001 | 0.004 |
| Variance of income | 0.003 | 0.003 | 0.003** | 0.0007 | 0.008** | 0.001 | 0.014** | 0.003 |
| Pension | −0.029 | 0.050 | 0.0006 | 0.008 | 0.005 | 0.030 | 0.008 | 0.066 |
| Adjusted/Pseudo $R^2$ | 0.129 | | 0.049 | | 0.097 | | 0.131 | |

\* Indicates statistical significance at the 10% level.

\*\* Indicates statistical significance at the 5% level.

*Notes*: This table reports OLS and quantile regressions of the determinants of the ratio of financial net worth to permanent income. Models include additional demographic controls including age, sex, race, marital status, number of children, education, regions, and a dummy for whether the respondent is born in the United States.

*Source*: See Table 9-1.

TABLE 9A-3  Determinants of Financial Net Worth Accumulation in the 1992 HRS

| | Total Sample | | Low Education Sample (High School or Less) | | | | | |
| | | | 1st Quartile | | Median | | 3rd Quartile | |
| | Coeff. | Std. Err. | Coeff. | Std. Err. | Coeff. | Std. Err. | Coeff. | Std. Err. |
|---|---|---|---|---|---|---|---|---|
| *Constant* | 3.560 | 4.069 | 0.094 | 0.614 | 0.572 | 1.582 | 2.756 | 4.202 |
| *Seminar* | 0.127 | 0.099 | 0.051** | 0.015 | 0.088** | 0.041 | 0.070 | 0.115 |
| *Health* | | | | | | | | |
| Excellent health | 0.257** | 0.099 | 0.025* | 0.015 | 0.027 | 0.040 | 0.137 | 0.109 |
| Very good health | 0.198** | 0.091 | 0.060** | 0.014 | 0.064* | 0.037 | 0.114 | 0.098 |
| Good health | 0.145* | 0.087 | 0.023* | 0.013 | −0.004 | 0.035 | 0.077 | 0.094 |
| *Pos./Neg. shocks* | | | | | | | | |
| Past unemployment | 0.001 | 0.059 | −0.02** | 0.009 | −0.025 | 0.024 | −0.064 | 0.067 |
| Past shocks | −0.249** | 0.061 | −0.04** | 0.009 | −0.115** | 0.025 | −0.25** | 0.069 |
| Received inheritances | 0.166** | 0.080 | 0.033** | 0.012 | 0.183** | 0.034 | 0.225** | 0.093 |
| Money from relatives | 0.055 | 0.117 | 0.052** | 0.019 | 0.034 | 0.050 | 0.010 | 0.137 |
| Money from insurance | 0.473** | 0.137 | 0.082** | 0.021 | 0.243** | 0.058 | 0.737** | 0.157 |
| *Risk aversion* | | | | | | | | |
| High risk aversion | −0.038 | 0.096 | 0.002 | 0.014 | −0.009 | 0.039 | 0.115 | 0.105 |
| Medium risk aversion | −0.038 | 0.121 | 0.035* | 0.019 | 0.019 | 0.050 | 0.143 | 0.135 |
| Moderate risk aversion | −0.081 | 0.123 | 0.010 | 0.019 | −0.050 | 0.050 | −0.011 | 0.135 |
| *Subjective expectations* | | | | | | | | |
| Expectation to live to 75 | 0.017 | 0.101 | −0.010 | 0.015 | −0.035 | 0.041 | 0.024 | 0.112 |
| Expecting SS more gener. | 0.061 | 0.095 | −0.005 | 0.014 | 0.025 | 0.038 | 0.0007 | 0.105 |
| Expecting house price up | −0.277** | 0.095 | −0.04** | 0.015 | −0.046 | 0.039 | −0.200* | 0.105 |
| Expected to give help to family | 0.116 | 0.091 | 0.030** | 0.014 | 0.031 | 0.037 | 0.093 | 0.104 |

|  | | | | | | | | |
|---|---|---|---|---|---|---|---|---|
| *Bequests and help* | | | | | | | | |
| Bequests | 0.291** | 0.059 | 0.063** | 0.009 | 0.148** | 0.024 | 0.341** | 0.068 |
| Parent alive | −0.038 | 0.064 | 0.011 | 0.010 | −0.017 | 0.026 | −0.024 | 0.072 |
| Can rely on help | −0.019 | 0.057 | 0.008 | 0.009 | 0.022 | 0.024 | 0.036 | 0.065 |
| *General attitudes* | | | | | | | | |
| Heavy smoker | −0.165** | 0.072 | −0.02** | 0.011 | −0.058* | 0.030 | −0.194** | 0.082 |
| Heavy drinker | −0.144 | 0.131 | −0.007 | 0.020 | −0.054 | 0.053 | −0.008 | 0.138 |
| No regular exercise | −0.049 | 0.058 | −0.012 | 0.009 | −0.06** | 0.024 | −0.024 | 0.066 |
| Talk to doctor about health | 0.127* | 0.065 | 0.012 | 0.010 | 0.047* | 0.027 | 0.114 | 0.075 |
| *Income and wealth* | | | | | | | | |
| Permanent inc./1000 | −0.003 | 0.003 | 0.002** | 0.0005 | 0.003** | 0.001 | 0.004 | 0.004 |
| Variance of income | 0.017** | 0.008 | 0.006** | 0.001 | 0.011** | 0.003 | 0.023** | 0.011 |
| Pension | 0.021 | 0.062 | −0.002 | 0.009 | −0.001 | 0.025 | −0.005 | 0.071 |
| Adjusted/Pseudo $R^2$ | 0.105 | | 0.028 | | 0.076 | | 0.121 | |

* Indicates statistical significance at the 10% level.
** Indicates statistical significance at the 5% level.

*Notes:* See Table 9A-2. Estimates refer to the sample of respondents with high school education or lower.

*Source:* See Table 9-1.

TABLE 9A-4 Determinants of Total Net Worth Accumulation in the 1992 HRS

|  | Total Sample | | | | | | | |
| --- | --- | --- | --- | --- | --- | --- | --- | --- |
|  | Total Sample | | 1st Quartile | | Median | | 3rd Quartile | |
|  | Coeff. | Std. Err. | Coeff. | Std. Err. | Coeff. | Std. Err. | Coeff. | Std. Err. |
| Constant | −2.044 | 6.148 | −2.061 | 3.112 | −4.044 | 5.454 | −1.904 | 7.108 |
| Seminar | 0.149 | 0.133 | 0.308** | 0.069 | 0.175 | 0.124 | 0.019 | 0.164 |
| *Health* | | | | | | | | |
| Excellent health | 0.560** | 0.164 | 0.304** | 0.088 | 0.455** | 0.149 | 0.907** | 0.195 |
| Very good health | 0.195 | 0.154 | 0.186** | 0.081 | 0.291** | 0.139 | 0.407** | 0.181 |
| Good health | 0.170 | 0.152 | 0.218** | 0.078 | 0.264* | 0.136 | 0.432** | 0.177 |
| *Pos./Neg. shocks* | | | | | | | | |
| Past unemployment | −0.290** | 0.096 | −0.142* | 0.050 | −0.313** | 0.088 | −0.344** | 0.117 |
| Past shocks | −0.522** | 0.093 | −0.293** | 0.050 | −0.392** | 0.087 | −0.571** | 0.115 |
| Received inheritances | 0.672** | 0.112 | 0.293** | 0.061 | 0.507** | 0.106 | 0.813** | 0.138 |
| Money from relatives | 0.723** | 0.158 | 0.359** | 0.085 | 0.728** | 0.150 | 0.794** | 0.200 |
| Money from insurance | 0.797** | 0.208 | 0.561** | 0.108 | 0.760** | 0.198 | 0.641** | 0.252 |
| *Risk aversion* | | | | | | | | |
| High risk aversion | 0.009 | 0.139 | 0.124* | 0.072 | 0.131 | 0.128 | 0.369** | 0.165 |
| Medium risk aversion | 0.106 | 0.173 | 0.140 | 0.092 | 0.166 | 0.161 | 0.421** | 0.208 |
| Moderate risk aversion | −0.093 | 0.181 | 0.167* | 0.095 | 0.231 | 0.168 | 0.103 | 0.218 |
| *Subjective expectations* | | | | | | | | |
| Expected to live to 75 | 0.078 | 0.166 | −0.128 | 0.088 | 0.036 | 0.153 | −0.018 | 0.198 |
| Expecting SS more gener. | −0.125 | 0.149 | 0.021 | 0.078 | 0.045 | 0.137 | −0.139 | 0.184 |
| Expecting house price up | −0.452** | 0.153 | −0.236** | 0.082 | −0.447** | 0.141 | −0.489** | 0.186 |
| Expected to give help to family | 0.359** | 0.143 | 0.079 | 0.074 | 0.284** | 0.132 | 0.551** | 0.176 |

*Bequests and help*

| | | | | | | | |
|---|---|---|---|---|---|---|---|
| Bequests | 1.115** | 0.089 | 0.543** | 0.047 | 0.877** | 0.083 | 1.288** | 0.110 |
| Parent alive | −0.142 | 0.102 | 0.034 | 0.053 | 0.023 | 0.094 | −0.180 | 0.124 |
| Can rely on help | 0.008 | 0.088 | 0.084 | 0.046 | 0.135* | 0.082 | 0.194* | 0.109 |
| *General attitudes* | | | | | | | | |
| Heavy smoker | −0.479** | 0.119 | −0.287** | 0.065 | −0.433** | 0.112 | −0.702** | 0.146 |
| Heavy drinker | −0.324 | 0.203 | −0.232*** | 0.110 | −0.102 | 0.188 | −0.094 | 0.238 |
| No regular exercise | −0.268** | 0.093 | −0.176*** | 0.050 | −0.219** | 0.087 | −0.286** | 0.114 |
| Talk to doctor about health | 0.309** | 0.106 | 0.084 | 0.056 | 0.157 | 0.099 | 0.460** | 0.129 |
| *Income and wealth* | | | | | | | | |
| Permanent inc./1000 | −0.033** | 0.006 | −0.001 | 0.003 | −0.013** | 0.006 | −0.036** | 0.008 |
| Variance of income | 0.007 | 0.005 | 0.003 | 0.004 | 0.021** | 0.005 | 0.026** | 0.005 |
| Pension | 0.174* | 0.102 | 0.189** | 0.054 | 0.186** | 0.094 | 0.164 | 0.126 |
| Adjusted/Pseudo $R^2$ | 0.158 | | 0.112 | | 0.113 | | 0.130 | |

*Notes*: This table reports OLS and quantile regressions of the determinants of the ratio of total net worth to permanent income. Models include additional demographic controls including age, sex, race, marital status, number of children, education, regions, and a dummy for whether the respondent is born in the United States.

* Indicates statistical significance at the 10% level.

** Indicates statistical significance at the 5% level.

*Source*: See Table 9-1.

TABLE 9A-5 Determinants of Total Net Worth Accumulation in the 1992 HRS

| | Total Sample | | Low-Education Sample (High School or Less) | | | | | |
| | | | 1st Quartile | | Median | | 3rd Quartile | |
| | Coeff. | Std. Err. | Coeff. | Std. Err. | Coeff. | Std. Err. | Coeff. | Std. Err. |
|---|---|---|---|---|---|---|---|---|
| *Constant* | 4.485 | 8.556 | −1.939 | 3.418 | −0.915 | 5.813 | 0.632 | 14.238 |
| *Seminar* | 0.085 | 0.209 | 0.272** | 0.089 | 0.134 | 0.146 | 0.131 | 0.373 |
| *Health* | | | | | | | | |
| Excellent health | 0.561** | 0.207 | 0.243** | 0.084 | 0.464** | 0.145 | 0.862** | 0.373 |
| Very good health | 0.233 | 0.190 | 0.203** | 0.084 | 0.451** | 0.131 | 0.355 | 0.338 |
| Good health | 0.052 | 0.182 | 0.113 | 0.079 | 0.304** | 0.125 | 0.271 | 0.321 |
| *Pos./Neg. shocks* | | | | | | | | |
| Past unemployment | −0.225* | 0.124 | −0.109** | 0.054 | −0.269** | 0.086 | −0.275 | 0.224 |
| Past shocks | −0.452** | 0.128 | −0.270** | 0.058 | −0.344** | 0.091 | −0.420* | 0.231 |
| Received inheritances | 0.895** | 0.169 | 0.474** | 0.075 | 0.658** | 0.121 | 0.993** | 0.310 |
| Money from relatives | 0.736** | 0.246 | 0.436** | 0.113 | 0.825** | 0.178 | 0.757* | 0.450 |
| Money from insurance | 0.994** | 0.288 | 0.602** | 0.129 | 0.971** | 0.203 | 0.519 | 0.516 |
| *Risk aversion* | | | | | | | | |
| High risk aversion | 0.022 | 0.202 | 0.192** | 0.088 | 0.110 | 0.141 | 0.440 | 0.343 |
| Medium risk aversion | 0.275 | 0.254 | 0.253** | 0.111 | 0.337* | 0.178 | 0.331 | 0.451 |
| Moderate risk aversion | −0.056 | 0.258 | 0.265** | 0.114 | 0.053 | 0.182 | 0.059 | 0.449 |
| *Subjective expectations* | | | | | | | | |
| Expected to live to 75 | 0.137 | 0.213 | −0.116 | 0.095 | 0.049 | 0.149 | −0.078 | 0.377 |
| Expecting SS more gener. | −0.071 | 0.199 | 0.101 | 0.086 | 0.096 | 0.137 | −0.047 | 0.355 |
| Expecting house price up | −0.568*** | 0.200 | −0.277** | 0.090 | −0.537** | 0.139 | −0.425 | 0.357 |
| Expected to give help to family | 0.107 | 0.191 | 0.059 | 0.082 | 0.255* | 0.133 | 0.198 | 0.353 |

| | (1) | (2) | (3) | (4) | (5) | (6) | (7) | (8) |
|---|---|---|---|---|---|---|---|---|
| *Bequests and help* | | | | | | | | |
| Bequests | 1.118** | 0.124 | 0.513** | 0.055 | 0.860** | 0.087 | 1.280** | 0.226 |
| Parent alive | 0.006 | 0.134 | 0.035 | 0.059 | 0.175* | 0.095 | 0.120 | 0.243 |
| Can rely on help | −0.035 | 0.121 | 0.024 | 0.053 | 0.070 | 0.085 | 0.321 | 0.223 |
| *General attitudes* | | | | | | | | |
| Heavy smoker | −0.367** | 0.151 | −0.284** | 0.070 | −0.357** | 0.108 | −0.481* | 0.277 |
| Heavy drinker | −0.422 | 0.276 | −0.256** | 0.125 | −0.221 | 0.190 | −0.269 | 0.460 |
| No regular exercise | −0.227* | 0.123 | −0.091* | 0.054 | −0.165* | 0.086 | −0.271 | 0.224 |
| Talk to doctor about health | 0.183 | 0.137 | 0.073 | 0.061 | 0.063 | 0.096 | 0.247 | 0.250 |
| *Income and wealth* | | | | | | | | |
| Permanent inc./1000 | −0.038** | 0.007 | 0.004 | 0.003 | −0.012** | 0.086 | −0.038** | 0.014 |
| Variance of income | 0.043** | 0.017 | 0.031** | 0.007 | 0.030** | 0.012 | 0.062** | 0.027 |
| Pension | 0.392** | 0.130 | 0.269** | 0.057 | 0.220** | 0.091 | 0.397** | 0.237 |
| Adjusted/Pseudo $R^2$ | 0.155 | | 0.121 | | 0.124 | | 0.132 | |

*Notes*: See Table 9A-4. Estimates refer to the sample of respondents with high school education or lower.

\* Indicates statistical significance at the 10% level.

\*\* Indicates statistical significance at the 5% level.

*Source*: See Table 9.1.

# Notes

[1] Author's computations among others is from the US Department of Labor's Abstract of 1998 Form 5500 Annual Reports.

[2] Cf. McCarthy and Turner (1996), Bernheim (1995, 1998), Bayer, Bernheim, and Scholz (1996), Clark and Schieber (1998), Madrian and Shea (2001), Bernheim and Garrett (2003), Clark d'Ambrosio, McDermed, and Sawant (Chapter 10, this volume).

[3] The implementation of new techniques to elicit information about wealth in the HRS has led to rather accurate wealth reports. For a thorough examination of the quality of HRS data and comparisons with other data sets, see Juster and Smith (1997) and Smith (1995), and the Data Appendix.

[4] An excellent examination of subjective probabilities in the HRS is provided in Hurd and McGarry (1995) and Hurd (1996). See Lusardi (1998) analyzes the probability of losing one's job next year and how this variable can be used to construct a measure of the variance of earnings.

[5] Special authorization is needed to access Social Security records. For detail on the construction of Social Security wealth, see Mitchell, Olson, and Steinmeier (2000).

[6] Alan Gustman and Tom Steinmeier provided the imputed Social Security wealth data; see Gustman and Steinmeier (1999a,b).

[7] For a detailed explanation of the construction of the pension data, see Venti and Wise (2001).

[8] For a more detailed discussion of the importance of business owners to explain wealth accumulation, see Hurst and Lusardi (2004) and Gentry and Hubbard (2000).

[9] Whether business equity represents accumulation for retirement is unclear.

[10] The description of the sample is provided in the Data Appendix.

[11] HRS respondents are asked whether "they plan to leave a sizable inheritance to their heirs." Here, I have grouped together all respondents who answered "yes" to this question, although several degrees of certainty exist (very likely, likely, etc.).

[12] For detail on the construction of this variable, see Lusardi (1998).

[13] Social Security wealth is calculated as the present value of the Social Security benefit payable in the form of an annuity from retirement until death. The variable I consider refers to the HRS respondent entitlement as of 1992; see Mitchell, Olson, and Steinmeier (2000) for calculations of Social Security wealth.

# References

Bayer, Patrick, Douglas Bernheim, and J. Karl Scholz. 1996. "The Effects of Financial Education in the Workplace: Evidence from a Survey of Employers." NBER Working Paper 5655.

Barsky, Robert, Miles Kimball, Thomas Juster, and Matthew Shapiro. 1997. "Preference Parameters and Behavioral Heterogeneity: An Experimental Approach in the Health and Retirement Study." *Quarterly Journal of Economics* 62(2): 537–579.

Bernheim, B. Douglas. 1995. "Do Households Appreciate Their Financial Vulnerabilities? An Analysis of Actions, Perceptions, and Public Policy." *Tax Policy and Economic Growth*. Washington, DC: American Council for Capital Formation: 1–30.

—— 1998. "Financial Illiteracy, Education and Retirement Saving." In *Living with Defined Contribution Pensions*, eds. Olivia Mitchell and Sylvester Schieber. Philadelphia: University of Pennsylvania Press: 38–68.

Bernheim, B. Douglas and Daniel Garrett. 2003. "The Effects of Financial Education in the Workplace: Evidence from a Survey of Households." *Journal of Public Economics* 87: 1487–1519.

Clark, Robert and Sylvester Schieber. 1998. "Factors Affecting Participation Rates and Contribution Levels in 401(k) Plans." In *Living with Defined Contribution Pensions*, eds. Olivia Mitchell and Sylvester Schieber. Philadelphia: University of Pennsylvania Press: 69–97.

Employee Benefits Research Institute (EBRI). 1996. "Participant Education: Actions and Outcomes." *Issue Brief* 169. Washington DC: EBRI, January.

—— (EBRI). 2001. "Retirement Confidence Survey (RCS), Minority RCS, and Small Employer Retirement Survey." *Issue Brief* 234. Washington DC: EBRI, June.

Garman, Thomas. 1998. "The Business Case for Financial Education." *Personal Finances and Worker Productivity* 2(1): 81–93.

Gentry, William and Glenn Hubbard. 2000. "Entrepreneurship and Household Saving," NBER Working Paper 7894.

Gustman, Alan and Tom Steinmeier. 1999a. "Effects of Pensions on Savings: Analysis with Data from the Health and Retirement Study." *Carnegie-Rochester Conference Series on Public Policy* 50: 271–324.

—— 1999b. "What People Don't Know about their Pensions and Social Security: An Analysis Using Linked Data from the Health and Retirement Study." NBER Working Paper 7368.

——, Olivia S. Mitchell, Andrew Samwick, and Thomas Steinmeier. 1999. "Pension and Social Security Wealth in the Health and Retirement Study." In *Wealth, Work and Health*, eds. James Smith and Robert Willis. Ann Arbor, MI: University of Michigan Press: 150–208.

Haliassos, Michael and Carol Bertaut. 1995. "Why Do So Few Hold Stocks?" *Economic Journal* 105(432): 1110–1129.

Hurd, Michael. 1996. "Labor Market Transitions in the HRS: Effects of the Subjective Probability of Retirement and of Pension Eligibility." Rand Working Paper.

—— and Kathleen McGarry. 1995. "Evaluation of the Subjective Probabilities of Survival in the Health and Retirement Study." *Journal of Human Resources* 30: S268–S292.

—— and Julie Zissimopoulos. 2000. "Inadequate Retirement Savings: An Experimental Approach to Understanding Saving Behavior." Rand Working Paper.

Hurst, Erik and Annamaria Lusardi. 2004. "Liquidity Constraints, Household Wealth, and Entrepreneurship." *Journal of Political Economy* 112(2) April: 319–347.

Juster, Thomas and James Smith. 1997. "Improving the Quality of Economic Data: Lessons from the HRS and AHEAD." *Journal of the American Economic Association* 92(440): 1268–1278.

Lusardi, Annamaria. 1998. "On the Importance of the Precautionary Saving Motive." *American Economic Review* 88(2): 449–453.

—— 1999. "Information, Expectations, and Savings for Retirement." In *Behavioral Dimensions of Retirement Economics*, ed. Henry Aaron. Washington, DC: Brookings Institution Press and Russell Sage Foundation: 81–115.

Lusardi, Annamaria. 2000. "Saving for Retirement: The Importance of Planning." *Research Dialogue* 66, New York: TIAA–CREF Institute.

——2002. "Explaining Why So Many Households Do Not Save." Dartmouth College Working Paper.

——2003. "Savings and the Effectiveness of Retirement Seminars." Dartmouth College Working Paper.

——2003. "Preparing for Retirement: The Importance of Planning Costs." *National Tax Association Proceedings.*

——, Ricardo Cossa, and Erin Krupka. 2001. "Savings of Young Parents." *Journal of Human Resources* 36(4): 762–794.

Madrian, Brigitte and Dennis Shea. 2001. "The Power of Suggestion: Inertia in 401(k) Participation and Savings Behavior." *Quarterly Journal of Economics* 66(4): 1149–1187.

McCarthy, David and John Turner. 1996. "Financial Sophistication, Saving and Risk Bearing." Washington DC: US Department of Labor Working Paper.

Mitchell, Olivia S., Jan Olson, and Thomas Steinmeier. 2000. "Social Security Earnings and Projected Benefits." In *Forecasting Retirement Needs and Retirement Wealth*, eds. Olivia S. Mitchell, P. Brett Hammond and Anna Rappaport. Philadelphia: University of Pennsylvania Press: 327–359.

Moore, James and Olivia S. Mitchell. 2000. "Projected Retirement Wealth and Saving Adequacy." In *Forecasting Retirement Needs and Retirement Wealth*, eds. Olivia Mitchell, P. Brett Hammond and Anna Rappaport. Philadelphia: University of Pennsylvania Press: 68–94.

Smith, James. 1995. "Racial and Ethnic Differences in Wealth in the Health and Retirement Study." *Journal of Human Resources* 30(Suppl.): 158–183.

US Department of Labor, Pension and Welfare Benefits Administration. *Abstract of 1998 Form 5500 Annual Reports.* Pension Plan Bulletin N. 11, Winter 2001–2002. Washington, DC.

Venti, Steven and David Wise. 2001. "Choice, Chance, and Wealth Dispersion at Retirement." In *Aging Issues in the United States and Japan*, eds. S. Ogura, T. Tachibanaki, and D. Wise. Chicago, IL: University of Chicago Press: 25–64.

Vissing-Jorgensen, Annette. 2002. "Limited Asset Participation and the Elasticity of Intertemporal Substitution." *Journal of Political Economy* 110(4): 825–853.

Warshawsky, Mark and John Ameriks. 2000. "How Prepared Are Americans for Retirement?" In *Forecasting Retirement Needs and Retirement Wealth*, eds. Olivia Mitchell, P. Brett Hammond, and Anna Rappaport. Philadelphia, PA: University of Pennsylvania Press: 33–67.

Weir, David and Robert Willis. 2000. "Prospects for Widow Poverty." In *Forecasting Retirement Needs and Retirement Wealth*, eds. Olivia Mitchell, P. Brett Hammond, and Anna Rappaport. Philadelphia, PA: University of Pennsylvania Press: 208–234.

# Chapter 10

# Sex Differences, Financial Education, and Retirement Goals

*Robert L. Clark, Madeleine B. d'Ambrosio,
Ann A. McDermed, and Kshama Sawant*

Many labor market differences have been documented between men and women, including in occupational choice, labor force attachment, hours of work, job tenure, and pay. Yet, little is known about sex differences in retirement objectives, retirement saving, and responses to financial educational events. This chapter examines sex differences in initial retirement goals and responses to financial education seminars. Responses are measured as revised retirement targets and changes in saving and investment behavior.

This is an important issue because women tend to have smaller accumulations in their basic and supplemental retirement plans, they are more likely to be employed in occupations requiring lower skills and less education, they have fewer years of job tenure, and they tend to have lower annual earnings. Consequently, women may be less prepared financially for retirement than men, and they may also be less able to enhance their retirement saving due to the prospects of lower earnings during their working lives. Developing an adequate financial plan is also very important for women, given their long life expectancies, greater chances of becoming widowed, and higher probabilities of needing nursing home care late in life. Secretary of Labor Elaine Chao was quoted on this problem stating as "Americans are saving too little, often dangerously too little. The average 50-year-old has less than $40,000 in personal financial wealth. And the average American retires with only enough savings to provide about 60 percent of former annual income. The problem is especially acute for women and minorities" (*USA Today*, 2003). Smaller account balances and lower annual

The authors acknowledge the cooperation of many consultants in TIAA-CREF Consulting Services who administered the surveys in conjunction with seminars around the country. They also thank Pirie McIndoe, Al Gonzalez, and Brian Usischon, of the TIAA-CREF Raleigh-Durham Office, for their assistance in pre-testing the survey and Robert Romano, of the TIAA-CREF Sales Support, for his efforts in coordinating the integration of the surveys with the financial education seminars. Paul Mulvey played a major role in the design of the survey. Juanita Kreps contributed to the development of the overall project. Mike Sitar provided research assistance. Research support was provided by the TIAA-CREF Institute.

saving rates must indicate that women have set lower goals for retirement income. Alternatively, women could have similar retirement goals as men but they could be making larger and more systematic errors in their retirement saving behavior. Finally, if women invest more conservatively than men, similar saving rates might yield different account balances at the end of a working career.

Mismatches in retirement goals and saving behavior for both men and women may be the result of inadequate knowledge of financial markets and the saving process.[1] If true, then workers should respond to financial education by altering either their goals (age of retirement and retirement income) and their saving behavior (changing the amount that they save each year or changing their investment allocations). If workers are on track to achieve their retirement goals, participation in financial education events should not alter their saving behavior. Instead, the educational experience should confirm that the household has set realistic retirement goals and is making reasonable choices to achieve these objectives.

To assess the role of financial education on individual retirement saving, we examine participants in retirement education seminars and estimate how they respond to the information presented regarding how financial markets work, the need to set specific retirement goals, and the retirement saving process. The behavior of men and women is examined separately to determine whether there are significant differences by sex.[2]

## Individual Responsibility for Retirement Saving

The structure of retirement plans has changed substantially, significantly increasing the role of workers in the determination of their retirement income. Though the proportion of the labor force covered by any type of pension plan has remained relatively stable at around 50 percent over the past 25 years, coverage rates in defined benefit (DB) plans have plummeted, while participation in primary defined contribution (DC) plans has grown rapidly. In addition, workers in large organizations, are often covered by supplemental pension plans, which are almost exclusively some type of DC plan. Thus, DC plans are now the dominant plan type for primary employer-provided pensions.[3]

In most DB plans, full-time employees are automatically included in the plan after meeting minimum participation standards, and retirement benefits typically depend on earnings histories and years of service. Thus, DB participants are generally not required to make participation, contribution, or investment decisions. In contrast, DC plans are based on individual accounts into which the company and employees contribute funds. In many cases, and especially for 401(k) plans, participation is typically voluntary, so each worker must decide whether to make any annual contribution and the size of annual contributions. In addition, each participant must decide how to invest the periodic contributions and when and how to rebalance his individual accounts. Workers must determine their desired retirement ages and level of retirement income, and then they must make appropriate saving decisions to achieve these goals. Otherwise they will arrive at retirement with insufficient resources.[4]

Economic theory provides a structure for considering the allocation of time and resources over the lifetime. Under certain restrictive conditions, such life-cycle models can solve for the optimal age of retirement, required saving rates, and retirement income levels. Most of these models assume that individuals have perfect knowledge, that they understand financial markets, and that they know the risk–return distribution of all assets. With this knowledge, people can make the appropriate consumption and saving decisions to maximize their well-being.

Evidence from the real world however, suggests that many workers suffer from limited knowledge of financial markets and are under-informed about how much they need to save to achieve a retirement income goal (MacFarland, Marconi, and Utkus, Chapter 6, this volume; US Senate Committee, 2002; Bernheim, 1998). For example, a recent survey indicated that one-third of workers aged 56–65 report that they will need 50 percent or less of their income during their final working years to live comfortably in retirement (*USA Today*, 2003).[5] In fact, it appears that most households will actually require 70–80 percent of pre-retirement income in order to have the same level of consumption in retirement.

It seems obvious that increased financial education and awareness would be beneficial to people considering how to save for their retirement. However, researchers know little about the linkages between financial education, setting retirement goals, and the impact of enhanced financial education on the likelihood of achieving the necessary saving to reach these goals.

In what follows, we evaluate the impact of participation in financial education seminars on retirement goals and retirement saving behavior. Specifically, we evaluate whether participants in such seminars revised their expected retirement ages and the desired level of retirement income desired in retirement. Further, we examine whether financial education prompts participants to change their saving behavior by making specific changes in the amounts they save, how they invest their retirement assets, and whether they intend to acquire additional information.

## Prior Research on Financial Education and Retirement Saving

Many employers now provide some form of financial education for their workers, consisting of communications that explain company retirement saving options, general information about financial markets and economic conditions, and financial education or retirement seminars led by in-house staff, pension providers, or other experts. Sometimes such programs are intended to increase participation and contribution levels to help the company meet nondiscrimination standards. It is estimated that 40 percent of employers with 1,000 or more employees offer some type of financial education program (Arnone, 2002). But many of these programs appear to provide only minimal assistance to workers and some employers are concerned about the liability associated with providing financial advice to their employees. Some firms also subsidize the cost of their employees purchasing a financial plan.[6]

Relatively few studies have attempted to estimate the effectiveness of such educational programs in influencing retirement goals or retirement saving behavior. Bayer, Bernheim, and Scholz (1996) found that workers employed by firms that offered financial education programs had higher participation rates in and contribution rates to 401(k) plans, as compared to firms that did not provide this type of program.[7] That analysis indicated that seminars were the most effective type of communication. Sponsorship of financial education seminars was associated with a 12 percentage point increase in the participation rate of nonhighly compensated workers, and a 6 percentage point increase among highly compensated employees. Company-sponsored retirement seminars produced a one percentage point increase in the contribution rate of the nonhighly compensated, and no significant increase among highly compensated employees. This jump in contribution rates for nonhighly compensated is quite large, given that the average contribution rate for these employees was only 3 percent.

A study by Clark and Schieber (1998) examined data from 19 firms covering more than 40,000 employees to estimate the effect of company-provided written communications describing the retirement savings process, the need for workers to save, the national economic environment, and the characteristics of the company retirement plan. They found that such financial information played a significant role in boosting the probability of participating in a 401(k) plan, and in increasing contribution rates to that plan. Providing written documents to workers about retirement saving increased the probability of participating in the 401(k) plan between 15 and 21 percentage points. In addition, providing of information concerning the company's 401(k) plan increased the annual contribution rate by two percentage points, while generic financial and economic information had no significant influence on the contribution rate.

Using the Health and Retirement Survey (HRS), Muller (2000) evaluated the effect of financial education seminars on the allocation of investments in defined contribution plans. The 1992 wave of the HRS asked whether respondents had ever attended a retirement seminar, and this factor appeared to have no general effect on asset allocation. However, the investment allocation question from the HRS asked whether the household's assets were mostly or all in stocks, mixed, or mostly or all in bonds. This measure would naturally miss small and even medium-size adjustments to pension investments. Mullen did find that people having a high degree of risk aversion did tend to adjust their portfolios after participation in a seminar.[8]

Other studies have focused on the role of planning and the lack of financial literacy for retirement saving. For example, Lusardi (1999, 2000, Chapter 9, this volume) found that people who did not plan for retirement had lower net wealth and were less likely to invest in assets with higher expected returns such as equities. She also stated that extensive information is needed to plan adequately for retirement and that financial education programs are important to the planning process. Analysis by Madrian and Shea (2001), use the administrative records of a large employer to examine participation and saving behavior in the 401(k) plan before and after a 1-h retirement seminar. They find small but statistically significant effects of attendance at financial education seminars: Attendees had increased rates of participation in the 401(k) plan and greater diversification in their retirement plan portfolios. On the other hand, most seminar participants made no changes in their savings behavior. Though only a very short post-seminar period of observation was available.

While this limited literature to date suggests that financial education provided by employers can increase retirement saving and potentially alter the investment of assets in retirement accounts, the mechanism for how education alters retirement saving and investment decisions is unclear. Maki (2001) offers three routes by which individuals may use new information. First, financial education could increase household saving by causing the family to lower its discount rate. Second, increased knowledge could prompt the household to become less risk averse, and thus invest more in assets with higher risk and expected return. Finally, financial education programs could change the household's knowledge of its investment choice set. For example, the information could reveal to workers that it is impossible to achieve the current goal of retiring at a specific age with a certain level of income, using their current saving and investment strategy. Maki dismissed the first two possibilities and argued that greater knowledge of what is possible is the primary mechanism through which these programs alter household decisionmaking.

## Seminars and Surveys

To further explore the effectiveness of financial educational programs, it is necessary to have baseline information before the event, and then to collect participant responses after the event regarding their changes or plans for changes in financial planning based on the information provided. We implement this research design using survey responses of participants in a series of financial education seminars who completed pre and post-seminar surveys. Participants in the seminars were employees of colleges and universities, other educational institutions, and some nonprofit organizations, which attended seminars presented by TIAA-CREF consultants.[9]

Since the seminars were open to all employees of these institutions, participants include administrative, technical, clerical, and maintenance workers, as well as faculty members. Seminar attendees could be enrolled in a DC plan or a DB plan. The seminars are aimed at audiences in different life stages including newly hired employees, mid-career workers, and pre-retirees.[10] The objective of the seminars is to provide financial information to assist individuals in the retirement planning process. Seminar leaders discuss retirement goals such as the amount of money needed in retirement to maintain consumption levels, and the relationship between the retirement age and the annual saving needed to achieve retirement income goals. Considerable time in the seminars is devoted to examining risk–return characteristics of alternative investments.

We conducted several surveys of participants attending these financial education seminars over the period of March 2001 to May 2002. The first survey was administered to participants at the beginning of the seminar, and the second survey was completed at the end of the seminar before participants left the room. Survey I asked participants to report their retirement goals, their current account balances in retirement plans, their investment allocations, and their annual contributions to retirement accounts. Participants indicated the age at which they hoped to retire and the annual income they hoped to have in retirement as a percent of their final earnings. Respondents also were asked to indicate the likelihood that they would achieve these goals. Individuals reported details concerning their retirement accounts including account balances and how these funds were invested. Finally, people were asked to provide information on their age, sex, employment, years of service, marital status, education, earnings, household income, number of children, and occupation.

After completing the first survey, individuals participated in the financial education seminar for approximately one hour. At the conclusion of the seminar, participants were asked to complete the second survey. In this second survey, respondents indicated whether, based on the information provided in the seminar, they had changed their retirement age goals or revised the level of retirement income they desired. In addition, individuals were asked whether they intended to change their allocation of invested funds in their primary DC plan to include more equities or more bonds. If respondents had a supplemental retirement plan, they were asked if they intended to increase contributions or change investment allocations. Individuals who did not have a supplemental plan were asked if they planned to establish one.[11]

A total of 633 usable responses in which participants completed both surveys were obtained.[12] Appendix Table 10A-1 reports the sample means for Survey I; more detail appears in Clark and d'Ambrosio (2002). Women represented 53 percent of the respondents. On average, the women were four years younger than the male respondents and had 5 years less experience with their current employer. Female respondents had less schooling and were more likely to be in non-academic positions. For example, 44 percent of the women had no graduate degree compared to only 27 percent of the men. Among female respondents, 13 percent were in secretarial or maintenance positions, compared to less than 6 percent of the men. When the sample was limited to those in teaching and research positions, three fourths of all men were in tenured positions, compared to only 44 percent of the women, and 59 percent of the men were full professors, while only 28 percent of the women were at this rank.

These differences in tenure, education, and occupation are reflected in annual earnings and account balances. Annual earnings from the primary employer were 50 percent higher for the male respondents ($73,070 compared to $50,388). Lower earnings for women also produced smaller account balances in both basic pension plans ($514,801 for men and $191,461 for women) and supplemental retirement plans ($129,293 for the male respondents and $91,060 for the female participants). The investment allocation of retirement accounts between equities and bonds was not substantially different by sex. In the basic pension plan, women held 64 percent of their assets in equities and allocated 60 percent of new contributions to equities. By comparison, men held 64 percent of the account balances in equities and allocated 58 percent of new contributions to equities. In the supplemental plans, women held 67 percent of their account balances in equities and designated 63 percent of new contributions to the purchase of equities while men held 70 percent of their balances in equities and used 71 percent of new monies to purchase additional equities.

Female respondents to our surveys tended to report that they were more conservative investors than men. Almost half of the women indicated that they were either conservative or moderately conservative investors, as compared to 44 percent of the men. This finding is consistent with other surveys that report women are more likely to elect lower risk–lower return investment choices than are men. It is interesting that these sex differences in risk self-assessment seem to be at variance with the similarity in the allocation of pension funds.

## Establishing Retirement Goals

Turning to an analysis of desired age of retirement and target replacement rate (the level of retirement income compared to final earnings), we find that women had slightly lower targets. They indicated expected retirement ages of 63 years as compared to an average age of 64 years for the men, and a desired replacement rate of 79 percent compared to 81 percent for male respondents. To explain the differences in retirement ages across participants, we estimated a Logit probability model. In this specification, the probability of seminar participants setting retirement age goals younger than age 60, between ages 60 and 64, age 65, or over 65 was estimated as a function of individual and household characteristics. Demographic characteristics included in the analysis were age, marital status, and number of children. Human capital variables were education, occupation, and years of service with the employer. Measures of financial resources were household income, whether respondents were the sole income earners in their households, and whether their basic pension plans were defined benefit plans. Finally, to control for potential differences in financial knowledge before the seminar, an indicator variable for whether or not they worked with a financial advisor was included.

The results indicate strong differences in desired retirement ages by sex. Women who were married were almost 20 percentage points more likely to set their desired retirement age below 65, while the expected retirement age for men was unaffected by marital status. Women with fewer years of education were significantly more likely to report a lower desired retirement age. Women with only a college degree were 14 percentage points more likely to have retirement age goals under age 65, as compared to women who had graduate degrees. Men with children were 22 percentage points more likely to have an expected retirement age of 65 or more compared to men without children. The presence of children did not significantly affect the desired retirement age of women. Men working with a financial adviser were 20 percentage points more likely to set a retirement age goal of younger than age 65. Working with a financial adviser did not significantly affect women's desired retirement age.

Differences in retirement income goals before the seminar were also explored. Women with children were 10 percentage points less likely to set a replacement rate goal in excess of 85 percent. Surprisingly, women with higher annual earnings were more likely to set lower income replacement goals. Each additional year of service with the current employer raised the probability of a higher replacement rate target in excess of 85 percent, by one percentage point for both men and women. Men who were the sole earner in the household were 19 percentage points less likely to set retirement income targets of 85 percent or more. Men under age 45 were 23 percentage points more likely to set replacement rate targets in excess of 85 percent.[13]

Before they participated in the seminar, women had less confidence in their abilities to attain these retirement goals. On a scale of 1–10, women indicated that they had a level 7 confidence level in being able to retire at the desired age, but only a level 6 confidence level in their ability to achieve the retirement income goal. By comparison, the men had confidence levels of 8 on their retirement age goal and level of 7 on achieving the retirement income goal. After the financial education seminar, women were much more likely than men to alter their retirement goals. Sixteen percent of the women but only 6 percent of the men modified their expected age of retirement while women were twice as likely to raise their expected retirement age after the seminar than to lower it, while men were split almost equally between those that raised and lowered the retirement age goal. Among women, those who had initially hoped to retire early raised their expected retirement age after learning more about financial markets and the savings process. Almost a quarter of women who had initially indicated a desired retirement age of younger than 60 raised this target after the seminar, and the increase was by an average of more than 4 years. By contrast and regardless of their initial retirement goal, relatively few men tended to alter their expected retirement age.

Table 10-1 presents results of a Logit probability model explaining how these changes in retirement age goals varied across individual and household characteristics.[14] For women, characteristics significantly associated with changing retirement age goals were age and educational attainment. Compared to older seminar participants, respondents under age 45 were nine percentage points less likely to increase their desired retirement ages after the seminar. Individuals without advanced degrees were seven to 11 percentage points more likely to increase their target ages of retirement. For men, those with only a high school degree were one percentage point more likely to increase their retirement-age goal.

In response to the seminar, women were also much more likely to alter their retirement income goals (Table 10-2). Approximately 35 percent of the women changed their income target, versus only 20 percent of the men. Almost three quarters of women who modified their goal, raised their desired income replacement rate. Almost half of those women who had initially reported a desired replacement rate of less than 65 percent of final earnings raised their retirement income goal. Similarly, men with relatively low retirement income goals were more likely to increase their desired replacement ratio after the seminar.

Women who had only an undergraduate college degree were 11 percentage points more likely to increase their retirement income objective. Women who were enrolled in a DB pension plan were 14 percentage points more likely to increase their desired retirement goal, and male participants in DB plans were 10 percentage points more likely to increase their income replacement rate goals. Male sole earners were four percentage points more likely to reduce their income goal after the seminar, and men who were more conservative investors were one percentage point less likely to raise their income goal. Men and women who had only long-term savings objectives were four percentage points more likely to report that they were lowering their retirement income goals.

TABLE 10-1  Estimates of Post-Seminar Changes in Retirement Age Goals

| Variable | Lower Goal | No Change | Raise Goal | Significance Level |
|---|---|---|---|---|
| **I. Women** | | | | |
| *DB plan* | 0.00 | 0.00 | −0.01 | 0.83 |
| *Age* | | | | |
| Age 44 or younger | 0.06 | 0.036 | −0.09 | 0.02 |
| Age 45 and over | | | | |
| *Education* | | | | |
| High-school degree | −0.07 | −0.04 | 0.11 | 0.03 |
| College degree | −0.05 | −0.03 | 0.07 | 0.04 |
| Graduate/Professional degree | | | | |
| *Occupation* | | | | |
| Teaching/Research | | | | |
| Professional/Technical, other | | | | |
| Administration/Management | 0.02 | 0.01 | −0.04 | 0.27 |
| Secretarial/Clerical | 0.06 | 0.04 | −0.09 | 0.74 |
| Maintenance/Service | | | | |
| *Household income (% change)* | −0.00 | −0.00 | 0.00 | 0.56 |
| *Conservative investor* | 0.03 | 0.02 | −0.04 | 0.21 |
| *Focus of savings* | | | | |
| Saving objectives include short, intermediate, and long term | −0.03 | −0.02 | 0.05 | 0.25 |
| *Number of observations* | 13 | 178 | 21 | |
| *Percent of sample* | 6.1 | 83.9 | 9.9 | |
| **II. Men** | | | | |
| *DB plan* | −0.03 | −0.00 | 0.03 | 0.14 |
| *Age* | | | | |
| Age 44 or younger | −0.03 | −0.00 | 0.03 | 0.25 |
| Age 45 and over | | | | |
| *Education* | | | | |
| High-school degree | −0.01 | −0.00 | 0.01 | 0.08 |
| College degree | 0.01 | 0.00 | −0.01 | 0.46 |
| Graduate/Professional degree | | | | |
| *Occupation* | | | | |
| Teaching/Research | | | | |
| Professional/Technical, other | | | | |
| Administration/Management | 0.01 | 0.00 | −0.02 | 0.38 |
| Secretarial/Clerical | 0.05 | 0.00 | −0.05 | 0.10 |
| Maintenance/Service | | | | |
| *Household income (% change)* | −0.00 | −0.00 | 0.00 | 0.69 |
| *Conservative investor* | 0.03 | 0.00 | −0.02 | 0.16 |

TABLE 10-1 *Continued.*

| Variable | Lower Goal | No Change | Raise Goal | Significance Level |
|---|---|---|---|---|
| *Focus of savings* | | | | |
| Saving objectives include short, intermediate, and long term | −0.00 | 0.00 | 0.00 | 0.97 |
| *Number of observations* | 6 | 167 | 6 | |
| *Percent of sample* | 3.3 | 93.2 | 3.3 | |

*Notes*: Table entries are the marginal effects derived from the estimated coefficients in Logit equations. Derivatives are evaluated at sample means.

*Source*: Authors' estimates.

## Saving and Investment Choices

Though women had much lower account balances in their retirement plans than did men, prior to the seminar, there were relatively small differences in investment choices for account balances and in the allocation of new contributions. Building on the new information provided in the seminar, the evidence shows that women were much more likely to increase their retirement saving and alter their investment choices. Among persons without a supplemental retirement plan, 48 percent of the women but only 33 percent of the men indicated that they would establish such a plan in the future. Among those who already had a supplemental plan, 53 percent of women compared to only 33 percent of the men planned on increasing their annual contributions. Women were also more likely to report that they would alter their investment choices in both basic and supplemental pension plans.

Table 10-3 reports marginal effects from sex-specific Logit estimations of the probability of establishing a supplemental pension plan among individuals who did not have such a plan prior to the seminar. Women whose basic pension plan was a DB plan were 40 percentage points more likely to indicate that they would establish a supplemental plan after the seminar, than those whose basic pension was a DC plan. Women aged 60 and over were 36 percentage points less likely to start a new supplemental plan, as compared to younger women. The likelihood of opening a new plan was 23 percentage points greater for women with a long-term savings horizon. For men, each 10 percent increase in the proportion of total household income derived from their earnings was associated with a seven percentage point increase in the likelihood of establishing a supplemental plan. Those with five or fewer years of employment with their current employer were 67 percentage points more likely to open a new supplemental retirement

TABLE 10-2  Estimates of Post-Seminar Changes in Retirement Income Goals

| Variable | Lower Goal | No Change | Raise Goal | Significance Level |
|---|---|---|---|---|
| **I. Women** | | | | |
| *DB plan* | −0.06 | −0.08 | 0.14 | 0.04 |
| *Age* | | | | |
| Age 44 or younger | 0.02 | 0.03 | −0.05 | 0.50 |
| Age 45 and over | | | | |
| *Education* | | | | |
| High-school degree | −0.03 | −0.05 | 0.08 | 0.38 |
| College degree | −0.05 | −0.07 | 0.11 | 0.08 |
| Graduate/Professional degree | | | | |
| *Annual earnings (% change)* | −0.00 | −0.00 | 0.00 | 0.12 |
| Respondent sole income earner | 0.00 | 0.00 | 0.00 | 1.00 |
| Conservative Investor | 0.02 | 0.03 | −0.06 | 0.35 |
| Works with financial adviser | −0.00 | −0.00 | 0.01 | 0.92 |
| *Focus of savings* | | | | |
| Long term | 0.05 | 0.07 | −0.12 | 0.06 |
| *Number of observations* | 19 | 130 | 54 | |
| *Percent of sample* | 9.3 | 64.0 | 26.6 | |
| **II. Men** | | | | |
| *DB plan* | −0.04 | −0.06 | 0.10 | 0.12 |
| *Age* | | | | |
| Age 44 or younger | 0.01 | 0.02 | −0.04 | 0.60 |
| Age 45 and over | | | | |
| *Education* | | | | |
| High-school degree | −0.03 | −0.05 | 0.09 | 0.32 |
| College degree | 0.02 | 0.04 | −0.06 | 0.30 |
| Graduate/Professional degree | | | | |
| *Annual earnings (% change)* | −0.00 | −0.00 | 0.00 | 0.20 |
| Respondent sole income earner | 0.04 | 0.07 | −0.11 | 0.04 |
| Conservative investor | 0.04 | 0.05 | −0.01 | 0.04 |
| Works with financial adviser | 0.02 | 0.03 | −0.05 | 0.28 |
| *Focus of savings* | | | | |
| Long term | 0.04 | 0.07 | −0.11 | 0.05 |
| *Number of observations* | 10 | 142 | 25 | |
| *Percent of sample* | 5.6 | 80.2 | 14.1 | |

*Notes*: Table entries are the marginal effects derived from estimated coefficients in the Logit equations. Derivatives are evaluated at the sample means.

*Source*: Authors' estimates.

TABLE 10-3  Estimates of Post-Seminar Changes in Retirement Saving Behavior

| Variable | Plans to Establish Supplemental Plan | Plans to Increase Contributions to Supplemental Plan |
| --- | --- | --- |
| **I. Women** | | |
| DB plan | 0.40 (0.04) | −0.01 (0.91) |
| Age | | |
| Age 44 or younger | −0.06 (0.69) | −0.12 (0.39) |
| Age 45–59 | | |
| Age 60 and over | −0.36 (0.04) | −0.26 (0.05) |
| Married | 0.25 (0.32) | 0.13 (0.32) |
| Occupation | | |
| Teaching/Research | | |
| Professional/Technical, other | | |
| Administration/Management | 0.11 (0.39) | 0.12 (0.24) |
| Secretarial/Clerical | −0.06 (0.67) | 0.28 (0.07) |
| Maintenance/Service | | |
| Annual earnings (% change) | −0.00 (0.17) | 0.00 (0.41) |
| Earnings % household income | 0.00 (0.50) | 0.00 (0.42) |
| Worked for employer 5 years or less | 0.02 (0.90) | |
| Conservative investor | −0.11 (0.44) | 0.21 (0.05) |
| Works with a financial adviser | −0.11 (0.36) | 0.14 (0.19) |
| Focus of savings | | |
| Short term | | |
| Long term | 0.23 (0.10) | 0.27 (0.15) |
| Multi-period focus | 0.27 (0.11) | 0.30 (0.14) |
| Number of observations | 73 | 102 |
| **II. Men** | | |
| DB plan | −0.07 (0.66) | 0.09 (0.49) |
| Age | | |
| Age 44 or younger | −0.05 (0.66) | 0.32 (0.09) |
| Age 45–59 | | |
| Age 60 and over | 0.04 (0.73) | −0.27 (0.02) |
| Married | 0.12 (0.46) | −0.03 (0.83) |
| Occupation | | |
| Teaching/Research | | |
| Professional/Technical, other | | |
| Administration/Management | 0.22 (0.36) | |
| Secretarial/Clerical | 0.16 (0.12) | |
| Maintenance/Service | | |
| Annual earnings (% change) | 0.00 (0.22) | 0.06 (0.66) |
| Earnings % household income | 0.01 (0.05) | −0.00 (0.82) |
| Worked for employer 5 years or less | 0.67 (0.00) | |

TABLE 10-3 *Continued.*

| Variable | Plans to Establish Supplemental Plan | Plans to Increase Contributions to Supplemental Plan |
|---|---|---|
| *Conservative investor* | 0.03 (0.81) | 0.04 (0.69) |
| Works with a financial adviser | −0.00 (0.98) | 0.11 (0.23) |
| *Focus of savings* | | |
| Short term | | |
| Long term | 0.14 (0.51) | 0.02 (0.94) |
| Multi-period focus | 0.15 (0.63) | 0.11 (0.71) |
| Number of observations | 58 | 94 |

*Notes*: Table entries are marginal effects derived from the estimated coefficients. Derivatives evaluated for each observation and averaged over the sample. Levels of significance are shown in parentheses.

*Source*: Authors' estimates.

plan. Thus, younger, low-wage women who were concerned about the future were the ones who were responding to the information provided in the seminar.

Similarly, women aged 60 and over were 26 percentage points less likely to increase contributions to existing supplemental retirement plans than younger women. Women who were secretarial or maintenance workers were 28 percentage points more likely to increase contributions. Women with a longer-term outlook were 27 percentage points more likely to report their desire to increase pension contributions. Women who reported that they were more conservative investors were 21 percentage points more likely to indicate a desire to increase contributions to supplemental plans. Men younger than age 60 were 27 percentage points more likely to increase annual contributions to a supplemental retirement plan than men 60 and older.

Among participants whose basic retirement plan was a DC plan, women more often indicated that they would alter their investment allocations after the seminar. Forty-four percent of the female participants, but only 35 percent of male participants, reported a plan to rebalance their accounts in their basic plans. A similar response was found among those with supplemental plans, with 40 percent of the women indicating a desire to alter the investment strategy in their supplemental plans, compared to only 26 percent of the men.

We also provide sex-specific Logit estimates of the probability of participants indicating that they planned to change the investment allocations in their basic and supplemental retirement plans (see Table 10-4). Women in

TABLE 10-4  Estimates of Post-Seminar Changes in Investment Allocation

| Variable | Plans to Change Allocation in Basic Plan | Plans to Change Allocation in Supplemental Plan |
|---|---|---|
| **I. Women** | | |
| *DB plan* | | −0.20 (0.11) |
| *Age* | | |
| Age 44 or younger | 0.15 (0.22) | −0.06 (0.67) |
| Age 45–59 | | |
| Age 60 and over | 0.06 (0.63) | 0.04 (0.79) |
| *Married* | 0.14 (0.15) | 0.11 (0.31) |
| *Children* | −0.01 (0.90) | |
| *Occupation* | | |
| Teaching/Research | | |
| Professional/Technical, other | | |
| Administration/Management | 0.15 (0.13) | −0.045 (0.67) |
| Secretarial/Clerical | −0.26 (0.07) | −0.19 (0.25) |
| Maintenance/Service | | |
| *Earnings % household income* | −0.00 (0.9) | −0.00 (0.17) |
| *Conservative investor* | 0.18 (0.07) | 0.030 (0.79) |
| *Works with a financial adviser* | −0.18 (0.07) | −0.08 (0.47) |
| *Focus of savings* | | |
| Short term | | |
| Long term | −0.00 (1.00) | 0.08 (0.68) |
| Multi-period focus | −0.04 (0.83) | 0.27579 (0.256) |
| *First seminar* | −0.08 (0.42) | 0.16 (0.17) |
| *Account balance* | −0.00 (0.02) | |
| *Percent equities* | 0.01 (0.75) | |
| *Number of observations* | 121 | 98 |
| **II. Men** | | |
| *DB plan* | | −0.07 (0.56) |
| *Age* | | |
| Age 44 or younger | −0.24 (0.04) | −0.04 (0.78) |
| Age 45–59 | | |
| Age 60 and over | −0.09 (0.31) | −0.01 (0.95) |
| *Married* | 0.06 (0.62) | 0.16 (0.12) |
| *Children* | −0.01 (0.90) | |
| *Occupation* | | |
| Teaching/Research | | |
| Professional/Technical, other | | |
| Administration/Management | 0.01 (0.88) | 0.03 (0.73) |
| Secretarial/Clerical | −0.02 (0.95) | −0.07 (0.70) |
| Maintenance/Service | | |

TABLE 10-4 *Continued.*

| Variable | Plans to Change Allocation in Basic Plan | Plans to Change Allocation in Supplemental Plan |
|---|---|---|
| *Earnings % household income* | −0.00 (0.15) | −0.16 (0.16) |
| *Conservative investor* | 0.11 (0.21) | 0.17456 (0.09) |
| *Works with a financial adviser* | −0.07 (0.40) | 0.16 (0.09) |
| *Focus of savings* | | |
| Short term | | |
| Long term | 0.10 (0.70) | 0.05 (0.77) |
| Multi-period focus | 0.03 (0.93) | 0.38 (0.20) |
| *First seminar* | 0.17 (0.05) | 0.07 (0.50) |
| *Account balance* | −0.00 (0.11) | |
| *Percent equities* | 0.01 (0.01) | |
| *Number of observations* | 129 | 93 |

*Notes*: Table entries are marginal effects derived from the estimated coefficients. Derivatives are evaluated for each observation and averaged over the sample. Levels of significance are shown in parentheses.

*Source*: Authors' estimates.

secretarial and maintenance positions were 26 percentage points less likely to alter their investment allocations in basic plans, and 19 percentage points less likely to change allocations in supplemental plans. Those with larger account balances in basic plans were also less likely to change allocations in these plans. Female participants working with a financial adviser were 18 percentage points less likely to want to make changes in their basic plan accounts, and 8 percentage points less likely to alter allocations in their supplemental accounts. Women who reported that they were more conservative investors were 18 percentage points more likely to want to make changes in their basic plan account balances after the seminar. Women whose primary retirement plan was a DB plan were 20 percentage points less likely to alter their investment allocations in their supplemental plan.

Men under the age of 45 were 24 percentage points less likely to make changes in their investment strategy for their basic pension plan than were older participants. Those men who were attending their first financial education seminar were 17 percentage points more likely to make changes in the allocations in their basic plans. Each 10 percent increase in equities, as a percent of total assets in basic pension plan accounts, was associated with a six percentage point increase in the probability of changing account allocations.

## Conclusion

As Alan Greenspan (2002) recently noted:

[E]ducation can play a critical role by equipping consumers with the knowledge required to make wise decisions when choosing among the myriad of financial products and providers. This is especially the case for populations that have traditionally been underserved by our financial system . . . In addition, comprehensive education can help provide individuals with the financial knowledge necessary to create household budgets, initiate savings plans, manage debt, and make strategic investment decisions for their retirement or children's education. Having these basic financial planning skills can help families to meet their near-term obligations and to maximize their longer-term financial well being.

Our analysis indicates that individuals respond to financial education by altering their retirement objectives. After participation in a financial education seminar, many attendees report that they are likely to alter their retirement goals, and in most cases, this means increasing the expected age of retirement. After the seminar, individuals who had initially indicated a relatively low retirement income goal were more likely to raise their income objectives. These responses indicate that the information provided in the seminar showed participants that they were not on track to reach their retirement goals. Responses include deciding to work longer, saving more, opening new retirement accounts, or changing their investment strategies. The results also indicate that women seem more responsive to financial education programs than men.

Future analysis will allow us to determine the extent to which seminar participants actually acted on their stated intentions to alter their retirement savings. If participants did not follow through on their intended changes, additional analysis will be needed to determine whether they have reassessed their plans after the seminar, whether they simply ignored the need to make changes, or whether their economic circumstances have changed. Meanwhile, our findings support the hypothesis that financial education is important to achieving retirement goals. Financial education programs can help people reassess their retirement saving plans and increase the likelihood that retirement dreams will be achieved. Clearly financial education can play an important role in setting retirement goals and developing long-term saving plans that enable workers to retire at the desired age with sufficient resources to provide the expected level of retirement income.

# Appendix

TABLE 10A-1　Sample Summary Statistics by Sex

| Variable | Mean | |
|---|---|---|
| | Female | Male |
| Number of observations | 335 | 293 |
| Age | 52.6 | 56.4 |
| Years of service | 13.1 | 17.7 |
| Number of children | 1.5 | 1.9 |
| Education attainment | | |
| Percent with high-school degree | 14.4 | 6.8 |
| Percent with college degree | 30.0 | 19.8 |
| Percent with masters degree | 33.6 | 27.6 |
| Percent with doctoral degree | 18.0 | 36.8 |
| Percent with professional degree | 3.9 | 8.8 |
| Annual household income (dollars) | 94,559 | 110,569 |
| Earnings from primary employer (dollars) | 50,388 | 73,070 |
| Type of investor | | |
| Conservative | 5.1 | 8.5 |
| Moderately conservative | 43.4 | 35.9 |
| Moderately aggressive | 39.7 | 43.1 |
| Aggressive | 11.6 | 12.3 |
| Retirement age goal | 62.9 | 64.2 |
| Likelihood of achieving retirement age goal (scale 1–10) | 7.8 | 7.6 |
| Retirement income goal: Percent of final working year's income | 79.2 | 80.5 |
| Likelihood of achieving Income goal (1–10) | 6.0 | 7.1 |
| Plan to work after retirement (percent) | 50.3 | 53.1 |
| Financial seminars previously attended | 2.1 | 2.3 |
| Currently working with financial adviser (%) | 24.3 | 26.5 |
| Basic pension plan | | |
| Percent with DC pension | 79.2 | 84.8 |
| Account balance (dollars) | 191,461 | 514,801 |
| Investment allocation in equities (percent) | 63.9 | 63.5 |
| Employee contribution rate | 7.2 | 7.5 |
| Employer contribution rate | 8.5 | 8.4 |
| Allocation of contribution to equities | 59.1 | 58.2 |
| Supplemental pension plans | | |
| Percent currently making contribution | 50.1 | 49.0 |
| Account balance in dollars | 91,060 | 120,293 |
| Percent in equities | 66.7 | 70.4 |
| Annual contribution in dollars | 5,048 | 6,005 |
| Contribution as a percent of salary | 9.7 | 8.5 |
| Allocation of contributions to equities | 62.7 | 70.9 |

TABLE 10A-1 *Continued.*

| Variable | Mean | |
|---|---|---|
| | *Female* | *Male* |
| *Type of employment (percent of respondents)* | | |
| Secretarial/Clerical | 12.6 | 0.7 |
| Teaching/Research | 24.7 | 38.9 |
| Administrative/Management | 28.4 | 22.4 |
| Maintenance/Service | 0.3 | 5.1 |
| Other professional/technical | 18.5 | 19.6 |
| Other | 6.1 | 3.1 |
| Retired | 4.9 | 6.9 |
| Not currently employed | 4.0 | 3.1 |
| *Tenure Status of teaching/ research* *(percent of those responding)* | | |
| Tenured | 44.3 | 74.4 |
| Tenure-track, non-tenured | 20.4 | 7.2 |
| Non-tenure track | 35.2 | 18.4 |
| *Rank of teaching/ research (percent responding)* | | |
| Instructor | 34.7 | 7.9 |
| Assistant professor | 21.7 | 24.7 |
| Associate professor | 15.9 | 7.9 |
| Professor | 27.5 | 59.2 |

*Source*: Authors' estimates.

# Notes

[1] In some cases, individuals might lack motivation to determine saving strategies as the result of a large menu of investment options offered by their retirement plans. Iyengar, Huberman, and Jiang (Chapter 5, this volume) found that participation rates in 401(k) plans decline significantly as the number of available investment options increases.

[2] Clark et al. (2003) examined the responses of these seminar participants using a pooled sample of men and women. That analysis showed important differences by sex in the effect of financial education on retirement goals and savings behavior, indicating the need for more detailed assessment including the estimation of sex-specific response functions.

[3] The transition to defined contribution plans has been driven by changes in government regulations and tax policy boosting the administrative costs of defined benefit plans and making defined contribution plans more desirable (Clark and McDermed, 1990; Hustead, 1998). In addition, labor force changes have reduced the likelihood of lifetime employment with the same firm and thus increased the demand for more portable pensions. Employment shifts toward sectors with DC plans have also accelerated the growth of such plans (Gustman and Steinmeier, 1992; Ippolito, 1997).

[4] Potential changes in the Social Security system may further increase the need for individuals to enhance their understanding of financial markets and the retirement savings process. For instance, some proposals to reform the Social Security system include individual accounts as a component of retirement benefits, which if adopted, would place even greater responsibility on individual workers in the determination of retirement income goals. Other reform proposals would reduce future Social Security benefits, which would also require workers to be responsible for saving a greater portion of their retirement income (Advisory Council on Social Security, 1997; President's Commission to Strengthen Social Security, 2001).

[5] The 2003 Retirement Confidence Survey also found that half of all workers believed that they would need less than 70% of their preretirement income to live comfortably in retirement (EBRI, 2003).

[6] Bernheim and Garrett (2000) and Bayer, Bernheim, and Scholz (1996) assess employer-provided financial education programs.

[7] Other studies using the same survey include Bernheim (1998) and Bernheim and Garrett (2000).

[8] This finding is somewhat odd since "high degree" of risk aversion is the second highest of four risk aversion categories used in the analysis, and individuals with "extreme risk aversion" (the highest category) did not have any significant reaction to financial education.

[9] TIAA-CREF is a large financial services provider with over $250 billion in assets. It is the primary retirement system for almost three million people employed by education and research organizations.

[10] Since participation in these programs is voluntary, self-selection is obviously an issue. Some participants might have done little in the way of retirement planning but begin to worry; such persons might be predisposed toward changing in their goals and behavior, and thus they could be more likely to respond after the seminar. Other individuals might be retirement planners and attend seminars to learn even more. For this group, seminar information may merely ratify past behaviors, so they would be less likely to change saving behavior afterward. Duflo and Saez (this volume) also discuss the issue of selection bias in seminar participation and the subsequent response to surveys.

[11] Approximately 3 months after the seminar, participants were sent a third survey by regular mail or email. This time we asked whether the person had actually made changes in his saving behavior. Results from this third survey are not yet available.

[12] Thirty-six seminars were held at 21 universities, other educational institutions, and nonprofit organizations. In addition, 24 community-based seminars were held in seven different areas. In total, 2,157 people attended part or all of these seminars and 725 individuals completed some parts of the two surveys for a response rate of 34%. The sample included in the analysis contains 633 usable surveys in which participants completed both Survey I and Survey II. Some individuals arrived after the seminar had begun and were not given either of the surveys. In addition, some participants who have completed Survey I left the seminar early and did not complete Survey II.

[13] Tables of Logit equations for retirement goals prior to attendance at the seminar are available from the authors on request.

[14] In this equation, certain variables are created by combining several categories of answers on the surveys. For example, a variable indicating conservative investors includes those that indicated that they were either conservative or moderately conservative.

# References

Advisory Council on Social Security. 1997. *Report of the 1994–1996 Advisory Council on Social Security*. Washington: USGPO.

Arnone, William. 2002. "Financial Planning for Employees Post-Enron," *Benefits Quarterly* Fourth Quarter: 35–41.

Bayer, Patrick, Douglas Bernheim, and Karl Scholz. 1996. "The Effects of Financial Education in the Workplace: Evidence from a Survey of Employers." Stanford University Working Paper.

Bernheim, Douglas. 1998. "Financial Illiteracy, Education, and Retirement Savings." In *Living with Defined Contribution Pensions*, eds. Olivia Mitchell and Sylvester Schieber. Philadelphia: University of Pennsylvania Press: 38–68.

—— and Daniel Garrett. 2000. "The Determinants and Consequences of Financial Education in the Workplace: Evidence from a Survey of Households." Stanford University Working Paper.

Clark, Robert and Madeleine d'Ambrosio. 2002. "Saving for Retirement: The Role of Financial Education." TIAA-CREF Institute Working Paper 4-070102-A.

—— and Ann McDermed. 1990. *The Choice of Pension Plans in a Changing Regulatory Environment*. Washington: American Enterprise Institute.

—— and Sylvester Schieber. 1998. "Factors Affecting Participation Rates and Contribution Levels in 401(k) Plans." In *Living with Defined Contribution Pensions*, eds. Olivia Mitchell and Sylvester Schieber. Philadelphia: University of Pennsylvania Press: 69–97.

——, Madeleine d'Ambrosio, Ann McDermed, and Kshama Sawant. 2003. "Financial Education and Retirement Savings." TIAA-CREF Institute Working Paper 11-020103.

Employee Benefit Research Institute (EBRI). 2003. "Findings from the 2003 Retirement Confidence Survey (RCS) and Minority RCS." *EBRI Notes*, July.

Greenspan, Alan. 2002. *Hearings on the State of Financial Literacy and Education in America*. Prepared statement to the US Senate Committee on Banking, Housing, and Urban Affairs, February 6.

Gustman, Alan and Thomas Steinmeier. 1992. "The Stampede Towards Defined Contribution Plans." *Industrial Relations* 31: 361–369.

Hustead, Edwin. 1998. "Trends in Retirement Income Plan Administrative Expenses." In *Living with Defined Contribution Pensions*, eds. Olivia Mitchell and Sylvester Schieber. Philadelphia: University of Pennsylvania Press: 166–177.

Ippolito, Richard. 1997. *Pension Plans and Employee Performance*. Chicago: University of Chicago Press.

Lusardi, Annamaria. 1999. "Information, Expectations, and Savings for Retirement." In *Behavioral Dimensions of Retirement Economics*, ed. Henry Aaron. Washington: Brookings Institution and Russell Sage Foundation: 81–115.

—— 2000. "Saving for Retirement: The Importance of Planning." *Research Dialogue* 66. New York: TIAA-CREF Institute.

Madrian, Brigitte and Dennis Shea. 2001. "Preaching to the Converted and Converting those Taught: Financial Education in the Workplace." University of Chicago Working Paper.

Maki, Dean. 2001. "Financial Education and Private Pensions." Paper presented at the Conference on Public Policies and Private Pensions at the Brookings Institution, September 21–22.

Muller, Leslie. 2000. "Investment Choice in Defined Contribution Plans: The Effects of Retirement Education on Asset Allocation." Washington: Social Security Administration Working Paper.

President's Commission to Strengthen Social Security. 2001. *Final Report.* http://csss.gov/reports.

*USA Today.* "Take July 4 as a Reminder to Save, Save, Save," Thursday, July 3, 3B.

US Senate Committee on Banking, Housing, and Urban Affairs. 2002. *Hearings on the State of Financial Literacy and Education in America.* February 6.

# Chapter 11

# Retirement Security in a DC World: Using Behavioral Finance to Bridge the Expertise Gap

*Jason Scott and Gregory Stein*

Defined contribution DC plans can provide real retirement security, but only if participants utilize them appropriately and make informed investment decisions. Yet, it has proved to be a challenge to provide the necessary expertise to support good decisionmaking in the DC context. Many employers have offered educational materials with fairly limited success, partly because these educational materials have often been relatively generic and difficult for people to apply to their own circumstances and situations. To make things a bit easier for employees, some employers have considered purchasing advisory services for their employees. An obstacle to this approach, from the employer's point of view, has been legal liability: Companies feared that if they selected advisers for their employees, then the company might be liable for any losses employees sustained.

Three factors have contributed to a dramatic shift in employer opinion regarding the provision of advisory services for employees. First, the US Department of Labor (USDOL) issued an advisory opinion in May 1998 which stated that it was legal for sponsors to offer advice. The DOL then reaffirmed that employers had the responsibility of selecting and monitoring the advice provider; then, assuming prudent selection and monitoring on the part of the employer, the advice provider was liable for the actual advice given. A second contributing factor was a spate of Enron-like corporate scandals. These scandals, and resulting lawsuits, demonstrated that employers bore some degree of responsibility for helping their employees manage their pension plans. A third factor contributing to changing attitudes was simply that more large employers began to offer advisory services, so subsequent employers did not have to be the first to offer advice.

The combination of these three factors has produced a dramatic change in the willingness to offer advice, so that today, many plan sponsors now believe that offering advisory services actually *reduces* their legal liability. Nevertheless, even while employers have grown more comfortable with the notion of providing advice, changing employee behavior remains a difficult task. This chapter explores some of the different techniques used to provide advice to employees and relates the experiences of Financial Engines, Inc., a provider of advisory services to sponsored retirement plans, to some of the current issues and hypotheses in behavioral finance.

In what follows, we first describe the market background associated with advisory services to pension-covered employees. We explore the two main employer goals for advisory services, namely disclosure and retirement security. Next we provide some background on how the services and products from Financial Engines fit into this general marketplace, and we discuss reaching the employee for disclosure purposes: What approaches have been used, their relative performance, and what explains the differences. Corroborating a hypothesis from the behavioral finance literature, we show how even seemingly small improvements in convenience can have a significant impact on the ability to reach employees. Finally, we analyze evidence on the impact of adviser and personal statements on participant behavior. The Adviser, in particular, went through a significant redesign that focused participants on fewer choices.

## Market Background

Before diving into the specific details, it is important to understand the key features of DC-related advisory services. When employers hire a company to provide advisory services to their employees, they are generally looking to accomplish one or both of the following goals:

1. *Disclosure.* Disclose to employees regarding their DC plan, help employees understand how much risk they are taking, what their retirement prospects are, and how much or how little they should expect from their DC plan.
2. *Retirement security.* Help employees make better decisions regarding investment risk and savings levels; employees should have sufficient saving and diversification to maximize their chance of a secure retirement.

The first goal arises from concerns regarding legal liability. Employers may be concerned that their employees might make saving and investment mistakes, so the fundamental requirement for the first goal is communication. The second goal involves changing individual behavior to improve retirement prospects. There are both legal liability and paternalistic aspects to this goal. If poor retirement finances might result in lawsuits, then changing behavior to improve retirement outcomes could reduce legal liability. Of course, some companies are primarily motivated by liability considerations, but many others genuinely want to help employees secure their retirement futures. For the latter employers, altering behavior is the success metric for advisory services.

## The Financial Engines Approach

Financial Engines, Inc. seeks to help companies with these two objectives, by applying to the individual's retirement problem some of the best practices used by pension asset managers (fund style and performance attribution, Monte Carlo simulation, mean–variance optimization, etc). In practice, this has meant giving employees two things. First, the approach provides employees with a retirement forecast to help them set realistic expectations. Based on their current saving and investment decisions, the forecast shows employees how much money they can expect annually in retirement if their investments perform well, average, or poorly. Communicating the forecast and related information to employees delivers on the employer's disclosure objective. Second, the company provides specific recommendations for saving and fund allocation to help employees improve their retirement forecasts. Persuading individuals to act on these specific recommendations helps to accomplish the second employer goal of improving retirement security.

"Personal Statements" and "Online Advice" are two core services that Financial Engines currently offers.[1] Personal Statements are sent to investors via electronic or regular mail, aimed at reaching all employees. Personal Statements first provide each participant with a personalized forecast of the reasonable range of outcomes he can expect given his specific investments, saving rate, and time horizon to retirement. Though analogous to a social security projection, this forecast also includes an assessment of the range of likely outcomes (upside, median, and downside), instead of just a point estimate. Additionally, the statement indicates how to improve the forecast, in ways that depend on the particular participant. For example, participants who do not fully take advantage of an employer match receive an analysis that shows the forecast improvement as a result of additional saving. Participants who take an extreme risk position (either conservative or aggressive) are shown the impact of a more diversified portfolio. As a result, the Personal Statement provides both an educational forecast and suggestions for change.

Our second tool, the Online Adviser, allows employees to get a realistic forecast of the range of income they can reasonably expect from their current retirement benefits. In addition it offers specific saving and investment recommendations to help improve the retirement forecast; and monitors progress to retirement and sends alerts if changes are necessary. Since Personal Statements are relatively new (released broadly in the Fall of 2002), there was yet little information available for analysis. In contrast, more information is available on the Adviser.

## Reaching the Participant

It would be that assessing participants' current situation was described as one of the key goals in this marketplace. In the present context, the participant must currently log on to the Financial Engines website.[2] Adoption of the Online Adviser, therefore, occurs when the participant registers for the Adviser service. To analyze adoption patterns, we drew a sample of companies from the Financial Engines' data warehouse. The sample was limited to corporations with 10,000 or more participants in their 401(k) plans, to avoid the issue of mixing data from very large and very small organizations. It should be noted that adoption does not all occur on the first day the Online Adviser is made available; rather the online medium is on-demand, adoption occurs fairly uniformly over any given time period. To address this issue, the sample was restricted to corporations that had made the Adviser available for at least one year as of the end of 2002.[3]

Overall adoption results at these large firms are reported in Table 11-1. The adoption percentage for each company is defined as the number of participants adopting the Adviser service, divided by the total number of plan participants (including terminated and retired participants). These are fairly significant barriers that limit the maximum adoption that reasonably can be expected. Financial Engines currently has no ability to communicate effectively with participants who are terminated or who are retired employees. In addition, Internet and plan provider access are sometimes difficult to measure, and in some cases, these barriers can exclude half or more of the eligible population from adopting the Adviser service. No adjustment has been made for Internet or plan provider access.[4]

Adoption rates average 18 percent in the 15 companies that have offered the service at least one year. Restricting the sample to companies that have offered the service at least 2 years boosts the average adoption rate to

TABLE 11-1  Current Adoption at Large Corporations[a]

|  | Average Adoption (%) | With Electronic Communication (%) | Without Electronic Communication (%) | Sample Size (Companies) |
|---|---|---|---|---|
| *Years since rollout*[b] |  |  |  |  |
| 1+ | 18.2 | 24.4 | 8.9[c] | 15 |
| 2+ | 28.0 | 33.9 | 10.1[c] | 4 |
| 3+ | 40.3 | 40.3 | N/A[3 c] | 2 |
| *Adoption measured at*[d] |  |  |  |  |
| 6 months | 10.1 | 13.5 | 4.9 | 10 |
| 1 year | 13.2 | 17.3 | 7.2 | 10 |
| 2 years | 21.1 | 27.1 | 9.1 | 3 |

*Notes*:
[a] Large is defined as 10,000 or more DC plan participants.
[b] Sample: 15 companies, ~450,000 participants, rollout date prior to 1/1/02.
[c] All companies with 3 or more years of data have electronic communication.
[d] Sample: 10 companies, ~379,000 participants, rollout date prior to 1/1/02.

*Source*: Authors' computations.

28 percent, while companies with 3 or more years have adoption rates of 40 percent. Of course, as the sample gets smaller, there is a large potential for company idiosyncrasies to skew the results. Corporations with three or more years of history are on average smaller in our sample (18,000 participants versus 30,000 for the larger sample). In addition, as "early adopters," these firms may be different from other large corporations. Such caveats aside, adoption does seem to significantly increase with time since the Adviser was first made available.

One of the most effective ways of encouraging employees to utilize the Financial Engines website is to send participants an email announcing the availability of the service. Including a link in this email that immediately brings the participant to the Financial Engines website makes trying the program extremely easy. By contrast, sending the participant a hard copy via regular mail means he must locate a computer, access the Internet, and type in a URL to achieve the same results.

One of the findings from the behavioral finance literature is that apparently small barriers can have large effects on behavior. It might be thought that employees would be willing to spend a bit of time to arrive at a proper plan for retirement investment, and saving decisions. But plan design can have a potent impact. For example, a DC plan could be structured to allow any employee who wishes to enroll in the plan (positive election enrollment), or plan rules could state that every employee is automatically enrolled unless he actively chooses to exit the plan (negative election enrollment). Companies tend to go to great lengths to inform employees about their choices and make reversing the default straightforward. Yet, this small change in plan design has a huge impact on participation. One hypothesis is that employees follow the "path of least resistance," and thus any barrier can cause employees to stick with the default choice (Choi et al., 2002).

Three alternatives have been proposed to explain this result (Duflo and Saez, Chapter 8, this volume). First, the result could stem from employees inferring some information from their employer's selection of the default. Second, employees may just not take the time to think about retirement. Finally, the default may be a commitment device to protect individuals from themselves. Table 11-1 provides evidence on the impact of reducing the barriers to adoption. Some companies provide an email with a link to the Online Adviser, while others do not, and the startling differences in behavior emerge. Of the 15 large sponsors, nine allow electronic communications while six do not. At those using electronic communications, adoption rates are almost 25 percent, while they are 9 percent if electronic communications are not used. The sample gets extremely small when examining companies that offered the Adviser more than 2 years, but the effect appears to be magnified.

Levels of adoption appear to be higher the longer the time since the Adviser service has been offered. It is possible that the effect of electronic communications could be due to differences in the amount of time since the service was first offered. For example, participants in companies with electronic communications have exposed about 7 months longer than those in companies lacking electronic communication. The bottom panel of Table 11-1 looks at interim adoption results to assess the impact of this difference.

Interim adoption results are also available for a sub sample of the main data set. Ten of the 15 companies in the base sample had interim adoption data available, corresponding to certain points in time (e.g. 6 months after rollout, one year after rollout, and 2 years after rollout), as opposed to current adoption rates. For the ten companies with available data, the average adoption rate at the 6-month point was about ten percent, which rose to 13 percent at the 1-year mark. The impact of electronic communication does not change after controlling for time since rollout. Firms having electronic communication averaged 13 and 17 percent adoption at the 6-month and 1-year mark, respectively. In contrast, companies without electronic communication averaged only 5 and 7 percent adoption at the 6-month and 1-year mark, respectively.

Clearly, electronic communication can have a significant impact on adoption rates.[5] Since barriers are relatively low for an employer-provided website for financial advice, the results seem to corroborate the "path of least resistance" hypothesis. They also support the hypothesis that employees simply do not take much time to think about retirement. It is hard to believe that the signaling mechanism is somehow dramatically stronger for an employer that offers online advice and allows electronic communication as compared to one that simply offers online advice.

Data from Financial Engines participant satisfaction surveys also corroborate the lack of time hypothesis. While these surveys dealt with many issues, they are very interesting for examining the question of non-adoption. Table 11-2 reports results on non-adopters in three recent surveys. The

TABLE 11-2  Non-Adopter Survey Results

| Reasons why have not tried FE | Survey Date | | |
|---|---|---|---|
| | June 2001 | March 2002 | June 2002 |
| Didn't know it was available as an employee benefit (%) | 25.1 | 48.6 | 37.8 |
| Haven't had time to try it (%) | 53.3 | 33.3 | 43.3 |
| Don't think I need help with my investments (%) | 3.8 | 3.5 | 3.7 |
| Don't want to use an Internet-based service (%) | 4.8 | 2.4 | 3.9 |
| Other (%) | 13.2 | 12.3 | 11.4 |
| Non-adopter (number) | 827 | 869 | 1,787 |

*Source*: Authors' computations.

results are remarkably consistent across waves: between one quarter and one half of the non-adopters surveyed indicated they did not know the benefit existed. An additional one-third to one half indicated they just had not found the time to try the Adviser. Averaging across all surveys, lack of time is reported as the single largest barrier. Interestingly, fewer than 5 percent listed the reason as not needing financial advice, and a small similar number indicated they were unwilling to use the Internet.

If convenience can have such a large impact, it implies that many participants are simply unwilling to spend time planning for retirement. These results are broadly consistent with MacFarland, Marconi, and Utkus (Chapter 6, this volume), who find that many people are "disinclined to be interested in the key activities or attitudes needed to make informed choices." Their analysis suggests that one-third or more of the working population may be avoiding thinking about retirement issues.

The survey results, and the prominence of small barriers, imply that providers must either improve convenience or eliminate the need for participants to proactively go online. Two approaches have been explored to incorporate these insights, one involving improving communication and convenience through enhanced provider integration, and a second which removes the online barrier altogether, by repackaging information available in the Adviser service in an offline format like a Personal Statement. Our data are still preliminary, but indications are that both approaches can enhance the reach of advisory services.

## Provider Integration

Though electronic communication does seem to enhance adoption, sending information via email has two significant shortcomings. First, some employers will not or cannot communicate with their employees via email. Second, participants who receive an email communication may not be interested in delving into their retirement planning when they get the email at work. For these reasons, provider integration is one form of electronic communication that overcomes both of these shortcomings.

Provider integration can mean a variety of things. When participants use a 401(k) provider website, they usually check their account balances, update their contribution rates, or adjust their investment mixes. In its simplest form, provider integration means alerting a participant to the availability of financial assistance at a relevant juncture so participants who are updating their investment mix could be asked if they would like to view the recommendations from the advice provider. Or participants who are updating their saving rates could be presented with an analysis that illustrates the impact of increasing saving on retirement wealth. The appeal of provider integration is that it overcomes the two main weaknesses of email communication. Even if a company does not actively communicate with employees electronically, many of these employees will still visit provider sites to maintain their accounts. Also, offering an analysis when the participant requests a change ensures that the participant has at least overcome the mental barrier of finding time to update his 401(k).

We have recently launched a pilot version of a provider integration approach which links to the Adviser, conducted at a Fortune 500 company. The pilot was started when roughly 9 percent of participants had adopted the Adviser service, several months after making the Adviser available. Projections suggested that the likely adoption rate after another year would have been 14 percent, assuming no other communication programs. Just 3 months into the pilot, adoption had risen from 9 to 13 percent, a 44 percent increase, and adoption expected to exceed 20 percent, a year into the pilot. It should be possible to enhance rates further, since participants currently must accept an Investor Services Agreement during the transfer from the plan provider to Financial Engines, yet some participants fail to do so. A small adjustment to this practice could have a significant impact on the number of participants that receive advice. Importantly, the potential improvement would be greatest for sponsors without electronic communication, since "path resistance" is dramatically reduced for their employees. Further, since provider integration levels the playing field between sponsors that do and do not allow electronic communications, it provides an opportunity to test the hypothesis that electronic communication results stem from sponsor selection bias rather than a differential effect from the communication method.

## Personal Statements

Another approach to improving reach is Personal Statements, which eliminate the online barrier by offering much of the information in a paper format. The benefit of this approach is that participants need not actively request an online financial analysis; instead, participants are mailed, or emailed, a Personal Statement for their own 401(k) plan. The statement provides each participant with a retirement forecast, and also illustrates how the participant could improve his retirement situation through saving more, diversifying, etc. since Personal Statements are relatively new, first released in 2002, little data are available to date. Table 11-3 reports some initial survey information collected by a company currently using Personal Statements, which indicates that about two-thirds of the participants can recall receiving a Personal Statement. This represents a substantial increase in reach, relative to the Online Adviser.

## Changing Participant Behavior

Reaching the participant satisfies the employer's disclosure requirement, and it also provides useful information to help him make informed decisions. In

TABLE 11-3  Personal Statement Survey Results[a]

|  | Responses (%) |
|---|---|
| *Recently, you were sent a Personal Retirement Forecast[b] from your employer.* | |
| *Do you recall receiving your Personal Forecast?* | |
| Yes | 66.2 |
| No | 17.6 |
| Not sure | 16.2 |
| *Since reviewing your forecast,[b] have you made any changes to your 401(k)* | |
| *account (such as increasing your savings or changing your* | |
| *investments)?* | |
| Yes, I have already made some changes. | 16 |
| No, but I plan on making some changes. | 52 |
| No, I do not plan on making any changes. | 32 |

*Notes*:
[a] 3,138 surveys were mailed, and 142 were completed and returned.
[b] "Forecast" in this context refers to the Personal Statement.

*Source*:  Financial Engines.

addition, some firms seek to change participant behavior to improve actual retirement security.

Behavioral finance, as a field, is concerned with understanding the behavior and biases of individuals as they relate to financial decisions. In the present context several studies are relevant. For instance, Iyengar and Lepper (2002) examine the relationship between the number of choices offered to consumers and their resulting decisions. They found that extensive choice attracted more attention, but that limited choice motivated actual purchases in a food context. Iyengar, Huberman, and Jiang (Chapter 5, this volume) relate the impact of choice to 401(k) participation. They show that the number of fund choices negatively influences the participation rates after controlling for a number of other factors. This is probably because a large and confusing number of choices may create a barrier sufficient to discourage participants from enrolling in the 401(k).

## The Adviser Redesign

To test these ideas, Financial Engines redesigned the Online Adviser in late 2002. The major change was how choices were communicated to participants. Prior to the redesign, the participant was given a range of choices for each of the major retirement decisions: Saving, investment risk level, and allocation to company stock. For example, suppose a participant was currently contributing $2,000 a year to his 401(k) plan. Prior to the redesign, the participant would have been encouraged to choose from five potential saving levels: ($0, $2,000, $3,000, $5,000, and $10,000). The impact of the retirement forecast was described for each level of saving. A participant also could input his own level of saving if his was not one of the five choices given.[6]

The redesign completely changed this framework. Instead of offering a range of choices, the participant is now provided with a single alternative to consider. Continuing with the saving example, suppose the employer matches employee contributions up to $3,500 for this participant. In that case, the initial saving choices would be limited to staying at the worker's current level of saving ($2,000) or switching to a level of savings that fully utilized the employer match ($3,500). A wider range of choices was still available, but the participant had to actively request the range. For each of the major retirement decisions, the redesign presented a single focal alternative and concentrated the participant's attention on the binary decision of staying where he was switching to a single alternative.

Another part of the redesign involves the Advice Action Kit (AAK), a screen in the Adviser service that summarizes changes between the participant's current situation and the new strategy he or she has selected. The AAK is a strong measure of impact, because it is only requested to facilitate implementation. It is not interactive, and it is rendered as a printable list of instructions necessary to implement the plan. For this reason, AAK data is believed to represent a serious retirement plan on the participant's part.

Our analysis of over 34,000 AAKs roughly split between pre- and post-redesign, appears in Table 11-4. The top row 4 reports results for the saving

TABLE 11.4  AAK Analysis

| Action | Percentage of Sample (Prior to Redesign) | Percentage of Sample (Post-Redesign) | Sample Size |
|---|---|---|---|
| Save more[a] | 31[b] | 45[c] | 24,040 |
| Adjusted risk[d] | 35 | 51 | 33,427 |
| Reduced stock, full sample[e] | 14[f] | 30[g] | 34,589 |
| Reduced stock, initial stock level > 0% | 28[f] | 60[g] | 17,412 |

*Notes*:

[a] Approximately 6% of the sample decided to save less in both cases.

[b] Median saving increased from $3,240 to $5,468 per annum.

[c] Median saving increased from $2,700 to $5,551 per annum.

[d] "Adjusted Risk" implies a change in portfolio volatility in excess of 5% of market volatility. (~55 bps as of April 2003).

[e] Less than three percent of the sample actually increased company stock in both cases.

[f] Median ending stock allocation is 37%. Median stock reduction was 69%.

[g] Median ending stock allocation is 28%. Median stock reduction was 82%.

*Source*: Authors' computations.

decision.[7] Prior to the redesign, 31 percent of the sample decided to save more, and after the redesign, 45 percent were saving more. In addition, while ending saving levels were comparable, the increase in savings was about $500 more in the post-redesign sample. The redesign also influenced the number of participants willing to change their investment risk level. Prior to the redesign, about one in three participants created an action plan with a materially different risk level from their original portfolio. After the redesign, this proportion increased to one in two.

The largest change perceived related to the company stock decision. Prior to the redesign, 14 percent of AAKs identified a desire to reduce company stock; after the redesign, this proportion increased to 30 percent. The magnitude of proposed changes also increased after the redesign. Before, the median ending level of company stock was 37 percent and after the redesign, the median ending stock allocation was 28 percent. The company stock results are somewhat understated, in that only half the available sample actually started with a positive amount of company stock. Limiting the sample to these participants, the fraction that reduced company stock pre- and post-redesign was 28 and 60 percent, respectively. This evidence corroborates the hypotheses that fewer and more direct choices are much more likely to generate action, compared to "choice overload."[8]

The pilot also allowed us to explore the effectiveness of this approach on changing participant behavior via provider integration. Preliminary data indicate that it is very important to be able to process fund transfers and savings adjustments directly from the Financial Engines website, without having to print the instructions and then go to the provider website to effect the change. In 3 months of data available from the pilot, the transaction incidence is *five times* higher for participants using the integrated approach as compared to those using other sources.

Limited survey data are also available to address the reach of Personal Statements, shown in the lower panel of Table 11-3. The results prove interesting. Of those surveyed, 16 percent had already made a change, and another 52 percent intending to make a change to either their saving level or investment mix. Of course, there is a gap between intending to make a change and actually making a change, when self-control and procrastination problems play a significant role (Benartzi and Thaler, 2004).

## Conclusions

Our research shows that communication methods can alter fundamental life decisions such as saving and investment levels. We corroborate this by examining the likelihood that employees utilize an employer-provided online advisory benefit. We find that employees who receive an email regarding the availability of the advisory service are much more likely to use it, than to those who receive a hard copy version in the mail. Also we find that the reason participants do not avail themselves of the service is primarily due to lack of time, since they readily admit the need for help. We further explored the impact of a redesign of the online advisory service. Reducing the number of choices employees were given from five to two increased by 40–100 percent the frequency with which individuals altered their behavior. Last, we evaluated data from a pilot version of provider integration, which reduces the barriers to action by offering services when individuals are most likely to be receptive. We find that lower barriers are associated with roughly double the adoption rate, and roughly five times the action rate.

Clearly, there is still work to do to help ensure retirement security in DC plans. Nevertheless, we conclude that insights from behavioral finance can have a large real-world impact on the decisions people make, and ultimately on their retirement well-being.

## Notes

[1] Discretionary asset management may also be useful for addressing the needs of many investors with little time for or interest in investing, but our focus is not that market.

[2] Integrating the forecast on the provider website could overcome this constraint.

[3] One company was excluded from the analysis because participants were required to enter credit card information prior to adoption. These "participant pay" arrangements are no longer offered because the barriers were too large for participants to reasonably overcome.

[4] In some situations, participants first have to create an account with their plan provider before using the Adviser.

[5] We acknowledge that, the fact that a sponsor allows electronic communication could proxy for other factors influencing adoption. For example, those sponsors may be more likely to have an Internet-enabled workforce, or they may have a higher percentage of white-collar workers.

[6] The saving level choices were selected to be "focal" in some way. Typical choices included the participants' current saving level, a level that exhausted the employer match, and the maximum saving level allowed.

[7] All AAK data is not available since easily accessible AAK logs have only recently been created. In addition, not all AAK logs have complete saving information.

[8] Fund transactions and savings adjustments are enabled directly from the Financial Engines website (without having to go to the provider site) for a few providers. The "transaction enabled" AAK data corresponds to approximately a 5% subsample. Results from this subsample did not materially differ from results in Table 11-4.

## References

Benartzi, Shlomo and Richard Thaler. 2004. "Save More Tomorrow: Using Behavioral Economics to Increase Employee Saving." *Journal of Political Economy* 112(1) February: 164–187.

Choi, James, David Laibson, Brigitte Madrian, and Andrew Metrick. 2002. "Defined Contribution Pensions: Plan Rules, Participant Choices, and the Path of Least Resistance." In *Tax Policy and the Economy*, ed. James Poterba. Cambridge, MA: MIT Press, pp. 67–113.

Iyengar, Sheena S. and Mark R. Lepper. 2002. "When Choice is Demotivating: Can One Desire Too Much of a Good Thing?" *Journal of Personality and Social Psychology* 76: 995–1006.

# Chapter 12

## Adult Learning Principles and Pension Participant Behavior

*Victor Saliterman and Barry G. Sheckley*

Many analysts suggest that American workers may not have enough money to support themselves during their retirement years. During 2001, for example, American households saved only 1 percent of their annual income (Conger, Drinkwater, and Dighe, 2002). According to the Employee Benefit Research Institute (EBRI) the median retirement account balance of US workers was under $15,000 in 2001; fully 25 percent of employees do not participate in retirement plans; and the average annual contribution rate was a low 6 percent of pay (Holden and Van Derhei, 2003).

Decisionmaking research (Selnow, Chapter 2, this volume) offers perspectives on boosting retirement savings based on concepts such as risk perception and rule-based processes (Weber, Chapter 3, this volume); costs and benefits of choices (Iyengar, Huberman, and Jiang, Chapter 5, this volume); and "money attitudes" (MacFarland, Marconi, and Utkus, this volume).

Many of the economic models, however simply "describe investors as they are" implying that these models cannot explain how to change investors' approaches to decisionmaking (Statman, Chapter 4, this volume). This analysis perhaps explains why Duflo and Saez (Chapter 8, this volume) report that an intervention planned to influence voluntary decisions had no impact on increasing enrollments in retirement savings programs—individuals in the treatment group (those who attended a retirement "fair") participated in a 401(k) at the same rate (9 percent) as did those who did not attend the fair. To resolve the retirement savings problem, the approach of accepting 401(k) participants "as they are"—and presenting decision choices accordingly, even to the point of making options prescriptive—may have to be supplemented with tactics for changing how participants think about their retirement plans. Educational programs designed for this purpose, however, have a poor track record. For example, in a recent EBRI (2002) survey, 41 percent of workers recalled receiving educational material or participating in seminars about retirement planning and savings, yet almost three out of four (72 percent) made no changes as a result.

Perhaps the design of these educational programs is problematic. For example, when asked, employees assigned a "C" grade to the retirement education programs offered by their employers (CIGNA, 2002). Additionally Weber (this volume), indicated that educational programs which present abstract information, emphasize statistical figures, and focus on far distant future consequences may fail to elicit "visceral" reactions to the potentially serious consequences of their retirement saving choices. While interventions based on behavioral decisionmaking models have promise for heightening retirement savings, we posit that supplemental approaches are also needed—especially when increasing voluntary contributions is a goal. One option may be to augment current programs with educational services designed according to research-based principles of how adults learn best. Accordingly, this study explored the proposition that participants who receive information about their retirement savings in accord with research-based principles of how adults learn best will markedly increase contributions to their retirement plans.

## Research-Based Principles of Learning

Since the 1940s, the metaphors of mind-as-computer and learning-as-information-processing have dominated educational practices (Mayer, 1996). The source of the metaphor is the input–throughput–output design of a computer. Learning processes, when depicted as "computer-like," are described as occurring serially, one after another. The senses (akin to a keyboard) activate a step-by-step process in which the cerebral cortex (akin to a computer processor) pulls information from memory (akin to hard drive files). A cognitive process such as reasoning (akin to a software program) is then used to analyze the information. Following this metaphor, thinking and reasoning, involve processes similar to finding and opening files on a computer. To support this process, instruction simply has to deposit data into a computer file; the mind-as-computer then locates and uses the data as necessary.

Thinking, learning, and therefore instruction, are more complex than depicted by the mind-as-computer metaphor, however. Research indicates that the brain actually operates, not as a computer, but as a jungle-like network intricately connected to the body's biology (Edelman, 1991). As described by Damasio (1994), the human brain and human body make up an "indissociable organism, integrated by means of mutually interactive biochemical and neural regulatory circuits (including endocrine, immune, and autonomic neural components)" (p. xvii). Many current theorists, including Damasio (1999), LeDoux (1996), and Edelman and Tononi (2000), spotlight the limits of the mind-as-computer metaphor and related data-depositing instructional programs. Numerous research studies indicate that only about 10–20 percent of information learned in classrooms that follow the mind-as-computer model is ever used in other settings (Baldwin and Ford, 1988). Researchers who understand the workings of the human brain emphasize that the complex emotional and visceral nature of learning must be supported by instruction that mirrors these affective and experiential processes (Damasio, 2003).

As an alternative to the mind-as-computer approaches to instruction the American Psychological Association's Board of Educational Affairs (APA, 2003), drawing on a comprehensive review of the research literature, concluded that educational practices were most effective when the learner—not the information to be learned—was the primary focus of educational practice. The principles for learner-centered instruction developed by this group—augmented with research on how adults learn best (Keeton, Sheckley, and Krechje-Griggs, 2002)—provide a template for designing educational services to influence how participants in 401(k) plans think about and plan for their retirement. Following the principles outlined in Table 12-1, educational services for individuals in retirement plans would be designed to engage participants as goal-directed and self-regulating learners who are poised to take responsibility for their own learning. Additionally, the services would aid participants in cultivating and developing retirement savings plans consistent with their personal goals and aspirations. The services would also assist participants to integrate new information about retirement options into their prior knowledge about saving for retirement, their personal values about money, the cultural norms that guide their financial thinking, and their prior investment experiences.

Since retirement planning requires a well-developed repertoire of thinking and problem-solving skills, effective educational services must engage participants in activities that help them develop such skills (e.g. reflection on their own strategies or interactions with others who are more knowledgeable about retirement). Since effective retirement planning requires individuals to plan, monitor, and evaluate their own decisions, educational planning services would assist participants in setting reasonable savings goals, selecting appropriate planning strategies, monitoring their progress towards these goals, and devising ways to address problems as they occur. Ideal educational services would also be described as a "warm hearth," in that they would provide a setting that embraced individual differences, respected diversity in all its forms, cultivated participants' positive beliefs about themselves as retirement planners, encouraged positive emotions such as curiosity, and dampened negative thoughts such as excessive fears, anxieties, or ruminations about failure. At their best, educational services would kindle participants' natural curiosity to learn, by engaging participants in novel tasks relevant to their own personal interests and providing for their personal choice and control. Finally, instead of following a one-size-fits-all format, effective educational programs would respect and embrace participants' unique strategies, approaches, and capabilities for learning.

TABLE 12-1 Principles of Learning with Related Practices

| Principle | Related Practice |
|---|---|
| • Successful learning is an intentional process of constructing meaning from information and experience | • Actively engage participants as goal-directed and self-regulating individuals who assume personal responsibility for learning about their retirement options |
| • Successful learning, the acquisition of complex knowledge and skills, is a process that occurs over time with support and instructional guidance | • Gain participants' commitment to persist in developing retirement plans and to invest considerable time and energy in a process to create plans that are consistent with their personal aspirations and interests |
| • Successful learning is a process of integrating new knowledge with a learner's prior knowledge and understanding | • Engage participants in linking new knowledge about retirement options to prior experiences, and using the new knowledge to refine their retirement plans |
| • Successful learning is a process that requires an expansive repertoire of thinking and reasoning strategies | • Engage participants in reflection about their retirement plans, and interactions with others who are knowledgeable about retirement options |
| • Successful learning is a process that involves higher order strategies for selecting and monitoring mental operations | • Engage participants in reflections on how they think and learn, setting reasonable retirement savings goals, selecting potentially appropriate retirement planning strategies, monitoring their progress toward these goals, and devising ways to address problems if they occur |
| • Successful learning is a process influenced by environmental factors including culture and social relations | • Provide a supportive environment for discussions about retirement, a setting that embraces diversity in all its many forms including cultural norms about money, savings, and retirement |
| • Successful learning is a process influenced by a learner's emotional states, beliefs, interests, goals, and habits of thinking | • Cultivate participants' positive self-beliefs about themselves as retirement planners. Encourage positive emotions such as curiosity to |

TABLE 12-1 *Continued.*

| Principle | Related Practice |
| --- | --- |
| | dominate over negative emotions (e.g. anxiety or panic) and related thoughts (e.g. ruminating about failure) |
| • Successful learning is a process in which creativity, higher order thinking, and natural curiosity all contribute to motivation to learn | • Engage participants in novel tasks related to retirement that are relevant to personal interests, and provide for personal choice and control |
| • Successful learning is a process that is influenced by social interactions, interpersonal relations, and communication with others | • Provide participants with opportunities to interact and to collaborate with others about retirement options |
| • Successful learning is a highly individual process | • Embrace participants' unique strategies, approaches, and capabilities for learning about retirement options |

*Source*: Author's analysis.

## Adults as Learners

The principles and practices outlined in Table 12-1 apply equally to adults and children, even though "learning" for most of the last century was conceived of as an activity for the young, a perspective that led Malcolm Knowles (1978) to describe adult learners as a "neglected species." The notion that "old dogs cannot learn new tricks," first introduced in the 1930s (Lorge, 1936), was based on the Wechsler "deterioration quotient" (Wechsler, 1958). According to this formulation, human "intelligence" increased until around 20 years of age and then began a slow and steady decline that continued through the life span. Follow-up research confirmed this pattern, but only when learning and intelligence were measured as the "fluid" ability of working memory to perform tasks such as memorizing strings of numbers (Rogoff and Gardner, 1984). According to Welford (1993), "While many studies suggest that adult memory declines with age, these results are inconsistent with the common observation that most people as they grow older seem to cope very well with the tasks and problems of everyday life."

## Adult Learning as Re-Cognition

The principles and practices outlined in Table 12-1 are also consistent with research indicating that adult learning is best conceived *not* as process of remembering (akin to recalling information stored in computer files), but rather as a process of re-cognition: "Seeing" the relationships between new information and knowledge gained from prior experiences. As Kolb (1984) observed, all learning is re-learning, since experience always intervenes. The difference between learning-as-memory (based on the mind-as-computer metaphor) and learning-as-recognition (based on current research on how the brain actually functions) can play out in different approaches to retirement planning. Programs following the mind-as-computer approach focus on filling up data files in the mind with numbers, statistics, projections, and related information. In contrast, programs that followed a learning-as-perception approach, following the research-based practices outlined in Table 12-1, engage individuals in an ongoing process of re-cognition that helps them "see" how information about investments has both immediate and long-term relevance to their lives.

According to the learning-as-recognition viewpoint, participants, when confronted with novel information such as that presented in retirement planning communiqués, will work to "see" if a relationship exists between this new information and a former event or experience. If such a link, or analogy, can be made, individuals will use this analogy to reason, judge, and make decisions about the relevance or viability of the new information (Gentner and Markman, 1997).

This analogy mapping process is not always effective, however. Amidst its many astounding features, the human mind does have a tendency to resolve issues in the simplest way possible, sometimes using surface similarities to establish links between new information and a prior experience (Holyoak and Thagard, 1997). When presented with new information about investing for retirement, participants may process the information using, for example, a simplistic "banking" analogy. The banking analogy may be useful for the moment because it has worked for them in previous situations related to money and investments. For the banking analogy to be most effective, however, participants will have to come to a re-cognition of how it must be restructured to embrace the complexities of investing for retirement.

## Adults as Self-Directed Learners

The principles and practices outlined in Table 12-1 are also consistent with research on how adults plan and carry out their learning. In his groundbreaking research, Tough (1979) found that adults spent over 100 h per week in intentional efforts to gain and retain knowledge. Most of this learning (73 percent) was self-planned, and did not involve working with teachers in classroom settings. Adults actively focused their learning on problems and issues of interest to them. They did not pursue learning just because others—teachers, spouses, or financial advisers—deemed a topic to be "important."

Since these results ran counter to many educational practices, they spawned a good deal of follow-up research that confirmed the original findings. The results were so consistent that "effective" adult learning is now described as "self-directed," "self-planned," or "autonomy-enhancing" process (Candy, 1991).

Self-direction, however, does not mean that adults learn best when left alone without guidance to assist their learning (Brookfield, 1985). Instead, as adults direct their efforts to resolve genuine problems, they can benefit from guidance and information that will enhance their learning (Merriam and Caffarella, 1999).

## Influencing Participant Behavior

We pose the following proposition in this study: Participants who receive information about their retirement savings in accord with research-based principles of how adults learn best will markedly increase contributions to their retirement plans. This is explored in two separate case situations. The first involves using research-based principles and practices of how adults learn best to influence participants who called into a service center for any reason whatsoever to increase contributions to their retirement accounts. The second used research-based principles of how adults learn best to prompt participants to increase their retirement savings through targeted communication and education programs.

### Case 1: Participant Service Center

Agents who work in the CIGNA Retirement & Investment Services (CR&IS) Participant Service Center (PSC) provide information to more than 2,200 callers each day. When participants contact the PSC, they can check on the status of their accounts, change their contributions, change the distribution of their investments, arrange for loans, or receive information on a wide array of retirement and financial topics. In most cases, they call searching for information about 401(k) loans, reallocating investments, or making withdrawals. Many also call to request distribution forms or to inquire about the status of a check that will provide payment for either a loan or with-drawal. Prior to this research project, very few (if any) participants called to voluntarily increase contributions to their retirement accounts.

Before this research project began, the PSC operated in a manner common to most call centers. Handling calls as quickly and as efficiently as possible was a top priority. Representatives gave prompt answers to questions. Requests were handled briskly. Coaches monitored representatives in terms of the call volume they handled as well as number of transactions completed. Representatives had no explicit responsibility for trying to influence participant behavior; rather their role was a reactive one. They listened to callers' requests and responded as effectively and efficiently as possible. The more calls they handled, the better.

During the summer of 2002, the PSC embarked on a research project to determine whether research-based principles on adult learning could be used to influence participants to increase contributions to their retirement plans, irrespective of the original purpose of their call. A process for influencing participant behaviors in this manner, termed the "Consultative Approach," adhered to the research-based principles and practices of how adults learn best summarized above. As such, it included three interactive steps: (i) Assess, (ii) Educate, (iii) Influence.

When callers contacted the PSC, agents following the Consultative Approach worked quickly to assess the caller's situation. Factors such as age, prior history of activity, length of time in the plan, nature of the request, and similar items were considered. Additionally, representatives would listen "between the words" to see if they could pick up cues (e.g. tone of voice, issues raised by the participant, background noises, and the like) to make a personal connection with the caller.

Next, the representative would engage in a dialogue for the purpose of educating and influencing the participant's views about saving for retirement. The representative would probe to test the caller's understanding of retirement planning options: "What age would you like to retire? Did you know that you are not taking full advantage of your retirement options?" If an opening appeared (e.g. if the customer said "Tell me more about the options I'm not using fully"), representatives would lead the caller through a process of re-cognition to help him rethink the roles of different options in his retirement plan. During the dialogue, the representative would provide expert information about positive and negative impacts of decisions each participant contemplated.

Finally, the representative would direct the process toward having the caller make a decision that would lead to a result such as increasing contributions, changing investment choices, or choosing alternatives to taking a loan against a retirement plan. The caller's decision, in turn, would help the representative assess the caller's situation and perhaps continue the discussion on a related topic, set arrangements for the representative to send additional information, plant a seed that may prompt a participant to consider future actions, or set up a time for a follow-up call to discuss additional options for retirement planning.

By using the consultative process, agents adopted an "instructional" stance when answering calls. Instead of merely reacting to participant requests, representatives worked as "educators" who guided participants through focused discussions about preparing financially for retirement. In this role, agents engaged participants as "learners in disguise" who could be vulnerable to a "teachable moment," in that callers sought information about retirement plans for the purpose of using this information. From an instructional viewpoint, the caller's queries provided agents-as-educators with insights about how the caller was thinking about and conceptualizing retirement planning. With all this information at hand, representatives-as-instructors could then prompt participants to think about their retirement in broader, more complex terms and thereby influence them to take advantage of retirement options they were not using (e.g. employers' matching contributions).

Table 12-2 outlines changes in participant contributions achieved during the project. The first column represents an average of each indicator from January 2001 through August 2002, the period before the start of the research project. In September 2002, the project began, and the next three columns off comparisons with the baseline measures. Each row in Table 12-2 lists indicators that document increases in contributions to defined contribution (DC) plans associated with the Consultative Approach.

During the 20 months prior to the use of the Consultative Approach, PSC agents handled almost 46,000 calls each month related to DC plans. This number remained relatively constant over the course of the project, suggesting that changes in participant behavior involving their DC plans were not related to an explosion of interest about DC plans among participants. Their concerns, in terms of numbers of DC calls per month, were relatively stable from January 2001 through June 2003.

One indication of the results achieved using the principles of how adults learn best is evident in the measure "total number of contribution calls/month" (Table 12-2, row 2). From January 2001 the inception of the

TABLE 12-2  Summary of Results Achieved using Consultative Approach

|  | Average Prior 20 Months | Average Sept.–Nov. 2002 | Average Dec. 2002–Feb. 2003 | Average Mar.–June 2003 |
|---|---|---|---|---|
| Total number DC calls/month | 45,813 | 45,620 | 47,058 | 43,418 |
| Total number contribution calls/month | 2,050 | 4,817 | 5,068 | 3,864 |
| Number contribution increase calls/month | Negligible | 1,372 | 1,555 | 1,557 |
| Percent contribution increase calls | Negligible | 28.5 | 30.8 | 43.0 |
| Total dollar increase/month (annualized) | Negligible | 2,134,557 | 3,063,397 | 2,864,649 |

*Source*: Authors' analysis.

research project, an average of about 2,000 calls/month came to the PSC regarding DC contributions. When the Consultative Approach began, however, this number more than doubled to an average of 4,817 calls during the September–November 2002 period. Previously, few if any callers contacted the PSC to voluntarily increase their contributions, hence the "negligible" entry in the first cell of row 3 in Table 12-2. With the use of the Consultative Approach, however, about 1,400–1,500 participants/month discussed contributions to their DC plans during their calls. Additionally, as portrayed in row 4, the percentage of calls related to increasing contributions grew steadily from 28 percent during the September–November 2002 period to 43 percent during the March–June 2003 period. Finally, and perhaps most importantly, row 5 indicates the overall financial impact related to the use of the Consultative Approach. Before, there were very few if any increases in contributions that could be tracked to participants' contact with the PSC. Afterwards, contributions rose steadily from about $2,000,000 per month (annualized) during the September–November, 2002 period to about $3,000,000/month (annualized) during 2003. The gains were likely even larger than reported in Table 12-2, however, since the figures listed in the Table 12-2 do not include employer matching contributions that may have accompanied participants' contribution increases. Anecdotal information suggests that a similar level of success occurred in areas such as convincing participants to avoid drawing loans from their 401(k) accounts.

Cost-benefit analyses also underscore the success of the program. Start-up costs (approximately $200,000) as well as recurring costs such as accommodating increased talk-time per call (approximately $200,000/year) were largely offset by annual revenues from increases in assets under management (e.g. $200,000 for 2003). Additional gains were experienced in terms of lower employee turnover, which went from over 50 percent in 2001 to under 10 percent in 2003, at a saving estimated at approximately $700,000/year. Further, agents reported that using the Consultative Approach made their work more satisfying, and morale and teamwork yielded estimated gains of approximately $150,000/year.

## Case 2: Communications and Education Programs

Using the research-based principles of how adults learn summarized in Table 12-1, CR&IS also customized its educational and communication activities to embrace individual client differences in background, interests, and life stage. No activities began until an assessment of participants' needs and specific goals was completed (see left-hand side of Figure 12-1). Additionally, targeted programs—consisting of communications (e.g. print materials, emails, and statements), informational resources (e.g. call service center, Internet site), and educational activities (e.g. workshops)—were offered in an integrated manner over a 6–12 week period (see Figure 12-1 middle). These programs

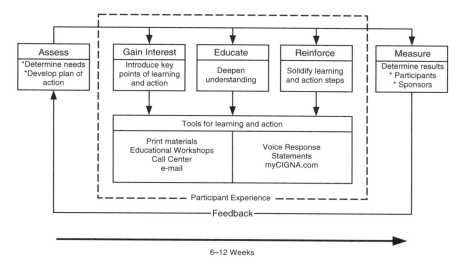

Figure 12-1. Communications and education delivery model.

*Source*: Authors' analysis.

and activities were targeted on specific topics of interest to the participants (e.g. getting started in the plan, maximizing workplace savings, staying abreast of fund changes, managing asset allocations, consolidating retirement accounts).

Each targeted program engaged participants in a process of re-cognition that allowed them to think through how the information pertained to their individual retirement situations. First, individuals were introduced to key ideas as they related to specific life stage issues and related problems. Using straightforward assessment tools, participants determined their "investor profiles,"—drawing on their current financial situation, their life stage, and their preferences for taking investment risk. From this information, a plan of action was developed. Next, opportunities were provided for participants to deepen their understanding through focused educational workshops. Finally, activities and events were planned to help participants solidify their re-cognition of how the information pertained to their individual retirement situation.

By engaging participants actively over a 6–12 week period, in a process of reframing their ideas of retirement planning, the communication and educational events helped participants weave the "vocabulary" of retirement planning into the ongoing conversation of their lives and, in the process, take actions that moved them closer to a financially secure retirement. Additionally, curricula used in the workshops were completely revised to make them more problem-based, more focused on issues each participant brought to the workshops, and more centered on interactions among participants.

The educational and communication activities were evaluated with both qualitative and quantitative measures. In addition to assessing levels of learning, intended action, and participant satisfaction with a program, researchers also measured actual actions taken. As each program concluded, it was evaluated based on program goals; for example, the number of eligible non-participants who enrolled in a plan, the percentage increase in contributions, changes in portfolio allocations, rollover of eligible retirement accounts to the plan sponsor's retirement plan. To ensure the accuracy of its measures, CR&IS engaged independent accountants, to review results. The findings were then used to assess the impact of the educational and communication events on participants' behaviors (see right-hand side of Figure 12-1). Using this feedback, the cycle started anew.

When the "traditional" format used during January–March 2002 period is compared with the "adult learning based" format that took hold during November–December 2002, the results underscore the benefit of reinforcing the "save for retirement" message with an integrated set of activities. During the January–March 2002 period, results are available for activities with one plan sponsor. With this sponsor, a workshop with 20 or so participants using a standard lecture format realized a total increase in contributions to retirement plans of about $65,000. This program was not integrated with other programs in a way that reinforced the "save for retirement" message. During November–December 2002, results are available for a similar set of three workshops—also enrolling about 20 or so participants—with other plan sponsors. These workshops, however, were part of an integrated and targeted series that took place over time to reinforce the "save for retirement" message. These November–December Targeted Programs were also personalized to participants, in that they led participants through a re-cognition process of rethinking their retirement options. These programs resulted in an average gain of $230,000 in deferrals per program.

Though the database is small for this comparison, the trend suggests that in terms of increased contributions, initiatives based on research-based principles of how adults learn best were effective in influencing participant behavior.

## Conclusions

Policymakers, financial service providers, and employers face a daunting challenge. Many pension plans allow individuals to take advantage of tax-efficient options for building retirement savings. Not only do these plans benefit from the ease of payroll deduction, but also employee contributions are often complemented by an employer match. Furthermore, extensive resources are poured into educating individuals about saving, investing, and retirement planning. Nevertheless, people are persistently slow to prepare adequately for the financial demands of retirement. Saving rates and amounts saved are insufficient for many to enjoy a financially secure retirement.

Our research suggests that programs founded on research-based principles of how adults learn best can influence participant investment decisions so as to provide them with a more secure retirement. Financial service providers can build on principles of how adults learn best by using a learner-centered process to guide participants through a re-cognition of how they can use information about investment options to devise effective financial plans. The techniques work best when they engage learners as active, self-determining individuals who will benefit most from assistance that helps them to reflect on and make informed choices about their retirement saving plans.

# References

American Psychological Association Board of Educational Affairs. 1995. "Learner-centered Psychological Principles: A Framework for School Redesign and Reform." www.apa.org/ed/lcp.html.

Baldwin, Timothy T. and J. Kevin Ford. 1988. "Transfer of Training: A Review and Directions For Future Research." *Personnel Psychology* 94(2): 192–210.

Brookfield, Stephen D. 1985. "Self-Directed Learning: A Critical Review of Research." In *Self-Directed Learning: From Theory to Practice*, ed. Stephen D. Brookfield. San Francisco: Jossey-Bass: 5–16.

Candy, Philip. 1991. *Self-direction for Lifelong Learning*. San Francisco: Jossey-Bass.

CIGNA Retirement and Investment Services. 2002. "Workplace Report on Retirement Planning." Hartford CT.

Conger, Tom, Cynthia Drinkwater, and Atul Dighe. 2002. "Delegate Resources: 2002 National Summit on Retirement Savings." Washington, DC: International Foundation of Employee Benefit Plans, Inc.

Damasio, Antonio R. 1994. *Descartes' Error: Emotion, Reason, and the Human Brain.* New York: Avon Books.

—— 1999. *The Feeling of What Happens: Body and Emotion in the Making of Consciousness.* New York: Harcourt Brace & Company.

—— 2003. *Looking for Spinoza: Joy, Sorrow, and the Feeling Brain.* New York: Harcourt, Inc.

Edelman, Gerald M. 1991. *Bright Air, Brilliant Fire: On the Matter of the Mind.* New York: Basic Books.

—— and Giovani Tononi. 2000. *A Universe of Consciousness: How Matter Becomes Imagination.* New York: Basic Books.

Employee Benefit Research Institute (EBRI). *2002 Retirement Confidence Survey.* Washington, DC.

Gentner, Dedre and Arthur B. Markman. 1997. "Structural vs. Syntactic Matching: Analogy Entails Common Relations." Paper presented at the Nineteenth Annual Conference of the Cognitive Science Society. Stanford University, Stanford, CA.

Holden, Sarah and Jack Van Derhei. 2003. "401(k) Plan Asset Allocation, Account Balances, and Loan Activity in 2001." Employee Benefit Research Institute (EBRI). www.ebri.org/pdfs/0303ib.pdf.

Holyoak, Keith J. and Paul Thagard. 1997. "The Analogical Mind." *American Psychologist* 52(1): 35–44.

Keeton, Morris T., Barry G. Sheckley, and Joan Krechje-Griggs. 2002. *Effectiveness and Efficiency in Higher Education for Adults: A Guide for Fostering Learning.* Dubuque, IA: Kendall/Hunt Publishing Company.

Knowles, Malcolm. 1978. *The Adult Learner: A Neglected Species*, 2nd edn. Houston: Gulf.

Kolb, David A. 1984. *Experiential Learning: Experiences as the Source of Learning and Development.* Englewood Cliffs: Prentice-Hall.

LeDoux, Joseph. 1996. *The Emotional Brain: The Mysterious Underpinnings of Emotional Life.* New York: Simon and Schuster.

Lorge, Ivan. 1936. "The Influence of the Test upon the Nature of Mental Decline as a Function of Age." *Journal of Educational Psychology* 27: 100–110.

Mayer, Richard E. 1996. "Learners as Information Processors: Legacies and Limitations of Educational Psychology's Second Metaphor." *Educational Psychologist* 31(3/4): 151–161.

Merriam, Sharan B. and Rosemary S. Caffarella. 1999. *Learning in Adulthood: A Comprehensive Guide*, 2nd edn. San Francisco: Jossey-Bass Publishers.

Rogoff, Barbara and William Gardner. 1984. "Adult Guidance of Cognitive Development." In *Everyday Cognition: Its Development in Social Context*, ed. Barbara Rogoff and Jean Lave. Cambridge: Harvard University Press: 95–116.

Tough, Allen. 1979. *The Adult's Learning Projects: A Fresh Approach to Theory and Practice in Adult Learning*, 2nd edn. Toronto: Ontario Institute for Studies in Education.

Wechsler, David. 1958. *The Measurement and Appraisal of Adult Intelligence.* Baltimore: Williams & Wilkins.

Welford, Alan T. 1993. "The Gerontological Balance Sheet." In *Adult Information Processing: Limits on Loss*, ed. John Cerella, John Rybash, William Hoyer, and Michael L. Commons. San Diego, CA: Academic Press: 3–12.

# Part IV
# Implications for Retirement Payouts

# Chapter 13

# How do Retirees Go from Stock to Flow?

*John Ameriks*

In funded defined contribution (DC) pension systems, plan participants accumulate assets in designated accounts over time for use in retirement. Given the tax subsidies accorded to these saving mechanisms, it seems clear that a first-order public policy issue is whether DC pensions and other retirement savings will enable retirees to maintain an "adequate" flow of consumption in retirement. Indeed, in both the popular press and the academic literature, there has been a great deal of focus on this question (cf. Easterlin, Schaeffer, and Macunovich, 1993; Engen, Gale, and Uccello, 1999; Moore and Mitchell, 1999; Warshawsky and Ameriks, 1999; Holden and Vanderhei, 2002; Wolff, 2002).

In order to assess the adequacy of retirement saving for the support of consumption in retirement, it is clearly necessary to specify, or model, saving behavior prior to retirement. It is also important to model *spending* behavior after retirement. It seems fair to say that assumptions made about retirement spending behavior have remained relatively unnoticed in the policy debate regarding the "adequacy" of retirement savings. For example, many assessments or estimates of the "adequacy" of DC pension plans often presume that retirees will use their retirement plan balances to obtain a life annuity (e.g. Holden and Vanderhei, 2002). Many well-known commercially available retirement planning software programs designed to assess retirement savings adequacy utilize similar assumptions. Such an assumption is consistent with the simplest form of a life-cycle model of consumption, in which there is no bequest motive (Brown et al., 2001).

Yet such an approach is likely to be too simplistic, in view of the fact that many retiring workers seem to maintain at least part of their retirement assets for purposes other than the immediate purchase of a stream of life-contingent income payments at the time they retire. Because many people appear to strongly desire alternatives to life annuities as a distribution mechanism for their retirement assets, the question arises as to how people will choose to utilize the stock of assets that they have accumulated in their

The views expressed are solely those of the author and do not represent the opinions of his current or past employer. The author is solely responsible for any errors.

pension accounts to finance an "adequate" flow of consumption in retirement. In a recent paper, Munnell et al. (2002) argue that as people are given more control over how they dispose of their pension plan assets, psychological or behavioral biases may lead them to (i) elect to receive distributions from their retirement plans as "lump sums", and (ii) subsequently choose to save too much of those assets (i.e. reduce their consumption below what is optimal). Indeed, this argument is similar to the argument that behavioral biases may cause undersaving before retirement. If behavioral biases lead some individuals to undersave before retirement, is it not also possible that other biases could lead them to underspend in retirement? Others believe that the form of benefits in retirement is not a significant issue, and that such choices are simply a reflection of differences in preferences.

Here, we do not intend to resolve this debate, since doing so would require extensive data on all sources of wealth, coupled with detailed information on consumption, that we currently lack. Instead, we focus on an examination of the range of distribution mechanisms used by TIAA-CREF participants. These data illustrate the extent to which retired and retiring individuals in a DC pension arrangement utilize a variety of different mechanisms to finance flows of income in retirement. These mechanisms include a range of annuity options, as well as many forms of distributions that do not involve a life-contingent form of income. The evidence indicates some striking trends over time. In particular, following the introduction of non-annuity income options in 1989, there has been a significant decline in the use of immediate life-contingent annuity payments among those beginning to take periodic income from their retirement accumulations. In addition, the data show significant variation both over time and by demographic characteristics in the types of income options chosen by participants.

## Retirement Rates and the Changing Nature of Retirement

When people move from the "accumulation" phase of a pension arrangement to the "distribution" phase, it generally involves a transition from work to retirement. Before examining patterns in the use of income options, we briefly review participant retirement patterns. There has been a large decline in the retirement rates of TIAA-CREF participants aged 69 and above since 1987, apparently related to the end of mandatory retirement in higher education in 1994 (Ameriks, 1999). Researchers also showed that over the same period, there was very little change in the retirement rates among participants younger than age 69. A larger study of faculty members also showed a similar pattern, with most of the decline in retirements at later ages concentrated at large research universities (Ashenfelter and Card, 2002). Figure 13-1 presents updated information on estimated rates at which participants retired in the year 2000. The base for each percentage

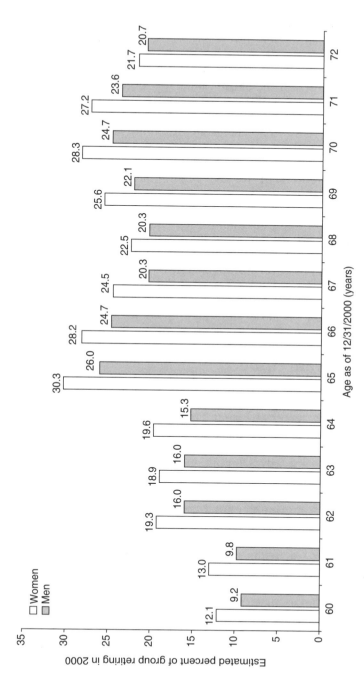

Figure 13-1. Estimated retirement rates for TIAA-CREF participants by sex, 2000.

*Notes:* Data show the fraction of each age/gender group who were making contributions to a TIAA-CREF pension annuity contract in 1999 but not in 2000. This is an estimate of retirements occurring in each year based on available data; contributions may of course stop for many reasons, but at the ages listed are likely to be largely a result of retirements.

*Source:* Author's calculations based on TIAA-CREF data.

(the number of "workers") in each group is the number of individuals who made any contribution to a retirement annuity contract in the year 2000, and the numerator (the number who "retire") is the number of those same individuals who either (i) no longer had a deferred annuity contract at TIAA-CREF as of 2001, or, (ii) remitted no additional contributions on their retirement annuities for the entire calendar year 2001.[1]

The most interesting aspect of these data is that retirement rates for all ages are similar to those documented earlier (Ameriks, 1999).[2] Women are slightly more likely to "retire" than men at all ages, there are peaks at typical retirement ages (62, 65, and 70), and age-specific retirement rates are all within few percentage points of earlier estimates. Overall, these data suggest that the incidence of "retirement" has changed significantly (declined) only for those aged 69 and above.

One difference is that older individuals appear to be waiting to begin receiving *any* form of income from their retirement assets. For women aged 65, the fraction of retirees starting to receive distributions within a year of retirement fell from 89 percent in 1987–90, to 81 percent in 1994–96; for men aged 65, the decline was from 90 percent in 1987–90, to 82 percent in 1994–96 (Ameriks, 1999). More recent data for those retiring at age 65 in 2000 confirm the trend: Among men, 78 percent received some form of distribution by the end of 2001, while among women, only 72 percent elected to receive some form of distribution by the end of 2001.

## Retirement Income Options

We now turn to data regarding the patterns in the selection of income options by those who **have** elected to begin an income stream. The data we use for this case study are drawn from TIAA-CREF (Teachers Insurance and Annuity Association-College Retirement Equities Fund). This is a not-for-profit organization and it is the largest private pension provider in the United States, managing nearly $300 billion in total assets for more than 2 million individuals. TIAA-CREF serves mostly employees at institutions of higher education and research, the majority at private institutions, where the sponsor offers a variety of investment options through employer-sponsored pension arrangements. Through such plans, participating employers and employees may make periodic contributions to accumulate assets for use in retirement. For many participants, these assets represent a major source of retirement income, in retirement as the assets are accumulated as a part of an employer-sponsored pension arrangement, rather than a supplemental arrangement (in contrast to many private-sector 401(k) plans).[3] Participants can choose from among several distribution options:

### Life Annuity Options

Two types of annuities may be used by participants to generate life-contingent income: *A single-life annuity*, which will provide income as long as the annuitant is alive; and *a joint-life annuity*, which provides some income payments as long as *either* of two annuitants (typically an individual and a spouse) live. Three different survivorship options are available under the joint-life annuities; the option selected determines the level of payments made following the death of one of the annuitants: The "Two-thirds to Survivor" option provides for two-thirds of the annuity benefit to continue to the survivor. The "Half to Second Annuitant" option specifies that if the primary annuitant pre-deceases the second annuitant, one half of the annuity benefit will be paid to the survivor; however, if the second annuitant predeceases the first, there will be no change in the benefit.[4] Finally, the "Full to Survivor" option provides for no change in the benefit upon the death of either one of the annuitants.

Because annuity assets are pooled, some retirees worry that in the case of a very early death, they will "lose" the assets used to purchase an annuity. In other words, some view purchase of an annuity as a "risky" proposition, rather than a means to reduce risk. One way that insurers deal with this concern is by giving annuitants the option to elect a *guarantee period*, or perhaps more accurately a "minimum payment period" when beginning an annuity income stream (either single or joint-life). This period is simply a length of time during which income payments will be made to the annuitant(s) or a designated beneficiary, *regardless* of whether the annuitant(s) is alive. In other words, during the guarantee period, income payments from the annuity are *not* life-contingent. If the annuitant(s) dies before the end of this guarantee/"minimum payment" period, payments will continue to a designated heir or other beneficiary. After the expiration of the guarantee period, continued payments are, however, contingent on the life of the annuitant(s).[5]

Payments under each of these annuity options are supported in large part by the pooling of mortality/longevity risk across annuitants unique to the life annuity. Because life-contingent annuity income payments are only made to living annuitants, periodic payments to annuitants can be higher over their expected lifetimes than would be possible in the absence of such a pooling arrangement.[6] In the absence of strong bequest and precautionary motives, there should be significant demand for such arrangements among individuals who are risk averse from the point of view of economic theory (Yaari, 1965; Brown, Davidoff, and Diamond, 2003; see also Brown et al., 2001). Yet the size of the immediate annuity market is strikingly small. A number of empirical studies have analyzed aspects of the operation and pricing of annuities offered on the private market in an attempt to resolve this apparent puzzle (cf. Friedman and Warshawsky, 1990; Mitchell et al., 1999; Brown et al., 2001). This research has illustrated that the implicit cost of private annuities has varied significantly over time and across carriers, and it depends heavily on the individual's private assessment of his own mortality prospects. These studies have concluded that while pricing issues may indeed make purchase of an annuity unattractive to some individuals, theory would still suggest much greater demand for immediate annuities than is currently observed.

## Variable Annuity Payments

An important feature of TIAA-CREF's pension annuities is that all involve at least some variable component. This means that the level of annuity income received by annuitants may change over time, based on overall performance of the annuity investment accounts (for CREF annuities) or dividend crediting rates (for TIAA annuities). Retirees choose whether such changes will regularly occur either on a monthly basis or an annual basis. For immediate annuities based on CREF accounts, initial income payments to annuitants are set using a current mortality table and an assumed interest rate of 4 percent. Annuity payments may then rise or fall to the extent that the overall performance (investment performance, mortality experience, and the expense experience) of the account since the last payment change exceeds or falls short of the assumed rates. If overall performance of the account exceeds the 4 percent assumption, the next income payment will be higher than the last. Similarly, if it falls short of the assumed 4 percent, the payment will be lower. This form of annuity can lead to volatility in payment levels over time, but it allows the annuitant to maintain exposure to the financial risks and return of various investments if so desired, while reducing exposure to longevity risk.[7]

In contrast to CREF annuities, TIAA annuities provide a minimum guaranteed amount of income as well as a variable component. The income change process for the variable component of TIAA annuities involves a significantly more complicated set of calculations than for CREF annuities, though the principles involved are similar. TIAA annuities have historically generated significantly lower levels of income volatility from period to period than CREF annuities (King, 1995; Hammond, 1996). Two types of payment distribution methods are used with TIAA annuities: a "standard" method, intended to generate a stable level of nominal payments, and a "graded" payment method, designed to generate a stream of increasing payments to at least in part offset adverse effects of inflation (cf. King, 1995).

Annuitants may choose to receive variable annuity payments from CREF investment accounts based on stock market investments, historically less volatile assets such as bonds, or use payments from TIAA to obtain a guaranteed income stream. They can also elect to receive income from a combination of these accounts and can mix several sources of income to create an overall "income portfolio." In addition, annuitants can change or periodically "reallocate" the combination of accounts that they use during the payout process, if desired. Over 95 percent of those receiving life annuity income receive at least some payouts from TIAA, and more than half receive at least some income from CREF. Detailed patterns in the portfolio-related details of annuity income decisions are an important area for future research, but they are beyond the scope of this chapter, which focuses on how annuity and non-annuity options are used, as opposed to investment allocation decisions across those categories.

## Non-Annuity Options: IPRO, MDO, and SWAT

In addition to the variety of life-annuity options, non-annuity options became available in 1989, following the introduction of the Interest Payment Retirement Option (IPRO). This enables retirees at least age 55 but younger than $69\frac{1}{2}$ to choose to receive the interest credited on their TIAA traditional annuity accumulations as income. Under this income option, the principal amount of the TIAA accumulation is preserved until a later date, when it must be either converted to a life annuity, a Minimum Distribution Option (MDO) contract, or otherwise withdrawn. The option was intended for use by those who would like to begin to receive some income from their retirement accumulations but might not yet desire to begin a life annuity.

The MDO contract was introduced in 1991. Federal regulations require that most retirement plan participants receive (and include in their taxable income) minimum distributions from their tax-deferred retirement assets by April 1 following the year they retire, or the year they reach age $70\frac{1}{2}$, whichever comes later.[8] Those who do not satisfy the requirements are subject to a nondeductible tax penalty equal to half of the amount that should have been distributed. The MDO mechanism provides income payments from accumulated retirement assets that are just large enough to avoid the federal tax penalties associated with failure to take distributions from tax-deferred retirement assets at the required rate. Unlike the IPRO, a participant beginning an MDO contract may have the option, but is not required, to change to another distribution option. The minimum distribution program can be subsequently converted to a life annuity in most cases; alternatively it can continue as long as assets remain to be distributed.

Systematic Withdrawals and Transfers (SWAT) were automated in 1996 and have been used increasingly ever since. Under this systematic withdrawal plan, a participant simply selects a schedule payment amount to receive (specifying either a fixed dollar amount, or a percentage of assets, as desired). These regular withdrawals or transfers will then be made from the accumulations according to that schedule, as long as assets remain. The level of these withdrawals must meet the minimum distribution requirement for those subject to it, or a tax penalty will apply. The participant can change the schedule of withdrawals as desired and retains the flexibility to convert to other options at a later date if desired.

This chapter focuses on the use of the life annuity, MDO, IPRO, and SWAT options, as each of these options generates a periodic stream of retirement income.[9] The issue of to what extent participants use various forms of ad hoc or lump-sum distributions is an important one, but it is beyond the scope of the current article. Without detailed additional survey data from individuals, there is no way to determine how, or even if, withdrawals or rollovers from TIAA-CREF are ultimately spent, converted to annuities, or otherwise utilized.

## The Level of Income Payments

When making a decision regarding an income stream, participants must decide how much periodic income the choice will generate. Several options are available.

### Life Annuities

The level of initial income provided by a life annuity depends on several factors. For example, the level of income obtainable from a single-life annuity is based on the survival probabilities of one individual, while a joint-life annuity reflects the expected survival/mortality patterns of two individuals. In addition, the interest rate used to price the annuity is an important factor, and the election of guarantee periods and various survivorship options (for joint-life annuities) are also a factor in determining the size of the periodic income payments. Finally, *all* TIAA-CREF pension annuities involve at least some variable component, so income after the first year of payments may change to the extent that investment performance or dividend crediting rates change.

Table 13-1 compares initial income streams obtainable from a hypothetical single life annuity at various starting ages, with various guarantee options. Table 13-1 shows the amount of initial income available from a single life annuity, based on three different interest rate assumptions and three different retirement ages. It also shows how payment levels are affected by the addition of a guarantee period. Finally, it should be noted that in general, as a result of federal law, the sex of the participant can be used in the determination of annuity benefit levels from retirement plan assets, as unisex mortality tables must be used to price the annuity income flow. This table illustrates three points:

1. Initial income payments per dollar annuitized grow as the interest rate rises used to price the annuity. For example, for a 65-year-old, a 4 percent interest rate generates payments of $686 per year per $10,000 annuitized. This rises to $830 at 6 percent, and $982 at 8 percent. Thus the initial rate at which the annuity is issued has a large impact on the level of starting income.
2. The size of initial income payments per dollar annuitized rises as the age of the annuitant rises.
3. Having a guarantee option lowers the amount of income payable by the annuity at any given age and interest rate. The cost of the guarantee

TABLE 13-1  Initial Hypothetical Single-Life Annuity Income Levels by Interest Rate, Annuitant Age, and Guarantee Period

| Interest Rate and Age | Annualized Income Per $10,000 (in $) | Payment Level w/Guarantee Period | | | |
|---|---|---|---|---|---|
| | | None (%) | 10 years (%) | 15 years (%) | 20 years (%) |
| *4 percent* | | | | | |
| Age 65 | 686 | 100.0 | 97.8 | 94.9 | 90.9 |
| Age 70 | 780 | 100.0 | 95.9 | 91.0 | 84.8 |
| Age 75 | 913 | 100.0 | 92.4 | 84.4 | 75.7 |
| *6 percent* | | | | | |
| Age 65 | 830 | 100.0 | 97.6 | 94.9 | 91.4 |
| Age 70 | 923 | 100.0 | 95.7 | 91.1 | 85.8 |
| Age 75 | 1,056 | 100.0 | 92.3 | 84.9 | 77.5 |
| *8 percent* | | | | | |
| Age 65 | 982 | 100.0 | 97.5 | 94.9 | 92.0 |
| Age 70 | 1,072 | 100.0 | 95.6 | 91.4 | 86.9 |
| Age 75 | 1,203 | 100.0 | 92.2 | 85.6 | 79.3 |

*Notes*: Annualized income above is monthly income times 12; not a once-a-year annual annuity payment. Payments are based on Annuity 2000 Mortality Table (Merged Gender Mod 1) with ages set back 2 years. Listed percentages are a percent of the annualized amount of income for each row.

*Source*: Author's calculations.

rises with participant age, in terms of the level of payments relative to an annuity with no guarantee period.

Table 13-2 presents a similar comparison for a joint life annuity. Here, the baseline level of income is for a "Two-thirds to Survivor" option without a guarantee period. Table 13-2 does not show how interest rates affect payments as it assumes a 6 percent rate; however, the relation is similar to the single life-annuity case. Table 13-2 does show similar patterns with regard to annuitant age and the election of a 20-year guarantee period. It also shows that the age of the two annuitants and the particular survivorship option elected can interact to raise or lower the level of income relative to the baseline case.

## Income from Non-Annuity Options

The level of initial income available from non-annuity pay out options generally does not depend on as many factors as are involved in annuity calculations. In the case of IPRO, the amount of income is dependent on the participant's accumulation in TIAA and current interest rates credited

TABLE 13-2 Initial Hypothetical Joint-Life Annuity Income Levels by Annuitant Ages, Survivorship Option, and Guarantee Period (Assumes Interest Rate of 6%)

| Age of Primary and Secondary Annuitants | Annualized Income Per $10,000 Annuitized (in $) | Two-thirds to Survivor | | Half to Second Annuitant | | Full Benefit to Survivor | |
|---|---|---|---|---|---|---|---|
| | | No Guarantee (%) | 20-Year Guarantee (%) | No Guarantee (%) | 20-Year Guarantee (%) | No Guarantee (%) | 20-Year Guarantee (%) |
| *Primary 65* | | | | | | | |
| Secondary 65 | 794 | 100.0 | 98.9 | 97.9 | 97.1 | 92.0 | 90.6 |
| Secondary 70 | 830 | 100.0 | 98.3 | 95.2 | 94.0 | 90.9 | 88.7 |
| Secondary 75 | 872 | 100.0 | 97.3 | 92.0 | 90.3 | 89.0 | 85.9 |
| *Primary 70* | | | | | | | |
| Secondary 65 | 830 | 100.0 | 98.3 | 100.0 | 98.7 | 90.9 | 88.7 |
| Secondary 70 | 874 | 100.0 | 97.2 | 97.4 | 95.4 | 90.4 | 87.0 |
| Secondary 75 | 925 | 100.0 | 95.7 | 94.2 | 91.3 | 89.1 | 84.0 |
| *Primary 75* | | | | | | | |
| Secondary 65 | 872 | 100.0 | 97.3 | 102.6 | 100.5 | 89.0 | 85.9 |
| Secondary 70 | 925 | 100.0 | 95.7 | 100.1 | 96.8 | 89.1 | 84.0 |
| Secondary 75 | 988 | 100.0 | 93.3 | 96.9 | 92.1 | 88.6 | 80.9 |

*Notes*: Annualized income above is monthly income times 12; not a once-a-year annual annuity payment. Payments are based on Annuity 2000 Mortality Table (Merged Gender Mod 1) with ages set back 2 years. Percentages in table are as a percent of the annualized income amount in each row.

*Source*: Author's calculations.

on TIAA accumulations. Depending on the history and timing of the person's contributions to TIAA, the total level of payments available via IPRO will vary. As of July 2003, the highest interest rate being credited by TIAA was 7.25 percent (for contributions received in 2000 on a RA/GRA), while the lowest was 3 percent (for contributions made between 7/1/2003 and 9/30/2003 to an SRA/GSRA). Thus, as of this date, IPRO payments could generate initial income payments equal to between 3 and 7.25 percent of the total accumulation ($300–725 per year per $10,000 of TIAA accumulation) depending on when contributions to TIAA were made. Relative to annuity payments for those aged 61–69, IPRO generally provides income payments that are somewhat lower than initial annuity payments (on the order of 20–40 percent lower), depending on the age of the annuitant and the annuity option selected.

The initial amount of income under the MDO can also vary depending on the age of the participant when distributions begin, and, if applicable, on the age of the designated beneficiary (and his relation to the participant). For someone who will be 71 at the end of the year in which distributions are first required, the minimum required distribution is approximately $382 per year per $10,000 of accumulation (assuming the beneficiary is not a spouse more than 10 years younger). This initial income level is substantially below the level of initial income payments available from life annuities to participants at this age (on the order of 50–60 percent lower). Systematic Withdrawals can, of course, provide an arbitrary amount of income, as long as the accumulation supports the payments (and as with all distribution mechanisms, rules regarding early withdrawals and the minimum required distributions must be respected with regard to accumulations). The point is that the choice of income option can dramatically affect the amount of initial income provided to a participant from his retirement assets. Individuals electing to take non-annuity options (other than SWAT) are choosing to receive significantly lower initial payments. All participants receive materials each year showing what their initial income payments would be, assuming the use of specific life annuity options. At retirement, they are also furnished with retirement illustrations showing how their choice of income option will affect their income levels. It is extremely unlikely that participants are unaware that higher initial income payments could be derived through the use of life-annuity options.[10] The choices that individuals are making, therefore, do appear to be made both willingly and voluntarily, reflecting consideration of the available options.

## Longitudinal Patterns in the Selection of Retirement Income Options

Next we turn to evidence on the changes in the use of various types of income streams over time at TIAA-CREF spanning the period 1975–2001.

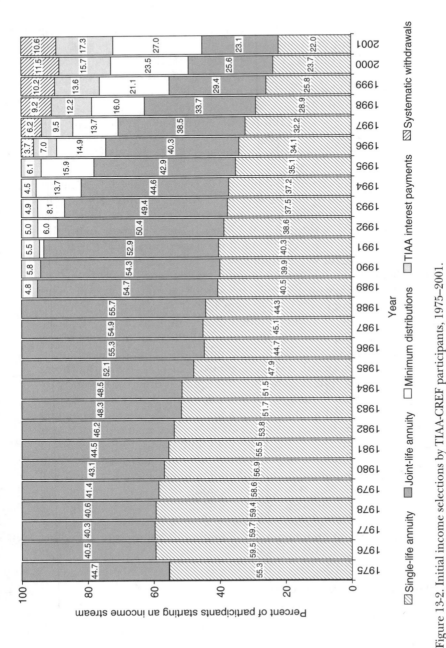

Figure 13-2. Initial income selections by TIAA-CREF participants, 1975–2001.

*Notes:* Participants combining different types of income streams are counted once for each type. Includes only those starting their first income stream.

*Source:* Author's calculations based on data from TIAA-CREF Retirement Services Actuarial.

These data show some remarkable changes over time. In 1975, the only distribution option available to TIAA-CREF participants was the life annuity (either single- or joint-life). Figure 13-2 shows that from the late 1970s through 1984, the single-life annuity was used by a (slight) majority of those starting an income stream from their retirement assets. From 1985 to 1988, the joint-life annuity became more popular, covering larger fraction of participants than the single-life annuity. Part of this shift in choice may be due to the passage of the Federal Retirement Equity Act of 1984, which provided that married employees (or employees who were married when they earned retirement benefits) under a plan governed by ERISA could select an option other than a two-life annuity under which the spouse is designated as the second annuitant *only* if the spouse agreed in writing to forego the two-life benefit. Figure 13-1 also shows that after the introduction of non-annuity options in 1989, there has been a dramatic decline in the proportion of participants selecting a life annuity. As of 2001, only 45 percent of those starting an income stream for the first time chose to use the life annuity, split roughly evenly between the joint-life and single-life options. We also see that after its introduction in 1989, few people selected the IPRO option (5 percent of those beginning any income stream); and its use subsequently showed a slight relation to 1994. Thereafter, the popularity of this distribution mechanism climbed, tripling in terms of its share among those starting income payments (rising to 17 percent in 2001). Since 1991, the greatest growth has been in the use of the MDO. In 1991, only 1 percent of those starting an income stream used the MDO, but of 2001, MDO is by 27 percent of those who start any income stream at all.

## Patterns in the Selection of Annuity Options

### Patterns by Sex

Table 13-3 presents data on various life-annuity options selected by individuals beginning an annuity income stream over the period 1995–2001. Table 13-3 is divided into three sections, with the top panel (Panel 1) simply breaking the relevant annuitant population into two groups, which are then analyzed separately. Panel 2 focuses on those electing a single-life annuity, and Panel 3 on those electing a joint-life annuity.

Confirming earlier studies (King, 1996), recent data show that female participants are significantly more likely to choose the single-life annuity option than their male counterparts. In 2001, 68 percent of the females beginning life-annuity income chose a single-life option, while only 30 percent of men did so. This pattern is only slightly changed from 1995, when 68 percent of females chose the single-life and 26 percent of males did so. An obvious reason for this could be differences in marital status among the female and male participants beginning an income stream. Unfortunately, historical data on marital status of participants are not available.

TABLE 13-3  Initial Annuity Income Option Sections, by Sex (1995 and 2001)

| Annuity Options | Men | | Women | |
|---|---|---|---|---|
| | *1995 (%)* | *2001 (%)* | *1995 (%)* | *2001 (%)* |
| **Panel 1: Single versus joint** | | | | |
| Single-life annuities | 25.9 | 29.5 | 67.6 | 68.0 |
| Joint-life annuities | 74.1 | 70.5 | 32.4 | 32.0 |
| *Total* | 100.0 | 100.0 | 100.0 | 100.0 |
| **Panel 2: Single-life annuities** | | | | |
| No guarantee | 35.0 | 32.3 | 33.7 | 28.4 |
| 10-year guarantee | 24.1 | 30.5 | 30.5 | 33.9 |
| 15-year guarantee | 16.2 | 14.3 | 14.0 | 15.7 |
| 20-year guarantee | 23.9 | 22.9 | 21.2 | 21.9 |
| Installment refund | 0.9 | 0.0 | 0.6 | 0.0 |
| *Total* | 100.0 | 100.0 | 100.0 | 100.0 |
| **Panel 3: Joint-life annuities** | | | | |
| *Full to survivor* | | | | |
| No guarantee | 8.8 | 10.0 | 7.1 | 9.2 |
| Any guarantee | 63.9 | 60.8 | 58.6 | 57.9 |
| All | 72.7 | 70.8 | 65.7 | 67.1 |
| *Two-thirds to survivor* | | | | |
| No guarantee | 3.1 | 4.3 | 2.2 | 1.9 |
| Any guarantee | 17.7 | 17.7 | 13.9 | 14.1 |
| All | 20.8 | 21.9 | 16.1 | 16.0 |
| *Half to 2nd annuitant* | | | | |
| No guarantee | 1.4 | 1.6 | 2.3 | 2.8 |
| Any guarantee | 5.0 | 5.6 | 15.9 | 14.1 |
| All | 6.4 | 7.3 | 18.3 | 16.9 |
| *Total* | 100.0 | 100.0 | 100.0 | 100.0 |

*Notes*: "Guarantee" refers to the election of a length of time during which annuity payments are not life contingent. "Installment refund" is a guarantee option available on a negligible number of older contracts.

*Source*: Author's calculations.

There are only a few other notable changes over this time period. Among women, there has been a slight increase in the election of a guaranteed period on the single-life annuity: of the women choosing a single-life annuity in 1995, one-third did so without opting for a guarantee period, while as of 2001, only 28 percent did not elect a guarantee. (As the data show, the largest increase was in the election of a 10-year guarantee.) In addition, there was a very slight increase in the fraction of female annuitants choosing the "Full to Survivor" survivorship option from 1995 to 2001. There was a corresponding decline in the fraction of women choosing the "Half to Second Annuitant Option," while the use of the "Two-thirds to Survivor Option" has remained fairly flat. Among men choosing the single-life annuity option, there was a similar slight increase in the use of the 10-year guarantee period from 1995 to 2001. In 1995, 35 percent of males using the single-life annuity did so without electing a guarantee period; while in 2001, 32 percent did so. At the same time, the use of the 10-year guarantee rose from 24 to 31 percent in 2001. The evidence for men indicates only a very slight change in the use of the various survivorship and guarantee options under the two-life annuity.

For both men and women choosing a joint-life annuity, the data show a strong preference for the use of the "Full-to-Survivor" option. In addition, among both men and women there is a strong preference for guarantee periods. Among those electing single-life annuities, roughly two-thirds chose a guarantee period, while among those electing a joint-life annuity, over 85 percent opted for a guarantee period.

## Patterns by Age

Figure 13-3 depicts time-series patterns in the age distribution of individuals beginning annuity income over the period 1980–2001.[11] It shows that the fraction of annuitants beginning income streams before the age of 65 rose gradually from 36 to 44 percent from 1980 to 1987, and it has remained roughly constant ever since. At the same time, the fraction beginning annuity income at age 65 has fallen by roughly half (from 38 to 17 percent) since the early 1980s. There has been a fairly steady increase in the proportion beginning annuity income at ages 66–69, and a significant increase, followed by a decline after 1991, in the fraction beginning annuity income at ages 70 or 71. The fraction starting annuity payments after the age of 71 increased slightly in the 1980s, then fell through the early 1990s, and it appears to be growing again in the early part of the twenty-first century.

There appears to be little change in the average age at which non-annuity distribution options are used. Since its introduction, the average age of participants using the minimum distribution option has been between 71 and 72—this is, of course, consistent with the fact that regulations require most retirees to begin taking minimum distributions by April 1 of the year following the year in which they turn $70\frac{1}{2}$. At the same time, the average age among those using only IPRO or SWAT is much younger: These averages have varied between 63 and 64 years. In the case of annuity income streams, the average age of participants has increased by a year over the period 1988–2001, rising from 63 to 64. Overall, the data show a striking increase in the overall age at which participants are beginning to start any income stream at all: The average age at which participants begin to receive *any* income stream rose from 63 in 1988 to 66 in 2001.

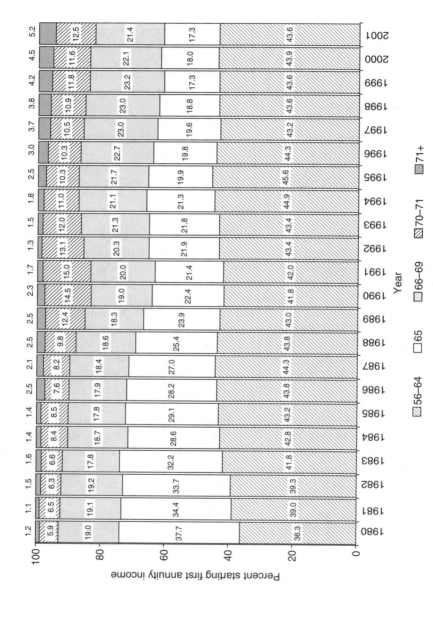

Figure 13-3. First life annuity issue by age, 1980–2001.

*Source:* Author's calculations based on data from TIAA-CREF Retirement Services Actuarial.

## Settlement Sequences

Until 1989, the only type of income stream available to participants was the life annuity, yet the participant was not required to convert all accumulated assets to an annuity. As more income options have become available over time, with features tailored to individuals at different points in the transition to retirement, many participants have used more than one income option. (As of 2001, less than 10 percent of those beginning an income stream used more than one form of distribution initially.)

Table 13-4 illustrates the use of alternative income options by those starting an income stream for the second time conditional on having chosen a single type of distribution for the first stream. For example, of those whose first income choice was a life annuity only, the table shows that 56 percent added and/or switched to another life annuity on starting a second stream, while 41 percent added an MDO contract. A small minority added IPRO or SWAT streams. For those whose first stream was an MDO contract, half started a life annuity contract as their second choice. While some of this may be the conversion of MDO contracts to life annuities, the pattern does not necessarily mean participants are converting their MDOs to annuities: Many participants still working after age $70\frac{1}{2}$ may have to take minimum distributions from accumulations earned under a prior employer's plan— thus, their first income stream is minimum distributions, although they are still working. When they do retire, they must begin to take income from their current employer's plan as well, which they may decide to take as an annuity. Almost all others with MDOs only who make a second choice elect to start another MDO stream. For those whose first choice is IPRO only, nearly 60 percent begin an annuity as their second choice, while 21 percent

TABLE 13-4 Patterns in Second Income Stream Selection, 1989–2001

| Initial Income Selection | Added and/or Switched to | | | | | |
|---|---|---|---|---|---|---|
| | Life Annuity (%) | MDO (%) | IPRO (%) | SWAT (%) | More Than One (%) | Total (%) |
| Life annuity only | 55.5 | 41.1 | 1.3 | 2.0 | 0.1 | 100.0 |
| MDO only | 50.1 | 46.4 | 0.0 | 3.2 | 0.3 | 100.0 |
| IPRO only | 58.0 | 20.6 | 9.1 | 8.7 | 3.5 | 100.0 |
| SWAT only | 10.5 | 19.4 | 13.2 | 55.9 | 1.0 | 100.0 |

*Notes*: Includes all participants who initially chose a single income option and who make a second income option decision at least one calendar year after their first election. "MDO" indicates minimum distribution, "IPRO" is TIAA interest payments, and "SWAT" is a systematic withdrawal plan.

*Source*: Author's calculations.

choose MDO. Finally, of those who begin an income stream with SWAT only, the second choice of about 11 percent is a life annuity, 19 percent choose an MDO, and 13 percent choose IPRO (the remaining individuals begin another SWAT stream).

## Discussion and Conclusions

Our evidence on the payout choices of TIAA-CREF participants evaluated changes over the period 1995–2001. We show that as non-annuity distribution options became available to retirees, more of them elected not to use a life-contingent annuity as a form of payout, at least at or near the time of retirement. More retiring individuals are electing to allow assets in their employer-sponsored retirement plans to continue to accumulate without taking distributions; use "temporary" or "transitional" mechanisms for distribution of assets that do not involve life-contingencies; and receive only the minimum amount of distributions needed to avoid federal tax penalties.

We also find that the frequency of retirement at ages younger than 69 remained roughly constant throughout the 1990s. It is, however, likely that at least some of the changes in the usage of income options, and in the observed postponement of the usage of retirement assets to generate income, may be related to the changing nature, rather than the incidence, of retirement at many US colleges and universities. As retirement has become less of a discrete transition from working full-time to not working at all, participants may not need to receive distributions from their retirement assets. The abolition of mandatory retirement rules in 1994, and changes in the tax treatment of Social Security payments, have also altered the set of financial constraints facing retirees over time. Increased part-time work after "retirement" and lower tax penalties on Social Security payments may also have increased the tax advantage of maintaining assets in tax-deferred vehicles.

Another important issue is that annuitization is generally an irreversible investment decision, so people may perceive some benefit to maintaining their option to start an annuity income stream at a later date. Those who began income streams without annuitizing over the last decade have used MDOs and IPROs.[12] An IPRO is by its very nature an interim income choice: At some point it must be annuitized or converted to minimum distribution. The growing use of this option is therefore perhaps quite consistent with retirees taking a "wait and see" attitude with regard to annuitization.

The decline in annuitization may be a cause for worry among some, but it is unclear whether "corrective" policy responses are needed. To the extent that people value bequests, or that precautionary motives for saving are a factor, lack of annuitization may simply reflect differences in preferences. Hence some of the patterns documented here could indicate that people do not view maximization of life-contingent retirement income at the point of retirement as the sole purpose of their retirement savings. Our evidence, as well as prior studies (e.g. Laitner and Juster, 1996) indicate substantial demand for "refund" features on immediate life annuity contracts, both single-life and joint-life. The widespread election of such options is strong evidence suggestive of a significant bequest motive.

If one admits the possibility that individuals are not well informed or rational, other explanations can be allowed. For example, Munnell et al. (2002), argue that as a consequence of psychological biases, older people may overvalue a "stock" of unannuitized assets relative to a "flow" of annuity income. If there is a psychological reluctance to give up a stock of assets, the result may be both underconsumption and unintended bequests. Unfortunately, it is not clear how one could determine whether the economic benefits of greater annuitization would offset the psychological costs. Along the same lines, it is also possible that people may not be understanding how annuities work at retirement. Indeed, basic concepts regarding how and why annuities are an effective and efficient means for financing consumption are not generally understood even among some financial professionals. This may play a role in their declining usage as participants are offered more choices in the distribution phase.

A related issue concerns the increasing use of MDO. Just as Madrian and Shea (2001) found, for 401(k) plan members it is possible that the decisions of at least some retiring participants may reflect inertia in decision-making, coupled with the existence of the MDO "default" (i.e. a choice that results when no alternative, well-considered selection is made) for income in retirement. Prior to 1989, the life annuity was the "default" (and only) option for receiving an income stream from a TIAA-CREF pension. After 1991, the MDO effectively became the "default" option, so in the absence of considering an alternative choice, in order to avoid tax penalties, participants may use the MDO. It is even possible that individuals perceive the minimum distribution required by tax law as a "government sanctioned" distribution mechanism for their retirement assets. Certainly for pre-retirees, there is significant inertia with regard to asset allocation decisions: Many workers never make asset allocation changes even after long periods of time and large fluctuations in financial markets (Ameriks and Zeldes, 2001). Likewise, we suspect that at least some participants might adopt the MDO at age $70\frac{1}{2}$, become more or less comfortable with the amount of income it provides, and then never reconsider the decision. Whether this is happening, and what the implications of such behavior might be, are important areas for future research.

The current menu of non-annuity distribution options has been available to retirees for less than a decade. Hence, people who were presented with non-annuity options are still relatively young, and it will take several years before it will be clear how successfully they combined income options to finance the full span of their retirements. It will also take time to learn whether they will make use of the annuity options available to them later in life.

## Notes

[1] We lack information that would allow us to determine how many members of this "retiree" group may have changed pension carriers or simply changed jobs rather than retiring. It seems reasonable that career changes at these ages are relatively infrequent; this calculation is perhaps the best estimate we can currently produce of whether individuals have retired. Note also that these estimates do *not* remove those for whom payments have stopped as a result of death.

[2] These data are not strictly comparable to the earlier study, because the 1999 study tracks one cohort of participants over time, whereas our data here look at retirement in the overall participant population at a single point in time. For example, the retirement rates estimated here are slightly (1–5%) higher at younger ages, in part reflecting higher turnover rates among those who entered the system recently than among those of the same age who have participated for several years.

[3] More information describing the organization, how it operates, and its history can be found in Greenough, 1990.

[4] This form of benefit and the "Full benefit to survivor" option are used in many of the annuity arrangements made through defined benefit (DB) plans. The "Two-thirds to Survivor" option is not typical of most DB plans; this option is the only one that results in lower benefits to the primary annuitant upon the death of the secondary annuitant.

[5] Essentially, the guaranteed period combines a period-certain annuity (i.e. a reverse amortization) *without* a life contingency, with the purchase of a *deferred* contingent life annuity that begins after the amortization is complete.

[6] For further description and details regarding the use of annuities to provide income in retirement, see Mitchell and McCarthy (2002).

[7] The mathematics of variable annuities as well as further details related to the structure of CREF annuities are described in greater detail in Brown, Mitchell, and Poterba (2002).

[8] The rules governing minimum distributions have had an interesting and convoluted history. The IRS issued final regulations governing the required minimum distributions in April 2002 that clarified and simplified some provisions related to minimum distributions. For a detailed discussion and analysis of the regulations, see Warshawsky (1998, 2001).

[9] Another form of non-annuity benefit available to most TIAA-CREF participants is cash withdrawals in the form of a Transfer Payout Annuity (or TPA) and/or a Retirement Transition Benefit (RTB). The RTB is a lump-sum withdrawal that can be used at the point of retirement in conjunction with the beginning of life annuity income, while the TPA is a form of period-certain annuity that must be used to liquidate TIAA balances under the terms of retirement plans that do not allow lump-sum withdrawals from TIAA.

[10] For all payment mechanisms (other than an extremely low and therefore indefinitely supportable level of fixed systematic withdrawals) the amount of income that the participant will receive will change over time, reflecting investment performance

and other factors. All TIAA-CREF pension annuities have a least some variable component.

[11] These data differ slightly from those presented by King (1996), as a result of difference in the way that ages and start dates are prepared here. The overall patterns are very similar.

[12] Of course, the SWAT mechanism has been available for a significantly shorter period of time.

## References

Ameriks, John. 1999. "The Retirement Patterns and Annuitization Decisions of a Cohort of TIAA-CREF Participants." TIAA-CREF *Research Dialogues* 60. TIAA-CREF.

Ameriks, John and Stephen P. Zeldes. 2001. "How Do Household Portfolio Shares Vary with Age?" Columbia University Working Paper. New York.

Ashenfelter, Orley and David Card. 2002. "Did the Elimination of Mandatory Retirement Affect Faculty Retirement?" *American Economic Review* 92(4): 957–980.

Brown, Jeffrey, Thomas Davidoff, and Peter S. Diamond. 2003. "Annuities and Individual Welfare." NBER Working Paper 9714.

——, Olivia S. Mitchell, and James Poterba. 2002. "Mortality Risk, Inflation Risk, and Annuity Products." In *Innovations in Financing Retirement*, eds. Olivia S. Mitchell, Zvi Bodie, P. Brett Hammond, and Stephen Zeldes. Philadelphia: University of Pennsylvania Press: 175–197.

——, Olivia S. Mitchell, James Poterba, and Mark Warshawsky. 2001. *The Role of Annuity Markets in Financing Retirement.* Boston: MIT Press.

Easterlin, Richard A., Christine M. Schaeffer, and Diane J. Macunovich. 1993. "Will the Baby Boomers Be Less Well Off Than Their Parents? Income, Wealth and Family Circumstances Over the Life Cycle in the United States." *Population and Development Review* 19(3): 497–522.

Engen, Eric M., William G. Gale and Cori E. Uccello. 1999. "The Adequacy of Retirement Saving." *Brookings Papers on Economic Activity* 2: 65–187.

Friedman, Benjamin and Mark J. Warshawsky. 1990. "The Cost of Annuities: Implications for Savings Behavior and Bequests." *Quarterly Journal of Economics* 105(1): 135–154.

Greenough, William C. 1990. *It's My Retirement Money—Take Good Care of It: The TIAA-CREF Story.* Homewood: Irwin.

Hammond, P. Brett. 1996. "Real Bonds and Inflation Protection for Retirement." TIAA-CREF *Research Dialogues* 47.

Holden, Sarah and Jack L. Vanderhei. 2002. "Can 401(k) Accumulations Generate Significant Income for Future Retirees?" *EBRI Issue Brief* 251.

King, Francis P. 1995. "The TIAA Graded Payment Method and the CPI." TIAA-CREF *Research Dialogues* 46.

—— 1996. "Trends in the Selection of TIAA-CREF Life-Annuity Income Options, 1978–1994." TIAA-CREF *Research Dialogues* 48.

Laitner, John and F. Thomas Juster. 1996. "New Evidence on Altruism: A Study of TIAA-CREF Retirees." *The American Economic Review* 86(4): 893–908.

Madrian, Brigitte C. and Dennis F. Shea. 2001. "The Power of Suggestion: Inertia in 401(k) Participation and Savings Behavior." *Quarterly Journal of Economics* 116(4): 1149–1187.

Mitchell, Olivia S. and David McCarthy. 2002. "Annuities for an Ageing World." Pension Research Council Working Paper 2002–12.

——, James Poterba, Mark Warshawsky, and Jeffrey Brown. 1999. "New Evidence on the Money's Worth of Individual Annuities." *American Economic Review* 89(2): 321–360.

Moore, James F. and Olivia S. Mitchell. 1999. "Projected Retirement Wealth and Saving Adequacy." In *Forecasting Retirement Needs and Retirement Wealth*, eds. Olivia S. Mitchell, P. Brett Hammond, and Anna M. Rappaport. Philadelphia: University of Pennsylvania Press: 68–94.

Munnell, Alicia H., Annika Sundén, Mauricio Soto, and Catherine Taylor. 2002. "How Will the Rise in 401(k) Plans Affect Bequests?" Center for Retirement Research at Boston College *Issues in Brief.*

Warshawsky, Mark J. 1998. "Distributions from Retirement Plans: Minimum Requirements, Current Options, and Future Directions." TIAA-CREF *Research Dialogue* 57.

—— 2001. "Further Reform of Minimum Distribution Requirements For Retirement Plans." *Tax Notes* 91(2): 297–306.

—— and John Ameriks. 1999. "How Prepared Are Americans for Retirement?" In *Forecasting Retirement Needs and Retirement Wealth*, eds. Olivia S. Mitchell, P. Brett Hammond, and Anna M. Rappaport. Philadelphia: University of Pennsylvania Press: 33–67.

Wolff, Edward N. 2002. *Retirement Insecurity: The Income Shortfalls Awaiting the Soon-to-Retire.* Washington DC: Economic Policy Institute.

Yaari, Menahem E. 1965. "Uncertain Lifetime, Life Insurance, and the Theory of the Consumer." *Review of Economic Studies* 32: 137–150.

# Chapter 14

# Annuities and Retirement Well-Being

*Constantijn W. A. Panis*

The economic position of the elderly has improved dramatically over the past several decades. In 1960, 35 percent of individuals aged 65 and older lived below the poverty line; today, only 10 percent are poor (US Bureau of the Census, 2002). This impressive gain is the result of a combination of public policy and private initiatives. The generosity of Social Security and Medicare was increased steadily, and the 1974 Employee Retirement and Income Security Act (ERISA) promoted private retirement savings. Yet, the outlook for the next generation is more clouded. The leading edge of the baby boom generation is now around 57 years old, and more workers than ever will be retiring in the next decade. This generation will retire at a younger age, spend more years in retirement than their parents, and will live longer. The life expectancy of a 65-year-old today is 82.9 years old, more than 4 years higher than in 1960 (Centers of Disease Control, 2001). At the same time, older people are less likely to enjoy lifelong guaranteed pension benefits. In 1978, some 38 percent of American workers were covered by a pension that guaranteed a lifelong benefit, compared to only 21 percent in 1998 (USDOL 2001, 2002). Instead, workers more often participate in 401(k) and similar plans (up from 7 percent in 1978 to 27 percent in 1998). If the funds in such plans were invested wisely, they can be substantial but they still offer no insurance of income security over many years of life in retirement. If the rate of return disappoints, there may not be much principal remaining. Almost everyone has Social Security, but system benefits may need to become less generous to cope with projected deficits. The most widely discussed reform proposal, personal accounts, could involve a shift similar to what happened with employer-provided pensions.

Concerns about the financial security of future retirees have until recently been muted by extraordinary stock market gains and corresponding wealth

The author thanks Sandra Timmermann, Daniel Rosshirt, Olivia Mitchell, John Turner, Sara Rix, Jeffrey Brown, and Amy Finkelstein for helpful comments; David Rumpel for careful programming assistance; and James Chiesa for outstanding editorial assistance. This work was made possible in part with financial support from the Mature Market Institute at the Metropolitan Life Insurance Company.

accumulation among baby boomers. But the recent downturn of the stock market and corporate bankruptcies have focused attention on the vulnerability of future retirees to investment risks. Much less discussed— but potentially even more painful—are longevity risks, that is, the risks that ever-longer-living Americans outlive their 401(k) and other savings and end up poor.

This chapter studies two measures of retirement well-being: Self-reported satisfaction with retirement, and the number self-reported of depressive symptoms. We are particularly interested in the association between the degree of annuitization and subsequent retirement well-being. Do people prefer being relatively rich at retirement, with a large amount of their own money readily available to be spent as flexibly as they wish? Or would they rather have the comfort of knowing they have a steady income in perpetuity? Our answers afford a peek into the well-being of the next generation of retirees.

## Analysis Sample

Our empirical analysis uses the Health and Retirement Study (HRS), a longitudinal nationally representative survey of older Americans' financial matters, health, expectations, demographics, and participation in the labor force. It began in 1992 with 7,700 households that included someone aged 51–61; spouses were also included, regardless of age, for a total of over 12,600 respondents. These persons have then been re-interviewed every other year, barring death or loss of contact. A survey of older persons began in 1993 with 6,050 households including someone at least 70 years old. Again, spouses of any age were included, for a total of over 8,200 respondents. Re-interviews were conducted in 1995, 1998, and 2000, and along the way, several birth cohorts were added to make the survey representative of the non-institutionalized US population aged 51 and older. In what follows, our analysis mainly uses information from all cohorts in the 2000 survey wave; in some cases, however, earlier waves or only a subset of the respondents (such as retirees only) are used.

In 2000 the most recent year for which we have data, 2000, the sample was 59 percent female and 41 percent male; respondents were 51 percent "completely retired" and 49 percent not. The sample as a whole was predominantly married people, though this is more true of men than of women (78 versus 55 percent). Women were much more likely to be widowed (30 percent, versus 9 percent for men). Income, not surprisingly, varied substantially between the retirees and others. The median for retirees (in 2000 dollars) was about $28,500, while before retirement it was about $54,700.[1] More than 22 percent of the non-retired group received over $100,000 in income, while only 6 percent of the retired did. Wealth, on the other hand, did not vary much between retirees and others.

# Empirical Results Regarding Well-Being in Retirement

We first consider workers' expectations prior to retirement. When asked what they expected would happen to their living standard when they retired, just over half of the HRS respondents said it would stay about the same.[2] Most of the remainder thought their standard of living would decline somewhat (36 percent) or a lot (6 percent), while only 7 percent thought it would improve. Women were somewhat more pessimistic than men, and women who used to be married (separated, divorced, or widowed) were particularly so (11 percent thought their living standard would decline a lot). The poorest 10 percent of the population (in terms of net worth), as might be expected, was more pessimistic than average. However, a remarkable percentage (19 percent) thought their lot would improve, perhaps because of eligibility for government programs such as Social Security, Supplemental Security Income (SSI), and Medicare. Surprisingly, workers with a pension were about as likely as those without one to expect a decline in their living standard.

Turning to the post-retirement experience, we next asked whether the reality lined up with expectations. The HRS did not directly query retirees to compare their standard of living with that of their pre-retirement years, but it did ask whether their retirement years have been better, about the same, or not as good as the years just before retirement. Almost half the retirees (48 percent) thought their retirement years were better; another third (34 percent) rated them about the same, and only 18 percent stated that their retirement years were not as good. It, thus, appears that most retirees were pleasantly surprised by their standards of living in retirement. Alternatively, it is possible that people's standard of living did not enter strongly into their judgments of whether their retirement years were "better."

Reality exceeded expectations not only with respect to retirement living standards, but also with respect to health. When 50–54-year-olds were asked about the chances that health would limit their work activity during the next 10 years, the average response was 36 percent. However, when persons (including retirees) 10 years older were asked whether they had an impairment or health problem that limited the kind or amount of paid work they could do, only 28 percent responded affirmatively.

We also explored several measures of well-being in retirement. The first is a direct question on satisfaction: "All in all, would you say that your retirement has turned out to be very satisfying, moderately satisfying, or not at all satisfying?" The second is a compound measure of mental health during the past week, similar to the Center for Epidemiologic Studies Depression (CES-D) scale (Radloff, 1977). The CES-D scale is based on 20 self-reported questions designed to assess symptoms of depression. The HRS administers an abbreviated version with just nine questions:

Now think about the past week and the feelings you have experienced. Please tell me if each of the following was true for you much of the time during the past week.

- [. . .] you felt depressed.
- You felt that everything you did was an effort.
- Your sleep was restless.
- You were happy.
- You felt lonely.
- You enjoyed life.
- You felt sad.
- You could not get going.
- You had a lot of energy.[3]

For each item, the answer could be "yes," "no," "don't know," or "refused." We explored each individual item as well as a composite score. The composite score increments by one for every "yes" on the six items expressing negative feelings, and for every "no" on the three positive items (happy, enjoyed life, lot of energy). The composite score ranges from zero (no sign of depression) to nine (strong signs of depression).

First, we assess how satisfied respondents are in retirement, without regard to any comparisons. In 2000, fully 59 percent said their retirement had turned out to be "very satisfying," and another third said it had been moderately satisfying. Only 8 percent stated that their retirement was "not at all" satisfying. Percentages did not vary much between men and women.

Though most people found retirement very satisfying, some were clearly more satisfied than others. What are the main factors responsible for differences in retirement satisfaction? Our analysis (Table 14-1, first three columns) shows that the most important factors were health and financial resources in retirement, as measured by household income or wealth. People who described their health as excellent or as very good were much more likely to find retirement very satisfying than those who described it as fair or poor. Satisfaction also varied substantially with income, as about two-thirds of retirees with household incomes in the $30,000–$50,000 bracket and 74 percent of those above $50,000, stated they found their retirement very satisfying, compared to only 40 percent of those with incomes below $15,000. The pattern for wealth is the same. "Wealth" refers to household net worth, or the value of all assets, including financial assets, housing, and vehicles, minus mortgages and other debts. Over three fourths of retirees with net worth above $400,000 found their retirement very satisfying, compared to only 38 percent of retirees with net worth under $50,000. Age and marital status were also of some importance. Older retirees were more

TABLE 14-1 Retirement Satisfaction and Depression Symptoms by Demographic and Socioeconomic Characteristics

| | Retirement Satisfaction (%) | | | Number of Depression Symptoms (#) | | |
|---|---|---|---|---|---|---|
| | Not at All | Moderate | Very | 0 | 1–3 | 4-plus |
| *Total* | 8.3 | 32.9 | 58.9 | 27.9 | 51.8 | 20.3 |
| *By sex* | | | | | | |
| Female | 7.8 | 33.7 | 58.5 | 25.5 | 50.7 | 23.8 |
| Male | 8.8 | 31.9 | 59.3 | 30.5 | 52.9 | 16.5 |
| *By health* | | | | | | |
| Excellent | 2.7 | 14.3 | 82.9 | 51.8 | 42.4 | 5.8 |
| Very good | 1.5 | 22.2 | 76.3 | 41.3 | 50.5 | 8.2 |
| Good | 4.6 | 33.8 | 61.5 | 25.5 | 58.4 | 16.1 |
| Fair | 10.2 | 42.8 | 47.1 | 12.7 | 54.5 | 32.8 |
| Poor | 27.2 | 41.5 | 31.4 | 4.4 | 38.5 | 57.1 |
| *By household income* | | | | | | |
| 0–14,999 | 14.3 | 45.5 | 40.1 | 16.3 | 50.1 | 33.6 |
| 15K–30K | 7.7 | 34.7 | 57.6 | 24.2 | 53.7 | 22.1 |
| 30K–50K | 5.8 | 27.0 | 67.2 | 32.5 | 52.0 | 15.5 |
| ⩾ 50K | 4.0 | 22.3 | 73.7 | 36.8 | 50.6 | 12.6 |
| *By household wealth* | | | | | | |
| 0–49,999 | 16.8 | 45.1 | 38.1 | 15.8 | 51.0 | 33.2 |
| 50K–150K | 8.7 | 37.0 | 54.3 | 22.4 | 54.2 | 23.4 |
| 150K–400K | 4.5 | 28.1 | 67.4 | 31.4 | 52.8 | 15.9 |
| ⩾ 400K | 2.6 | 20.7 | 76.7 | 37.7 | 48.9 | 13.5 |
| *By age* | | | | | | |
| <60 | 19.8 | 36.2 | 44.1 | 26.1 | 47.1 | 26.9 |
| 60–64 | 11.6 | 32.1 | 56.3 | 30.8 | 51.2 | 18.0 |
| 65–74 | 7.5 | 32.0 | 60.5 | 31.1 | 51.0 | 17.9 |
| 75–84 | 5.7 | 33.8 | 60.6 | 24.6 | 53.8 | 21.5 |
| 85+ | 5.1 | 31.8 | 63.0 | 17.9 | 54.6 | 27.5 |
| *By marital status* | | | | | | |
| Never married | 8.7 | 34.9 | 56.4 | 24.8 | 58.4 | 16.9 |
| Married | 7.5 | 30.2 | 62.3 | 31.7 | 51.9 | 16.5 |
| Separated/divorced | 17.6 | 39.8 | 42.6 | 23.0 | 51.1 | 26.0 |
| Widowed | 6.7 | 36.4 | 57.0 | 20.2 | 51.1 | 28.8 |

*Note*: First three columns sum to 100%; last three columns sum to 100%.

*Source*: 2000 Health and Retirement Study.

satisfied than younger ones. (Below we discuss whether this is an age or a cohort effect.) Married people and those who never married were more satisfied with retirement than those who were once married but now widowed, separated, or divorced.

Next we turn to the depression scores described above. Among retirees in the 2000 wave, 28 percent reported no sign of depression during the week before the interview, 25 percent reported one symptom, 27 percent two or three symptoms, and the remainder reported four or more symptoms. One in six retirees stated that he felt depressed for much of the prior week, one in three slept restlessly, and one in five felt sad much of the prior week. However, 89 percent were happy much of the time and 93 percent enjoyed life. Differences by sex are of interest as well. While women reported approximately the same levels of satisfaction with retirement as men, they showed more signs of depression than men. Women responded "yes" more often on all six negative items, and "no" more often on all three positive items. In particular, they more often felt depressed (19 versus 14 percent), lonely (22 versus 15 percent), and sad (25 versus 15 percent).

Returning to the composite depression score, the last three columns of Table 14-1 show the distribution of number of depression symptoms by sex, health status, household income, household net worth, age, and marital status. We collapsed the 0–9 scale into three items: No symptoms of depression, 1–3 symptoms, and 4 or more. We find the same patterns as for satisfaction with retirement. (The simple correlation between the 3-item retirement satisfaction response and the 10-item composite depression score was −0.40.) Mental health strongly correlated with general self-reported health: More than half of those who stated that their health was excellent reported no symptoms of depression, whereas more than half of those in poor health reported four or more depression symptoms. Individuals with higher incomes or higher net worth reported fewer signs of depression. Elderly retirees reported more symptoms of depression than younger retirees, except for very young retirees. Married individuals reported fewer signs of depression than, in particular, separated, divorced, and widowed retirees.

## Annuitization and Retirement Satisfaction

Financial resources which play an important role in predicting post-retirement satisfaction may take two forms: annuities and bequeathable wealth. Social Security provides an annuity, private saving builds wealth, and private pensions may provide an annuity, wealth, or both. We now explore how well-being in retirement correlates with the degree of annuitization of retirement resources. Theoretically, according to a simple life-cycle model, people ought to value their annuitized pension more highly than non-annuitized wealth (Brown and Warshawsky, 2001).

Not every pension entitles its holder to an annuity. Only the so-called "defined benefit" (DB) plans provide lifelong benefits based on the number of years worked for the employer and the salary in the last few years before retirement. By contrast, widespread 401(k) plans and the other so-called "defined contribution" (DC) plans do not provide a lifelong benefit.

In those plans, workers and their employers generally contribute funds to accounts owned by the workers. Tax treatment apart, these DC plans are not much different from other savings, so while they do not result in life-long guaranteed pension benefits, they are available to support retirement spending.

Defined contribution pension plans have become increasingly popular and are now the most common source of pension coverage. As mentioned above, the fraction of workers covered primarily by a DB pension plan went from 38 percent in 1978, to 21 percent in 1998. The fraction of workers with a DC plan as their primary pension went from 7 to 27 percent (USDOL 2001, 2002) over the same period. Workers with DB plans that switch jobs sometimes settle their pension entitlement with a lump sum payment and put the money in an Individual Retirement Account (IRA); IRAs have essentially the same features as DC plans.

Some DC plans allow the beneficiary to convert his or her balance into an annuity upon retirement. Surveys of medium and large firms show that only 27 percent of full-time 401(k) participants had this option in 1997, down from 34 percent in 1993 (Mitchell, 2000). The fraction may be higher in larger firms: on the 2000 National Compensation Survey, showed in a General Accounting Office analyses that 38 percent of DC plan partici-pants in large firms had the option to convert their plan balance into an annuity (GAO, 2003). In practice, very few retired workers take the option to annuitize. Hurd and Panis (2003) found that only 7 percent of HRS respondents with a DC plan who retired from their jobs converted the bal-ance into an annuity. For all practical purposes, DC plans thus do not, at present, provide a lifelong benefit.

We define two measures of the degree of annuitization. Both are ratios which use as the denominator expected total retirement resources, that is, bequeathable wealth plus the expected discounted value of income from Social Security and DB pensions. Bequeathable wealth is measured as net worth. Here, we define "Social Security reliance" as the ratio of the expected discounted value of income from Social Security to expected total retirement resources. It ranges from 0 (for individuals without Social Security entitle-ment) to 1 (for individuals without any savings or pension entitlement). Similarly, we define the "pension annuity ratio" as the ratio of the expected discounted value of income from DB pensions and privately purchased annuities, to expected total retirement resources. It, too, can vary between zero and one.

Our empirical analyses shows, for the HRS sample, that the more people relied on Social Security for financing their consumption in retirement, the less satisfied they were with retirement (Table 14-2, first three columns). This result arises mainly because heavy Social Security reliance implies little or no private pension and private saving. In other words, retirees who rely heavily on Social Security tend to be poor. This interpretation is confirmed

TABLE 14-2  Retirement Satisfaction and Depression Symptoms by Degree of
           Annuitization

| | Retirement Satisfaction (%) | | | Number of Depression Symptoms (#) | | |
|---|---|---|---|---|---|---|
| | Not at All | Moderate | Very | 0 | 1–3 | 4-plus |
| *By Social Security reliance* | | | | | | |
| 0–25 | 5.7 | 26.4 | 67.9 | 31.7 | 51.1 | 17.3 |
| 26–50 | 5.6 | 32.2 | 62.2 | 28.1 | 52.7 | 19.1 |
| 51–100 | 13.1 | 43.0 | 43.9 | 18.3 | 52.0 | 29.7 |
| *By pension annuity ratio* | | | | | | |
| No pension | 10.6 | 35.1 | 54.3 | 25.9 | 50.3 | 23.8 |
| 1–25 | 4.4 | 28.9 | 66.7 | 27.2 | 53.6 | 19.2 |
| 26–100 | 3.5 | 27.0 | 69.5 | 32.1 | 52.6 | 15.3 |

*Note*: First three columns sum to 100%; last three columns add to 100%.

*Source*: Author's computation using the 2000 HRS.

in a multivariate analysis that controls for household wealth (see the
Methodology Appendix).

By contrast, the more people felt that they could count on lifelong guaranteed pensions, the more satisfied they were with their retirement. About half
of retirees had no DB pension: that is, their pension annuity ratio was zero. Of
these retirees, 54 percent said they had a very satisfying retirement. One in
four retirees had a pension annuity ratio of 1–25 percent; among them,
67 percent were very satisfied. Among the remaining one in four retirees, who
could finance more than 25 percent of their consumption in retirement from
DB pensions, 70 percent reported having a very satisfying retirement.

The last three columns of Table 14-2 report the same breakdown for
depression symptoms. As before, the same pattern arises as for satisfaction
with retirement: The more retirees relied on Social Security for their consumption, the more signs of depression they reported, and the greater the
fraction of consumption that could be financed from pension annuities, the
fewer signs of depression were reported. Furthermore, satisfaction among
persons with lifelong guaranteed pensions lasted longer than among those
without (Table 14-3, first three columns). Satisfaction among persons without
any DB pension or privately purchased annuity tended to decline the longer
they were retired (from 58 percent very satisfied shortly after retiring to
47 percent 10 years later). The same was not true of persons with DB
pensions; their satisfaction remained approximately constant over the duration of their retirement. The explanation may be that persons without a DB
pension were becoming increasingly anxious about outliving their savings.

The last three columns of Table 14-3 confirm this pattern for depressive
symptoms: retirees with a DB pension were better able to maintain their

TABLE 14-3  Retirement Satisfaction and Depression Symptoms by DB Pension
Receipt and Retirement Duration

| Years Retired | Retirement Satisfaction (%) | | | Number of Depression Symptoms (#) | | |
|---|---|---|---|---|---|---|
| | Not at All | Moderate | Very | 0 | 1–3 | 4-plus |
| Without a DB pension | | | | | | |
| 0–1 | 10.9 | 31.4 | 57.7 | 33.3 | 47.0 | 19.7 |
| 2–4 | 13.5 | 32.3 | 54.2 | 28.6 | 49.9 | 21.5 |
| 5–10 | 11.7 | 36.3 | 52.0 | 28.4 | 47.2 | 24.4 |
| 10+ | 14.6 | 38.6 | 46.9 | 24.1 | 48.0 | 28.0 |
| With a DB pension | | | | | | |
| 0–1 | 5.6 | 30.5 | 64.0 | 33.9 | 53.2 | 12.8 |
| 2–4 | 4.1 | 27.3 | 68.6 | 33.3 | 53.2 | 13.5 |
| 5–10 | 5.3 | 28.5 | 66.2 | 33.4 | 52.1 | 14.5 |
| 10+ | 5.4 | 27.3 | 67.3 | 30.3 | 52.7 | 17.0 |

*Note*:  First three columns sum to 100%; last three columns sum to 100%.

*Source*:  Author's computations, 1992–2000 HRS.

mental health. While both retirees with and without a DB pension experienced increasing numbers of depression symptoms over time, the rate of
increase was markedly slower for DB pensioners.

These results also shed light on the relationship between age and retirement satisfaction shown in Table 14-1, where, satisfaction increased with
age. In Table 14-3, satisfaction stays the same or declines with increased retirement duration, which is correlated with age. (Both Tables 14-1 and 14-3
are based on cross-sectional outcomes from the 2000 HRS.) A potential
explanation is that the age relationship could reflect a cohort effect: the
oldest-old, who lived through the Great Depression, appeared to be more
content with less money than the younger generation. Another possibility
is that the oldest-old have had time to adjust to income losses, whereas
younger retirees might compare their retirement income to recent pre-
retirement earnings and find the ratio not to their satisfaction.

One may suspect that the positive relationship between pension annuity
ratios and retirement well-being is due to income rather than pension
annuity ratios themselves. Indeed, retirees with higher household incomes
were more likely to receive a pension, for them, pension annuity ratios may
be proxy for income. Table 14-4 addresses this issue: looking down the
first three columns, the relationship between income and satisfaction is
clear. But the more interesting comparison is within rows: at any income
level, retirees with a DB pension were more likely to be very satisfied than
those without. Having a DB pension increased satisfaction by about as
much as moving one income category up. For example, retirees with total

TABLE 14-4  Relationship Between Retirement Satisfaction and Pension Annuity
Ratio, by Income Category

| Household Income | Percent Very Satisfied | | | Percent with Zero Depression Symptoms | | |
|---|---|---|---|---|---|---|
| | Zero Pension Annuity Ratio | Medium Pension Annuity Ratio (1–25) | High Pension Annuity Ratio (26–100) | Zero Pension Annuity Ratio | Medium Pension Annuity Ratio (1–25) | High Pension Annuity Ratio (26–100) |
| Under $15,000 | 39.2 | 50.8 | 50.4 | 16.4 | 14.5 | 18.8 |
| $15,000–30,000 | 54.5 | 62.0 | 62.4 | 24.8 | 23.4 | 23.8 |
| $30,000–50,000 | 61.2 | 70.4 | 72.1 | 30.7 | 32.3 | 34.5 |
| $50,000 or more | 70.2 | 78.4 | 75.6 | 36.7 | 34.2 | 38.4 |

*Source*: Author's evaluation of 2000 HRS.

household income between $15,000 and $30,000 and with a DB pension
were about as likely to be very satisfied (62 percent), as were retirees with an
income above $50,000 but without the security of a lifelong guaranteed
pension income (61 percent).

The last three columns of Table 14-4 illustrate the depression counterpart
of retirement satisfaction. They report the fraction of respondents without
any reported depression symptoms by pension annuity ratio and household
income. The same pattern emerges as with retirement satisfaction, though it
is not as sharp. The appendix contains a multivariate (ordered probit)
analysis with controls for income and several other factors. In that model,
pension annuity ratio has the expected negative sign and is significant.

## Risk Aversion and Retirement Satisfaction

One further factor of potential interest is respondent risk aversion. The HRS
asked respondents to imagine they were faced with a choice between two
jobs: One that would guarantee their current family income for life, while
the other would have a 50 percent chance of doubling income for life and
a 50 percent chance of cutting it by a third. The expected value of the
second alternative was 33 percent higher than the first, yet three out of four
respondents took the safe choice, and were thus relatively risk-averse. More
of them (61 percent) were very satisfied with their actual retirement than
were the more risk-tolerant who took the second choice (51 percent).

This choice is similar in some respects to the choices available to everyone before retirement: They can put money into an arrangement that will
pay an annuity, or they can invest it in ways that might make them wealthier
during retirement but have the risk of leaving them worse off. This choice

involves two sources of uncertainty: Rate of return on accumulated saving, and remaining length of life. Even if the saving builds to greater wealth than with an annuity, the saver can come out worse off. He or she may live so long that the saving is exhausted before death.

## Long-Term Planning and Retirement Satisfaction

Our evidence conclusively shows that satisfaction with retirement was higher among retirees who had engaged in some sort of financial planning activity. In the 2000 data, 10 percent of respondents, generally those age 50+, had long-term care insurance coverage, and of those 71 percent reported being very satisfied in retirement, compared to only 58 percent among those without. This may well have been fueled by anxiety about large medical expenses: In 1993 and 1995, respondents age 70 or older with long-term care insurance were somewhat less likely to predict exhaustion of savings during the next 5 years due to medical expenses than those without (28 versus 32 percent). More broadly, approximately one in every four respondents to the 1992 and 2000 surveys reported having attended a meeting on retirement or retirement planning. Among those who had attended a meeting, 71 percent reported having a very satisfying retirement in 2000, compared to 55 percent among those not having attended a meeting. In 1993 and 1995, about one of every seven respondents age 70 or older had a financial adviser. Here again, those with an adviser were more satisfied in 2000 than those without (71 versus 60 percent very satisfied).

People with higher incomes were more likely to engage in long-term planning. As with pension annuity ratio, one may thus suspect that our planning measures (long-term care insurance, retirement planning, and financial adviser) reflect income differences and that their correlation with retirement satisfaction is purely due to income. This is not the case. Similar to what Table 14-4 showed for pension annuity ratio, we tabulated retirees' level of satisfaction by household income and long-term planning activities. For any income level, there was a 11–13 percent increase in the likelihood of high satisfaction with retirement if a person had attended a planning or other type of retirement meeting. The results for having purchased long-term care insurance and having a financial adviser held up similarly within income category.

## Conclusions

Our analysis documents how Americans experience retirement. Using several measures of expectations, we have shown that retirement tended to be a more positive experience than expected for many Americans. Yet, satisfaction in retirement varies widely across individuals and is positively influenced by good health and financial resources. We also find that older retirees tended to enjoy greater satisfaction, partly due to a cohort effect: Perhaps as a result of having lived through the Great Depression, the oldest-old are more content with fewer resources.

The main thrust of our study concerns the importance of annuitization, that is, the extent to which retirees can finance their consumption with life-long guaranteed income streams, as opposed to liquid saving. We find that those with greater annuitization were more satisfied in retirement, and they maintained their satisfaction throughout retirement. By contrast, retirees without lifelong annuities have become somewhat less satisfied over the years. The guaranteed income benefits may reduce anxiety about the risks of outliving one's savings and ending up in poverty. These findings are reiterated using measures of well-being in retirement, namely self-reported symptoms of depression. Our findings, thus, have direct implications for retirees of tomorrow, in view of the long-term trend away from DB pensions that pay a guaranteed benefit for life, and toward DC pensions, which tend not to pay lifelong benefit streams. If future retirees are less likely to be annuitized, this could drag down future retiree well-being.

Of course, this problem could be offset by providing DC plan participants with access to a lifelong guaranteed monthly payment (i.e. an annuity). Currently, only one in four 401(k) participants already has such an option, and for many, the security that a conversion brings will enhance their satisfaction and mental health for many years to come. But the evidence suggests that few retirees with a DC plan, only about 7 percent, chose to annuitize (Hurd and Panis, 2003). Why do so few DC plan beneficiaries annuitize their balance? First, annuity products may be perceived as expensive. This is not because of insurance company profits but because of adverse selection: People that annuitize tend to live longer than the average person in the population (Brown et al., 2001; Mitchell and McCarthy, 2002). Second, retirees may worry about unexpected large expenses, such as for medical care. This concern may be mitigated by new annuity products that incorporate long-term care insurance (Warshawsky, Spillman, and Murtaugh, 2002). Third, retirees may desire to maintain liquid assets to bequeath to their children. It is not clear how important such bequest motives are for household asset allocation and consumption decisions (Brown and Warshawsky, 2001). Fourth, would-be annuitants may worry about the lack of protection against inflation in current US annuity products. But Brown, Mitchell, and Poterba (1999) found that, for plausible levels of risk aversion, people attach only modest value to inflation protection. Fifth, retirees may be concerned that they will outlive the insurance company. Indeed, the long-term financial instruments that would be needed to match long-term obligations from annuities are currently not available in financial markets (Mitchell and McCarthy, 2002). Sixth, consumers appear to have only limited understanding of the longevity insurance that annuities offer. Many tend to focus more on the risk of dying early than of living long (American Council of Life Insurers, 1999). Consistent with this perspective, GAO would like pension plan sponsors to educate participants about the various risks that they face at and after retirement (GAO, 2003).

Another novel result we report is greater satisfaction among individuals who had engaged in long-term planning, from attending a retirement planning meeting or by purchasing an insurance policy for long-term care. These results are robust to controls for income and many other factors, though it is possible that people who engage in long-term planning activities are also prudent types that prepared themselves for retirement in more ways than we looked at. Nevertheless, these results coupled with those from other studies suggest that successful risk management enhances retirement well-being (Ameriks, Chapter 13, this volume; Drinkwater and Sondergeld, Chapter 15, this volume; Lusardi, Chapter 9, this volume; Weber, Chapter 3, this volume).

## Methodology Appendix

This appendix offers additional results reported in the text. Table 14A-1 shows estimation results of two ordered probit models. Retirement satisfaction is the outcome of the first specification; the second pertains to the number of depressive symptoms. We present specifications that control for both household income and household net worth; the results are robust to a variety of alternative specifications. Most importantly, the relationships between pension annuity ratio and retirement well-being hold up after controlling for financial resources, health, sex, and marital status. The higher the fraction of sustainable consumption financed from lifelong guaranteed pension benefits, the greater is retirement satisfaction and the fewer depression symptoms reported. Holding constant the values of all other covariates, a 10 percentage point increase in pension annuity ratio decreases the chances of being not at all satisfied in retirement from 7.1 to 6.5 percent, and increases the probability of being very satisfied from 61.0 to 62.7 percent. (The multivariate analysis sample is slightly smaller than that in Table 14A-1 because of missing covariate values.) Similarly, a 10 percentage point increase in pension annuity ratio boosts the probability of reporting zero depression symptoms from 27.8 to 28.4 percent and decreases the chances of four or more symptoms from 20.1 to 19.7 percent.

The relationships between Social Security reliance and our two measures of retirement well-being are not significant after controlling for other covariates. In other words, the relatively low satisfaction and high depression found among retirees with high Social Security reliance is at least in part due to their low wealth or low income from other sources, rather than to Social Security reliance itself. However, Social Security benefits are in some respects preferable over private pensions, for example, because of the protection against inflation that Social Security offers. It is therefore somewhat puzzling to not find significant effects in the same directions as with respect to pension annuity ratio.

TABLE 14A-1  Ordered Probit Model Estimates of Retirement Satisfaction and
            Depression Symptoms

|  | Retirement Satisfaction (0 = Not at all, 2 = Very) | Number of Depression Symptoms (0–9) |
|---|---|---|
| Pension annuity ratio | 0.53** | −0.21** |
| | (0.07) | (0.06) |
| Social Security reliance | −0.09 | −0.07 |
| | (0.07) | (0.07) |
| Ln(household income) | 0.11** | −0.03 |
| | (0.02) | (0.02) |
| Ln(household wealth) | 0.10** | −0.05** |
| | (0.01) | (0.01) |
| Health (1 = excellent, 5 = poor) | −0.33** | 0.43** |
| | (0.01) | (0.01) |
| Male | −0.03 | −0.16** |
| | (0.03) | (0.03) |
| Separated or divorced | −0.17** | 0.15** |
| | (0.05) | (0.05) |
| Widowed | −0.05 | 0.24** |
| | (0.04) | (0.03) |
| Never married | 0.18 | 0.02 |
| | (0.10) | (0.08) |
| Age | 0.02** | 0.00 |
| | (0.00) | (0.00) |
| Pseudo-$R^2$ | 0.11 | 0.07 |

*Notes*: Standard errors in parentheses. Significance: * = 5%, ** = 1%. Satisfaction and depression specifications include two and nine ordered probit thresholds, respectively.

*Source*: Author's calculations, 2000 HRS.

The other covariates in Table 14A-1 are consistent with their corresponding univariate pattern. Household income and wealth are both positively correlated with satisfaction and negatively with depression symptoms, while the opposite holds for poor health. There was no net difference in satisfaction between men and women, but women tend to report more symptoms of depression. Individuals whose marriage was disrupted by separation, divorce, or widowhood report lower levels of satisfaction and more symptoms of depression than lifelong bachelors and married people. Satisfaction increases with age, even controlling for other factors, but has no net effect on depression symptoms.

Not shown is that the multivariate analysis also verifies the earlier finding that risk-averse individuals are more satisfied with their retirement than the risk-tolerant. Surprisingly, however, some other expected relationships involving risk aversion do not show up. First, while one might expect the risk-averse to choose jobs that promise lifelong pensions, their pension security (pension annuity ratio) is no greater than that of the risk-tolerant. Second, while both risk aversion and pension security correlated positively with greater satisfaction in retirement, their interaction is insignificant. In other words, the risk-averse do not derive more satisfaction in retirement from income guarantees than the risk-tolerant. One might also expect that individuals with longer-than-average expect that life spans would appreciate lifelong guaranteed pensions more than others, so that the interaction between survival chances and pension annuity ratio should be significant. Respondents were asked to assess their own chances of living to age 85. Those reporting higher survival chances (controlling for age) also report greater satisfaction, but there is no disproportionate difference for retirees with high levels of lifelong pension security.

## Notes

[1] All monetary figures given in this chapter are in real 2000 dollars.

[2] For detailed results see Panis (2003).

[3] This item is not among the standard 20 CES-D items, but the HRS administers it in the same manner as the other eight items.

## References

American Council of Life Insurers. 1999. "Positioning and Promoting Annuities in a New Retirement Environment." Task Force on Annuity Messages.

Brown, Jeffrey R. and Mark J. Warshawsky. 2001. "Longevity-Insured Retirement Distributions from Pension Plans: Market and Regulatory Issues." National Bureau of Economic Research Working Paper 8064. Cambridge, MA.

——, Olivia S. Mitchell, and James M. Poterba. 1999. "The Role of Real Annuities and Indexed Bonds in an Individual Accounts Retirement Program." National Bureau of Economic Research Working Paper No. 7005. Cambridge, MA.

——, Olivia S. Mitchell, James M. Poterba, and Mark J. Warshawsky. 2001. *The Role of Annuity Markets in Financing Retirement.* MIT Press.

Centers of Disease Control. 2001. "Deaths: Preliminary Data for 2000." *National Vital Statistics Reports* 49–12, Department of Health and Human Services.

General Accounting Office. 2003. *Private Pensions: Participants Need Information on Risks They Face in Managing Pension Assets at and during Retirement.* GAO-03-810, July.

Hurd, Michael D. and Constantijn W. A. Panis. 2003. "An Analysis of the Choice to Cash Out, Maintain, or Annuitize Pension Rights upon Job Change or Retirement." RAND Working Paper. Santa Monica, CA.

Mitchell, Olivia S. 2000. *New Trends in US Pensions.* Pension Research Council WP 2000–1. Philadelphia, PA.

—— and David McCarthy. 2002. "Annuities for an Ageing World." National Bureau of Economic Research Working Paper No. 9092. Cambridge, MA.

Panis, Constantijn W. A. 2003. "Annuities and Retirement Satisfaction." RAND CORPORATION Working Paper DRU-3021. Santa Monica, CA.

Radloff, Lenore S. 1977. "The CES-D scale: A Self-report Depression Scale for Research in the General Population." *Applied Psychological Measurement* 1: 385–401.

US Bureau of the Census. 2002. "Poverty in the United States: 2001." *Current Population Reports*: 60–219. US Government Printing Office.

US Department of Labor (USDOL). 2001. "Abstract of 1997 Form 5500 Annual Reports." *Private Pension Plan Bulletin* 10, Winter 2000–2001. US Department of Labor, Pension and Welfare Benefits Administration, Office of Policy and Research.

——2002. "Abstract of 1998 Form 5500 Annual Reports." *Private Pension Plan Bulletin* 11, Winter 2001–2002. US Department of Labor, Pension and Welfare Benefits Administration, Office of Policy and Research.

Warshawsky, Mark J., Brenda Spillman, and Chris Murtaugh. 2002. "Integrating Life Annuities and Long-Term Care Insurance: Theory, Evidence, Practice, and Policy." In *Innovations in Financing Retirement*, eds. Zvi Bodie, Brett Hammond, and Olivia Mitchell. Philadelphia, PA: University of Pennsylvania Press: 198–221.

# Chapter 15

# Perceptions of Mortality Risk: Implications for Annuities

*Matthew Drinkwater and Eric T. Sondergeld*

This chapter reviews recent research investigating how retirees and near-retirees perceive and manage mortality risks. Of particular interest are the implications of decision processes regarding mortality risk for annuity buying behavior. For example, if people assume that they will not live very long in retirement, they will be less motivated to convert a portion of their assets into guaranteed lifetime income, than if they were concerned about outliving assets. Understanding the decisionmaking process is important for at least two reasons. First, faulty decisions regarding mortality risk will stress the resources of family members, government programs, and society in general. Greater reliance on income annuities and other products could alleviate this burden (Bodie, Hammond, and Mitchell, 2000). Second, retirees themselves tend to report greater satisfaction when they possess guaranteed income sources, aside from social security (MetLife, 2002; Sondergeld, Drinkwater, and Jamison, 2002*b*; Panis, Chapter 14, this volume).

The primary mortality risk facing people during their working years is dying too soon, a fact that boosts the demand for traditional life insurance. For retirees, by contrast, the primary mortality risk is dying later than expected, or living longer than financial resources can support people's desired standard of living. Longevity risk can thus be defined as the possibility that a person will outlive his savings and be forced to reduce his living standard. A related concern for married retirees is spousal mortality risk, defined as the possibility that one spouse will die and cause a significant decrease in the surviving spouse's standard of living. This is, of course, a concern at any life stage but, married retirees may face particularly negative consequences when widowed compared to working age individuals. For example, especially for older women, the loss of a spouse can reduce social security benefits, pensions, and annuity income. Moreover, the death of a partner can also bring about the loss of non-financial benefits such as care-giving and other support.

To confront longevity risk, individuals can delay retirement to a later age if they believe that this decision could reduce their risk of outliving savings or increase their chances of maintaining a desired living standard during retirement. The insurance industry markets products designed to protect against both losses, due to earlier or later-than-expected death. To insure against the risk of living longer than expected, people can annuitize a portion of their assets, using employer-sponsored retirement plan assets, Individual Retirement Account (IRA) balances, or deferred annuity assets, or they can purchase lifetime annuities. Choosing a "joint and last survivor" annuity allows the income stream to continue (often at a reduced rate) upon the death of the first or pre-specified annuitant, thereby addressing spousal mortality risk. Along with annuities, life insurance can mitigate the financial impact of a spouse's death by providing a tax-free lump sum payment, all or part of which could be converted into an annuity.

## Mortality Risk Perceptions

While it is straightforward to explain how individual insurance products help address mortality risk, it is difficult to measure how people recognize it and make decisions to handle it. As Weber (this volume) describes, this risk perception is often driven by affective processes which may ultimately lead to suboptimal risk management. It is therefore interesting that, on average, older people appear to be relatively good at predicting their life expectancy (Sondergeld, Drinkwater, and Jamison, 2002*b*). Depending on the mortality table chosen, retirees and those within 2 years of retirement mis-estimate their longevity only slightly (Table 15-1). Retirees were found to underestimate their life expectancy by 2.5 years when their estimates were compared to an actuarial mortality table developed for annuitants, but they overestimate by one year when compared to a general population mortality table. Women tend to be much less optimistic than men: Female retirees' subjective estimates are as much as 5 years too low. Hurd and McGarry (1997) also demonstrate that subjective survival probabilities aggregate to life table averages.

Nevertheless, mortality remains a difficult concept for people to understand, one that many prefer not to contemplate. Consequently, consumers

TABLE 15-1  Subjective Longevity Expectations Less Actuarial Life Expectancy

| Mortality Table | | Males | Females | All |
| --- | --- | --- | --- | --- |
| Annuity 2000 Basic | Near-retirees | 0.1 | −2.5 | −1.2 |
| | Retirees | −0.9 | −5.0 | −2.5 |
| US (SSA AS 107) 1990 | Near-retirees | 3.4 | −0.3 | 1.6 |
| | Retirees | 2.7 | −1.5 | 1.0 |

*Notes*: Actuarial life expectancy determined using the Annuity 2000 Basic Table (Johansen, 1998) and Social Security Administration Actuarial Study (SSA AS107; Bell, Wade, and Goss, 1992). Near-retirees are aged 50–70 within 2 years of retirement; retirees are aged 55–78 and retired (self-defined).

*Source*: Sondergeld, Drinkwater, and Jamison (2002*b*).

often use life expectancies when retirement planning exercises. A recent study found that one-third of retirees, and 46 percent of near-retirees, assumed that they would live to a certain age when they were planning the details of their retirements (Sondergeld et al., 2003*b*). The problem is that using this benchmark exposes them to the risk of outliving their planning horizon. Indeed, 11 percent of the retirees surveyed had already outlived their earlier determined planning horizons. One reason consumers take this viewpoint is that prevailing retirement planning software programs virtually all use life expectancy as the default planning horizon (Sondergeld et al., 2003*a*). While some programs incorporate techniques (such as Monte Carlo simulation) that treat future investment returns as a stochastic variable, they still assume a retiree's date of death is deterministic. To counter such determinism, consumers must learn that life expectancy is only an average; but it is not terribly helpful for planning retirement needs. Illustrations that make use of survival probabilities for each year of retirement can be much more instructive in demonstrating the likelihood of an individual surviving to specific ages, and married individuals should understand that the chance of at least one spouse in the couple surviving to older ages is much greater.

Previous research has not examined how mortality risk is perceived by the general public, relative to other concerns faced by retirees and those near retirement. To evaluate how seniors perceive mortality risk, we surveyed near-retirees and retirees regarding a variety of retirement risks to determine the level of concern regarding each. We found that survey respondents were more concerned with health-related risks, and even financial and investment-related risks, as compared to mortality risks (see Table 15-2). Only one in five near-retirees expressed major concern about the impact that outliving assets could have on their living standard in retirement.

It appears that there are two explanations for this result. First, people tend to be more concerned with outcomes that could affect them in the short run, as compared to those of a more long-term nature (Selnow, this volume). Second, many people do not fully understand the implications or likelihood of living long, or at least beyond their life expectancies.

## Decisionmaking and Judgment

Psychological research has amply demonstrated that people are systematically biased in their assessments of future events, in such a way that the likelihood of negative consequences tends to be minimized (Taylor and Brown, 1988; Weber, Chapter 3, this volume). Moreover, this bias is most pronounced for estimates about one's self; not only will the future be good, it will be especially good for oneself in particular. For example, when asked to predict whether a specific negative event (e.g. becoming ill, becoming depressed, having an accident) might happen to them, people have a tendency to assign a lower chance of these events happening to them than their peers

TABLE 15-2 Perceived Impact of Retirement Risks on Standard of Living

| Risk | Near-Retirees | Retirees |
|---|---|---|
| Prescription drug costs (%) | 47 | 48 |
| Health care costs | 45 | 37 |
| Long-term care costs | 37 | 35 |
| Prolonged stock market downturn | 36 | 29 |
| Provide for spouse if you die | 31 | 31 |
| Tax increases | 30 | 33 |
| Inflation | 29 | 32 |
| Provide for you if spouse dies | 22 | 22 |
| Interest rate decline | 20 | 25 |
| Outlive your assets | 20 | 16 |
| Assistance which may be needed by other family members | 14 | 13 |

*Notes*: Figures represent percent of survey respondents indicating "major concern" about the impact that each item could have on their standard of living in retirement. Near-retirees are aged 50–70 within 2 years of retirement; retirees are aged 55–78 and retired (self-defined).

*Source*: Sondergeld, Drinkwater, and Jamison (2002*b*).

(Fiske and Taylor, 1991). Similar results are obtained when the subject matter involves mortality estimates. In a recent study of retirees, more than six in ten believed it was likely they and their spouse would outlive the average life expectancy by more than 10 years (Society of Actuaries, 2002). Sixty-nine percent of retirees said it was "very likely" or "somewhat likely" that an average 65-year-old would have to spend at least some time in a nursing home before death. Yet, the percentage drops when retirees are asked about themselves: only 43 percent say it is "very likely" or "somewhat likely" that they will have to spend some time in a nursing home before death.

A tendency to positively distort information may promote mental health, but it can also have serious negative implications. For instance, if most people underestimate the chance that their spouses will die early in retirement, or that they or their spouses will live long enough to spend all of their assets, then they will be less likely to take action and delay retirement or insure against these risks. Furthermore, mortality estimates have been wrong in the past, and there is no absolute consensus on how human life expectancy might shift in the future (Bodie, Hammond, and Mitchell, 2000; Korczyk, 2002). Other research suggests that having more imprecise probabilistic beliefs can lead to overly conservative decisionmaking, which in turn can produce suboptimal financial asset allocations (Lillard and Willis, 2001).

Even if individuals did have valid and reliable information regarding the probabilities and costs associated with future negative events, there is no guarantee that they could process it in a fully rational manner (Yaari, 1965).

Indeed, recent research uncovering various cognitive biases and heuristics used during the decisionmaking process seems to imply that rational processing may not be the norm when retirement risks are involved (Kahneman and Tversky, 1979). Brothers (2002) describes how chosen retirement ages can be determined by anchor and adjustment heuristics. In that framework, the worker uses peers' retirement ages as a baseline, and adjusts his or her own, relative to his or her "anchor." Especially if a worker does not believe that he or she will live very long in retirement (or, alternatively, that he or she will not face catastrophic healthcare costs), later retirement may be seen as a "loss" and hence avoided. This may explain the recent survey of prospective retirees which showed that longer subjective life expectancies are not associated with older expected retirement ages; in fact, those with longer subjective life expectancies have lower expected retirement ages (Society of Actuaries, 2002).

People's retirement timing decisions could also be "incorrectly" chosen for other reasons. For example, subjective survival probabilities can embody individual information not reflected in a life table based solely on age and/or gender (Hurd, Smith, and Zissimopoulos, 2002). Even when observable covariates such as socio-economic status are controlled for, people may incorporate personal private information. Indeed, Hurd and colleagues have shown that subjective survival probabilities can predict actual measured mortality, and that people are less likely to claim early (i.e. reduced) social security benefits when they believe they have a high survival probability (Hurd and McGarry, 1997; Hurd, McFadden, and Merrill, 1999; Hurd, Smith, and Zissimopoulos, 2002). For example, using information from the Health and Retirement Study (HRS), Hurd and McGarry (1997) found that participants who had died between data collection waves had significantly lower subjective survival probabilities than those who survived. Related research has also shown that although fewer men delay the onset of social security benefits than would be expected from optimizing theoretical models, men with longer life expectancies tend to delay longer than men with shorter life expectancies (Coile et al., 2000).

The decision to delay the receipt of a lifetime benefit such as social security, however, cannot be equated with the decision to surrender a portion of assets for an income stream in the form of a payout annuity. Besides the difference in liquidity implications, usually the decision to annuitize also involves an additional choice between a lifetime, a joint and last survivor, or a non-lifetime payout. As will be discussed later in this chapter, lifetime payouts are not always a popular choice. However, as annuity-writing companies have long observed, the average life expectancy for a group of annuitants is generally longer than that of the general population (termed "adverse selection"; Mitchell and McCarthy, 2001). Clearly, people's knowledge of their own mortality plays some role in the decision to voluntarily annuitize.

Some research has demonstrated a rational link between key factors and annuitization decisions, even when the overall annuitization rate is less than what would be expected if people sought optimal solutions. Using the HRS, Brown (1999) showed that the decision to annuitize responds to mortality risk, marital status, risk aversion, and the presence of other annuitized wealth (e.g. Social Security benefits). Hence, annuitization should be more attractive for nonmarried individuals and those with higher longevity prospects, higher risk aversion, or fewer annuitized wealth sources. It is these individuals that will require more wealth than others to replicate the well-being achieved through annuitization (i.e. they have a higher "annuity equivalent wealth"). Brown found that, as annuity equivalent wealth increased, so did the plan to annuitize.

## Planning Approaches

Conventional advice regarding retirement income planning recommends that people select a finite time horizon (e.g. how long they expect to be retired; invest in a diversified portfolio subject to their risk tolerance, and, from that, determine how much they can "safely" withdraw annually to supplement their income. This advice mirrors the approach commonly used in accumulating assets for retirement, where the goal is to determine how much one must save each year to accumulate a desired asset level by the assumed retirement date. In retirement, the calculation is how much to take out, rather than put in, so that there are funds remaining at the "end of retirement." In both cases, the individual is effectively solving for the payment of an annuity certain.[1]

Of course, risks associated with longevity are not the only factors retirees face: Other risk factors include health problems, disability, and death of spouse. Traditionally, these have been covered by employer provided insurance even after retirement, but such coverage has declined overtime. For instance, the percentage of employers offering retiree health insurance dropped from 50(44) in 1993 to 36(29) by 2000 for employees retiring early (for Medicare-eligible retirees; GAO, 2001). Twenty years ago, about 40 percent of the private sector workforce was covered by defined benefit (DB) pensions, but this figure has been halved today.

## Insurance Products for Mortality Risk

As discussed earlier, the responsibility for addressing mortality risks has increasingly fallen on individuals rather than companies or the government. Next we explore the use of individual insurance products to protect against these risks.

## Annuities

The main financial product for managing mortality risk is the annuity, which transfers longevity risk from the individual to a private insurer.[2] The main reason people offer for buying these products involve their tax-deferral characteristics and investment growth potential, besides the lifetime payout aspect (Brown et al., 1999; Sondergeld, Tumicki and Terry, 1999). For example, when asked why they bought an annuity, 41 percent of recent buyers cited the savings or favorable tax features; but only 12 percent mentioned retirement income. In fact, fewer than a quarter of recent buyers understood that their annuity had the ability to create a lifetime income stream! Moreover, much of the growth in annuity assets reflects investment gains in variable annuities, much of which has evaporated due to the recent decline in stock prices; assets in fixed annuities were mainly level over the past 5 years. In short, the individual annuity market has grown, but this growth may not reflect increased attention to the risk-management features of annuities.[3] Indeed each year, roughly one percent of deferred annuity assets are annuitized; the vast majority of contract terminations result from surrenders and exchanges (Beatrice, Drinkwater, and Sondergeld, 2002; Drinkwater, Sondergeld, and Terry, 2002). Sales of immediate annuities have increased somewhat but they remain a small fraction of total annuity sales and retiree wealth.

Other consumer surveys also point to an under-utilization of payout features. Individuals who retired 1998–2001 and had the opportunity to take a lump sum distribution from their employer-sponsored retirement plans were asked: Whether their plan had an annuity option available, and whether they elected to receive an annuity (Sondergeld, Drinkwater, and Albrycht, 2002a). Among retirees with a DB plan (including those who additionally had defined contribution, DC plans), only 49 percent were aware that an annuity payout option existed in their plans, and 17 percent were "not sure" if this option was available. Among retirees with only a DB plan, just 34 percent knew that their plans had an annuity option. Among retirees who said that an annuity option was available, 21 percent chose the option. However, among this same group, only half of those who had only a DB plan chose the annuity payout option. Twenty-two percent of those with both a DB and DC plan took an annuity; only 10 percent of those with only a DC plan chose an annuity. The presence of a DB plan—even one that offered lump sum distributions—thus appeared to promote annuitization. With a continued decline in the popularity of DB plans, it seems plausible that the overall annuitization rates will fall further, unless people become aware of and take advantage of annuity offerings in DC plans.

When annuitization does not occur directly from the employer plan itself, it could happen after assets are transferred to some other retirement portfolio such as a deferred annuity. Among the 51 percent of retirees who chose to rollover the funds or take cash distributions, 14 percent said that they invested the funds in an annuity. While it is unclear what type of annuity these funds were invested in, given the small proportion of immediate relative to total annuity sales we suspect the vast majority was invested in deferred, not immediate, annuities.

Another point is that even when individuals convert their assets into income, they are not obliged to choose a lifetime payout. For annuitizations of deferred annuities, a lifetime payout feature is chosen by only one quarter of annuitants according to a recent LIMRA study (Drinkwater and Sondergeld, 2003). Ameriks (Chapter 13, this volume) explains how increasing numbers of participants in one large DC plan have elected to delay or avoid lifetime income payouts, in favor of systematic withdrawals and minimum required distributions. The percentage of buyers choosing lifetime income among immediate annuities has remained steady at approximately 60 percent from 1997 to 2001. Meanwhile, the proportion of married couples choosing joint and last survivor coverage—which can help to address spousal mortality risk—is also low (around 30 percent in 2001).

In sum, ownership of an annuity product is not synonymous with mortality risk transfer. Against the backdrop of falling traditional pension plan coverage such evidence indicates that people are becoming less protected over time from mortality risk.

## Life Insurance

Another source of protection against mortality risk is life insurance. During the retirement years, in-force life insurance can represent an additional source of income, either from cash value withdrawals (from permanent policies), or from conversion of the tax-free benefits following a spouse's death. Depending on the situation, individual life insurance or first-to-die policies can be purchased on either or both spouses. Though many people have this protection during their working years, life ownership drops off as people retire from jobs and leave group coverage behind. Concomitantly, retirees may find their individual term insurance policies expire, or they may be unwilling (or unable) to keep up with scheduled premium increases. Life insurance ownership among married people is more prevalent at ages 46–55 with 81 percent owning group or individual policies in 1998 compared to age 66 or higher with 63 percent owning (Terry and Bryck, 1999). At older ages, individually underwritten policies are likely to be prohibitively expensive. This fact helps to explain the miniscule proportion of buyers over the age of 60: among married individuals who bought individual life insurance policies in 2001, only three percent were over 60 (unpublished data, LIMRA International). When married people without life insurance die early in retirement, this can expose surviving spouses to substantial hardship when income sources are also cut off or sharply reduced.

## **Market Implications**

We have argued that for many people approaching retirement, mortality risks seem to rank low on a list of issues that includes more immediate concerns such as prescription drug costs and plunging stock values. People tend to have difficulty envisioning their life, health situation, and finances far into the future, and when they do not think that risks will befall them, they may not be motivated to address these issues.

Of course, these challenges are not new for the annuity industry. To the extent such biases are a natural feature of human decisionmaking, they have been present for many years. Nevertheless, in the past, these risks were covered by public (Social Security) and private (DB pension) sources. In the future, both of these sources will recede, leaving people increasingly exposed to mortality risks. As a result individuals are increasingly burdened with the responsibility of protecting themselves.

In the United States, at least, the annuity industry has done a good job emphasizing the asset accumulation phase. The next test for annuity providers will be to emphasize the product's ability to convert assets into a lifetime income stream. Yet, an explanation of product features, by itself, will not necessarily boost annuity sales or greater rates of annuitization. Companies must also learn how their customers frame decisions involving mortality risks, such as when to retire, whether to allow their life insurance policies to lapse, whether to purchase life insurance or modify existing coverage, and whether to annuitize a portion of their assets. Furthermore, they must understand how other retirement risks are perceived and prioritized. Other challenges for providers include compensation and product design. With the shift from accumulation to distribution, companies may need to consider innovative techniques to reward distribution partners who encourage annuity owners to annuitize. To address other objections to annuitization, providers should explore creative product designs. Already, more providers are promoting the liquidity features of their immediate annuities. New product designs may combine long-term care insurance with income annuities which can help to offset adverse selection pressures. Income annuities with inflation-indexed payouts should also be considered, which would not only mitigate the longevity risk but inflation risk as well (Brown, Mitchell, and Poterba, 2002).

## Future Research

Further investigation is needed on conditions in which consumers tend to insure against mortality and other retirement risks. There is no general agreement yet regarding the optimal method of educating different types of consumers, but research could help determine education techniques which increase general subject knowledge and influence behavior (Clark et al., Chapter 10, this volume; MacFarland, Marconi, and Utkus, Chapter 6, this volume). For example, focus group participants that initially reacted negatively to the concept of annuitization warmed to the concept after discussing it for some time (Sondergeld, Drinkwater, and Jamison, 2002b). During the focus groups, participants reacted to a series of scenarios of future income with and without annuitization. Graphic illustrations, showing how saving can be drained over the course of a retirement may have been instrumental in changing attitudes to annuitization. It would also be useful to learn how consumers would prefer to plan for retirement. As MacFarland, Marconi, and Utkus (Chapter 6, this volume) describe, retirement education programs should reflect the heterogeneous nature of peoples' planning preferences. The financial services industry will then be in a better position to find ways to effectively use insurance products to manage retirement risks.

## Notes

[1] In accumulating a desired amount, $L$, by retirement, one needs to solve for the annual contribution, $p_1$, such that $L = p_1 * s(n_1, i_1)$ where $s(n_1, i_1) = [(1 + i_1)^{n_1} - 1]/i_1$ and is the future value of an $n_1$ period annuity certain that earns $i_1\%$ per period. Upon retirement, the payment, $p_2$, is solved for and is the amount of income that can be created from the accumulated amount $L$, such that $L = p_2 * a(n_2, i_2)$ where $a(n_2, i_2) = [1 - (1 + i_2)^{-n}2]/i_2$ and is the present value of an $n_2$ period annuity certain that earns $i_2\%$ per period.

[2] For an overview of life annuities' importance in retirement security, see Mitchell, 2002.

[3] Many annuity providers added enhanced death benefits, living benefits, and other risk management features to their annuity products in recent years. It is not known whether these new features are responsible for the majority of increases in annuity sales.

## References

Beatrice, Daniel Q., Matthew Drinkwater, and Eric T. Sondergeld. 2002. *The 2001 Individual Annuity Market: Sales and Assets.* Windsor, CT: LIMRA International.

Bell, Felicitie C., Alice H. Wade, and Stephen C. Goss. 1992. *Life Tables for the United States Social Security Area.* Actuarial Study No. 107, SSA Pub. No. 11-11536. Washington, DC: USGPO.

Bodie, Zvi, P. Brett Hammond, and Olivia S. Mitchell. 2000. "Analyzing and Managing Retirement Risks." In *Innovations in Retirement Financing,* eds. Olivia S. Mitchell, Zvi Bodie, P. Brett Hammond, and Stephen Zeldes. Philadelphia: University of Pennsylvania Press: 3–19.

Brothers, Linda S. 2002. "An Individual's Chosen Retirement Age: When Is the Economically Feasible Retirement Age Chosen Over the Anchor Provided by Known Others?" SOA Monograph M-RS02-2. Schaumburg, IL: Society of Actuaries.

Brown, Jeffrey R. 1999. "Private Pensions, Mortality Risk, and the Decision to Annuitize." NBER Working Paper No. 7191.

——, Olivia S. Mitchell, and James M. Poterba. 2002. "Mortality Risk, Inflation Risk, and Annuity Products." In *Innovations in Retirement Financing,* eds. Olivia S. Mitchell, Zvi Bodie, P. Brett Hammond, and Stephen Zeldes. Philadelphia, PA: University of Pennsylvania Press: 175–197.

Brown, Jeffrey R., Olivia S. Mitchell, James M. Poterba, and Mark J. Warshawsky. 1999. "Taxing Retirement Income: Nonqualified Annuities and Distributions from Qualified Accounts." *National Tax Journal* LII(3): 563–592.

——— 2001. *The Role of Annuity Markets in Financing Retirement.* Cambridge, MA: MIT Press.

Coile, Courtney, Peter Diamond, Jonathan Gruber, and Alain Jousten. 2000. "Delays In Claiming Social Security Benefits." NBER Working Paper 7318.

Drinkwater, Matthew and Eric T. Sondergeld. 2003. *The Annuitization Study: Profiles and Attitudes.* Windsor, CT: LIMRA International.

Drinkwater, Matthew, Eric T. Sondergeld, and Karen R. Terry. 2002. *Annuity Persistency Study.* Windsor, CT: LIMRA International.

Fiske, Susan T. and Shelley E. Taylor. 1991. *Social Cognition.* New York: McGraw-Hill.

General Accounting Office (GAO). 2001. *Retiree Health Benefits: Employer-Sponsored Benefits May Be Vulnerable to Further Erosion.* May. Washington, DC: USGPO.

Hurd, Michael D. and Kathleen McGarry. 1997. "The Predictive Validity of Subjective Probabilities of Survival." NBER Working Paper 6193.

Hurd, Michael D., Daniel McFadden, and Angela Merrill. 1999. "Predictors of Mortality Among the Elderly." NBER Working Paper 7440.

Hurd, Michael D., James P. Smith and Julie M. Zissimopoulos. 2002. "The Effects of Subjective Survival on Retirement and Social Security Claiming." NBER Working Paper 9140.

Johansen, Robert J. 1998. "Annuity 2000 Mortality Tables." In *Transactions of the Society of Actuaries, 1995–1996 Reports,* ed. Society of Actuaries. Schaumberg, IL: Society of Actuaries: 263–291.

Kahneman, Daniel and Amos Tversky. 1979. "Prospect Theory: An Analysis of Decision Under Risk." *Econometrica* 47(2): 263–291.

Korczyk, Sophie M. 2002. *Back to Which Future: The U.S. Aging Crisis Revisited.* Washington, DC: AARP.

Lillard, Lee A. and Robert J. Willis. 2001. "Cognition and Wealth: The Importance of Probabilistic Thinking." Presented at Third Annual Conference of the Retirement Research Consortium, Washington, DC. May 17–18.

MetLife. 2002. *MetLife Retirement Crossroads Study: Paving the Way to a Secure Future.* New York: Metropolitan Life Insurance Company.

Mitchell, Olivia S. 2002. "Developments in Decumulation: The Role of Annuity Products in Financing Retirement." In *Aging, Financial Markets and Monetary Policy,* eds. Alan Auerbach and Heinz Herrman. Berlin: Springer-Verlag: 97–125.

Mitchell, Olivia S. and David McCarthy. 2001. "Estimating International Adverse Selection in Annuities." Pension Research Council Working Paper 2001-12.

Mitchell, Olivia S., James M. Poterba, Mark J. Warshawsky, and Jeffrey R. Brown. 1999. "New Evidence on the Money's Worth of Individual Annuities." *American Economic Review* 89(5): 1299–1318.

Society of Actuaries. 2002. *Retirement Risk Survey: Report of Findings.* Washington, DC: Mathew Greenwald and Associates and EBRI.

Sondergeld, Eric T., Elaine F. Tumicki, and Karen R. Terry. 1999. *Deferred Annuity Buyer Study: Attitudes.* Windsor, CT: LIMRA International.

Sondergeld, Eric T., Matthew Drinkwater, and Charles J. Albrycht. 2002*a*. *Opportunities in the Pension Rollover Market: Employee Perspective.* Windsor, CT: LIMRA International.

Sondergeld, Eric T., Matthew Drinkwater, and Kent Jamison. 2002*b*. *Retirement Risks: How They Are Viewed And Managed.* Windsor, CT: LIMRA International.

Sondergeld, Eric T., Robert S. Chamerda, Matthew Drinkwater, and Daniel Landsberg. 2003*a*. *Retirement Planning Software.* Windsor, CT: LIMRA International.

Sondergeld, Eric T., Matthew Drinkwater, and Kent Jamison. 2003*b*. *Retirement Planning: The Ongoing Challenge.* Windsor, CT: LIMRA International.

Taylor, Shelley. E. and J. D. Brown. 1988. "Illusion and Well-Being: A Social Psychological Perspective on Mental Health." *Psychological Bulletin* 103(2): 193–210.

Terry, Karen R. and Sally A. Bryck. 1999. *Trends in Life Insurance Ownership Among Americans: The Spiraling Decline Continues.* Windsor, CT: LIMRA International.

Yaari, M. E. 1965. "Uncertain Lifetime, Life Insurance, and the Theory of the Consumer." *Review of Economic Studies* 32(2): 137–150.

# Index